A Living Man From Africa

NEW DIRECTIONS IN NARRATIVE HISTORY

JOHN DEMOS AND AARON SACHS, Series Editors

The New Directions in Narrative History series includes original works of creative nonfiction across the many disciplines of history and related social sciences. Based on new research, the books in this series attain the highest standard of scholarship while fully embracing narrative storytelling and stylistic innovation. The works in the New Directions in Narrative History series, intended for the broadest general readership, enable us to better understand the past, present, and future of our world and its people.

A Living Man
From Africa

*Jan Tzatzoe, Xhosa Chief and Missionary, and the
Making of Nineteenth-Century South Africa*

Roger S. Levine

Yale
UNIVERSITY
PRESS
New Haven & London

Published with assistance from the Kingsley Trust Association Publication Fund
established by the Scroll and Key Society of Yale College
and from the foundation established in memory of Amasa Stone Mather
of the Class of 1907, Yale College.

Copyright © 2011 by Yale University.
All rights reserved.
This book may not be reproduced, in whole or in part, including illustrations,
in any form (beyond that copying permitted by Sections 107 and 108 of the
U.S. Copyright Law and except by reviewers for the public press), without
written permission from the publishers.

Yale University Press books may be purchased in quantity for educational, business,
or promotional use. For information, please e-mail sales.press@yale.edu (U.S. office)
or sales@yaleup.co.uk (U.K. office).

Designed by
Set in Electra type by Newgen North America.
Printed in the United States of America.

Levine, Roger S.
  A living man from Africa : Jan Tzatzoe, Xhosa chief and missionary, and the making
of nineteenth-century South Africa / Roger S. Levine.
     p. cm. (New Directions in Narrative History)
  "Published with assistance from the foundation established in memory of Amasa
Stone Mather of the class of 1907, Yale College"—T.p. verso.
  Includes bibliographical references and index.
  ISBN 978-0-300-12521-4 (cloth : alk. paper)
  1. Tzatzoe, Jan, b. ca. 1792–1868. 2. Xhosa (African people)—Kings and rulers—
Biography. 3. Missionaries—South Africa—Biography. 4. Christians—South Africa—
Biography. 5. Tzatzoe, Jan, b. ca. 1792–1868—Political and social views. 6. Social
change—South Africa—History—19th century. 7. South Africa—History—To 1836.
8. South Africa—History—1836–1909. 9. South Africa—Colonization. 10. South Africa—
Ethnic relations—History—19th century. I. Title.
  DT1768.X57L48 2011
  968.00496'39850092—dc22
  [B]
                                                                                        2010019085

A catalogue record for this book is available from the British Library.

This paper meets the requirements of ANSI/NISO Z39.48–1992 (Permanence of Paper).

10 9 8 7 6 5 4 3 2 1

To my grandparents,
Eileen and Solly Berman
and Lydia Sagankahn Levine and Jules Levine,

and my parents,
Janet Levine and Franklin "Sandy" Levine

For their strength and sacrifice in embarking for foreign lands.

Lemali enkulu-na siyibizile?
Lemali wako-na siwubizile?

This great price, have we called for it?
This home of Thine, have we called for it?

(*Ulo Tixo Mkulu*, *The Great God*, Ntisikana's Great Hymn, circa 1818)

Contents

Preface ix
Acknowledgments xi
Maps xiv

Introduction 1
Kelso, Scotland, 1837 7

Part I

Xhosaland, 1810 11
Bethelsdorp, 1811–1815 21
Makana's Kraal, 1816 34
Kat River, 1816–1818 49
Fish River Valley, 1822 66
iQonce, 1825–1832 74
Buffalo River, 1833–1835 93
Queen Adelaide Province, 1835–1836 106

Part II

Charles Darwin in Cape Town 123
England, 1836 125
Great Britain, 1836–1838 142

PART III

Tzatzoe in Kuruman   161
King William's Town, 1838–1845   163
British Kaffraria, 1845–1868   175

Epilogue   193
Notes   197
Bibliography   265
Index   283

Photo gallery follows page 128

Preface

I was born in South Africa and raised with sunshine soaking into my skin, with the melodies of early morning bird song, with the sight of thunderclouds as they massed over the Highveld, with the smells of earth and smoke and crushed jacaranda blossoms, with the taste of Cadbury's chocolates. In 1984, we emigrated from a desperate and despairing country. I was eleven, but almost twelve. Unlike my father, who retains an iconic memory of his arrival in South Africa as a four-and-a-half-year-old in 1948—"Cape Town, steaming into the Bay early in the morning and seeing Table Mountain rise out of the mist"—I only vaguely remember our arrival in the United States.

But I can recall in detail and, as I write this and reread it, with intense emotion, our departure from Johannesburg. The unduly cheerful conversation. The leather back seat of my parents' friend's luxury car. The wintry afternoon light clarifying each bare branch of the trees that loomed above deserted avenues (in my memories we are the only car on the road). And much later, an overwhelmingly dark night. The plane climbing. The city's lights an illuminated tapestry below. Golden threads woven through a pitch-black background. Everything that was certain. Everything that I knew. Thinking: "OK. Here we go."

Thirteen years later, in the summer before I began graduate school at Yale University, I worked in the African department of Sterling Memorial Library. Every night, I returned to a stifling temporary apartment, sat cross-legged on the mattress that served as my couch, and savored a small section of Noël Mostert's epic history of the eastern Cape of South Africa. The fourteen-hundred-page *Frontiers* covers the one-hundred-year war from the 1770s to the 1870s between the Xhosa and the European invaders of their lands, and it seemed to secrete a mournful air. The eastern Cape seemed to grieve for the betrayal of its innocence, for the crushing of its brief moments of hope. And as a South African exile, Mostert lamented the loss of his motherland. The thrill of his brief trips home only added to the sadness of another departure. I left the book as enthralled as I had been during my first momentary glance at its opening pages.[1]

One character, in particular, in Mostert's account drew my attention. I followed the career of a Xhosa leader named Jan Tzatzoe with interest as he made his sporadic appearances in the text: as a convert and teacher at the missionary station of Bethelsdorp, as an ambassador in London, as a Xhosa general before the walls of Fort Peddie. I knew only that I wished to know more about this young man who seemed to have accomplished and risked so much, only to encounter the full weight of a racist colonial order.

Most of all, I wanted to tell his story.[2] And after three years of graduate classes and three more years of research in archives from Cape Town to Grahamstown to Parkhurst, South Africa, from Oxford to Colindale to London, England, from New Haven, Connecticut, to Cambridge, Massachusetts, I realized that I could.

Acknowledgments

I write these words from the open rooftop of a Swahili town house. Dawn has appeared suddenly over an ancient stone town; a morning breeze stirs in the palm trees and the Islamic call to prayer echoes from mosque to mosque. Lamu is a site of journeys, of ongoing movement and exchange and cultural contact, and, as such, it seems an appropriate location in which to reflect upon the multitude of people and institutions that have assisted me in the making of this book.

One sees in the ruins of the Swahili coast the same basic building blocks of coral masonry, geometric design, narrow streets, airy courtyards and bedrooms, and deep cisterns from which the current stone houses and towns are formed. In a similar fashion, the underlying structure of this book draws upon the accumulated wisdom and pedagogical skill of my many teachers, including Kevin Mattingly, Patty Smith, Carly Wade, Sandra Sanneh, Robert Harms, Louis Warren, Karl Jacoby, Melvin Ely, Ben Carton, Leonard Thompson, Robin Winks, Gail Gerhart, Ciraj Rassool, Paul Landau, Jim Scott, Howard Lamar, Johnny Faragher, John Demos, Lamin Sanneh, Jay Gitlin, and Mart Stewart.

Every house is created from raw building blocks, without which even the grandest vision remains just that. For the acquisition of the material from which this project was built, and the material itself, I must thank Yale College, Yale University, and the Yale Graduate School; the Williams Pickens family; the Yale History Department; the Yale Center for International and Area Studies; the Program in Agrarian Studies, Yale University; the American Fulbright Association; the History Department of the University of the Western Cape; Riana Coetzee and the South African Fulbright Commission; the Giles Whiting Foundation; the Yale Center for British Art; the Howard Lamar Center for the Study of the American West; Deans Rita Kipp and John Gatta, and the Faculty Development and Research Grants Committee, of Sewanee: The University of the South. I also drew heavily upon the archival resources of the institutions mentioned below. I am specifically indebted to Museum Africa and the Cape Archives for their permission to reproduce the images that I have included in the text.

Even with an underlying framework and raw materials, one needs a multiplicity of experts to build any significant structure. I must thank the staff of the Yale University Library system and that of the Sterling Library Microform room in particular; Erika Le Roux and the staff of the Cape Archives, Cape Town; Stephanie Victor and the staff of the Amathole Museum, King William's Town; Michelle Pickover and the staff of the Cullen Library, University of Witwatersrand; the staffs of the South African Library, Special Collections at the University of Cape Town, the Brenthurst Library, the Cory Library at Rhodes University, Museum Africa, and the British Library; Cari Shepherd and the Interlibrary Loan office of Sewanee's duPont Library.

In the tradition of stone houses, this project was constructed floor by floor, and room by room. New expertise was required for each addition and remodel after my initial dissertation. My thanks to Richard Roberts, Benjamin Lawrance, and Emily Osborn; David Miller of The Garamond Agency; Robert Ross; Richard Price; the audiences who responded to my presentations at Yale University and Duke University; Tina Campomizzi; Nicholas Hollingshead for his mapmaking; and James Goodman. For believing in my work and shepherding it through the publication process with the utmost professionalism, special thanks to Christopher Rogers, Laura Davulis, and Margaret Otzel of Yale University Press. Robert Harms, Lamin Sanneh, John Demos, Aaron Sachs, Paul Landau, Nancy Jacobs, and Andrew Bank provided invaluable assistance through their support and encouragement, and, not least, through detailed readings of various stages of my manuscript. Without them, I would never have been able to follow my vision in this work.

A house must function above all as a site of changing communities, of family and friends, in which truths are told, support is given, stories shared, dreams dreamed, and jokes made at one's expense. For all of the above, thanks to the members of the History Department of the University of the Western Cape, Cape Town; Susie Newton-King; Ciraj Rassool and Patricia Hayes; Michael Jones; Diana and Peter Rich; Lily Gureff and the Rosenberg and Berman families for their hospitality in Cape Town and Johannesburg; the Bermans of Toronto; Pamela Schirmeister and Everett Seymour; Tom and Carol Migdalski; Max Lamont; Jim Copland; Larisa Grawe and Derek Desantis; John Brittingham; Chris Harper; Albert Buchman; Ruramisai Charumbira; Fiona Vernal;

Brian Peterson; Christian McMillen; the Writing History group at Yale University, especially John Demos, Aaron Sachs, and Adam Arenson; faculty members and friends at Sewanee, and the History, IGS, and Environmental Studies departments in particular; my students at Yale, Brown, and Sewanee (special thanks to my Spring 2010 junior tutorial); Lacy Johns; Sewanee's "New" Faculty, including alums Ken Walsh and Liza McCahill and recently arrived Nick Roberts; Dodie Mcdow and Alison Norris; Wiebe and Joanna Boer; and Wei Yang. For their support academically, and in every other way since before this project was even conceived, my mentor and friend since my junior year at Yale, Robert Harms; my brother, Antony Bugg-Levine; Wiebe Boer; Dodie McDow; and my boyz, Francisco Arsuaga, Greg Blanton, Bryan Just, Ian Kahn, Marc Ramdeen, Ray Rast, Joe Scotto, and Petie Stringer.

Any solidity or pleasing design that the reader finds in this book benefited enormously from the help of everyone listed here; the cracks, and chipped plaster, and irregular window frames are, of course, the fault of no one but me. Finally, if I could fill every whitewashed wall of a stone house with my barely legible script, I would still not have enough space to elaborate on the gratitude I feel toward my grandmothers, Eileen Berman and Lydia Sagankahn Levine, and my parents, Janet Levine and Sandy Levine, for their constant love and support, and the multiplicity of ways they have assisted in this endeavor. So, instead, I will attach a small plaque, inscribed with unadorned letters, to the wall in the entrance foyer. It will read: "For my parents and grandparents, to whom all thanks is due."

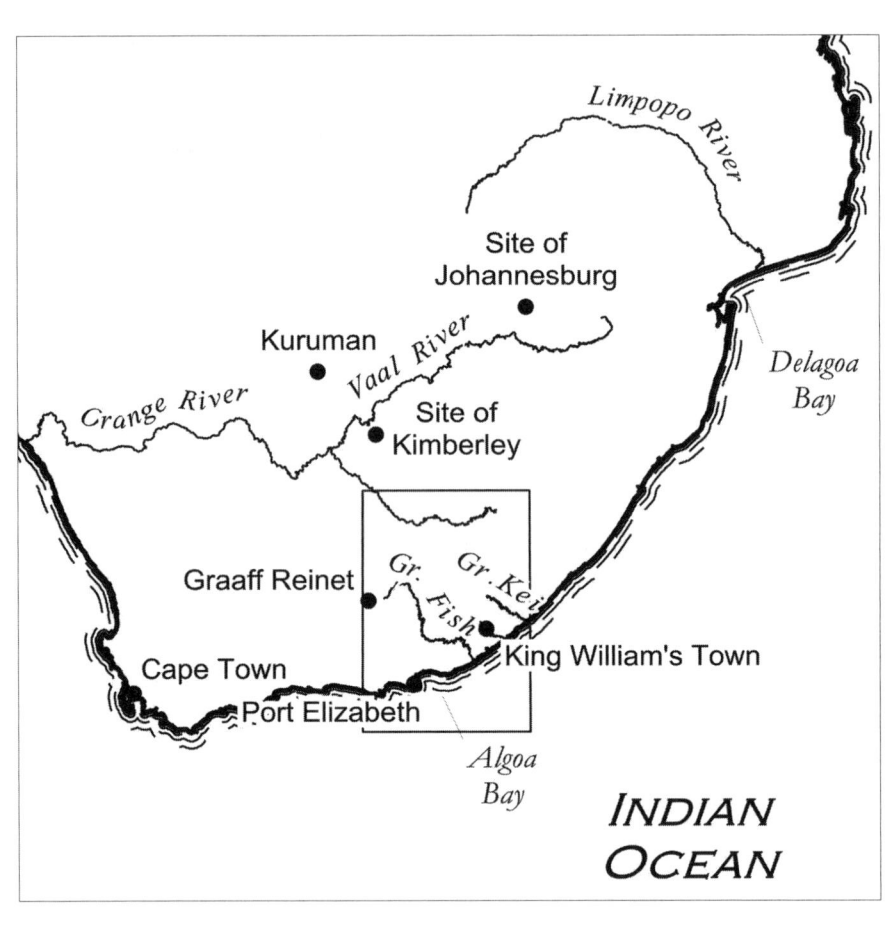

Map 1.1 Map of South Africa

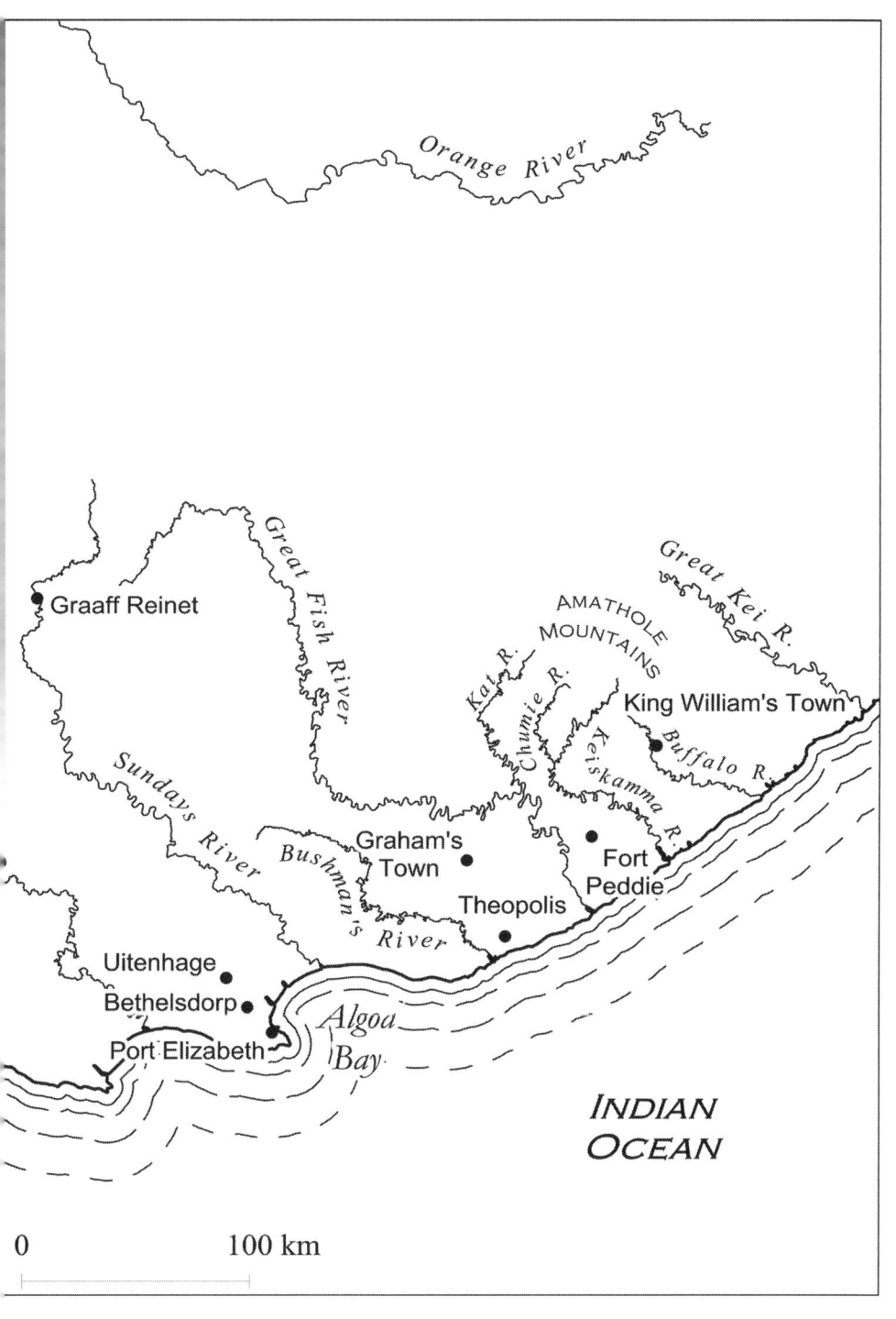

Map 1.2 Map of Eastern Cape

Introduction

Born around 1792 in the eastern Cape region of South Africa, Jan Tzatzoe was an African leader and intermediary who flourished in the European world of the missionary, Reverend Read, who helped raise him from boyhood, and the African world of his father, Kote Tzatzoe, chief of the amaNtinde lineage of the Xhosa state, to whose people he eventually returned.[1] In South Africa and during a two-year trip to Great Britain, Tzatzoe interacted with both worlds, and with an emerging South African colonial world as an evangelist, diplomat, chief, and ambassador on the local, metropolitan, and imperial stage.[2]

Tzatzoe experienced, shaped, and, with an increasingly forceful voice, bore witness to the advent and imposition of colonialism in South Africa.[3] As an intermediary, Tzatzoe was actively engaged with mediating European colonialism and acquiring its best attributes. He was the subject of evangelical mission Christianity and its attempts to colonize the consciousness of Africans, but he also took on Christian beliefs and practices and mingled them with his own understandings. He negotiated the political realities of an emerging South Africa and attempted to establish a secure place for himself and his followers in their nexus. Tzatzoe came to resent and resist the constraints of British colonialism, and he ended his days an oppressed subject of a harsh colonial regime.[4]

The first half of the nineteenth century, in which Tzatzoe lived and worked, saw tumultuous social, economic, political, and cultural change on a global scale. In Europe and the United States, the Industrial Revolution gained momentum and the Napoleonic Wars redrew the map of Europe. Europeans and their descendents endeavored to impose their will over peoples as distinct as Australian Aborigines; the Cree Indians of Canada; the Creek, Seminole, and Cherokee Indians of the southern United States; and the Sikhs of northern

India. Tecumseh, Makana, and Simon Bolivar unified their followers in resistance, while similar figures arose in other colonial conflagrations. As the British ended their system of slave trading and abolished slavery itself, the practice became further entrenched in the southern United States and Brazil. A successful slave rebellion in Haiti sparked slave revolts throughout the Caribbean.

South Africa was one of the most violent, desperate, and tumultuous settings in the world at the time. British, Dutch and African cultures clashed, collided, and commingled.[5] At first, Europeans encroached haltingly onto African land. But as the region became arguably the most missionized region in the world, white domination became successfully entrenched. Africans ignored, acknowledged, absorbed, and confronted European colonialism and civilization. European evangelists, humanitarians, and colonial officials adapted to and mobilized African influences. Africans participated in the expansion of colonial control. They also provided formidable resistance to it. In the midst of this emerging colonial world, Jan Tzatzoe journeyed back and forth across vast political, cultural, and personal chasms.[6]

"Even when they study a single person's life," Jill Lepore writes of microhistorians, "they are keen to evoke a period, a mentalité, a problem.... [there is a] concentration on individual life experiences and how they can be probed for deeper meaning.... an endeavor to discern through the lives of individuals or families the broader contours of the social and cultural landscape."[7] During this period of fervent cultural and political appropriation and contestation, Jan Tzatzoe embodied African participation in several of the crucial issues of this colonial encounter: the coalescing of European and African religious thought and culture, the redefinition of African political authority, the construction of a colonial state apparatus and racial ideology, and humanitarian and African resistance to this construction. *A Living Man from Africa* investigates Tzatzoe's contributions in these realms of interaction between Africans and Europeans.[8]

There is an underlying tension within *A Living Man from Africa*, as there must be in any biographically oriented study, between the exceptional nature of Jan Tzatzoe's life (which makes it worthy of a book-length study) and its representative nature of the experience of other Africans. Jan Tzatzoe's life is exceptional because of the amount of historical data from which I have been able to re-create it and the diversity of roles in which Tzatzoe functioned as an intermediary.[9] It also points towards other African intermediaries and leaders who faced similar dilemmas of resistance and assimilation, of incorporating new religious and political structures, of mediating between competing powers.[10] An intermediary may be relegated to a life of marginality, but it is on the margins that the most far-reaching and important inter-cultural conversations take place.[11]

In *The New Biography*, Jo Burr Margadant argues that the "object of study for the new biographers is not just the construction of identities, but also and inevitably, the contested nature of inventing selves. Every social location offers a limited number of possibilities from which individuals can create a possible self."[12] Jan Tzatzoe's life as an intermediary personified the hybrid nature of the new selves being fashioned in the interstitial and highly contingent space created by the colonial encounter in South Africa. This period featured an unprecedented number of possibilities from which Africans could create, or indeed invent, many possible selves. These selves also reveal the inadequacy of the Manichaean dichotomies of resister or assimilator, pagan or Christian, barbaric or civilized that have been overturned in academic work but are still found in popular discourse.[13]

In order to explore the fashioning of new hybrid selves in the colonial encounter, *A Living Man from Africa* does not present a "modernist" or "positivist" life of Tzatzoe that follows the conventions of nineteenth-century biography by employing a "linear biographic construction" with an established notion of self. The narrative emphasizes the poignant predicament of Tzatzoe's life in the middle. With this approach, this book attempts to move beyond a biographical understanding in which a historian (as he digs more deeply and reads more closely) rescues his African subjects from posterity and grants them a compelling amount of historical "agency" in the historical setting in which their life was lived.[14] Instead, *A Living Man from Africa* engages with Jan Tzatzoe as a "person . . . always in the process of becoming, negotiat[ing] different historical contexts in all their vexed complexities."[15]

Since the arrival of democratic rule in South Africa, the vibrant field of South African autobiography and biography has seen massive growth. With the success of *A Long Walk to Freedom* and the numerous biographies of Nelson Mandela and, increasingly, other resistance leaders, popular political biography of Africans has risen to the forefront of public interest, while academic studies of political, artistic, and historical African lives have kept pace.[16] Besides adding the first book-length study of an intermediary in the colonial encounter, as noted above, this book contributes historical depth to this thriving field of African auto/biography. Currently, biographies situated in the early to mid-nineteenth century focus on political and military history and do not develop an understanding of the lived experiences of their subjects. Also, there are no existing studies of literate or Christianized Africans (Africans capable of fashioning the history of their own lives, or providing the materials for others to do so) for this period.[17] From the extensive records of Jan Tzatzoe's life, including a substantial amount of material attributable directly to him, this book uncovers the direct experience and unique voice of an African immersed in the era of colonial contact and establishment of colonial rule. This life and voice provide a new prism through which to view the colonial encounter and a foundation upon which later African lives might be re-evaluated.[18]

Tzatzoe moved between the eastern Cape of South Africa and Great Britain, interacting with representatives of both locations. As such, a study of his life "integrate[s] the local and the general. . . . [It provides] a synoptic view, bringing metropole and colony, colonizer and colonized, British and indigenous peoples into one frame, into a single analytical field, [in order to] reveal not merely a catalogue of differences and similarities, not just a series of intriguing parallels, but whole configurations, general processes, an entire interactive system, one vast interconnected world."[19] To both his supporters and detractors, Tzatzoe served as a unique figure in bringing the empire home to the British and transmitting its power to his countrymen in the eastern Cape.[20]

In South Africa and Great Britain, Tzatzoe became a symbol to humanitarians and sympathetic colonial officials of the civilizing power of British colonialism and Christianity. His life story and written and oral production were used in evangelical public campaigns that built on the legacy of the abolitionist movement. A key feature of these mass political campaigns was the exultant display or exhibition in Britain of redeemed Africans who could, literally, embody and speak to the drastic changes wrought in their lives. But such figures also became targets for those attempting to subvert reform, as they were accused of a lack of authenticity in their presentations and were held to be ciphers onto which reformers were projecting their own ideologies and agendas. Thus questions of literacy, authorship, and authenticity are important features of Tzatzoe's story.[21] Tzatzoe emerges as an original and compelling narrator and commentator on the colonial encounter, but his life was, at times, produced (or mobilized) in ways with which he did not agree or of which he was not aware.

With the advent of Dutch and British colonial expansion, the eastern Cape region in which Tzatzoe lived and worked became a border zone or borderland, or simply a border region. *A Living Man from Africa* employs this concept of a border region to build on the idea of a frontier as a zone of intercultural contact, where no one group has established political, economic, or cultural dominance. But to employ the notion of the frontier to describe the eastern Cape in the early to mid-nineteenth century is to downplay the long-term African presence in the area, as well as to diminish the harsh policies that enabled Europeans to expropriate African land and labor during this period.

Instead, this book situates Jan Tzatzoe's story in a border region and posits that such a region may be defined as a place of uncertainty and insecurity, in which intermediaries flourish because they address the need for information and certainty. In this sense, a border region ceases to exist (as a frontier "closes") when a colonizing power has sufficient military and political dominance to ensure security and assumes control over the production of knowledge.[22] This transition also drastically reduces the number of possibilities for creating hybrid selves, whose presence is a feature of the contingent period of early cultural contact in a border region.[23]

In the last two decades, many historians writing about South Africa (where conversations between European missionaries and Africans have been ongoing for centuries) have focused on the history of Christianity and missions as a way to analyze the culture and discourse of colonialism and African resistance.[24] Understanding language, William Worger has argued, is "key to the translation, exchange and transmittal of ideas" in this colonial encounter.[25] *A Living Man from Africa* explores Jan Tzatzoe's success as a religious, linguistic, and intellectual innovator in the regimented setting of European missions and the more syncretic settings of various Xhosa communities.[26] As an African evangelist in his own right, and a translator for many different European religious disseminators, Tzatzoe exemplified African involvement in the creation of language in the border region.[27] His work illustrates the intellectual and linguistic innovation that attended the spread of Christianity throughout Africa.[28] Tzatzoe and other African linguistic intermediaries might be thought of as the vanguard of an African intellectual tradition born in the colonial encounter.[29]

In its narrative orientation and presentation, this book is inspired by works from South African, African, Latin American, American, and Australian history.[30] It seeks to tell a good story, while getting the facts right and exploring interesting questions.[31] It gets its characters moving and engaged with the world.[32] The stories told about Africans often feature a downward trajectory—solidified by the use of the past tense—in which Africans are increasingly constrained by their environment, be it physical, cultural, religious, or political. *A Living Man from Africa* unfolds in the present tense so that the reader can gain a sense of a life that is under constant construction and become aware of the multiple possibilities of each historical moment of Tzatzoe's life.[33] In order that quoted text might be more easily integrated into the narrative, it has been italicized instead of the more usual practice of being placed within quotation marks.

One final note: the quoted text, as well as the archival record from which the narrative and analysis developed (except on rare occasions that are specifically indicated), are in English, translated by missionaries and colonial officials from Dutch, Cape Dutch, or isiXhosa originals that were not preserved.

Kelso, Scotland

1837

In Scotland, Jan Tzatzoe feels more at home than at any other time during his eighteen-month-long journey to Great Britain. The *wild* and *rough* mountains with their *fine trees* transport him back *to his native mountains and valleys*. Back to his family; to his father, Kote Tzatzoe, chief of the amaNtinde; to the people themselves; to the leaders of the Xhosa state; to the missionaries and colonial officials with whom and for whom he has worked, and even fought. All await his return to the Cape Colony, to Xhosaland, to South Africa.[1]

Shortly after six thirty P.M. on Friday, 4 August 1837, Tzatzoe ascends the stage of the Secession Church in Kelso. He has retained a slender build into his early forties and appears young for his age. A dark navy military-style jacket clinches tightly around his waist. It has eight large gold buttons and both its stiff-standing collar and sleeve cuffs are embroidered with fine gold thread in a two-rowed curlicue.[2]

Before an audience *composed of all denominations*—a gathering unprecedented in the estimation of the *Kelso Chronicle* for its size and sustained attention—Jan Tzatzoe speaks:

> I stand before you . . . A *living man from Africa*.

Part One

XHOSALAND

His Longing Desire to Return to Our Place

1810

In the early days of 1810 the Reverend James Read is about to cross the Cape Colony's eastern border at the Sundays River when his horse slips on a muddy slope and falls *on all fours*, trapping itself between two small trees. Read runs his hands over his body to reassure himself that all of its parts remain unbroken. Raindrops shatter beneath his feet, so unlike the drizzle of his English childhood that gently dripped off his hat brim. The wet red clay of the road coats the flanks of his horse and streaks his pants.[1]

Along with seven men who have accompanied him from the London Missionary Society's Bethelsdorp mission station, Read is officially on the hunt for stolen cattle.[2] But his real aim is to search for *our young Caffer Chief who had informed me of his longing desire to return to our place*. Read is looking for Jan Tzatzoe.[3]

Six years earlier, in 1804, Kote Tzatzoe, chief of the relatively poor amaNtinde lineage, or clan, of the Xhosa state, had spent some time among the rolling hills clad with knotted fynbos fur that rise above the vast semicircular sweep of Algoa Bay.[4] There, just inside the colony, he had entrusted his son to Read and his fellow LMS missionary, Johannes van der Kemp, to live and learn at the year-old Bethelsdorp mission station. The missionaries had quickly grown fond of the ten-year-old boy, who had left Bethelsdorp a few years later to return across the colonial border to his father and his natal land.[5]

In his attempt to locate Tzatzoe, Read is passing at his peril, and with begrudging permission from the local colonial official, the Landdrost of Uitenhage, Colonial Jacob Cuyler (an American Loyalist who had fled Albany, New

York, for Canada), across an expanse approximately one hundred and fifty miles wide, from Algoa Bay in the west to the Great Fish River in the east. This border region is a locus of cultural exchange, where two settlement zones meet and merge together on their margins.[6]

To the west, the European zone, where, since the start of the eighteenth century, European settlers have been trickling across the four hundred miles of mountains and open plains that separate Algoa Bay from Cape Town, the cosmopolitan seaport established by the Dutch East India Company in 1652 near the Cape of Good Hope.[7] Mostly Dutch and French Huguenot, these European settlers live off the output of small farms, large herds of cattle and sheep, and the skins and meat from hunting expeditions. Many of the European families settling the zone have brought slaves along with them. These individuals have been transported to the Cape from the length and breadth of the Indian Ocean world, the west coast of Africa, or were born into African captivity.[8]

Along with Read and Van der Kemp (whom the Dutch colonial government had recalled to Cape Town), Jan Tzatzoe had witnessed the military engagements through which the British (concerned about the Cape's importance in their wars with Napoleonic France) had wrested control of Cape Town and its hinterland from the Dutch in the early months of 1806. Since then, the European zone has been under British colonial control, but it remains authoritatively Dutch and sparsely populated. Roman Dutch law and Dutch bureaucratic structures remain in place. Most importantly, Dutch remains the language of the farmers and hunters, the traders and soldiers, the missionaries and interpreters.[9]

To the east, the Xhosa zone, where large numbers of densely settled Africans remain fully independent. Known to the colonists as Kafirs, or Caffres, following an old Arabic description of the peoples of the southeast African coast, in 1810 a population of between fifty and one hundred thousand people lives near and along the coast for three hundred miles from Algoa Bay past the Kei River. They call themselves amaXhosa, and maintain a fractious unity through a mutually intelligible language and an assertion of common descent from an early seventeenth-century ancestor, Tshawe. The Xhosa are descended from a millennia-old migration into southeastern Africa of agriculturalists and metalworkers, and their language and way of life is closely related to that of other states found on or near Africa's southeast and eastern coast. They reached the western limits of their zone (where rain-fed agriculture gave way to arid conditions) at least two hundred years before the area became a border region. Much like the Europeans to their west, the Xhosa rely upon livestock, hunting, and trading; their agriculture, however, is more sophisticated and prolific as a result of better rainfall in the land they control.[10]

Another group of people live (or have lived) in both zones. These are the mostly nomadic Khoisan pastoralists and foragers, known at the time as Hottentots and Bushmen, who predate both the Europeans and the Xhosa. The Xhosa have been in contact and conflict with the Khoisan for centuries, defending their herds from Khoisan raiders, expelling Khoisan families from valuable hunting and agricultural land, pushing them ever farther to the west toward the Cape of Good Hope but also integrating them as herders, hunters, guides, religious practitioners, and even family members. The Xhosa have incorporated three click consonants from the Khoisan into their language—the explosive plop produced by the tongue rocketing from the top of the mouth, the gentle tut from the front of the mouth, and the cluck from the side.[11] The Europeans have rapidly conquered the Khoisan in their zone, reducing them to a servant class on European farms and with European livestock ranchers under a quasi-legal situation that amounts to forced labor at worst and indentured servitude at best. Christian missionaries of varying denominations had come among these broken people and many of them have embraced the new religion.[12]

Over the course of the eighteenth century, the border region where the two zones meet has grown increasingly violent as the Khoisan remaining there have resisted colonization by the Europeans and Xhosa, and the two major groups in the area have crossed paths more frequently, competing for grazing land and raiding each other's cattle. In response to Xhosa incursions, and, primarily, to perfect their predatory excursions, the Dutch settlers and their Khoisan allies have developed a military system built around the commando, which is a small to medium-sized group of armed and mounted men who muster, strike, and retreat quickly (often driving captured cattle before them). This time period has featured three particularly intense eruptions of conflict within the border region that will later be identified as the First, Second, and Third Frontier Wars. The amaNtinde lineage of Jan and Kote Tzatzoe is among the most western of the Xhosa lineages. As a result, the amaNtinde have had a significant degree of integration with Khoisan groups; they have also faced considerable European pressure and influence.

After James Read's accident and in spite of the rain, the party from Bethelsdorp hurries to reach the Sundays River before sunset. The north-to-south course of the Sundays marks the official border of the Cape Colony and Xhosaland, hanging like a plumb line through the border region. Elephants pose a *great danger*. The beasts rush to the river after dark, *resisting every thing before them*, and there are *no paths but what are made by them*. The river has a *frightful appearance*, both banks guarded by one hundred and fifty paces of reed beds, in rows so orderly as to appear planted.[13]

Read is happiest at times like these, *indulging his great desire for itinerating*, putting the constricting life of the mission station behind him, sleeping on the ground, searching for new converts. The son of a carpenter from a small village in Essex in southeast England, the missionary is broad-backed, with a welcoming face dominated by bushy eyebrows. Read first cast his lines off from Britain during the waning moments of the eighteenth century. He and his fellow missionaries aboard the *Duff* were anxious—yet eager—to jostle with storms, to journey halfway around the world to a land of soaring mountains, crashing waves, wide sandy beaches, fecund and savage vegetation. But the French fleet captured the ship in the South Atlantic, ending its voyage to the famed South Seas, and ordering it back to England. *Being thus disappointed in his object*, Read turned, instead, toward the craggy cliffs of the Cape of Storms.[14]

Having crossed the Sundays, the party passes through broken country. Open plains mix with *large woods*. Fresh elephant dung and the uprooted carcasses of trees remind Read just how far he is from England's tamer shores. But as he rides up to the village of Sibi, a *young Caffra and subordinant chief of Conga*—perhaps it is the rain which has him in such a nostalgic mood—he sits tall in his saddle, swivels around for a panoramic view, takes in with pleasure the *vast fields of Caffra and Indian corn*, and cattle dotting the fields to the horizon, and remarks to himself that it bears a *strong European resemblance*.[15] Another English traveler will share Read's admiration and nostalgia for the broken border country, which is *totally different from that about the Cape, being covered with grass . . . of the richest green; and large tracts with a striking resemblance to English park scenery*.[16]

The coastline to the east of Algoa Bay is ragged and treacherous. Heading inland, a coastal belt of rainforest clings to the sides of steep inland mountain ranges that tower over plains that extend about thirty to fifty miles into the interior. Large open grasslands intercede between coast and mountain. Here, mimosa *with its delicate green, rich yellow blossom* is the dominant presence. Acacia trees stand guard, their crowns of toughened-green leaves and disproportionately severe *milk white* thorns thrust regally into the air. On steeper slopes, there are spiky-haired aloe, both large and small, and the *palm-like euphorbia, with its naked trunk*. Many types of heather. *Different jasmines, speck boom, ivy geraniums*. Like giant candelabras, rock outcroppings display proteas; squat, anti-diluvian cycads with fernlike leaves trailing upward like a squid's many tentacles; and most spectacular of all, the flamboyant Strelitzia, blossoms blazing with an orange glory that seems to combine the red of the soil with the yellow of the noonday sun.[17]

Precipitous river valleys furrow the entire region, replete with *strikingly beautiful* timber: *the rich foliage of the wild fig, the plum, and that of the gnarled and twisted elsewood . . . the cold green of the bending willow*. Approaching to within twenty miles of the coast, the trees grow larger. Along with Assegai and Ironwood, there are now Stinkwood, Coral trees, and most majestic of all, the soaring Yellowwood, its stubby branches feathered with tiny, waxy, leaves forming an endearing counterpoint to its massive, corrugated, trunk. At the ocean's edge, rivers greet the sea with marshy hands.

It is possible that Read sees the aftermath of the fires that are *sometimes the effect of chance, frequently of design*, and that serve to regenerate the grass while helping it fight off the spreading mimosa and acacia. Cattle come *galloping and bounding and playing*. Young Xhosa boys are in charge of the herds, which graze on sourveld on the upland leas in the springtime, while the young grass shoots are in their infancy. Sweetveld, eaten year round, is found lower down the mountains and in the river valleys.[18]

Chief Sibi greets the travelers hospitably, offers them as much green Indian corn, or maize, *which when boiled or roasted is very delicious*, as they can carry, and agrees to serve as their guide and their translator of the message of *eternal welfare* as they push further into Xhosaland. They move on in search of Kote Tzatzoe's village, visiting another Chief, Camma or Kama, *who with his son had always . . . much regard for the word of God*. In the twilight they emerge from the dark recesses of the woods, inhale deeply of the brackish air, brush beads of sea-spray off their cheeks, and ride the short distance uphill to Kote Tzatzoe's village.[19]

The chief's eldest son greets them with signs of *great friendship*. He slaughters a fat ox as a *treat* and supplies them with fresh corn and a *sufficient quantity* of milk. Jan Tzatzoe and his father are away on a hunting trip gathering the skins of antelope, and of lion and leopard if their luck is auspicious. The skins will be sewn into karosses, or toga-like garments, with the leopard skin garments reserved for the few with aristocratic status. As night settles over the dwellings, a runner is dispatched to inform the hunting party of Read's arrival.

Read has been given the chief's *house* in which to stay, but he finds it *unbearable*. The Xhosa houses are *shaped like bee-hives, formed on strong wicker-work frames*, and *thatched with reeds or grass*. They have a *low, narrow aperature* for a door, and a *round shallow hole in the center* for a fire. Women do the majority of the construction, with the men providing the four to six central timber supports. A flat mat lies on the earthen floor, but, typically, no other furniture is present. Read complains of the smoke from cooking which only partly escapes through the door and the thatched roof. The small space throngs with visitors night and day, and his clothes, washed clean by the rain after his encounter with the mud, are again *quite red* after a night of such close proximity with the *quite naked*, clay-daubed bodies of the Xhosa men.[20]

Read wakes to sunshine slanting through an open door. Compounds consisting of the houses of a man and his multiple wives, and his central cattle enclosure, are known as kraals, and they are generally located on the *side of [a] gentle hill*, the *entrances of the huts* facing the *rising sun*. Kote Tzatzoe's kraal is only distinguishable from those of his followers by its relative size and the *elephant's tail hanging from a pole near its entrance*. Activity is audible beyond the thin clay and dung-daubed walls of the hut: women and girls murmur to each other as they start cooking fires and leave to fetch drinking water from the stream down slope; boys fetch their willowy cattle prods and gather around the cattle enclosure, readying themselves and their charges for another day of grazing and dozing and swatting at flies; older men emerge from the huts to admire their cattle and enjoy the calm and comfortable temperature of the early summer morning.[21]

Most of the boys and men are dressed in antelope karosses. The women and girls wear short leather skirts. The clothing is decorated with brightly colored trade, or more subtle bone, quill, and stone, beading. Both sexes wear necklaces, bracelets, and anklets made of shell, ivory, and copper. The men tend to favor copper or brass armbands. As they prepare for the scorching day, the villagers cover their exposed skin with a mixture of reddish clay and animal fat to protect against insects and sunburn. The result is to make them appear to be carved from *polished bronze*.[22]

Young boys herd the cattle and move around during the day in search of pasturage. At night, they return to the village cattle kraals. It is not unusual for hyenas, lions, and leopards to prowl around these walls of amputated thorn bush limbs. The older men are responsible for the care of the animals and the production of fermented milk, which is a key component of the daily menu. Cattle are the preeminent source of wealth in Xhosa society, and powerful members of society, mostly associated with the aristocratic families, gain followers by disbursing cattle. Young men aspire to two or three cows in order to raise a large herd with which they might pay bride wealth.

Read eases into the sunlight. He looks down the hill to the foaming shoreline. To his left and right, about twenty kraals are arrayed along the hillside in a row. Each one contains an average of twelve huts and a cattle enclosure. Below the kraals are abutting gardens; he can see sorghum, maize, millet, pumpkins, melons, sweetcane, tobacco. Next *fine grass* and timber, and running through it a river with *fine fish* that is stained by wood tannins to a color resembling the tea that he is sipping for his breakfast.

In the morning air, he holds a service for his little group. To his surprise, many members of the village arrange themselves around him. They conduct themselves in an altogether different manner from usual, keeping *very quiet*. He repeats the message he has delivered so often. Spoken in Dutch, it is consumed by various translators and released in Xhosa. The *word of God*: the *birth, life, death, resurrection, and ascension of Christ, the resurrection of the dead, and the last Judgement*.[23]

Around noon, the advance guard of the hunting party, about twenty men accompanied by twelve oxen, race into the seaside village, all in a *breaking sweat*. The oxen are trained to follow three men chosen to be advance runners, and they do so with *great swiftness*. Oxen are used to carry men into battle as well as to charge en masse with lowered and sharpened horns into the enemy's ranks.[24]

The men are dressed in readiness for hunting or war. These activities are often interchangeable, and the practice and training from an early age for one often prepares for the other. As one visitor to Xhosaland notes, *not even a small bird can rise from the grass, within sight of a native, without being pursued, and brought down by the kirri, which he throws with unerring aim*. In addition to procuring meat and skins, hunting trips allow for scouting and maintenance of a defensive perimeter around a chief's territory. The soldiers wear a loin-cloth and a thin leather belt around their heads onto which is sewn two grey or blue crane feathers, giving the appearance of horns. They carry elliptically shaped, hardened-ox-hide shields about four feet high, and a sheaf of assegais or spears. The assegais can be hurled with great accuracy, or by breaking the shaft in half, used as a stabbing spear. So equipped, the men attack the *most fierce* lions and leopards, creeping close to them under cover of the shield and then stabbing with their spears. They also engage elephants and hippopotami. The crane feathers, worn only when men are engaged in hunting or war parties, designate those that wear them—like this group of men who've been hunting with Jan Tzatzoe and his father—as military veterans. According to Read, these elite warriors are used tactically like the *cavalry in our troops*, held in reserve during an attack and sent forward in a rush when the enemy's ranks break.[25]

Soon after the advance guard, Jan and Kote Tzatzoe arrive astride oxen. According to Read, there is *great joy in meeting*. Tzatzoe is now a man, a full member of Xhosa society. He has undergone a lengthy initiation process. Did Kote Tzatzoe recall him from Bethelsdorp for this purpose? Or had he made the trek of his own volition? He and his fellow initiates, boys in their late teens born within a few years of each other, were sent into seclusion for several months, most likely during the preceding winter. In the bush, their bodies were daubed from head to toe with white clay. They learned the stories and wisdom that gird their world. They had to endure, without crying out, the removal of their foreskin. On occasion, they visited local villages, participating in nightlong feasts and dances during which they wore an elaborate headdress and a skirt made of palm fronds. Their passage into adulthood concluded when the local leader, in this case, Kote Tzatzoe, called them out of seclusion. At one last ceremony, they were officially returned to the village and welcomed by the male elders, who gave them final instructions on how to fulfill their new duties.[26]

Tzatzoe's coming of age means that he is now considered his father's chosen successor in preference to his brothers; to Read, he is the only son of the *real wife of Tzaatzoe*. Kote Tzatzoe, like most of the Xhosa leaders, had waited until his age, and his accumulated wealth in cattle, enabled him to marry his most important wife (in this case Tzatzoe's mother) from the most prestigious royal family that he could, usually outside of the Xhosa state. The eldest son of the union of a chief and his *real* or *Great* wife is endowed with more status that his half-brothers and becomes the first choice in chiefly succession. By anointing the son of his Great wife, a chief guarantees that his successor will only come of age when the chief is old enough to hand over power.

The talk between the missionary, the chief, and his chosen son continues throughout the day. Visitors come to pay their respects, especially the members of the hunting party, as befits their elevated social status: all express their *great joy* upon seeing Read. The villages in which the Xhosa live are held together through kinship ties and the perceived strength of the leader of a lineage. With an abundance of territory into which to expand, villages tend to fissure.[27] As a result, leaders (who can behave in quite autocratic and hierarchical ways) cannot always resort to direct coercion and must cultivate and maintain the loyalty of their followers. Much of a leader's time is spent, as Kote Tzatzoe's is on this day, consulting with the senior men of the village, adjudicating disputes, conducting diplomacy with neighboring villages and ensuring the physical and spiritual health of the community.[28]

Sitting with Kote Tzatzoe and his son, Read is having trouble with the women who crowd around him, *begging handkerchiefs, beads &c*. They have cleaned out his pockets and are surprised to find him unwilling to part with his last handkerchief, *not being able to conceive the use of it upon my neck*. But he admires them for their seeming innocence, and he appreciates the fact that they, unlike the women of other African groups he has encountered, are *always clothed*. As the day progresses, he remarks on the men, who seem *entirely without any kind of work*, but derives satisfaction from the *great share of spirits both men and women possess*—he notices them *playing upon their gora's* (sic) (a stringed instrument), singing and making what appears to him to be *the most strange and childish gestures*.

Kote Tzatzoe inquires into the state of the missionary institutions and asks after Read's fellow LMS missionary, Johannes van der Kemp. Before meeting Read in Graaff-Reinet in 1801, Van der Kemp had lived in Xhosaland for two years doing a great deal of itinerant preaching and acquiring a Xhosa name, either Jank'hanna, most likely given to him in honor of his bald, and (unusually for the time) uncovered, head, or Nyengana, *meaning one who* has *appeared as if by accident*.[29]

Kote repeats his request for a Missionary to come to him and instruct him and his people. Read, who now has his own Xhosa name, Ngcongolo, which literally means a reed, tells him that Van der Kemp has applied to Colonel Cuyler for permission to go to the Tambookies, or amaTembu, a group to the northeast that is affiliated with the Xhosa mainly through aristocratic marriage ties, but whose lineages separated centuries ago. Kote Tzatzoe is *much grieved*; he asks why he is not considered to be as desperate for instruction as the amaTembu. Read attempts to placate him with a promise to visit as often as he can, to which the chief replies he should leave *no means for that purpose untried*.[30]

In the midst of the visits and greetings, Read has ascertained that Jan Tzatzoe, having crossed one threshold into adulthood, is excited by the possibility of re-crossing another and returning to Bethelsdorp. Tzatzoe's return to Bethelsdorp from Xhosaland has been the *matter of* Read's *prayer for the whole journey*. Tzatzoe does not know how his father feels about the matter, and he is reluctant to broach the subject. He asks Read to do so, and Kote Tzatzoe replies in the affirmative. The chief points out that he has only a few sons, and that Tzatzoe is still *very young*. As the son of Kote's Great wife, Tzatzoe will eventually inherit his father's leadership role. Kote expresses his hope that as much of Tzatzoe's *time as possibly he could spare might be devoted to a farther knowledge of those things which he*, the old chief, has *lived and probably* will *die a stranger to*.

Years earlier, Kote Tzatzoe, alone among the Xhosa royalty who visited Bethelsdorp in its early years, handed his child to Read and Van der Kemp. Now, he does so again. Tzatzoe passes back to one father from the other. He will be the first member of the Xhosa aristocracy to live voluntarily among the encroaching Europeans. He will be the first to learn Dutch, the language of the border region, to be trained in the construction of wagons, wheels, and wood-framed houses, to appreciate European habits and religious practices first hand. But the choice of Jan and Kote Tzatzoe will have consequences far beyond those they might imagine. Tzatzoe will live on the liminal fringe of two societies. Others will follow, but he will have no contemporaneous companions. Like a ship rounding the Cape of Good Hope and passing over the turbulent rapids where two great oceans and their contradictory currents converge—one flowing cold and clear from the southern seas, the other warm and turbid from the northern tropics—Tzatzoe will live his life awash in tumultuous and unpredictable waters.

Having secured their companion, Read and his party must leave immediately. The pass that Colonel Cuyler has granted them for their time across the border is about to expire. Europeans are forbidden to cross the boundary without official sanction. Although some do, they are considered runaways and subject to military justice. Jan Tzatzoe is able only to gather a few of his belongings and say quick farewells.

Members of the party walk and ride off toward the descending sun. A *vast number of men, women and children*, who show *much affection to their young chief* accompany them for *some distance*, then gradually drop off the pace, until the only retinue left is the sigh of the wind through the long grass. Just before they reenter the colony, the party passes through a grove of human skeletons, picked clean and bleached by years of lying abandoned in the veld. The jagged white bones of an English officer and twenty of his men—ambushed a decade earlier by the Xhosa warriors they were attempting to drive out of the country—lie scattered about in full sight.

BETHELSDORP

Oh Free Grace!

1811–1815

In 1811, a year after James Read's journey into Xhosaland to retrieve Jan Tzatzoe, Read's wife, Elizabeth, gives birth to the couple's fourth child and first son: James Read Junior. Read had married Elizabeth at Bethelsdorp, in June 1803, immediately after the missionaries established the station on an abandoned farm set on burning, windswept flats a few miles inland from the majestic reach of Algoa Bay. To Read's fellow missionary, Johannes van der Kemp, Elizabeth, on the day of her marriage, was a *young Hottentot girl, the inventory of whose earthly possessions are two sheep-skins and a string of beads to ornament her body*. In fact, Elizabeth was twenty-four and only two years Read's junior.[1]

Jan Tzatzoe lives in the Reads' Bethelsdorp household, which must serve as a sanctuary for him. There are no archival records that elaborate upon the intimate life of the Read household. No way to know which language Tzatzoe uses to communicate, or to describe the sleeping arrangements, the allocation of domestic duties, the tensions and kindnesses of everyday life. Does Tzatzoe watch the young James Read's first steps and hear him speak his first words? To what extent does Elizabeth serve as a surrogate mother to the young Xhosa man whose mother is likely also of Khoisan descent? The lives of Jan Tzatzoe and James Read Junior will be intertwined: two trees born of the same soil, growing so close at first as to appear as one, but then splitting apart and separately seeking the nourishment of sun, rain, and earth, their branches inscribing different silhouettes against the sky, their roots burrowing in different directions for security and sustenance.[2]

James Read misses most of his son's first year of life. In late 1811, he and Van der Kemp are called to Cape Town to testify before the British Governor of the Cape Colony and a new judicial circuit court the Governor has created. The court is investigating complaints of the mistreatment of the Khoisan living in and around Bethelsdorp and on settler farms. Read is indirectly responsible for bringing the matter to the attention of the colonial government. A year earlier, he had written a letter describing the injustices to the Directors of the London Missionary Society. The Directors enlisted the aid of one of their staunchest allies in Parliament, the noted abolitionist William Wilberforce, and thereby gained an entrée into the government offices responsible for administering the colonies. The political attention in London had forced the hands of the local Cape officials.[3]

During the summer of 1811 and 1812, as Read and Van der Kemp testify in Cape Town, the British colonial government flexes its military muscle in the border region. Seeking to ensure European access to prime grazing land, it conducts a sustained campaign against some, but not all, of the Xhosa chiefs and their subjects who live near the Sundays River. It is a brutal and one-sided conflict. The colonial military leader, Colonel Graham, expels the Xhosa (including Kote Tzatzoe) across the Fish River, a distance of almost one hundred miles. He does so with crushing efficiency—shooting women and children in the bush, burning crops and grain pits and homes, confiscating milk cows along with trophy cattle.

One hundred miles northeast of Bethelsdorp, on a plateau running between the Sundays and the Fish in the middle of the newly conquered territory, a nascent outpost struggles out of its military fortress and supply depot cocoon and emerges as a mercantile town. The collection of barracks, rickety wooden buildings, and dusty streets bears the name of the man who has endowed it with its hinterland and bequeathed its invidious inheritance: Graham's Town. The government extends its mandate to the Fish and demands a complete closure of the border. This directive is, of course, more rhetorical than practical. The new order does little to prevent traffic between both sides of the boundary. But its chilling message has an impact on Bethelsdorp. Surrounded by newly constructed military posts, the region's inhabitants know that the stitches that suture the border together are unlikely to be cut easily, but that once they are, the border will open and gush with blood.[4]

Jan Tzatzoe is around twenty years of age when James Read returns, alone, from Cape Town in early 1812. While Read was testifying in 1811 Van der Kemp had died unexpectedly. Upon his death, Read inherited his mentor's unenviable position. He is now seen as the individual most closely allied with the native inhabitants of South Africa, and in consequence, a bitter enemy to settler interests. At the time of their reunion in 1812, Tzatzoe is far removed from the boy, who Read will describe in 1836 as having been (upon their first meeting in 1804) *without even the piece of sheep skin, ignorant and debased as the rest of his nation*. After a year at Bethelsdorp, Tzatzoe has shed his antelope or animal skin kaross, forgone the Khoisan sheepskin garments, and acquired European dress. He has also adorned himself in a foreign culture.[5]

Despite the British reconquest and administration of the Cape since 1806, there are few British settlers in the colony and the use of English is restricted to conversations between them, and to official British correspondence (the frontier colonial officials conduct their day-to-day business in Dutch and report to Cape Town and London in English). Jan Tzatzoe is learning how to read and write in Dutch, which is the language of the border region. He is apprenticed to a carpenter and a wheelwright, and he dabbles in the *smith's work* and in general handicraft trades. He wears the ritual and spiritual vestments of mission Christianity, too, by attending the open-air prayer meetings and worshiping in the small wooden chapel.[6]

But in a testament to the power of Christian conviction among the missionaries and their converts, and their central belief in the primacy of God's grace and its ability to reveal itself, Tzatzoe is not considered a Christian merely because he lives in the missionary institution, attends services, and performs the role expected of an African who has demonstrated a commitment to European norms of dress, habit, and industry. The missionaries and their congregation wait for Jan to embrace Christ for himself.

In the winter of 1814, Read and several other Bethelsdorp brethren attend a conference of missionaries and so-called *native teachers* and converts in Graaff-Reinet, a major provincial center located about seven days, or seventy hours, by ox-wagon to their north in the semidesert terrain adjacent to the Karoo Desert.[7] *Their minds are most deeply affected*, and upon their return to Bethelsdorp, *a great revival of religion* takes place. *There was a general awakening of the people*, Read reports to the LMS, *and, in a short time, fifty persons were added to the church*.

Read exults at the awakening of Jan Tzatzoe, the *son of a Caffre chief*, who, *till now, discovered no regard to serious religion*. In fact, Read adds, Tzatzoe had been a *ringleader of the young people in their follies*:

> The conversion of this youth made a deep impression on the minds of many, especially his companions. Affecting scenes took place at some of their public meetings; the greater part of the assembly being bathed in tears, and crying for mercy; while the believing Hottentots wept for joy, on beholding so many of the heathen turned from darkness to light, and added to the church of Christ.[8]

On the first of October 1814, Jan Tzatzoe declares before the entire congregation that he is now with God, becoming entry number ninety-eight on the Roster of Adult and Infant Baptisms at Bethelsdorp.[9] Does the ceremony remind Tzatzoe of his Xhosa initiation? The baptismal water that coats like the white paint of the Xhosa? The presentation to the community? The exhortations to live under new rules as a new man?

The reasons for the spiritual outpouring are unclear. Some historical commentators might attribute it to a mass hysteria, with members of the community being swept before a wave of excitement and sense of common feeling. Others might say that anyone seen resisting the crowd would feel that they are threatening their status or, even, their very place in the institution. Still others might feel that the Khoisan men and women understand that in order to gain the benefits of life at the station with the access to property, capital, and redress to law that it bestows upon them, they need to give the missionaries what they seem to want most, by professing an internal recognition of a Savior and therefore the existence of sins for him to forgive, and by demonstrating this belief externally by living an orderly lifestyle, one within behavioral norms dictated by the missionaries. Others might see a final surrendering of old gods and a prior spirituality in the face of cultural and social breakdown and the hopeful embrace of a supposed source of new spiritual power. And lastly, there are those who would point to the actions of a higher and more bona fide presence, and leave it at that.[10]

For whatever reason it is adopted, the psychological power of the revival is real. It fundamentally transforms the behavior, professed beliefs, and actions of many of those at Bethelsdorp and will shape their lives in ways they cannot imagine. Jan Tzatzoe is no exception to this statement; in fact, he is one of its most potent exemplars.

Bethelsdorp is a thriving center of Khoisan life. The institution claims 500 men, women, and children as inhabitants. There are 1,521 horned cattle, 1,125 sheep, twenty-six horses, and four wagons. Around thirty men are employed as artisans: they saw timber, burn lime, and serve as wheelwrights, smiths, carpenters, and bricklayers. With the help of some of the men, the women work in the communal gardens, weave mats and baskets, shape sheepskins into blankets, and gather thatching material. Schools are held twice a day with reading, writing, and some *arithmatick*, but studies are *retarded* by a want of books. Upward of four hundred adults are on the baptismal rolls in addition to almost three hundred children. Many different types of people pass through the station's gates seeking information, succor in the form of gifts of food, protection from oppressive employers, or security in the grant of a small plot of land and a chance to add a few cattle to the station's large herds.[11]

During its decade of existence, there have been many visitors to Bethelsdorp from Xhosaland. This traffic is driven, in part, by the preponderance of Khoisan kinship ties among the Xhosa. The colonial authorities are wary of the close ties between the communities, and do their utmost to prevent them. But many people slip through the border and pass unnoticed into Bethelsdorp and back again. Others move back and forth as laborers, working on settler farms for several years in order to acquire livestock with which to return to Xhosaland. Some of the visitors also return with items garnered from missionary teachings.

After the spiritual firestorm, Bethelsdorp becomes a proper *Christian Society*. Its members are *exceedingly lively and zealous*. The LMS missionary, Reverend John Evans, delights in *upwards of 200 of the Heathen* worshiping every Sunday and singing *praises to Father, Son, and Holy Ghost*, often continuing until midnight. Their motion reminds him of the *zealous welsh*, and he is sure that he has never heard an instrument in England that is the equal of the melody of the *sweet voices* rising up into the *profound silence of the night*. Children and adults increase their school attendance. Senior members of the community itinerate, seeking to *spread abroad the knowledge of a Saviour*. Three hundred more members are added to the Church roll. The baptized are so overcome with *feelings* that they *faint away* and lie *senseless on the grass for a considerable time*. A young Khoisan woman named Sanna Oursen, *who said some time ago that if Christ would shew her mercy she would do any thing in the world for him*, has a revelation and volunteers to accompany a missionary's wife on a journey to a northern LMS mission. She will not be long absent from Bethelsdorp.[12]

In a testament to his newfound conviction, his aptitude, and his ability to communicate, Jan Tzatzoe participates fully in the ongoing revival at the station. He and a fellow lay preacher named Matroos undertake proselytizing excursions to nearby farms and to the town of Uitenhage, where the authorities bar the visits of European missionaries. In town, they speak to kitchen maids and artisans. The conversation that Reverend Evans has with a Khoisan man he meets on the roadside during this time suggests the tenor of Tzatzoe's conversations with local Khoisan farm workers and cattle herds:

> Where is your home? Evans asks.
>   *With the farmers*, the man answers.
>   *What does he say to you?*
>   *Work, work, work.*

> *Does he say something of Christ and your Soul to you?* Evans knows the answer, but the response is still shocking.
>
> *No, but he tells me I have no soul! He tells me to look at the ox, he is black, and has short hair like you, that is what you are!*
>
> Evans then questions the man about who created him. The Khoisan man is silent. He replies reluctantly.
>
> *The farmer told me that the devil of Christians made me and all the Blacks. How did he prove that?*
>
> *He took a mirror and placed it before us—Then said he, There is as much difference between my creator and yours, as there is between the white and black face which you see in the mirror!!*[13]

Tzatzoe also preaches to the Bethelsdorp congregation. And it is during the afternoon of 15 October 1815 that his words are first directly recorded. Marking one of the key ways in which his life will be unique in South Africa, Tzatzoe's speech inaugurates a lengthy paper trail that, through the years, will reveal his evolving opinions, thoughts, even feelings. This first recorded address demonstrates the depth of Tzatzoe's raw emotion. It also speaks to his intellectual engagement with Christianity. His words have biblical resonance, alluding directly to the first book of the New Testament, the Gospel of Matthew, and its account of the Sermon on the Mount:

> In the afternoon Jan Tzaatzoo (the Caffre Chief) preached—during his discourse he said—"Here we enjoy great priviledges [sic] by hearing the word of God, but the question is, are we as thankful for it as we ought to be—then he noticed the goodness of God to his own countrymen in giving them health and providing food and raiment for them while they never prayed to the true God for any of these things. Oh! (said he with a deep sigh) how shall it go with my poor parents and sisters, not knowing any thing of God—however I hope God will hear my feeble prayer, and send some faithful Missionaries there, telling them of the Savior of the world—he then wept and concluded.[14]

The phrase, *food and raiment*, is used quite often in the Bible. And the fifth chapter of Matthew reveals a nonjudgmental and omniscient God, who succors even those who do not pray to him: *He maketh his sun to rise on the evil and on the good and sendeth rain on the just and the unjust* (Matthew 5:45). Tzatzoe further invokes the Sermon on the Mount, with its references to food and raiment, to reinforce the faith of his Bethelsdorp audience. The passage also amplifies his concern that while the amaNtinde are being adequately clothed and fed by God, they need to hear the Word of God directly, so that they might choose righteousness (and its additional material benefits) for themselves:

Behold the fowls of the air: for they sow not, neither do they reap, nor gather into barns; yet your heavenly Father feedeth them. Are ye not much better than they?

And why take ye thought for raiment? Consider the lilies of the field, how they grow; they toil not, neither do they spin:

Wherefore, if God so clothe the grass of the field, which to day is, and to morrow is cast into the oven, shall he not much more clothe you, O ye of little faith?

Therefore take no thought, saying, What shall we eat? Or, What shall we drink? Or, Wherewithall shall we be clothed?

But seek ye first the kingdom of God, and his righteousness; and all these things shall be added unto you. (Matthew 6:26, 28, 30–31, 33)[15]

Jan Tzatzoe is flourishing in his new world, with its new language, ideas, and stories.

Grace showers down like the steady rain, which, in the unpredictable and unreliable climate of Bethelsdorp, is the greatest blessing of all.[16] The rains swell the institution's dairy herd and water its fields. A young man returns from a woodcutting expedition in tears. He recounts how he left Bethelsdorp in disgrace, Reverend Messer telling him, *Wenzel, you must not return as you go.* During his first days in the woods, he cut his foot so dangerously with an axe that his life hung *as on a thread*. His foot improved as he began *pleading for grace*. Later, he came across a large tree, but he found its interior *hollow and rotten, and good for nothing*. The resonance between the tree and his own self proved overwhelming:

> It was as if the Lord had said to him, "That is a picture of you! a fine youth but a deceitful and rotten heart." He fell down and cried out Yes Lord, but thou art gracious &c. He was unable to relate more of his story, but cried out, Oh Free Grace!

Children convert other children. Boys and girls as young as nine confess their sins. *His sins are greater than the largest mountain in the world*, one says, he would rather die than live in sin again. Two young girls want to *speak of Salvation*.

> *Why?*
> *Because my heart is sick*, the brave one confesses.
> *Why is it sick?*
> *Because of my many sins.*
> *What will you do with such a wicked heart?*
> *Bring it to the feet of Jesus.*[17]

A speech from one of the converts conveys the power of the Christian mission and its message that Jan Tzatzoe has wholeheartedly embraced and is actively spreading. The grace of God brings virtue and reward to individuals and to the community, a true empowerment:

> We are all Hottentots, we never had a house, we never were esteemed or considered human beings, we never were allowed into a farmers house, and to day we are here sitting together in a large white house. We never had a waggon, and now there are more than twenty waggons at Bethelsdorp belonging to us Hottentots. Look at the women! who never had any good clothes; now you see them sitting amongst us in white and several colours. We never had the honour of knowing any thing of God or his word, and now we can read and write,—and the greatest thing God has favoured us with, is the sending unto us poor Hottentots, his servants, explaining unto us daily his holy word.

The conversions at Bethelsdorp are distinctly personal. Old Jager explains to Read that Christ himself has sent him to be baptized. Read points out that Christ is in heaven. How can he speak so directly? *Yes, but he is likewise on earth*, replies Jager, *he says that he shed his blood for my sins, and that I must drink it or die, and I do not know how to drink his blood.*[18]

One note mars the chorus. Read and his colleagues attribute the backsliding of a few of the converts to the work of an enraged Satan, resentful of Christ's usurpation of his throne in the hearts of the Khoisan. Satan's *attacks* are primarily revealed in the *chief vice* of adultery, to which the climate and *situation is very favourable*. Unfortunately, in time, not even the most respected and devout of Bethelsdorp inhabitants will prove immune.[19]

Four short days after Tzatzoe's speech at the prayer service, at ten o'clock at night on 19 October 1815, a British dragoon rides into Bethelsdorp atop a sweat-soaked horse. Candles are relit. Faces loom in windows. The soldier carries letters from military and civil officials at Uitenhage. Scanned hastily by Read and his brethren in the twinkling light, the letters warn Bethelsdorp that information has been received from Graham's Town that the *Caffres intend to invade and desolate the district*. This time the war does not materialize. But in this uneasy border region, it is seemingly always the eve of war. Pregnant uncertainty weighs down the European farmers, the members of the missionary institutions, and the soldiers huddled in the border posts.

Xhosa warriors and colonial commandos do not breach the border, but the fragile boundary cannot contain Christianity. In the aftermath of Graham's war, the expulsion of the Xhosa across the Fish River, and the establishment of border posts and Graham's Town itself, additional opportunities have arisen for Xhosa people to hear the preaching of the word of God and to interact with those who profess the new faith. Visitors from Xhosaland to the border posts and mission stations have increased in number. The first sustained encounter with British force has shaken the faith of many who were previously isolated from the new power in the border region.

A Xhosa woman who had visited Bethelsdorp is said to have taken a *Bible with her, which she reads amidst groups of attentive people*. An account from early 1814 places the woman with a group of Xhosa who have *separated themselves from the others*, forming a *large Kraal of praying Caffres*. The members of the kraal send word to James Read that he need only light a signal fire on his side of the Great Fish River and they will come over to see him. An officer who crosses the Fish in search of stolen cattle receives a tumultuous reception. The mistaken word that a missionary has arrived has drawn Xhosa people from *every quarter*.[20]

The missionaries gain inspiration from the evident spread of Christianity, even if it has occurred outside of their control. And the colonial officials grow increasingly curious. News about the village of praying Xhosa comes with increasing frequency. There is a charismatic leader at its head. This man, known by many names including Makana, Links, and Nxele, has captured the imagination of Xhosaland—*the case of this Caffra is in every mouth*, Read writes. Makana is reported to be of *singular character*; he goes from place to place, *inviting the attention of the people to religion; declaiming himself against war; and exhorting his countrymen and the king himself to pray to the true God*. The new leader states that *Christ had revealed himself to him*. James Read is suspicious of this line of thinking, acknowledging this unease—*whatever may be thought or said of this circumstance*—in a line of a letter to his Directors in London. Nevertheless, Read reports, the man is exposing his countrymen to Christ and admirably telling them that enough blood has been shed, that all the Xhosa assagais must be thrown into the sea, and that no man might enter his village with any sort of weapon. Were he granted permission to leave a missionary with these people, Read speculates, the biblical proposition of Isaiah *would be literally fulfilled*.[21]

Ever since Van der Kemp arrived in South Africa in the late eighteenth century, he and his fellow missionaries had tried to establish a mission in Xhosaland. But colonial policy prevented any missionary inroads, and Van der Kemp withdrew to Bethelsdorp where his dream infected the likes of James Read. Read had kept the prospect of evangelical action alive by promoting Xhosaland in terms that hewed to the hyperbolic vision of the evangelical movement: the promise of 100,000 new souls, ready to be saved, living in a land of abundant rain, streams that ran year round, timber aplenty, thick, nutritious, grasses, plentiful game and rich soil.[22]

In August 1815, Makana visits Bethelsdorp to deliver a singular message. He states that Christ himself had shown him his hands and feet bearing the bloody marks of the crucifix, and told him to *go and tell the other Caffres of what he had seen and heard*. Christ had assured him that in the face of resistance to his teachings, he would use the moon's eclipse (that had been visible on the 21 June 1815) to *confirm the truths of what you say*. Finally, Makana asks for a Missionary to accompany Jan Tzatzoe back to Xhosaland to instruct Makana's people.[23]

Makana does not ask for a missionary for himself, nor does he seek to usurp European authority. Perhaps he understands the symbolic power inherent in the figure of Jan Tzatzoe as a means of mobilizing the Europeans to support his own endeavors? Perhaps he hopes to gain personal power from his association with the young man who has entered the European world? While at Bethelsdorp he has likely heard Tzatzoe preach, listened to him translate his conversations with the missionaries, and spoken with him at length as one of the few Xhosa speakers at the station. Perhaps he feels he should emulate Jan Tzatzoe? That Tzatzoe might be able to teach him?

Does Makana's request, coming as it does from a powerful Xhosa leader, in turn, inspire a sense of pride, or ambition, or destiny in Tzatzoe? He has undergone a significant spiritual experience and is active as a preacher in the neighborhoods surrounding Bethelsdorp. Have his thoughts turned to the people he left behind, to the spiritual succor he might provide for them? Does he feel an amniotic tide flooding his soul, impelling him back to the land of his mother and father?

Following Makana's visit, Read engineers a widespread campaign for a mission in Xhosaland. He has evidence of the pacifying effects of Christianity and a receptive African audience. He has a recently arrived European missionary, Joseph Williams, and his wife, Elizabeth, who have agreed to the task, and who meet Read's *chief qualifications for Missionaries in Africa: burning zeal for the conversion of the Heathen; ardent Love to their persons, for their souls sake; and Self denial to a high degree*. He knows that the government's representatives, flush with the scientific fever sweeping through the far-flung British Empire, are increasingly keen on natural history and the gathering of *curiosities*, such as giraffe skins. These items Read offers to do his *utmost to procure* in the lands beyond the colony. Best of all, he has Jan Tzatzoe—a *Caffre chief, qualified to promote the arts of civilization among the people, as well as to promulgate the gospel of Christ.*[24]

Read places his *Caffre chief* at the point of attack, as a symbol of progress and possibility, as a potential means to cultural mediation and understanding. Writing to Colonel Cuyler, Read emphasizes that the *Caffras are very anxious for instruction and* beg *that Jan Tzaatzoe and a Missionary might be sent to them*. Tzatzoe has been *instructed in the Christian religion . . . been taught to read and write in a common way, ha[s] learnt the carpenter trade,* is *of almost incomparable behaviour*, and has *been baptized into the Christian religion*. Read emphasizes that Tzatzoe is not a political or military threat, having such an aversion to the *present barbarous manners of the Caffras* that he has *no intention or desire to return to his country, except it is with a view to introduce Christianity and civilization among his countrymen*. Furthermore, the *young Chief* has *no intention of residing in Caffra Land*, but instead *a great desire to see his friends, and impart to them the import of that religion with which he has become acquainted*. Read offers to accompany Tzatzoe, *should there be no objection on the side of Government*. Such a *step*, he concludes, *might break the ice for future good and introductions of Christianity, among that most depraved race of mankind.*[25]

Read offers to send the young Xhosa man to speak with Colonel Cuyler in person. It is not known if this visit ever takes place. Cuyler, forwarding Read's letter to the colonial secretary in Cape Town, does not mention a meeting with Tzatzoe, but Tzatzoe will successfully interact with senior colonial officials in the future, for himself and on behalf of the missionaries. Perhaps it is an audience with Tzatzoe, or an acceptance of Read's pretext that he will only be accompanying Tzatzoe into Xhosaland, or a fear of a renewed Xhosa military threat—regardless, in a reversal of colonial policy that Read feels is *truly remarkable*, Cuyler has a change of heart.[26]

Cuyler carefully frames his letter to Cape Town. The decision is *so weighty a matter*, he cannot *myself decide upon it*. He worries that the *Solicited visit of Mr. Read* will *renew that connexion which has been with much labour and study separated . . . between the Hottentots of Bethelsdorp and the Kaffree people*. Cuyler *strongly recommend[s]* that a *proper Missionary[,] a man of Education and known principals, should be sent among the Kaffrees*. And further, that the Missionary should be *accompanyed by the young Kaffree Jan Catzoe mentioned in Mr. Reads Letter by which the undertaking will have a favorable Introduction*. But an *intercourse to be renewed with the present Inhabitants of Bethelsdorp who are many of them connected by consanguinity and others by marriage &c is in my humble opinion not at present adviseable*. These relationships lead to *friendly visiting parties* who can *only be looked upon as Spys and in league with Thieves.*[27]

Despite Cuyler's endorsement, Read's letter lies dormant in Cape Town. By 19 January 1816, Read has waited long enough. He composes a vexed letter directly to the Colonial Secretary in Cape Town. His language bypasses the obsequious meanderings and obfuscation of official discourse: *Sir! About four months ago I got several pressing invitations from the Caffras to proceed with the young caffra chief who is at our Institution.* Read has been waiting with *painful anxiety* for an answer. Proud as he is of the progress among the Khoisan in the Bethelsdorp region, the Xhosa to the east are a *People of superior natural Talents*, with a *country fertile in the extreme, well watered and wooded and offering every advantage to a civilized life*. And who but the *young chief* to embody this potential?

Read refers to Tzatzoe's great importance, to the improvements he has made. He has been instilled with the habits of industry and religion. He will serve as a beacon to Xhosa youth and will be able to assure their elders of the *principles and good intentions of the English Government*. Read is so confident in the personal impression that Tzatzoe can make that he asks the colonial officials to consult with the members of the Circuit Court who had met Tzatzoe when they sat in Uitenhage during 1815. Then, the day after James Read writes his letter, Jan Tzatzoe writes one of his own.[28]

Tzatzoe's letter, in Dutch, is addressed to a member of the Court, Mr. Bresler, and Bresler promises to forward it to Cape Town in *Jan's own hand writing*. Its formal diction indicates grammatical and rhetorical assistance. Does James Read do more than help? Does he write it himself? Dictate it? Whatever Read's contribution, Jan Tzatzoe speaks through the stilted compositional conventions of the time.

> Sir
>
> You will not take it amiss that I address myself to you in this Letter. I should not have dared to have taken this liberty had it not been for the kindness you showed me when at Uitenhage and Bethelsdorp.
>
> You know that my desires are very strong that my Nation should become acquainted with the things that belong to their eternal happiness that is to know the Lord Jesus Christ.
>
> I enjoy a Privilidge [sic] that no one of my Nation enjoys and I cannot rest till they enjoy the same.
>
> Mr Read has written twice to Government for permission for Missionaries to go but no answer has been received.

Now is my earnest request that you and Mr Jennings will use your interest with His Excellency to get my wishes satisfied. I shall always consider myself under obligation.
With much esteem I sign myself &c

Sir
Your obedient Servant
Jan Tzaatzoe[29]

MAKANA'S KRAAL

A Door to that Numerous Race is Opened

1816

In February 1816, less than a week after receiving Jan Tzatzoe's letter, the British Colonial Secretary in Cape Town, Colonel Bird, writes directly to James Read (the letter bypasses Cuyler while still relying on that official's positive recommendation); *trusting that success will attend the attempt*, permission is granted for Joseph Williams, Jan Tzatzoe, and a few Khoisan assistants to enter Xhosaland. A delighted Read writes with *unspeakable pleasure* to the Directors of the London Missionary Society: *a door to that numerous race is opened*.[1]

The British are having a difficult time administering the European settlement zone whose boundary they have recently extended. They have inherited its recalcitrant Dutch peasantry and frontiersmen, or Boers, who seem intent on disregarding British regulations, its dislocated Khoisan groups who refuse to surrender their migratory lifestyles for manual labor on colonial farms, and its constant visitors from Xhosaland about whose motives and beliefs little is known. Under martial rule, the British maintain tight control over the colonial subjects near their towns (the government is sufficiently strong, for example, to compel the missionaries' compliance, thus the repeated requests to Cape Town), but outside of the officials' immediate purview, laws and regulations are routinely broken. Rumors abound and rebound, of a Xhosa invasion of the colony, and worse, of the Boers combining forces with the Xhosa.

In sanctioning Read's Xhosaland mission, some colonial officials may wish to introduce the Xhosa, who have already witnessed the power of British military might, to the more compassionate aspects of their civilization. Others likely see that the missionaries will be able to gain access where soldiers cannot, providing invaluable knowledge of their current antagonists and potential future subjects. Or, perhaps, the capitulation results from a momentary cessation of Cape Town's daily harassing summer southeaster, allowing the colonial officials huddled behind Cape Town's stone walls an uplifting of spirits, a soothing of frayed nerves?

Next step for Bethelsdorp: prepare a convoy to deliver men and material into Xhosaland to establish a mission station. All supplies and farm implements must be carried in one or two ox-drawn wagons: axes, hoes, and saws; vegetable seed; carpentry tools, nails, and paint; a bell for the chapel; books and instruments of instruction. Read complains that the items, for the most part having been shipped from London, are stashed away in boxes that are too large to be easily moved around. Glass is the one item that remains elusive.

Read is also concerned about Jan Tzatzoe, *our young caffre*, as he calls him, who is now *some what under the character of a Missionary* but who lacks the missionary's requisite suit of clothing. Read wishes to make him a *coat of many colours*, and he dips into Missionary funds to purchase clothing for him. Does Tzatzoe, in turn, adopt Joseph's next act in the biblical tale, to dream a dream of his nation deferring to him as a leader? He must imagine many different possibilities and scenarios as his clothes are bought and fitted, as six weeks pass, and the preparations for departure grow more intense.[2]

Read asks Cuyler for permission to have five Khoisan men from Bethelsdorp accompany the party for *attendance and protection*. Cuyler agrees, but he stresses the importance of preventing communication of any sort between the *Hottentots of the Colony* and the *Kaffres*. Read, Williams, and Tzatzoe visit Cuyler in Uitenhage on 28 March 1816 to ask for last minute advice and instructions. They return home with a gift of ten pounds of gunpowder. The following Sabbath, Bethelsdorp holds a ceremony to bless those who are leaving, and Jan Tzatzoe is once more the focus of attention. In his many-colored coat, he stands before the congregation as the missionaries *set him apart* to the Lord's work. It is a *day much to be remembered*, in the words of James Read, a day when the promise of the mission to the Xhosa people is personified, when the symbol of Jan Tzatzoe meets the reality of personal feeling.[3]

The ceremony begins in the early morning, the Khoisan congregants sitting on the dusty ground in front of the dais. Brother Messer addresses Tzatzoe and the congregation from 1 Timothy 4:12–16:

> Let no man despise thy youth; but be thou an example of the believers, in word, in conversation, in charity, in spirit, in faith, in purity. Till I come, give attendance to reading, to exhortation, to doctrine. Neglect not the gift that is in thee, which was given thee by prophecy. Take heed unto thyself, and unto

the doctrine; continue in them: for in doing this thou shalt both save thyself, and them that hear thee.

James Read is a man whose oratory seems to rise to meet momentous occasions. Now, he feels the full weight of the years he has spent with Jan Tzatzoe. His address meditates on these biblical words, *Thou therefore, my son, be strong in the grace that is in Christ Jesus*:

> And the things that thou hast heard of me among many witnesses, the same commit thou to faithful men, who shall be able to teach others also.
> Thou therefore endure hardness, as a good soldier of Jesus Christ.

Read confesses in a letter that he writes later in the day that he can make the statement with the knowledge that *I could consider him my Son in two sences, as being so long (10 years) in my house as a child and 2ndly in a Spiritual relationship*. Does he articulate these thoughts to the crowd as he undertakes the final step of the ceremony and hands Tzatzoe a Bible? The father turning to the son, the son now grown up and moving away to become a Good Soldier of Jesus Christ.

The congregation bursts into *a bitter weeping*; of the five hundred present, there are *very few dry eyes*. Many in the gathering have grown up with Read's kind face peering out to them every Sunday. They have seen his close friendship with the boy who is now a man. Tzatzoe seizes his turn to speak. Again, he refers directly to Christ's Sermon on the Mount, this time quoting directly— *Seek ye first the kingdom of God, and his righteousness*. He continues in an autobiographical direction. *When he was very young*, he had *heard something* of the Missionaries. Knowing that his father was going to visit Bethelsdorp, he had begged to go along but had been denied permission. He decided to follow his father at a safe distance, only revealing his presence when a return journey was out of the question. Upon arriving at Bethelsdorp, he found the missionaries and their preaching *so agreeable* that he and Dr. Van der Kemp had asked his father for permission to let him stay. After several years, the *Lord was pleased to change his heart*, and here he is now.[4]

Perhaps intending his life's story to illustrate God's righteousness, Tzatzoe offers a new biography from the one he told prior to his baptism. Now, he is the spirit behind the decision to engage with the Europeans, their Christianity, and their civilization. His father's role is diminished. This new self-representation reflects a reshaping of memory to fit evangelical needs. It may well be closer to the truth. Years later, James Read will speak of Jan Tzatzoe arriving at Bethelsdorp with an *avowed wish . . . to acquire some knowledge of the language of white men, and of the arts of civilized life.*[5] Kote Tzatzoe, however, will by word and action dispute this new interpretation.[6]

Tears stain the memory of Tzatzoe's last day at Bethelsdorp. The traveling party is up early in the morning, brewing tea. They test the leather harnesses that encircle the bellies of the oxen. Will they be strong enough to carry the loads and yet flexible enough to shift with the jostling of the stony paths?

On 1 April 1816 the journey begins by following a newly cut road along the Sundays River to the mission station of Theopolis. But moving past Theopolis, the wagons are impeded by the characteristic tangled mass of trees and vines that clog up every river valley in the border region. The danger from unpredictable elephants is so great that the party stays up well past midnight, large fires burning to light the ravine. Finally breaking into a clearing, the exhausted and hungry group holds a prayer session in gratitude, with the *young chief Tzatzoo* presiding.[7]

As he prays for the Xhosa and their mission to them, Tzatzoe is *so much affected* that he cannot continue and another Khoisan member of the party finishes for him. Why this collapse, this failing of nerve and energy? Is it the overwhelming difficulty of the passage or the overpowering expectations being placed upon him? Perhaps the flooding emotions of the anticipated reunion with family, friends, and his father? Or a powerful sense of a divine presence and its mandate to serve as a vessel of grace, now that the fulfillment of its wishes is so near at hand?

The party passes through Graham's Town and survives an attack on one of its Khoisan members, who while chasing a honey bird to find a beehive runs into a buffalo instead.[8] From their camp on the summit of the Zuurberg, they look past the colonial boundary at the Great Fish River upon an extended vista of Xhosaland: from the craggy defiles of the Winterberg, over the jumbled hills, to the broken coastline.

Along with his spiritual son, James Read is experiencing surging emotions. As his companions light signal fires from their elevated perch and await the arrival of Xhosa guides to convey them across the dangerously elevated Great Fish—as they wait and continue to wait—Read reflects on his feelings. He is elated to see the country again and to know that a way is opening, that in a *wonderful circumstance* he can now look forward to *imparting to the Caffres the gospel*. But other thoughts crash in upon him, *suggestions* made to his mind, that he *should never cross the Fish River*.

The source of this psychological anxiety, so rarely revealed in early nineteenth-century accounts, is impossible to trace, but the premonitions prove false. After days of waning patience, just as Tzatzoe rises from his knees having concluded another prayer service, the Khoisan members of the party loom into view accompanied by *Caffre* companions. The party reassembles itself across the border. Clothes soaked during the river crossing are hung up to dry, and Read calls a meeting. He wants to fulfill a vow he made before the crossing, in an attempt to silence the demons in his head, by *offering public thanks to the Lord* and *devoting* himself *afresh to his service*. The water washing over the floorboards of the wagons has evidently carried his misgivings along with it.

No sooner has Read begun then he must interrupt his prayers. Following the panicked glances of the worshippers out to the woods, he sees an encircling mass of humanity, more than one hundred Xhosa men and women bedaubed in red paint and leather karosses with assegais in hand. The Xhosa group communicate that they come from the kraals of Makana, where they are taught to *abstain from blood-shedding, theft, witchcraft, and adultery*. The majority of the group begin begging for beads, buttons, and other baubles, but one woman in particular impresses Read by her earnestness in sitting down to *hear the word of God*. She tells him that she pities the others, *that if they felt what she felt*, they would not be asking for trade items but for the *word of God*.

The group from Bethelsdorp moves out, singing hymns as they go, and the Xhosa follow for a considerable distance, *seemingly delighted*. The melodies settle like mist over the landscape, diffusing into the wind seeking its way through the mimosa trees and the cacophonous chatter of insects and birds.

Venturing deeper into Xhosaland, attention begins to shift toward the chief's son in the party's midst. It is tempting to try to see and feel and understand and empathize with Tzatzoe, but Read does not make him the focus of his narrative account of the journey. He provides hints, and he reports scenes, incidents, even dialogue, but never feelings or emotions. Take the following lines:

> We spanned out at a little distance from a kraal of Caffres, many of whom were present at worship; and our brother Tzatzoo prayed, for the first time, in that language, which seemed to have a good effect.

Imagination can soar. Tzatzoe's young life had already seen many journeys. His conception of the possibilities of life was altered; he felt a divine presence that has shaped his thinking and feeling. And now from the realm of strangers—alien, yes, but kindred and kind—he has returned home. With him, inside of him, tapping the deepest core of his being, he has brought the power to move, to exhort, to convert, the power to redeem life itself; this he surely believes. The power to be an interpreter between the missionaries and the Xhosa chiefs and commoners with whom they will engage. The power that sprung from a source as comforting as that which an upset child derives from the embrace of a parent: the power of his mother tongue.

The first Xhosa village visited by the party is that of a chief named Kobus Congo, who awaits the party with two of his brothers and twenty of his *chief men*. He shakes hands with them as they enter the tramped-down and meticulously swept soil of the chief's kraal and promises to guide them to Makana's kraal. Tzatzoe preaches again in Xhosa. In all likelihood, he is positioned beneath a large tree, probably an acacia. Villages in Xhosaland, especially those containing the kraals of chiefs, often have such large meeting trees where the leaders of the community can gather in a circle in the shade.[9] At the conclusion of his service, the majority of the *great concourse of Caffres* who have assembled to hear the evangelists *retire to the bushes to pray*. There, Golana is *heard to pray thus*:

> O Taay (Jesus Christ) give me a heart to understand thy word! I believe thou canst do it: for that man (Tzatzoo) who preached it, is likewise a black Caffre.

On 19 April 1816, Tzatzoe's memories interrupt the monotony of shuffling feet and bellowing oxen. Passing over a plateau on their way to Makana's kraal, he looks up to recognize the spot where he first saw Van der Kemp, who had been without shoes, socks, or even a hat to shield the sun on his itinerant journey through Xhosaland in 1799. Tzatzoe's past and present is colliding with increasing frequency.

At Makana's village, on Sunday, 21 April 1816, about a thousand people gather to worship and to witness the strange visitors from the west. They hear first from Jan Tzatzoe, preaching in Xhosa from Galatians 1:3–5:

> Grace be to you and peace from God the Father, and from our Lord Jesus Christ. Who gave himself for our sins, that he might deliver us from this present evil world. To whom be glory for ever and ever.

Makana, who now goes by at least one more name, Langa, or the Sun, then begins to preach. Read is impressed by Makana's passion and potential, likening him to John the Baptist. But he is also perplexed by the syncretic nature of his teachings. Several years earlier, Makana had lived in Graham's Town where he evinced an *insatiable curiosity*, talking to military officers about war and to artisans about wheelwrighting or blacksmithing. A Dutch minister, Brother Van der Lingen, felt the full force of his *acute intellect*, as he questioned the doctrines being preached in chapel and returned to *puzzle* the preacher with *metaphysical subtleties or mystical ravings*.

Makana had begun to piece together Christianity, biblical verse, the tenants of Xhosa religion and idiom, and his own *wild fancies*, presenting an *extravagant religious medley* that involved God and his son, the *creation, the fall of man, the atonement, the resurrection, and other Christian doctrines*. As an example, on a later occasion, drawing on biblical imagery that will resonate with his pastoralist audience, Makana will urge a group of Xhosa to *stick fast to the word of God . . . as the Gum does to the Trees and as the roots of the Grass stand against the beast while they are plucking at the blade*.[10] Read senses a confused, yet kindred, spirit who has to merely *gain more light*. Makana needs guidance, but he represents specific evidence that the Bible is spreading, that success in converting the Xhosa is imminent.[11]

Makana is not the only Xhosa leader who has begun to embrace and perpetrate the spread of Christianity in Xhosaland. Another key figure, and one against whom Makana will be directly pitted in the future, is near at hand. Ntsikana will be remembered by many as the first great Xhosa Christian spiritual leader, an important political advisor, accurate seer, and composer of important Xhosa hymns. Growing up in the border region in an aristocratic family, as a boy, in 1799, Ntsikana was impressed by the preaching of Van der Kemp. Later, after securing a large inheritance from his father, he gained an elevated political position and following as a Xhosa chief. Just before Read and Tzatzoe's visit, he had a deeply personal conversion that involved seeing an extraordinarily bright ray of light strike the side of his favorite ox as he examined it in the dawn light. Like Joseph Smith, a contemporaneous prophetic figure with an illuminated vision living on an uneasy frontier, Ntsikana found himself transformed. He abandoned the social gathering to which he had been invited that day, and that evening washed off his red ochre body paint. In the morning, he emerged from his house humming the first of the hymns for which he would be remembered.[12]

Following Jan Tzatzoe's address to the large gathering, Makana speaks of the *Creation, the Fall of Man*, and *the Deluge*, proving his case by noting the presence of shells on the highest peaks of Xhosaland. For his Xhosa audience, who maintain a rigid physical and psychological division between the land and the sea—rarely swimming in the ocean and never taking to boats—and who are aware that the light-skinned strangers who have wrought havoc in past decades originally came from the ocean, the thought of the land submerged by water must be a terrifying and apocryphal vision.[13]

Makana continues, *upbraiding* the audience for their *blindness and hardness of heart*. His listeners are missing the signs of his message, which are scattered all about them. When they drink water, they do not realize that it is the *water of life*. When they walk through a grove of thorn-trees, they do not think of how Jesus, or Taay, was *crowned with thorns*. Dali, or the Creator—the name Makana employs for God in opposition to the missionaries who used the Khoisan-inspired appellation Thixo—had sent Nyengana (Dr. Van der Kemp) to them, but they had not listened. So Nyengana returned to the Khoisan, the *despised nation*, who had *received* the word. Dali then turned to Makana himself, a *raw Caffre*, to warn them, and now Nyengana's son, Read, and the *child Tzatzoo* are here to bear *witness to the word*.

Makana's message centers on the polygamous nature of Xhosa society. God had taken only one rib from Adam to make a woman, and had given him only one wife. Who are the Xhosa to challenge this precedent?[14] He seeks *obedience* to his proclamations; they are not mere suggestions. Without quick action, Dali will return again, this time bringing not water but fire that will sweep the land. Makana's listeners have likely witnessed the torture to death by fire of accused witches.

The meeting breaks up and Read quizzes Makana in private. The Xhosa preacher understands the general outlines of Christian teaching, such as the crucifixion and eternal punishment, but Read feels he lacks a *real knowledge of himself and of the gospel*. He also *entertains a most strange notion of his birth, as derived from the same mother as Christ*, but Read downplays the heresy. Surely, Makana intends this to mean his *new birth through which he might call Christ his brother*.

Makana's conversion occurred early in his life when he had been confronted by a crowd seeking to throw him into a large fire (presumably because he had been accused of witchcraft). But Taay had delivered him from the situation and told him to follow in Nyengana's footsteps, making Taay's will known to the Xhosa. Though a dispossessed commoner from the group with the lowest status among the Xhosa, Makana has recently been appointed as a chief. He confesses to Read that while his entourage is growing, he feels it his *duty* to keep preaching to them. One day, Taay would *breathe his wind into their mouths, ears, &c, and then they would be obedient*. Makana has merged the concept of the Holy Spirit from the New Testament and the breath of life, with the Xhosa notions of breath and spirit.[15]

On Monday, the paramount chiefs of those lineages of the Xhosa state located west of the Kei River arrive at Makana's kraal to discuss the feasibility and location of a mission station for Williams and Jan Tzatzoe. Tzatzoe's amaNtinde trace their descent back to the Xhosa's founding ancestor, Tshawe. Thus, they are accorded a fair amount of respect and independence and not held to be directly subservient to any other lineages. Their marginal size, however, leaves them constantly vulnerable.[16]

The political situation of Xhosaland is in flux because of the ongoing competition between the region's two major chiefs and rivals: Ndlambe, and his nephew, Ngqika. Ndlambe has given Makana his full backing and protection, and in turn, has gained renewed leadership status as the champion of the region's most effective spiritual leader. Ngqika, with whom Ndlambe has been locked in a decade's-long power struggle, has turned to the British across the colonial boundary for political assistance.

Read, Tzatzoe, and the Bethelsdorp party need to recognize, respect, and cultivate the power of Ndlambe (and Makana as his surrogate). But they have also set out from Algoa Bay with instructions from Colonel Cuyler to provide as much intelligence on Ngqika as they are able to gather, and crucially, with a predetermined desire to establish Williams and Tzatzoe's mission station in the territory that Ngqika controls. Jan Tzatzoe is the primary intermediary in this complex diplomacy. He is not only an interpreter of language, but of cultural idiom and diplomatic protocol.

The meeting convenes early in the morning. Of the assemblage of minor chiefs and their retinues, one group stands out: Kote Tzatzoe along with his four brothers and two sons. Read tells us nothing of Tzatzoe's reunion with his father, uncles, and brothers. Is Tzatzoe's family proud of his growing eloquence and importance to the missionaries? Is he happy? The young Xhosa man has regained the embrace of his family, has returned to a deeply felt part of his emotional being, and yet he has grown in ways that are beyond comprehension to those whom he had once held dearest. Once again in his young life, this time surrounded by his closest family and friends, does he feel quite alone?

Boklo, one of Tzatzoe's uncles, opens the meeting, thanking the chiefs for attending and thanking Taay for sending the missionaries with the word of God. While acknowledging that Makana's preaching has reached many Xhosa, he blames the defiance of others to a *corruption of their hearts*. Kobus Congo continues, noting his long acquaintance with Read, whom he calls Nyengana's son, and stressing that his father, Pato, had often told him that *man has an immortal soul* and that only a part of him dies upon physical death. He wants to know more about this, and will take on the Williams mission himself if none of the other chiefs volunteer to host it.

Ndlambe's brother and sons hope that the arrival of the missionaries will bring peace to the region. Ndlambe relates that he feels too old to understand the word. He would be happy to put a stop to raiding, cattle thieving, and witchcraft, but he could never give up his young wives. According to Read, this statement prompts an outburst from Jan Tzatzoe. Dispensing with the usual diplomatic protocol, he speaks out of turn and in direct opposition to his superiors and elders. Tzatzoe makes it clear that the missionaries have no *authority to command in such cases*. They cannot dictate behavior and custom, but only make *known the will of God*. Nevertheless, he continues, the Xhosas' *manner of living* is worse than beasts, *worse than cats and dogs*; they are in a most pitiful state that might only be rectified by listening to, and heeding, the word of God.[17] In coming years, missionaries in the border region will increasingly seek to constrain directly what they consider to be immoral behavior, and conflicts between them and the chiefs will increase. Tzatzoe himself will have to decide how best to spread his ideas about right and wrong, by suggestion as a missionary, or more directly, as a chief.

After the meeting, the chiefs breakfast in Read's new tent, the canvas of which is soon decorated by the red clay that covers the men's bodies and karosses. Though their *appearance* is *offensive*, Read notes, their *company* is *very agreeable*. Ndlambe agrees that Makana, as his surrogate, should point out an appropriate site for the mission station. Makana is intent on quizzing the missionaries on many religious and secular subjects including the character and role of the King of England and the nature of English government under a constitution.

Three days later, the travelers arrive at the newly founded residence of Kote Tzatzoe, who has settled with his family and followers on the banks of a river about thirty miles to the east of the Keiskamma. To the best of Read's knowledge, European settlers have not yet named the river, called the Umqonci by the Xhosa, and he names it the Somerset River, in honor of the Governor of the Cape Colony. But the Somerset, described by Read as one of the *finest Rivers in Caffre Land*, will become known to future generations as the Buffalo River.[18]

Kote Tzatzoe pleads for his son and Williams to establish the mission with him. He has selected the site on the river with the specific intention that, upon his return, Jan might make use of it. He pledges every means of assistance in converting the rocky grassland into farmland and creating irrigation canals. Sensing Read's reluctance, he presses his case. *You are my friends*, he says, *and thus, from the connection between us, I cannot permit you settling anywhere else*.

Read replies that he is worried that the chief will *introduce other customs*— and potentially inhibit the changes demanded by life in a mission. Kote Tzatzoe responds indignantly. He had not sent Jan away for an education, only to have him return and conform to the old ways of living and thinking. He had sent him to Bethelsdorp so that he might return and teach his father, his father's children, and his father's people, how they should behave. He will do nothing to constrain Jan's choice of how to dress, how to farm, and how to construct his home. He insists on the *first claim, especially on his son*.[19]

Read is notably silent on Jan's feelings about settling near his father. It appears he has little interest in attending to his father and his people's material needs. Instead, Read feels that Tzatzoe has aligned himself with the evangelical work of the intended mission, and believes as Read does that this work needs to take place closer to the colonial boundary, in Ngqika's territory, because those *Caffres dwelling on the borders seem in a moral sence* (sic) *to want the labours of missionaries most*.[20] Likely, Read fears that with its proximity to European influence, the border features a form of Christianity that is taking root and flowering rampantly without the careful pruning that only a European missionary might provide.

Early in the morning on 26 April 1816, Jan Tzatzoe takes leave of his family, blessing the kraal and committing it to God. One of his brothers weeps as the party departs. The party sets off again, with the intention of seeking Ngqika wherever they might find him. They travel back to Makana's kraal through a densely populated region, meeting up with groups of Xhosa every time they halt. In the afternoon, they encounter a large Xhosa hunting party consisting of fifty men leading twice that many hunting dogs.

Tzatzoe and Read spend several days visiting the kraals of lower-ranking chiefs. Then, at ten o'clock one night, Hendrik Noeka, Ngqika's interpreter, strides into their camp. Read is ecstatic, effusive in his praise of Noeka's ability to command respect among the Xhosa and to translate the words of the missionaries effectively, to *put word into our mouths*, as he terms it. This praise suggests that Read might have become dissatisfied with the ability of Jan Tzatzoe and his Khoisan companions to translate his words into Xhosa; more likely, he feels that Ngqika is the most important person he will visit on the journey and that every advantage he can take into the meeting is to be treasured.

Ngqika approaches his meeting with Read and Williams in the regal manner that is expected of a person whom Read describes as *His Majesty*. He advances with his retinue trailing behind him, shakes hands, and then with a little smile asks if he might conduct some important business among his subjects before consulting with the missionaries. He returns after an hour, causing the people who have been thronging the party's wagons to disappear into the surrounding vegetation. Read invites him into his tent, which step is accomplished with decorum, as the chief's guards form in rank outside the canvas walls.

In a delicate conversation, Ngqika makes it clear to Read that he is insulted that he has not been officially informed of the missionaries' visit, and of their request for a location for a mission. Read insists that visiting him has been his first priority, that he had asked Makana to send a message to this effect. Read then asks the chief where he might wish for the mission to be located. Ngqika replies in a circuitous fashion, asking for a complete report of the answers of the other chiefs, turning the question back to the missionaries and asking them where they would like to settle, before finally stating his inability to make the decision without final consultations. Without contact with the other chiefs, Ngqika says, he is but a *child*, unsure of how to act.

The meeting adjourns with the decision having been cast back to Williams and Tzatzoe, who beg for a day to consider their options. With the help of Tzatzoe's understanding of the subtleties of Xhosa diplomacy, Read decides that Ngqika clearly wants a mission station, but is afraid to make an outright case for one because he does not want to appear greedy or manipulative in the eyes of the other chiefs. The following morning, another bout of talks, until Read finally declares that *Mr. Williams has no objection to come and reside with him, if it is his wish, and if a proper place can be found*. Ngqika answers that *the whole country is before* them. The matter is settled when the party decides to reconnoiter the highly recommended Kat River valley.

The conversion turns to reflect the political concerns that Colonel Cuyler had insisted they cover. Read describes these talks in a passage that is noticeably missing from the report of the journey he sends to the LMS, but that features prominently in his report to Cuyler. Read reiterates the colony's concern with cattle raiding across the border region. The colonial officials hold Ngqika *responsible for the many lives constantly lost by thieving cattle*, as each Xhosa raid leads to colonial retaliation.[21] The government is obliged to protect its inhabitants, Read insists, but *if the caffres would conduct themselves better, Government would exert itself to make them happy*. Read also asks the chief and his headmen about reports that the Boers are attempting to fight the English and are trying to enlist the Xhosa's military aid. His enquiry is met with laughter. Ngqika and the other chiefs tell Read that they are glad to hear of the government's intention to introduce a system of trade across the colonial boundary in the form of regional markets, and that many of them have stockpiled ivory for this purpose.

The meeting returns to religious matters, and Ngqika expresses his astonishment that he might be able to pray in his own language. Years before, he attended services where Nyengana spoke in Dutch, but now the European missionaries have returned with a native Xhosa speaker in the person of Jan Tzatzoe. A final prayer service is held. Ngqika and his chief men, arranged in order of rank, sit to the missionaries' left. Their wives remove themselves from their husbands in public, and sit in the enclosed tent. Many people from the surrounding neighborhood sit before the group, women placing themselves behind the men.

One man has traveled two days to see the preachers. He appears sickly, but says that the *sickness* is *in his heart*. A year ago, his sins had been revealed to him, but he had not known what they were and tried to drive away the *convictions*. At a ceremony held to detect a witch, he had fallen down, close to death, and had seen a vision of a *glorious Person, so glittering* that his eyes grew dim in looking upon him. Then a voice had said this person could help him. Now, he knows that the missionaries are the people he was seeking.[22]

Tzatzoe leads the service, preaching with *great boldness* in the language of the people. Upon the conclusion of the prayers, members of the crowd disperse to the bushes. That afternoon, the Khoisan members of the party, with tears in their eyes, exhort the people in small groups, acquainting *them with the way of salvation*. Ngqika seems particularly moved. He remains with the party deep into the evening—as the young boys bring the cattle home to the kraals and the sunlight draining from the sky is met by an onrushing tide of darkness. When the dark emptiness of the night sky blazes with cold white light, Ngqika points heavenward and declares that *as impossible as it is to tell the stars, so impossible is it to tell my sins*.

He feels ashamed before the party, he tells them. Once, he could look upon Jan Tzatzoe as his own child, but now he looks upon him as his father. He will heed the word of God as it has returned to him. He can see that without Taay, he is *nothing*. If the Lord will only give him a little more strength, he prays, he will abandon his wives and cattle and live for Christ alone, and if his fellow Xhosa do not follow his example, he will leave them to join *God's people in Cape Town and England*. The night comes to an end as the small party, singing hymns, walks up the hill toward Ngqika's kraal.

On their journey back to the colony the party passes through the country of the Kat River, finding it, at first glance, *delightful*, but of little use for irrigation. Pausing to fashion a makeshift bridge to span the stream, the travelers camp near a Xhosa village whose members provide fresh milk. The following morning a guide takes them to a location where the river traverses several large plains with low banks, excellent conditions for the laying out of watercourses. Nearby Read can see *large forests of fine timber, which for ages cannot be exhausted, and excellent stone for building. Here we resolved, with God's will,* Read states, *the first station should be*.

Riding on through the rain, the party camps on a hill above another village. All night, loud noises reverberate up the hillside. In their fitful sleep, the party blames a dance ceremony held to detect a witch. But the following morning, as they descend the hill, the fog left over from the rainy night clears, and they see a group of about thirty elephants meandering *gently* away. Their gardens under threat, noise had served the Xhosa in place of firearms.

At each village they pass on their return voyage, Jan Tzatzoe gives an account of the *object* of the missionary party, and a *short sketch of the way of salvation*. Nearing the Fish River, the group stumbles across an elephant in a densely wooded glen. They hit it with five musket balls, but it does not topple. One of their *Caffre-guides*, a *little man, probably of Bushman extraction*, seeing the timidity of the men, rushes in with his assegai and inflicts two more wounds. Bleeding heavily, the elephant moves off, and two men decide to follow in order to salvage its ivory. Read asks the guide where he had gained such courage. Not from himself, he replies, but from God.

Red flames flash. Musket fire reverberates with booming echoes. The air is suddenly acrid; the atmosphere itself turned sour with gunsmoke and surprise. Read, Williams, and Tzatzoe have returned to Bethelsdorp to the customary discharge of guns. It is two o'clock in the morning on 16 May 1816. The following days rush by. Colonel Cuyler must be consulted immediately and reassured of the missionaries' resolve to convey all possible information on the movements and intentions of the leaders of Xhosaland. Cuyler is fascinated by the figure of Makana. Has he obtained the substance of his preaching from *inspiration*, the colonial official inquires of the missionaries, or has he been *told something by men*? Cuyler promises the nascent mission *any possible assistance*.[23]

Read consults his fellow voyagers and casts his mind back to the journey from which they have just returned. He composes letter after letter in the last days of May. To Cuyler. To the mission board in London. He must address this curious figure of Makana. For what if God truly speaks to a man from Xhosaland? He must also establish his faith in the ability of Williams and Tzatzoe to preach the right Word, to show the Xhosa that obedience to God means a better life for all.

All the while, Read is preparing for his own journey. He is satisfied that he has fulfilled Van der Kemp's intentions with regard to the Xhosa nation, has opened an *effectual door* through which will flow *the chief doctrines of truth*.[24] He has entrusted this task to his spiritual son. But he cannot be of any additional assistance. Beset by rumors of infidelity that he is scarcely able to deny (a young Khoisan woman will soon give birth to his child), Read intends to take his family and flee to the northern desert interior. Flee to seek clarification and comfort in the spare vistas. Flee with the hope that the hot, dry air will sear the self-doubt that flutters within and burn away the suffocating stench of immorality that follows him like a dark, buzzing effusion of flies. Read may have precious little shade from the cauterizing desert sun, but he will be sheltered from the moral judgment of the LMS and the harsh denunciations of the British government and its settlers. In the manner of his biblical heroes, he will return from the desert in due course.[25]

On 8 June 1816, the Bethelsdorp mission holds a service to bless two major transformations. Joseph Williams is ordained so that he can immediately baptize Xhosa converts at the new Kat River mission station. For his part in the service, James Read conducts a *laying on of hands*. Then he gives a *Sort of a charge from Christ's charge to Peter*:

> Jesus saith to Simon Peter, Simon, son of Jonas, lovest Thou me more than these?
> He saith unto Him, Yea, Lord; thou knowest that I love Thee. He saith unto him, Feed my lambs. . . . He saith unto him, Feed my sheep. (John 21:15–16)[26]

Following Williams's ordination, Jan Tzatzoe marries a Khoisan woman, Sanna Oursen. During the revival at Bethelsdorp in 1815, Sanna had been swept up and repented of her previous habits. Obeying a vow she made to Read that if God saved her she would undertake his bidding, she accompanied the Reverend Evans's wife north to the desert station at Lattakoo. It was a journey *respecting which she had so many fears*, but she performed the task admirably. As with Tzatzoe's life in the Read household, the historical record has not preserved any further information on Sanna Oursen and this transformative moment in Tzatzoe's life. Again, the intimate life of familial relationships, however tantalizing and important, remains veiled.

Williams preaches a farewell sermon from the verse, *Finally Brethren, pray for us*. Charged by the LMS to gain converts and convert the behavior of his charges, Williams knows that he and Tzatzoe and their families will also take with them on their journey to the Kat River the colonial government's missive to reconnoiter and report on the political terrain of Xhosaland. No disinterested party, they will be entering the most dangerous territory in the border region. Chiefs threaten each other. Powerful and charismatic men with conflicting spiritual visions await a new challenger. There is the simple matter of sustenance. Williams turns to the Word:

> Finally Brethren, pray for us, that the word of the Lord may have free course, and be glorified, even as it is with you: And that we may be delivered from unreasonable and wicked men: for all men have not faith. (2 Thessalonians 3:1–2.)[27]

Kat River

How is this, Major Fraser?

1816–1818

The European missionary is red-faced from the molten disdain of an alien sun. His exposed flesh has gained a jagged topographic profile, craggy with the welts of insect bites and the scratches of thorns. He crosses the frontier between white civilization and native barbarity, taking a long-suffering but nobly accommodating female companion along with him, to establish an outpost in the wilderness. In his grass hut, surrounded by swarming swarthy hordes and skulking carnivores, he dreams of a whitewashed stone chapel with glass windows that will allow his converts to peer out on the imperfect world from which his walls of God provide shelter. His people are arranged in orderly rows. They speak at appropriate moments. Their dress resembles his own.[1]

In many ways, the missionary adventure of Joseph Williams that begins in the winter of 1816 cleaves to the generic script. Williams will even die a martyr's death—though a poorly commemorated one. But another story of the Kat River mission can be told that differs from the heroic paean and that flows over the narrative embankments into which the events of the past have been channeled from Williams's day to the present.

While ivory hunters, Boer traders, and the occasional runaway have crossed from the Cape Colony into Xhosaland, Williams is, indeed, the first European to venture across the boundary intent on settling in the area as a fully recognized representative of the colony, of Christianity, and of British civilization. Williams does build a grass hut. He is surrounded by inquisitive Africans, some of whom attend his services, others of whom delight in presenting him and his wife, Elizabeth, with intimidating displays of martial prowess. With Elizabeth's assistance, he even teaches some Xhosa girls to sew their own European-style gowns and weave cottage-bonnets from rushes growing along the river.[2]

But in contrast to the enduring story being fashioned for the readers of periodicals like the London Missionary Society's *Transactions*, Williams is not set adrift in the African wilderness. He is intimately connected to the colony. When the seedlings in his garden—germinating from stock carried from Britain in the dank holds of oceangoing ships—succumb to the eastern Cape heat, he survives on food supplies bought with LMS funds and transported by oxwagon. And Williams is actively involved in tasks that are more political than ecclesiastical, more diplomatic than spiritual. The threats to his mission derive not from the resistance of faceless hordes to the disconcerting power of his teachings, but from the ongoing strife within the Xhosa state. Most of all, Williams is not alone.

Elizabeth Williams and her husband belong to a stratum of London society whose birthright is a paltry education that confers a lifelong legacy of spelling and grammatical errors, and toil at jobs that fall in between the daily menace of menial labor and the elevated status of artisan and business owner. Joseph's occupation as a carpenter allows him the leisure time to attend the old Independent chapel of Fetter Lane and to continually petition the LMS's *Committee of Examination*. From his first appearance before the Committee at age twenty-six, he is continually deferred and told to improve himself. He spends his spare time in the ensuing years not only mastering the required catechisms, but also improving his writing to the point where he can deliver lectures on *Theology* and the *old Testament*.

By 1814, while attending the Gosport missionary school and being educated in topics such as the *Office and Qualification of a Missionary and Conduct* and *Doctrine of Missionaries respecting Civil Government*, Williams finds the time to court the woman who is to become his wife. Elizabeth Rogers is working as a maid along with a young woman named Sarah Williams who is, most likely, Williams's sister or cousin and who becomes engaged to Williams's companion from Gosport, George Barker. On their way to serve in South Africa, Williams and Barker hold hurried marriage ceremonies.[3]

Elizabeth Williams is intellectually curious, and the letters she writes home to friends in London reveal a playful personality that seems to delight in, but not directly claim, an internal fortitude more than capable of confronting the manifest dangers of her position as a missionary's wife. Surprisingly, the language of Elizabeth's letters and, indeed, often entire segments of them, are almost identical to those found in the letters and journals submitted by Joseph Williams to his supervisors in London. That Elizabeth is the author of some of her husband's letters seems clear when they are compared to letters she writes to London after Joseph's death. It seems likely that Elizabeth is at her husband's side during his conversations with colonial officials and African chiefs and serves as his chief secretary and scribe.[4]

And to further complicate the canonical view, their mission is also Jan Tzatzoe's mission. Tzatzoe is the Williams's guide, translator, assistant evangelizer, and diplomatic envoy. He will play a central role in the survival and work of the mission.

On the morning of 15 June 1816, twenty-six individuals set out from Bethelsdorp for the Kat River. Joseph Williams and Elizabeth have an infant son, Joseph, who has been born while his parents have waited for permission to begin their mission. Jan Tzatzoe brings his new bride, Sanna Ourson, and her niece, Kaatze Kaatje Roe. There are six men, described by the colonial authorities as Hottentots, presumably all from Bethelsdorp: Windvogel Eksteen, Windshut Plaatje, William Kaarlus, Mattroos Joris, William Hans, and Jan Links. With the exception of Hans, all have wives and children who accompany them. Several months into their residence in Xhosaland, Williams will describe his men as failures—having spent the *most part of their lives in residence among the Caffres* they *are consequently not disposed for work.*[5]

It takes a little over three weeks for the group to reach the Fish River. On their journey past many Boer farms and military posts, they are encumbered by a particularly troublesome wagon. The European settlers and soldiers express their surprise to the Williamses that they are *not afraid to go among such savages thieves & robbers as the caffres* are *well known to be by all who* have *any acquaintance with them.* The prevailing opinion is that *nothing but powder and ball* will *do to bring such savages to their senses and that after they* have *sent a good lot of them to hell, then* will *be the time to go and preach salvation to them, and not before.*[6]

They add five cows to their baggage train at Captain Andrews's military post, but the sheep Williams is hoping to purchase cannot be found. This paltry amount of cattle will have to supply the milk that will be the mission's major food source. And upon entering Xhosaland, the small herd will represent the station's relative wealth and status. When compared to the thousands of head of livestock at the kraals of Makana, Ngqika, and Ndlambe, Williams's power and influence will appear limited.

An unusually dry winter is in part to blame for the scarcity of domestic animals. In the six days it takes the party to travel from the Fish to the Kat, they are not troubled by any of the inhabitants of the land or by wild animals. Water is remarkably *precious, as dear as the best liquid* was in England. The paucity of wildlife and domestic animals in the region can be explained by the fact that the higher elevation of the land surrounding the Kat River renders it poorly suited for winter grazing; better forage is available for man and beast lower down the tumbling hills, closer to the onrushing clouds of the ocean.

On 15 July 1816 the party decides to locate their mission at the base of a low-slung oblong hill where the Kat River, having descended from mountainous and crenellated heights, bursts through a tight gap in the topography and flows onto a broad plain that is still elevated above the local escarpment. With nearby hills for vantage points and the funnel effect of the gap through which the river plummets, the station is ideally situated to both attract and observe the traffic entering and departing the upper Kat River valley.[7]

The site is about fifteen miles from Ngqika's village, or Great Place—the term for the village of a chief—but relatively isolated from any other Xhosa villages. The party is surprised, therefore, to find a group of Xhosa men awaiting their arrival. The men crowd around, asking for food and beads in a manner that is *very pressing*. Tzatzoe translates as the men complain about a mounted party of Boers who had come a few days before and ridden off with thirty head of cattle. Williams must stammer in reply. He is not here to adjudicate property disputes. He questions the men. Do they know of the *existence of their never dying souls*? Are they consequently aware of the *necessities* to which they must attend for their souls' preservation throughout eternity? Williams finds them totally ignorant as to these matters.

It appears that the reality of the mission will not cleave to the sustaining vision in Williams's mind of enlightening spirituality flowing down upon a receptive audience, like scorching lava transforming all in its path. Perhaps it is this disappointment that triggers Williams to affix a sarcastic afterword to his diary entry describing the men's request: *as if I could help them*. Williams appears to be disturbed by the intrusion of political concerns into his spiritual undertaking, and in addition, with his political impotence in Xhosaland.

Jan Tzatzoe can serve as a guide for Williams to the meanings inherent in the conversations, the actions, and even the appearances of the African people among whom they have settled. For example, what appears to Williams as begging is, in fact, the etiquette of gift giving that attends meetings among the Xhosa.[8] But Williams will first have to ask. It does not seem that he very often does, because his journal is full of invective directed at people whose actions Tzatzoe could quite easily have explained. While for obvious reasons, Williams does not report any instances where Tzatzoe has to smooth over the friction caused by cultural misunderstandings, there seems little reason to doubt that this function becomes part of his work at the mission.

Before they have time to unpack their ox-wagons or to begin building a structure for worship, both Williams and Jan Tzatzoe are confronted with the principal, powerful, and at times, paralyzing predicament that will underlie their lives in Xhosaland, constrain their actions, and ultimately undermine their missionary work. However much they might try to fulfill the role of messengers of God's Word sent by a higher power—or at least, by a more enlightened segment of colonial society than the government itself—their presence in Xhosaland, and the actions and decisions they can and cannot take, will be viewed by the people among whom they have settled through the people's own understanding of the power and potential of the chiefs to whom they pay allegiance, but whose hold over them is tenuous at all times.

Their first encounter with the neighbors of their intended mission station does not reveal hunger for the Word, but a routine obligation that all Xhosa chiefs owe to the commoners who settle on their lands—the adjudication of property disputes, in particular those involving thefts of cattle. Indeed, the men might actually be seeking Tzatzoe's assistance in this matter. Williams does not mention that the men came to him directly; indeed, they seem uninterested in anything he might have to say. Williams and Tzatzoe will diligently carry on the work of God, but the initial visit is an ill omen for these efforts. As their stay in Xhosaland extends into years, Williams will grow increasingly frustrated by his political position. Writing to Major Fraser in November 1816, he will convey the complaint of a minor Xhosa chief, Jan Luza, against a Boer named Philip Opperman for taking away thirty head of cattle from his kraals. *This is now the third time of application to ask if they can get no recompense*, he will plead, *they plague me for an answer*.[9]

But as much as political appeals of the Xhosa among whom they live distract Williams and Tzatzoe from their spiritual work, the colonial government will prove even more troublesome. In a letter to James Read, written as the Kat River party strengthens its hold on its small section of riverbank, the Colonial Secretary, Colonel Christopher Bird, passes on word from the Governor that His Excellency's *greatest hope in permitting a Missionary establishment to pass into Caffraria, contrary to the policy antecedantly adopted, has been with the view of ensuring its cooperation in putting a stop to that system of plunder which has kept the Frontier so long in a state of ferment.*

Bird argues that if the missionaries can provide detailed intelligence of depredations committed by the Xhosa against the colonists, the government will be able to *shame* the Chiefs, who already *appear to feel the injustice of their conduct*, with specific evidence of infractions, and force them into making restitutions which they have hitherto refused to do by claiming ignorance of the specific parties involved. According to Bird, this *shame operating with those principles which your Brethren are labouring to impress them with*, can lead to the reform that all *anxiously desire*. Williams responds that he will provide information *respecting such Robberies as are committed by the Kaffers with pleasure*, but it is *very unlikely that their misdeeds should come to my knowledge*.[10]

Not that Williams seems to mind mixing political and theological lessons. The reason he is unlikely to hear of raids across the boundary, he admits in a letter to the LMS, is that he makes it a *point of my object to expose the evil of such conduct and also to condemn it*. Nevertheless, soon after agreeing to forward any information he may recover to Fraser, he finds himself *constantly perplexed* by letters from minor colonial officials inquiring about runaway slaves, missing cattle, rustled horses, and stolen muskets.

In addition to colonial demands, the mission is immediately incorporated into the political structures of the Xhosa state. As soon as Xhosa families begin to move to the mission (having been granted permission to do so by their chiefs), Ngqika *appoints* his interpreter, Hendrik Noeka, *chief of the people residing* with the missionaries. Thus it appears that while Jan Tzatzoe remains the public face of the mission, he is not able to parlay his association with the missionaries into an elevated political status within his father's society. Why does Tzatzoe remain with the mission when he might put his skills as an intermediary and his knowledge of Christianity to work in other ways in the border region?

Tzatzoe could try to emulate Makana and other Xhosa individuals who are allying aspects of the spiritual teachings of Christianity with Xhosa beliefs in order to recreate themselves as prophetic figures who have acquired access to both old and new powers. These figures like Makana can demand loyalty and tribute in the form of cattle. Or he could emulate other Xhosa figures who serve as diplomatic intermediaries between the Xhosa chiefs and the colony—at one point taking land, cattle, and wives from Ngqika, and at another being granted title to land within the colony by government officials.[11]

Tzatzoe remains allied with the mission, seeking to serve it. Does his conviction come from his conversion experience that had taken place through the agency of mission Christianity? Does he stay to further his spiritual life and his personal relationship with Christ. Or with his father? By serving the mission, Tzatzoe operates from within the ambit of colonial society, and preaches, at least in part, as its representative. He makes the Word available. When he claims its power, he does so on behalf of the mission, and not for himself, as individuals like Makana appear to do.[12]

Tzatzoe and the other Bethelsdorp men assist Williams as he builds a house woven from rushes, sixteen feet long, fourteen feet wide, and thirteen feet high. They also aid in his failed attempts at a garden and at plowing a field for wheat and maize. The cold dry ground refuses the iron teeth of the English plough, wrought as it was in a British factory for far more compliant earth. Gradually, gardens are cultivated and more permanent dwellings constructed. Williams begins to build a dam on the Kat River. Stone after rough stone tears at his hands and burdens his back, but his dream of a network of irrigation canals transforming the rich but desiccated land propels him forward. Assessing the reality of his situation, however, Williams immediately sends for a load of meal from the colony.[13]

Lessons for adults and children run by Williams and Tzatzoe start almost immediately. They are conducted in Dutch, which has held its place over English as the European lingua franca of the border region. On 21 July 1816 fifty to sixty people begin to learn the alphabet. They display *eagerness and constant perseverance* and their numbers gradually grow to reach one hundred and twenty over the coming year.[14] The mission also holds to a strict schedule of worship. Sunday is devoted to day-long prayer, in Dutch and Xhosa. The first meeting is just after sunrise; the second at nine o'clock to go over Sunday School subject matter; the third at eleven to *dispense the word of eternal life and after the same form as is common among dissenters*; the fourth in the afternoon similar to the third; and a fifth in the evening when Jan Tzatzoe climbs the dais and addresses the people *either from a single text or a large portion of the word*.

During the week there are two assemblies, the first soon after sunrise and the second after sunset. All the services share singing and prayer—the meetings open with a hymn whose first line declares *God has so loved the world* and goes on to *proclaim what God has done for the world in giving and punishing his son, his design in doing so and who will be benefitted by it & the last verse calls on sinners to believe and praise this wonderful deed*. Williams describes the hymn in his report to London, not because he rates it superior to any English hymns, but because it is *such blessed news* being heard by those who a *few days ago were sitting in the valley of the shadow of death*.

After visiting the Kat River mission, two of Jan Tzatzoe's brothers fall into a *state of derangement, powerfully affected under the Word of God*. With the waters of the Kat River, they wash away the red clay that coats their bodies, casting their ornamental brass rings and strands of beads into the stream. The brothers return home in an effort to hold Christian prayer meetings. Kote Tzatzoe and his people receive the brothers warily. Their behavior resembles that of individuals who are under the spell of witchcraft, or who have been called by the ancestors to intercede in the spirit world. The amaNtinde fear that *they should fall into the same snare*.¹⁵

As the station increases in size, Williams sees Satan's *strong hand* in the many excuses the local Xhosa offer for not attending services. Satan's *many willing servants* oppose the Word of Christ with *false suggestions, ridicule and threats*. They tell the faithful attendees that the chiefs will not brook their people settling at the mission *until the corn is sown, until the hunt is over, and then until the corn is cut*. In individual cases, for those that take the lessons from the station home and retire to the *bushes* to pray, there are direct and violent threats of murder.

Jan Tzatzoe will in later years fondly recall this time at the Kat River. It was a *quiet* time, he will say, a time when colonial patrols did not take up residence at the mission stations, a time when Xhosa visitors felt free to come and go. Tzatzoe will rate the Williams's evangelizing success highest among all the missionaries who will subsequently enter Xhosaland. He will attribute the *great impression* that the Word of God made *upon the people at that time* to the relative tranquility of the isolated station and the personal charisma of Williams, who *instructed the people in the Word of God, and told them to be better men*. He will give himself far too little credit.¹⁶

Tzatzoe is the critical figure at the station. Williams speaks through him in every conversation on the life of Jesus, on thefts of cattle, on improved farming methods, on the use of colonial currency. Tzatzoe gives flight to his words, and more importantly to the novel religious, political, and cultural concepts they often convey, by rendering them into the vocabulary of his childhood. Defending the mission, Tzatzoe is embroiled in the intrigues of the Xhosa royalty, and finds himself questioned from every side. He has to justify the actions of the Europeans who have given him this great gift of Christianity, but who seem to contradict its message with every cattle rustling commando and diplomatic sword swipe. Most of all, Tzatzoe reprises the role, performed by thousands and thousands of others for hundreds upon hundreds of years, of teaching a transfixed audience about the Gospel, the transformation it has wrought within him, and the ability of his listeners to harvest its blessings through the act of reading.¹⁷

On 14 August 1816 Ngqika arrives at the Kat River personally to examine the diplomatic and spiritual strength of the mission. The chief probes the institution as an anteater does an anthill with a quick thrust of the tongue here, a sustained, determined prod there. He seeks the sweet sustenance hidden within that might sustain his power. Yes, the reward contained inside might bite and pinch a couple of times on the way down, but it will invigorate once eaten. And if the hill refuses to cede its treasure in a polite and timely fashion, he has the brawny hindquarters, the muscled forelegs, the armored claws, to leave it strewn across the veld in disparate clods of dirt and dried grass. Better, though, to keep the hill whole and capable of renewing its internal bounty for repeat visits.[18]

Ngqika's retinue includes six of his wives, three counselors, forty soldiers, and his eldest son, Maqoma, who is eighteen. After a childhood spent near his mother's home herding cattle, honing his military prowess with assagai and knobkerrie, and hunting and exploring in the tangled mountainous vegetation surrounding the Kat River valley, Maqoma has recently returned from the circumcision rites. With a cohort of age-mates whose loyalty to him has been forged by their appreciation of his uncommon intelligence, charisma, and ambition—evident even at so young an age—Maqoma is beginning to test his father's authority.[19]

With Jan Tzatzoe translating and Maqoma listening intently, Williams and Ngqika, upon meeting, engage in the diplomatic protocol of Xhosaland by exchanging news. Williams is learning how to conduct himself with the etiquette due to the Xhosa royalty. Williams decides that Ngqika's news of Makana is *not worthy of writing*. It seems to concern a shift in Makana's theology or religious practice that runs contrary to the missionaries' preaching.[20] Although Ngqika emphasizes a potential conflict over religious ideology between Williams and Makana, in fact he is seeking to confront Makana's new political and popular appeal, and his alliance with Ndlambe.

Williams replies that instead of challenging Makana himself, as Ngqika urges, he will wait for *God to set him right, if he were a teacher raised up by God*. The news he can offer, he tells Ngqika through Tzatzoe, is *impossible to be made known and fully understood in one day*, news that is *forever telling and yet untold*. It is *joyful news to those who understand it in the heart*. The words seem to strike Ngqika deeply and he expresses his wish that all of his people could be at the Kat River to hear them, especially those who are *disposed to contend against* them. He has sent for all his people, he says, but they have refused to come. How should he *correct* those who are *disobedient* to him?

In Xhosaland, as in most societies, claims to political power are intimately intertwined with claims to spiritual power. Sometimes, as in the figure of Makana, political and spiritual power fuse together. The query hangs in the air. Williams launches into a theological explanation. As a King of his nation and appointed to that office by God to punish evildoers and protect those that do well, Ngqika is accountable to God for both his private and public actions. If he needs help with punishing evildoers, he should ask *God for direction who giveth wisdom to all men liberally.* But for now, if what he *professes* is *just and necessary*, he should rely on setting a good example and *friendly entreaty*, and let God take notice of their sins.

As Ngqika remains with the Williamses for the next sixteen days, learning the alphabet along with three of his wives, his requests are increasingly of the material kind: a long-stemmed stovepipe for smoking tobacco by the fire, a tobacco sack, an axe. He receives gifts from the LMS: handkerchiefs for his wives; knives and a looking glass; a coat, waistcoat, and shirt from James Read. Twice a day he calls for tea and bread, a request to which an exasperated Williams must cater while sending Tzatzoe to tell the chief that the missionary can ill afford these luxuries, that Williams himself must pay for them from the colony. A few months later, when Williams will ask Ngqika to discuss letters sent from the colony about the increasing frequency of thefts along the boundary, Ngqika will respond with requests of his own for the Governor—*two suits of Clothes, a great Coat, Hat and shoes, tea and tea kettle basins, sugar raw and candied, beads of all colours but all very small a little larger than a pin head and Looking glasses.*[21]

At times during the two weeks of his stay at the Kat River, Ngqika seems to genuinely grasp the opportunity to redeem his life, to submit to the higher power—he appears to be *affected by the Word* and especially by the singing of hymns—but in his initial conversation with Williams, he retreats from this potential internal transformation to the practicalities of the Word. With Tzatzoe translating, he asks Williams pointed questions: How had Williams become acquainted with God's Word? (He had heard it from people appointed by God for that purpose and read it in God's book, the Bible, and felt the *powerful spirit* convey the truth to him until his heart was *turn[ed]*.) How long does it take to find the Lord after a person starts looking for Him? (Only when men seek God as they do *silver and gold*, with a *whole heart*, do they find him.) Who had sent Williams to his country? (*Christ and those that loved Christ in England.*) How had those who first existed been made? (By God after a consultation between the *Father, son & holy Ghost.*) How then did so many nations exist now? (*From mans natural dislike to God and his law, an unwillingness to be under any restraint of the laws of men, the natural independent spirit in mankind.*)

Who is the Devil? Unable to employ the term "angel" Williams replies, *one of Gods chief Servants*, which Tzatzoe translates as *one of Gods chief soldiers.* The change that Tzatzoe makes from Devil as servant to Devil as soldier reflects his concern that in the Xhosa cultural context, the Xhosa term for servant would reflect too servile a meaning and would not convey the distinguished and important work of an angel. And why was he cast into hell? *Because of his dis-*

obedience and dissatisfaction with his situation. The interaction between Tzatzoe and Williams in the arena of translation (as revealed through Williams's writings) illustrates a compelling degree of equality. Williams understands that his efforts depend on Tzatzoe's abilities to translate into Xhosa, and he is willing to partner with the Xhosa man in the endeavor as well as to credit Tzatzoe's contributions.[22]

From 1816 to 1818 the Kat River mission meanders like the river it abuts. The African landscape around the mission houses takes on an English lilt—wheat fields and vegetable gardens accent thorn-bush cattle kraals and clearings. A pervasive atmosphere of fear and uncertainty shrouds the nascent mission and its quiet rhythms of prayer, manual labor, itinerant preaching, and school instruction. Elizabeth Williams is home alone with her baby when she hears an *unusual noise advancing towards* her hut. Outside, she is *immediately surrounded by a numerous body of Caffers, about twenty of whom* are *on horseback—all naked, and armed with weapons of war.* Numbers more approach *in all directions, all with spears and assagais in their hands; and* all have *a very alarming appearance.* The men on horseback *instantly dismount*, and Elizabeth expects to *be seized every moment.* She cannot communicate in any way with the men, but at length they learn that her husband is away tending to his dam in the river. They ride off with *great violence*, and she follows, with her *little boy in her arms* and a *trembling heart and limbs.* She expects to find Joseph murdered but instead he is peacefully at work, knee-deep in the river. The men are revealed to be *merely a party of* Ngqika's *warriors, who had been out hunting, and who called in on their way home to look at the poor missionary and his wife, who had brought back to them the Great Word, over the deep sea-water.*[23]

The institution is beset with reports of great disaffection within the Xhosa state with regard to its continued existence. Williams reports that Ndlambe has threatened to *come with his people and take all the cattle and murder us all.* In such moments of crisis, Williams turns to Jan Tzatzoe to mediate between himself, the mission, and the surrounding chiefs. Rather than accompanying the young interpreter, he sends him off alone, when, in a very real sense, his life and that of his family hang in the balance. Tzatzoe repeatedly travels to Ngqika's kraals in a diplomatic capacity. In September 1816 he assures Ngqika that the rumor being circulated claiming that the mission was established in Xhosaland in order to *betray* the Xhosa *into the hands of the English is false* and based on the provocation of frontier Boer settlers chafing under British rule.[24]

Tzatzoe's royal status likely gains him entry into the chiefs' councils more easily than if he were a Xhosa commoner. Once there, like all the participants in the council, he must rely on his oratorical skill and reasoning ability to present the challenging proposition of allowing the colonial intrusion in the form of the mission. On these diplomatic journeys Tzatzoe has to skillfully negotiate between competing agendas: that of Williams and his desire to build the institution and convert the local inhabitants; of the colonial government that makes continual demands upon the mission that affect its relationships with the various chiefs; of the chiefs themselves, who demanded obedience and respect; and of spreading his own religious convictions and ensuring his own political and economic status and security as well as that of the amaNtinde. Tzatzoe must negotiate these various interests, and his strategic response is to occupy the nexus of the competing influences—if one wind blows too strongly, he lets it blow him just far enough so that its strength is counteracted by another, or all three.[25]

In April 1817, the Governor of the Cape Colony, Lord Somerset, and a colonial delegation meet face to face with Ngqika, Ndlambe, and other Xhosa leaders at the Kat River mission. Ngqika must be cajoled into attending the conference. He is intimidated by the Governor's martial escort and by rumors that the colonists have come to revenge the death of a leading colonial official, Landdrost Stockenstrom, who had been ambushed in a previous frontier war, and whose son and official replacement, Andries, now sits at the Governor's side.

Finally, Ngqika places his confidence in Williams and Tzatzoe's reassurance, and after a day of windswept rain, at eleven o'clock on the morning of 2 April 1817 he arrives on the left bank of the Kat River with a retinue of three hundred soldiers. His *great distress and dread* so lock his limbs that he must be literally dragged across the river, arm-in-arm with Williams and the Landdrosts Cuyler and Stockenstrom.

The chiefs are led to a marquee whose sides have been raised to reveal the public nature of the discussions to be held within. Flanked by twin artillery pieces, the tent is surrounded on three sides by the colonial forces: *one hundred dragoons, detachments of the 83rd, 72nd, and Cape Regiments, and three hundred and fifty burghers armed and mounted.* Ngqika and Ndlambe sit on mats in a row to the right of the Governor's chair. Maqoma is directly behind his father, while other chiefs like Botomane, Enno, and Jalousa flank their superiors. While not mentioned directly by the colonial officials who record the minutes of the meeting, Jan Tzatzoe is also present and he sits among the chiefs, not next to Joseph Williams.

Translation occurs from English into Dutch and then into Xhosa by a man named Buttanje. Two Afrikaners check the translation for the colonial side;

Hendrik Noeka does so for Ngqika. The participants strain to make themselves heard over a *constant clucking* coming from the Xhosa warriors, whose sharp aspirations reverberate with the concussion of their stomping feet and echo in the damp valley air.

Somerset's goal in traveling so far from Table Mountain's soaring buttresses is to appoint Ngqika as the highest chief among the Xhosa west of the Kei River. The creation of a distinct hierarchy from among the scattered and ever shifting political allegiances of the Xhosa state has been a long-term goal of the colonial administrators who have ignored repeated avowals by various chiefs that none among them are capable of wielding such power.[26] Pushing ahead nonetheless, the colonial officials have asked Jan Tzatzoe (alone among the Xhosa) to provide lists of which people belong to which chief.[27]

Somerset addresses Ngqika directly. He wishes to renew the friendship between the colony and the *Kaffre nations* that had *formerly existed* in the border region before the current round of murders and *depredations*. Somerset holds out the promise of a renewed *bartering intercourse between the two nations*, and the possibility that Xhosa traders might come to Graham's Town twice a year to dispose of their goods. Ngqika will henceforth be held responsible for any stolen cattle, horses, or runaway slaves that remain in the country under his control, and he will need to punish the thieves. He will be accountable for the actions of the people to whom he gives his permission to enter the colony, an act to be signified by his granting them a copper gorget as a pass. Most crucially, he will have to allow colonial military patrols and commandos to follow the tracks of stolen cattle or horses out of the colony and into Xhosaland, where the patrols or commandos will be able to remove the requisite number of beasts from the first Xhosa kraal to which the tracks lead them, even if the animals have been moved deeper into Xhosaland, and regardless of whether or not the inhabitants played a role in the original raid. This set of regulations will come to be known as the *spoor law* in the colony, and the actions of colonial officials and settlers in enforcing its provisions (collectively identified as the commando, or patrol, system) will provide the largest source of conflict in the border region in the next decade and a half.

Somerset's official report to his superiors in London portrays a regal and eager Ngqika, his fears overcome, his *countenance expressive, his deportment firm, and his answers well weighed and wary*. The Ngqika of the colonial record reminds the Governor that many of the chiefs present at the meeting consider themselves independent of him, but he gratefully accepts Somerset's public acknowledgment of his position as first chief and voices the sole regret that more Xhosa leaders are not present to hear the endorsement.[28]

Some twenty years later, Tzatzoe will present an alternative view:

> The governor came to Kat River to Mr. Williams' station, and he then appointed Gaika as head over all the chiefs in Caffreland. Gaika said to the governor, "We do not do things as you do them; you have but one chief, but with us it is not so; but, although I am a great man and king of the other Caffres, still every chief rules and governs his own people." Gaika said to the governor, "There is my uncle and there are the other chiefs."
>
> The governor then said, "No; you must be responsible for all the cattle and the horses that are stolen." The other chiefs then said to Gaika, "Say, yes, that you will be responsible, for we see the man is getting angry;" for we had the cannon and artillerymen and soldiers and boors [sic] with loaded muskets standing about us. Gaika then complied. He said he would be responsible for all the cattle and horses stolen from the colony. The governor said moreover, that the Caffres were not to pass the Fish River; that the English were to drink on the other side of the river, and the Caffres were to drink on this side of the river; that the middle of the river was the boundary line.

The colonial muskets are pointed at Jan Tzatzoe as a member of the powerful Xhosa royal governing elite and not past him.[29]

By April 1818 the station is not only poor and powerless, but in grave danger. After his Xhosaland conference, Governor Somerset had grown increasingly upset with the unabated levels of cattle raiding across the border. Despite Ndlambe's strident denials of his peoples' culpability, Somerset mounted a punitive campaign against the subsidiary chief (in the imagined colonial hierarchy) with the intention of confiscating thousands of head of cattle. The news reached Ngqika at the Kat River mission. The gathering commando was incorrectly rumored to have instructions to come after him and not Ndlambe, and Williams and Tzatzoe were unable to contradict this information. Ngqika retreated to his Great Place, where Tzatzoe soon arrived to explain that Major Fraser had made it clear that he was after Ndlambe's cattle and not Ngqika's.

In late January 1818 Fraser led a party of three hundred British infantrymen and one hundred and fifty mounted Boers into Xhosaland. Ndlambe confronted him with two thousand warriors. Attempting to seize some cattle, the colonial force found itself surrounded on three sides by Ndlambe's men and retreated. Still looking for booty, the commando ransacked the surrounding countryside, attacking indiscriminately, and killing Xhosa men, women, and children, as well as seizing cattle from both Botomane's and Ngqika's people. Cutting wood near the Kat River station, Jan Tzatzoe could hear the echo of gunfire as it consumed the valley. A shocked and exasperated Ngqika immediately sent envoys to the institution, accusing the missionaries of *betraying* him *into the hands of these people*. Williams and Tzatzoe could only reply that they do not know what has happened, but that they had told Ngqika exactly what Fraser had conveyed to them.[30]

In the aftermath of the raid, the institution is left deeply damaged. Tzatzoe undertakes a personal diplomatic mission to Graham's Town to visit Fraser, who has not responded to Williams's correspondence, and who is in the delicate position of denying any wrongdoing in the conduct of his commando to an official colonial office inquiry. Instead, he is arguing for a case of mistaken identity, based on the fact that at least half of the chiefs from whom his commando is accused of taking cattle were not identified as being under Ngqika's control on the list Tzatzoe had submitted to the Governor at the Kat River conference in April 1817.[31]

Later, in England, Tzatzoe will recall the discussion:

> How is this, Major Fraser? You sent a letter to Ngqika to say, that you were not going to attack him; that the object of your commando was to attack Ndlambe; how is it that you have broken your word and attacked Ngqika's people?
> It would have been much better had you yourself gone to Ngqika and told him this; you have ruined us; Ngqika will never put any confidence in us.

Fraser replies, *Were those Ngqika's people that I attacked?*

> You knew very well that those people belonged to Ngqika; you were present when the governor had a conference with Ngqika on the Kat River; if the impression on your mind was that those people belonged to Ndlambe, you would not have gone through Trumpeter's Drift, but you would have come by Brun's Drift.

A chastened Fraser makes no effort to reply.[32]

The trip to Fraser underlines Tzatzoe's importance as an intermediary and diplomat. Tzatzoe acts decisively on behalf of himself and the mission when he confronts Fraser, who he believes is ignoring Williams's appeals. Tzatzoe also appears to be currying favor with Ngqika and trying to ameliorate the diplomatic damage that has occurred on account of colonial double-dealing.

When Tzatzoe returns to the Kat River, the Khoisan functionaries of the mission station decide to leave en masse for the colony. While fear over the wrath of Ngqika perhaps drives the decision, the threat also crystallizes ongoing tension between Williams and his assistants. As Williams notes in a letter to his supervisors dated 14 April 1818, the *people who came with me from Bethelsdorp are too much under the eye to escape notice here they have been repeatedly admonished but in vain at length I began to expose their inconsistency publickly they then stood up and abused me and now they return to Bethelsdorp.*[33]

The departures would be no *great loss*, Williams adds, except that Jan Tzatzoe has been *prevailed upon* to leave as well. Tzatzoe is the *only individual* to whom Williams can *speak with any satisfaction* and the *only suitable interpreter* he has with him. These are the only kind or complimentary words that Williams ever articulates with regard to Jan Tzatzoe. Elizabeth Williams never mentions him at all.

Joseph Williams blames Tzatzoe's *Good for nothing* wife for Tzatzoe's defection: *She has abused him from the time we were on our journey to the present period in a shameful manner.* According to Williams, Sanna Oursen has been accusing her husband of being *too intimate with the women who reside here she says all are his wives*. This accusation is one of the few glimpses available into Tzatzoe's personal relationships. Like one of the looking glasses that Ngqika requests from the colony, what image of Tzatzoe does it reflect back? Xhosa chiefs have many wives. Has Tzatzoe been assuming the patriarchal duties of a chief? Have the women of the mission station (who have sought its protection because they are unhappy or powerless in local Xhosa villages) looked to Tzatzoe as the equivalent of a village head to whom marital obligations are owed in return for physical and spiritual security? Cleary, in Sanna Oursen's view, her husband has been behaving in ways that do not conform to the sexual mores of the mission Christianity in which both have come of age and which are markedly different from those of Xhosaland. Her defiant actions and words suggest a marital relationship between the two that is uncharacteristic of the strongly patriarchal nature of Xhosa society. There will be no further intimations of infidelity on Tzatzoe's part, and future events will demonstrate that his marital bond will remain strong.[34]

In the immediate crisis of April 1818 Sanna Oursen adds another charge—that Williams is withholding food from her. This is not the first time Jan Tzatzoe has been caught between the exigencies of his family and friends and his deeply felt obligations to mission life. Despite having just returned from a diplomatic mission to save the institution, Tzatzoe sides with his wife and the Bethelsdorp people. Citing Sanna Oursen's unhappiness (but not referring to the charge of infidelity) and her complaints about the food, he asks Williams for permission to return to the colony. His about-face angers Williams, who insists that Tzatzoe *never made a complaint until now but on the contrary manifested the greatest satisfaction*, and he refuses to write Tzatzoe a pass to cross the colonial boundary. Williams tells him to write directly to the colonial officials to ask for permission. Tzatzoe turns to Ngqika instead and obtains one of the gorgets sent to the chief by Governor Somerset, which are intended to convey Ngqika's approbation of a subject's mission to the colony.[35]

On 28 August 1818 Jan Tzatzoe is living at the Theopolis mission station when the resident missionary, George Barker, receives word from Xhosaland that Joseph Williams has died five days earlier and that Elizabeth Williams, *surrounded by savages* and *with no one to give the deceased a decent burial*, remains at the Kat River. *Just as day began to break, his happy spirit took flight to be for ever with the Lord*, Elizabeth writes in her journal. With no European Christians to assist her, she orchestrates the construction of a coffin, the digging of a grave and the ceremonial last rites. *As soon as it was light, the people returned to work upon the coffin, and about eleven o'clock it was finished. I appointed four young men (in whose hearts, I trust, the Lord hath begun a work of grace) to put the body in the coffin. I then took my two fatherless infants by the hand, and followed the remains of my beloved husband to the grave, accompanied by the whole of the people and the children. When they put the body in the grave, I requested them to sing a hymn, after which we prayed.*[36]

With Tzatzoe on a rented horse, and a couple of other Khoisan assistants astride an ox, Barker sets out for Xhosaland. Their mission is not one of comfort but of rescue — a rescue that Elizabeth Williams, who has reprised the role of missionary by holding Sunday services and classes just a day or so after the funeral, seems reluctant to accept. The people of the institution beg her to remain, and she lies awake all night, her mind in distress: *To leave this people and the place where I had been living so happily, and where now the body of my dear husband lay, was like tearing my heart out.*

Finally, Robert Hart, a member of the colony who had preceded the missionary party to the station, prevails upon her to leave, arguing for the *impropriety of a lone woman, with two little children, remaining in such a place, without a protector*. Just an hour on the road back to the colony, they meet Barker and his companions. Barker is sympathetic to Elizabeth's pleas that she might be allowed to remain in the area until a new missionary deputation might be sent, but he reasons that a woman, alone, *can do nothing, or very little*, and that it is not *proper* for her to remain. No one raises the question of whether Jan Tzatzoe might fulfill this missionary role. Elizabeth asks Barker to visit the Kat River with her, to see the *earnestness of the poor natives for a teacher*, to fix the scene in his mind so that he might feel the compunction necessary to spearhead efforts to rapidly replace the Williamses. *But*, she must report in her journal, *it is ordered otherwise*. Through the dust kicked up by their mounts, Jan Tzatzoe and Elizabeth Williams look back on their home of over two years. The soil that has entombed Joseph Williams shimmers in the air.[37]

FISH RIVER VALLEY

To Enter and Proclaim Upon their Mountains

1822

After leaving the Kat River in 1818, Tzatzoe spends the next few years at the Bethelsdorp and Theopolis mission stations. He likely works as a carpenter and wheelwright and evangelizes as an itinerant preacher in the surrounding countryside. The missionaries at the station do not register his presence or actions. Some of the Christian adherents of the abandoned Kat River mission scatter; others gather under Ntsikana's leadership. Collectively, they will seed the many missionary institutions that will be established in Xhosaland in the 1820s and 1830s. By 1822 Jan Tzatzoe is crossing, once again, from the colony into Xhosaland.[1]

This time, his companions are not London Missionary Society missionaries but three ministers associated with the 1820 British settlers. In 1818 and 1819 ninety thousand applicants from throughout Britain had responded to a British government plan to fund the emigration of citizens who would settle the Albany province of the Cape Colony (the region between the Bushman's River and the Great Fish River that had been conquered from the Xhosa by Colonel Graham in 1811). Between April and June of 1820 five thousand settlers, organized into small parties under the leadership of wealthy patrons, arrived in Algoa Bay, eager to glimpse their grants of land. Most were disappointed. The grants were far too small to support pastoral activities, and the aridity of the region precluded intensive rain-fed agriculture. Thrust into an uncertain political situation in the border region, the settlers quickly streamed into the small towns in the region, especially Graham's Town.[2]

Tzatzoe leads the Reverend William Shaw, who has been ministering in the Wesleyan church in the small town of Salem, just south of Graham's Town, and dreaming of establishing a Wesleyan mission in Xhosaland. They are ac-

Fish River Valley, 1822

companied by two more Methodist 1820 settlers: Stephen Kay and the Reverend William Threlfall. The ministers are traveling to see Ngqika, in order to gain his permission to cross his territory and to establish a new mission, not among Ngqika's *Gaika tribes,* as Shaw terms them, but with the *A*mandhlambi under Ndlambe, the *A*magonakwaybi under Pato, or the *A*magcaleka under Hintza.[3] Jan Tzatzoe is their only guide and interpreter. He is more than that, too; he is a diplomat and an evangelist. He is also of vastly more importance to the journey than his companions realize.

As the sun sets behind them, Jan Tzatzoe and his traveling companions leave Graham's Town, heading east toward the Great Fish River. The path is an *exceedingly solitary one, leading through a bushy part of the country, infested by wild beasts, and traversed by wandering marauders.* During winter, darkness falls early. But the moon is full, and its *bright beam casts a cheering radiance upon the surrounding gloom.* The men continue through a preternaturally still night—*nature* seems *lulled to rest* and *all* is *silent around* them; the only sounds are the clip-clop of the horses' feet and the *occasional observations of the thoughtful travellers.* The staccato verbal exchanges surely help to allay overactive imaginations.

An opportunity for rest arrives when the moonlight limns the haphazard outline of a broken-down border post on the Great Fish River. Inside, a *poor English soldier* does his best by the party, *presenting* them with a *little refreshment,* and then, despite his being a *Roman catholic, unhesitatingly* joining them in their *evening devotions.* Kay passes an uncomfortable night on a *wooden couch* covered with *animal skins* and awakes at an *early hour* with *aching bones.* It is unlikely his fellow travelers fare much better.

Before continuing north along the course of the Great Fish toward Fort Willshire—a journey that should take them all day—the party gathers to examine the graves of several members of the Royal African Corps who had been killed in a frontier war that had convulsed the region in 1818 and 1819. Kay is *deeply affected while reading the different inscriptions on rude and rapidly decaying tablets, which the survivors had erected over the mangled relics of their comrades.*[4]

In October 1818, on the open upland below Ngqika's Great Place in the Amathole Mountains, at a site called Amalinde, Ngqika's son, Maqoma, led an army against Ndlambe and Makana. The army was decimated, and Ngqika fled the scene to appeal for assistance from Governor Somerset. The Governor stood by his word at the Kat River conference and sent a colonial force to punish Ndlambe. Under the leadership of a Colonel Brereton, the colonial commando captured 23,000 head of Xhosa cattle. Forced to counterattack, Ndlambe and

Makana invaded Albany province. While British reinforcements marshaled in Graham's Town in early 1819, Makana attacked the town on the morning of 22 April 1819. The British forces nearly succumbed, but blasts of cannon fire and the sharp shooting of Khoisan snipers serving with the British threw the Xhosa into retreat. Makana surrendered when his last intervention failed. He had promised that the ancestors of the Xhosa would rise from the sea to assist his cause. He was sent to Robben Island in Table Bay where he drowned during an attempted escape on 9 August 1820.[5]

The day proves unbearably hot and the country barren and sterile in the extreme. Winter in the region can feature such days when a hot and unsettling wind blows down the river valleys. Lunch is a *crust of bread* and a gulp of water in a *thicket*. The *little bower* is *consecrated* by a reading of a *portion of the Scripture* and a prayer committing the travelers to the *care and direction of Almighty God*. Soon after lunch, though, the river valley deepens. Its sides gain in depth and gradient. *Extensive and dense forests* of yellowwood, melkwood, and assegai bush coat the valley walls like algae covering a rock—a sweeping mass of subtly distinguishable shades of dark-green. Multiple vistas open, of *stupendous mountains and precipices* and the *beautifully serpentine course of the stream*. It is a *prospect of the most romantic description*.[6]

Fort Willshire is substantial and heavily garrisoned. The missionaries hold a service for two hundred troops. The fort is also the only site on the colonial boundary where there is a legal trade between colonists and Xhosa. Weekly trade fairs, such as the one witnessed by the party on Monday, 5 August 1822, begin with the boom of a cannon. At the signal hundreds of Xhosa ford the river seeking to exchange their animal and cattle skins, honeycombs, and other trade items for beads, buttons, brass jewelry, or iron pieces.[7]

The following morning, the travelers ride off toward the mountains that beckon from the northern horizon. Shaw cannot *avoid a smile* as he glances around at his companions. They are clothed in an *extraordinary sort of outfit*: sheepskin trousers ward off the thorns and burrs through which they will ride; *jackets* prove more *convenient than coats*; straw hats cover some heads, fur caps the others. All carry *haversacks slung over* their *shoulders* with their food, and an extra packhorse is burdened with the great coats and sheepskin blankets that will be needed in the evening chill. Tzatzoe carries a musket, another man a *fowling-piece*, or shotgun.[8]

Night finds the party gathered around a fire in a *small circular enclosure*, identified as a threshing-floor, in the home of a chief of a village on the way to Ngqika's. The leader has sent *his women* to the neighboring homesteads to issue an invitation to hear the preaching of the Gospel, and a large crowd is assembled. After a brief service, *all* are *requested to kneel before Jehovah, Maker of heaven and earth, and to keep silence while prayer* is *made unto him; which is strictly attended to.* There follows a lengthy and profound interchange, *respecting the Gospel,* between a local Xhosa man—who appears to delight his companions whenever he asks a question that temporarily *puzzles* the missionaries—and all three of the missionaries.

With each missionary jumping in when another falters, the discussion resembles a tag-team wrestling match. But the travelers have their own satisfaction when Tzatzoe, who is the medium through which the conversation flows, turns to them after relaying their answers and says: *Nu is hij stom,* or *Now is he dumb,* an acknowledgment that the objections have been fully accounted for.

It appears then that God requires men to pray all their lives, even to death: now this is too hard. If the Almighty would be satisfied with two or three days' praying, that might be done; but to pray all our lives, is too hard.

Tzatzoe translates the missionaries' answer: *Those who pray sincerely will soon find that it is not a hard work, but pleasing and delightful. A child finds it very difficult at first to attempt walking but soon takes great delight in running about.*

Another question: *But you say God is almighty, and can do all things: why does he not change me at once himself without sending teachers to tell me what I must be?*

And the response: *God is truly almighty, but he uses means to effect what he designs. It is the same with the soul as with the body: he could give us bread from heaven; but every one knows that he does not do so. Your women have first to dig the earth, and plant, and sow the seed; and he then sends rain upon it, whereby the corn and pumpkins are made to grow and become food. Even so it is in spiritual things. God sends teachers to proclaim his word: this you must hear and believe: repent of your sins, and pray that he will save you. Fear the Lord, and renounce the service of Satan, who leads you on in sin, in order to destroy you forever.*

The mention of Satan logically leads to the next question: *But why does not God change Satan first? We are told that he is very wicked; and I know that he troubles me and pushes me on to bad things. Why then does God not first convert him?*

And a fairly evasive answer: *Satan was the first sinner: no person tempted him; and as he sinned without being tempted, God cast him into hell, where he must remain forever. God will not have mercy on him: but upon man it hath pleased him to have pity; yea, him hath he loved, and given his only Son to die for us; so that "whosoever believeth shall not perish, but have everlasting life."*

The complexity and degree of engagement with the Gospel and its teachings evinced by the Xhosa skeptic, the *shrewd man* in the opposing corner, is quite surprising to both Kay and Shaw. Both men feel that the questions he asks convey *some idea of the acuteness which these natives occasionally display*.[9] But it is Kay, and not Shaw, who realizes Tzatzoe's central role in facilitating the exchange—indeed, in allowing it to take place at all. *The value of a pious interpreter is incalculable,* Kay remarks, *as he frequently opens our way to the minds of the people in the most happy and successful manner; introducing subjects in the precise form and phraseology that is most likely to arrest their attention, and impress the heart.*

The discussion is *clear proof* of Tzatzoe's ability to communicate to his Xhosa listeners not only the text of the Gospel, and its attendant liturgy, but, in addition, the stories and practices that attend the practice of mission Christianity—how it is lived, justified, exalted, and challenged. The intelligibility of Tzatzoe's translations can be measured by the extent to which they provoke questions and challenges from his Xhosa listeners. He is not presenting ideas and stories that can be dismissed—he is providing information that the Xhosa feel, at the least, needs to be debated before it can be incorporated into their ways of living and understanding the world.

While squatted around our evening fire, says Kay, *Tchadchoo, being a Kaffer himself, and experimentally acquainted with divine things, soon began to testify of these things to the sable visitors. His conversation with them gave rise to a number of interesting questions, all of which were proposed with becoming seriousness.*[10]

The next day, the party rides off to the east still searching for Ngqika who is reported to be near the Great Place of Kote Tzatzoe. They pass several small villages in country that is increasingly fertile and well watered and cross a stream that Shaw declares to be the *finest river I have yet seen in Africa*. Around noon, they enter a cattle enclosure unannounced. Inside, they see *fifty or sixty great stout fellows busily employed in cutting up an ox*, which they have just slaughtered and for which a large fire is already burning. *For some minutes,* the two groups gaze at each other in silence. Then, *at length,* the aging chief *recognizes his son in the interpreter,* as Kay puts it. Kote Tzatzoe rises to greet his son and welcome him.[11]

Everyone exchanges handshakes, and the party is provisioned with a twenty-pound share of beef, rendered *far from tempting,* adds Kay, by the *custom, by no means uncommon,* of rolling the meat in the dirt of the cattle kraal. At night, a well-attended service is held around a *large fire,* but the people are *rude and dissipated*, and it is *impossible to arrest their attention* or to gain their silence. There is no record of Jan Tzatzoe's reactions to these events. Is he immediately included in his father's circle of councilors? Is he present for the failed meeting? In their writings, Kay and Shaw do not solicit Tzatzoe's thoughts or offer observations on his personality. They even misread the events of the afternoon. Most likely, Kote and Jan Tzatzoe had recognized each other, but were observing the etiquette of greeting. Tzatzoe's moments of self-expression or self-reflection are remarkably rare in the historical record, leading to an inability on the part of an historian to speculate on his character. Therefore, an archival passage such as this one that describes Tzatzoe's familial interactions gains a heightened air and invites speculation. After his career at the Kat River and his current service, does Tzatzoe feel underappreciated, unrecognized? Clearly, at this point in his life, Tzatzoe is capable, forceful (in his conversations and dealings with colonial officials, missionaries, and Xhosa leaders), and focused. Does his father entreat him once again to stay at his side? Does Tzatzoe insist on adhering to the task at hand instead? Is he biding his time for a return? If so, what keeps him in the colony?

This particular arrival among the amaNtinde leads to an almost immediate departure, as Jan Tzatzoe informs Kay and Shaw that they must turn back toward the Chumie River in order to meet with Ngqika; *it would be wrong to proceed further without seeing the King*. The travelers are soon seated in front of Ngqika, who *leans on the breast of a man* to his left, in *true oriental style*. Tzatzoe has coached the group in the niceties of Xhosa diplomatic protocol, and, *agreeably to* his *advice*, they wait for quite a while before initiating the conversation. Ngqika continues to talk with his armed councilors.[12]

The delay allows the clergymen to observe Ngqika's appearance in great detail. He is not very tall, but *well-proportioned* and *good-looking*. Around his head he wears a leather band, embroidered with white and black beads in triangular shapes. His kaross is made out of leopard skins, and like other Xhosa men, it is his only garment. His *right fore-arm* is almost entirely *covered with metal rings*, while brass rings encircle both of his thumbs and the third fingers of each hand. On one ring, a single word, Hope, is inscribed.

After a *considerable time* has passed, Ngqika abruptly turns to the travelers and asks for news. The missionaries speak of kings, like himself, who live on islands in the ocean — they are referring to the South Seas — who have recently adopted Christianity along with their people, and who now, having been *induced to renounce their heathenish customs*, live in peace and happiness. But Ngqika seems particularly interested in any news of the reported death (which Ngqika immediately dismisses) of Makana. Before his surrender in 1819 Makana had prophesied that no matter what *force* was *employed against him, or wherever the white people might take him to,* their efforts would be for naught and he would return to his country and his countrymen.

And so, in 1822, Ngqika is not alone in Xhosaland in refusing to believe the reports of Makana's death and in awaiting his imminent return. But Kay had been in Cape Town during the attempted escape, and he had actually seen Makana's lifeless body *thrown out upon the beach.* He relays this information to Ngqika, who scoffs at the notion. The chief claims that all that is said on the subject is a *fabulous story, invented* for the Xhosa's *amusement.*

After the discussion of Makana's death, the missionaries turn the meeting to their formal request of being granted permission to travel to Pato's country near the coast and to establish a station there. The chief replies that he must convene his entire council in order to arrive at an answer. He promises to do so the next day. As the travelers prepare to depart, however, Ngqika calls Tzatzoe over to his side. The chief wants Tzatzoe to tell the missionaries to present him with the gifts they have brought to him, and to do so in his abode, in the *utmost privacy.* Kay takes the news particularly poorly. *Every shade of dignity, and all appearances of greatness, was now entirely thrown aside,* he writes later, *and in this sable ruler (sometimes designated King) we found a lying, sordid, avaricious, and beggarly wretch.* But Shaw is quite equivocal about the *beggarly* behavior, as Kay calls it. He understands it as diplomatic gift giving, noting it matter-of-factly in his account, and adding that in addition to the beads, pocket-knife, tinder-box, and copper for rings, he throws in his own handkerchief at Ngqika's request. It is unclear if, as Kay implies, Ngqika's requests exceed the standard diplomatic etiquette of gift giving.

The chief promises to gather his principal councilors in the morning to rule on the missionaries' request, and they ask permission to preach to the group as the following day is a Sabbath. They part on good terms, but a messenger meets the party on its way back to say that Ngqika has changed his mind and will, instead, depart for his *other residence.*[13]

The missionaries are *all a good deal chagrined.* Tzatzoe is reported to be *quite angry with the conduct of his King.* Tzatzoe may feel Ngqika is not behaving responsibly. As an intermediary, he might also feel that he has failed in his duties. A quiet Sunday passes, with services held in an *old thatched house,* referred to as *inhluka utixo,* or House of God. *The solemn assemblies will assume a still more pleasing aspect,* Kay concludes, *when circumstances allow them to lay aside their beast-skin mantles and procure decent clothes.* On Monday, as they are saddling their horses and readying for the journey back to the colony, Ngqika's messenger arrives to say that the chief has reconsidered and wishes to see them. There is snow topping the mountains over which they ride, making Kay nostalgic for home. This time, Ngqika gives permission for their intended mission, and the party turns for home.[14]

Having passed through terrain dense with Xhosa kraals, they come across a Xhosa hunting party near the Fish River. Over a hundred men have spread themselves in a circle and are slowly chasing the game in the center toward the hunters located at its one exit.[15] Galloping at full speed through this *bushy country*, Kay's horse stumbles into an ambush hole—a *deep pit dug by the natives for the purposes of ensaring game* and *completely concealed by the high grass growing around it*—throwing him from its back, over its head, and *entirely across the pit*. He lies on the ground, *almost senseless and altogether helpless* from the *violence* of the fall and a kick to the side of his head.

Jan Tzatzoe, who has been riding just behind him, comes quickly to his assistance. By a *remarkable interposition of divine Providence*, the injuries to Kay and his horse are not serious. The sharpened sneezewood stake that is typically driven into the bottom of a game pit—waiting to impale any creature unlucky enough to plunge in—has fallen and lies harmlessly on its side.[16]

IQONCE

He has always longed to return

1825–1832

Scythed by precipitous overgrown ravines, the Amathole mountains soar two thousand feet above the Chumie River valley. As they peak their ridges merge into a series of ascending buttes that resemble a school of dolphins departing for the interior of South Africa. The Chumie valley is one of the richest in Xhosaland. An *abundance* of timber is near at hand. Together with the Kat River valley that lies in the first drainage to the west and the highlands that feed both streams, the region is the economic and spiritual heartland of the Xhosa chiefs who support Ngqika, and, thereby, distinguish themselves from those who support Ndlambe. In 1825 the Amathole tower over a government mission station run by the Reverend John Brownlee.[1]

Brownlee had arrived at the Cape in January 1817 as a member of the London Missionary Society, but he soon resigned because of the scandal swirling around James Read's infidelity. Against the wishes of Brownlee and other newly arrived members of the missionary field the LMS had not expelled Read from their ranks, but allowed him to continue in his work at Lattakoo, their northernmost station in the colony. The conflict crystallized a shift in ideology within the LMS in South Africa. The radical evangelism of Van der Kemp and Read, which allowed and even encouraged interaction with the proselytized to the point of marriage, was being replaced by a conservative, culturally chauvinistic, and racially charged ideology that demanded, above all, that its agents adhere to accepted norms of British respectability that would not allow for marriage with Khoisan or African women, and certainly not condone adultery. By 1820 one of the newly arrived missionaries, Robert Moffat, would personally remove Read from his post, and send him back to the colony.[2]

Also in 1820, John Brownlee entered the Chumie Valley with his Cape-born wife, Catherine de Jager and an appointment letter from Colonel Bird that left little doubt that his main role as a government missionary at the Chumie would be to keep the Xhosa chiefs, particularly Ngqika, under surveillance. Jan Tzatzoe accompanied Brownlee to the Chumie at the station's founding, and from time to time helped the missionary itinerate and undertake an intensive study of the history and culture of the Xhosa people among whom he had settled, and especially, of their language. Tzatzoe visited Chumie with Kay and Shaw in 1822, and in 1823, he accompanied Shaw again, this time with the company of William Shepstone (on their way to found the mission station of Wesleyville). The Chumie institution also bore witness to the first document printed in Xhosa, when the Scottish missionary John Ross arrived with a small printing press in December 1823. In 1824, the press printed a Xhosa version of an elementary spelling-book, some hymns, the Lord's Prayer, and a *portion of Brown's catechism*.[3]

In addition to driving Brownlee into the hands of the government, Read's scandal had prompted the arrival of John Philip in South Africa in 1819. Philip, the self-taught son of a Scottish weaver, is a rotund man, possessed of prodigious energy and drive. Framed by dark, bushy sideburns and a full head of black hair, his face has sharply defined and delicate features.[4] Appointed by the Directors of the LMS to inquire into the state of their missions, Philip and his fellow investigator, John Campbell, wrote a blistering report back to London in December 1819.

Philip and Campbell described a failed missionary movement in South Africa, which they laid at the feet of Dr. Van der Kemp (a *man of learning, science, and genius but his mind delighted in philosophical abstractions, and his understanding was not sufficiently practical for the common place duties of a Missionary*), and his protégé, James Read (the *feeble Successor* of Van der Kemp). They accused Read of allowing Van der Kemp's books to rot on the *ground in the corner of an old house that was overflowed with water by every shower of rain*, while he allowed carpentry tools to rust, failing even to employ the *only plough ever sent to Africa by the Society*. In their opinion, Read's hyperbolic reports clearly overstated his accomplishments:

> With a few specimens of fruit from a solitary tree in his own Garden, which engaged his exclusive attention, he deceived the public, and led us to think that he was covering Africa with Groves of the Orange tree. . . . He had expected a crop where he had neither sown nor bestowed labour.

Echoing the ongoing shift in evangelical ideology, Philip and Campbell's report concluded by calling for a *new class of missionaries* for the Cape Colony. Unlike the more egalitarian thinking that drove the actions of men like Read and Van der Kemp, these new men of *"Character"* would be able to *sustain the complicated Characters of the Magistrate, the Father, the Master and the Minister of the Gospel*. Philip would remain in the colony to oversee the new LMS dispensation.[5]

By 1825 Brownlee is uneasy. He looks south from the Chumie, and sees the Wesleyans (after their trip with Tzatzoe in 1822) establishing a mission among Ndlambe's people. He looks east where the representatives of the Glasgow society will soon arrive. Brownlee feels that his Chumie mission is on its feet, and that his status as government missionary is *extremely prejudicial to his spiritual influence among the natives*.[6] Concerned about the progress of alternative mission Societies, Brownlee writes to Philip: *I cannot help wishing that you may turn your attention to this quarter of the heathen world, as the L.M.S. were the first who occupied this field*. He praises the original Kat River mission to which he had been assigned before Joseph Williams's death: *from the above Mission either directly or indirectly a foundation has been laid for the now existing Institutions in this country*. He also has kind words for Jan Tzatzoe, or *John Tzatzoo*, as he calls him. The Xhosa man can be more *extensively useful* in Xhosaland than at Theopolis. He has *connexions in this country, and a perfect knowledge of the language that renders him in some respects superior to any European Missionary particularly in translating*.[7]

Equally anxious about the imminent success of his missionary rivals, Philip sees the return of a valuable ally in Brownlee. It falls to him to write the necessary letters for the new mission, to request sufficient funds, to mollify Cape Town and London. Philip's work at the Cape since his arrival in 1819 has involved smoothing over the personality clashes and philosophical differences among his small group of LMS missionaries and, through his connections with the humanitarian movement in Great Britain, politicking on a grand scale for the rights of the oppressed Khoisan peoples remaining in the colony. Philip has been compiling notes for a history of the society's work in South Africa. He has spoken to Elizabeth Williams, James Read, John Brownlee, and many others who have attested to the importance of the Williams's mission at the Kat River and to Tzatzoe's role within it.[8]

In late July or early August 1825, after meeting with Brownlee, Philip completes a letter written in a *hasty scrawl* to the LMS Board of Directors. Wherever he has visited in the colony, he has been *very much pressed* to *renew* the LMS mission in Xhosaland—a goal that has been on his mind since he arrived in the colony only to discover that the government had prohibited the Society from appointing a successor for Williams at the Kat River. *Favourable signs have at last been given of the intimation of divine will.* And in the person of Jan Tzatzoe, the LMS is *in possession of means above those of any other Society for conducting a Mission in Caffreland*:

> Tzatzoe is not only the son of a Xhosa chief, but he is considered as a branch of the Royal Family in Caffre Land and as great respect is shewn to that distinction among the Caffres you will perceive the advantageous effects his labours are likely to be accompanied with. He is a truly pious and respectable young man and his attachment to our Society has often been tried in rejecting many proposals made to him by this Govt. and the Missionaries of other Societies to induce him to join them. From the day he left Caffreland, he has always longed to return as a missionary to his relations and countrymen.

Philip focuses on the figure of Jan Tzatzoe. Tzatzoe symbolizes the means by which the LMS may gain access to the Xhosa and the success of British evangelicalism and civilization. Tzatzoe's resonance as a symbol will continue to grow in the border region, in Cape Town, and in London. Philip recognizes his presence as an intermediary as a necessary condition for the mission. In the intriguing phrase that mentions that Tzatzoe has rejected *many proposals made to him by this Govt. and the Missionaries of other Societies to induce him to join them*, Philip implies that other Europeans have recognized Tzatzoe's symbolic and practical value.

Tzatzoe has had to contend with offers from other mission societies, and perhaps even the government itself. What offers have been made? For Tzatzoe to serve as an assistant to European missionaries? Or to head a mission on his own? Has the government sought him as a translator in their interactions with the Xhosa chiefs? Or in a more elevated and unprecedented capacity as a colonial diplomat or administrator? The archival record can provide no answers.[9]

Since leaving the Williams Mission in 1818, Tzatzoe has traveled back and forth throughout the border region. Yet, he has remained loyal to the LMS, not venturing off to start his own mission, not seeking out the amaNtinde in an effort to spread the Word. What continues to *attach* Tzatzoe to the LMS? Is it loyalty to James Read and the memory of Van der Kemp? Perhaps Sanna Oursen and her attachment to the mission stations of her childhood? Does Tzatzoe feel he still has much to learn in the colony? While it is tempting to speculate on his motivations—to suggest, for instance, that there is a docile aspect to Tzatzoe's character or personality, a lack of self-confidence or internal motivation, that can explain why he doesn't return on his own to Xhosaland—there are no openings into the past through which to reach for the truth or reality of any such insights. The fragments of the past that remain provide multiple and contradictory perspectives, and they must be considered in turn.

Philip had spoken to Tzatzoe in 1821 and 1823 at Theopolis, and he is convinced of Tzatzoe's *zeal for the conversion of his countrymen* and his *attachment to the LMS*. In return Philip has *assured* Tzatzoe that the *Mission to the Caffres will be renewed, if Providence should open a door to us into the Caffre country. We were both of opinion,* Philip writes, *that if the Government were to sanction the proposed attempt it could not well be made till we should have it in our power to send a suitable person along with him.* Is Philip glossing over Tzatzoe's impatience and eagerness here? Has Tzatzoe been asking why he might not return directly as a missionary to his relations and countrymen? Or has Tzatzoe, recognizing the value of British knowledge and connections, been biding his time, carefully waiting for a *suitable person* with whom he might work constructively. Is the choice of a new LMS mission to Xhosaland, and of its British missionary, in Tzatzoe's hands? Philip writes to the Scotsman:

> Brother Brownlee, if you find yourself at liberty to join John Tzatzoe and undertake such a Mission, the measure shall have my immediate sanction, and I shall instantly write home to the Directors and from what they know of my opinion of you, I am convinced they will give me a Bill of indemnity for what I have done.[10]

It is summertime, 20 January 1826. Brownlee, Jan Tzatzoe, and their families arrive on the banks of the iQonce or Buffalo River, approximately twenty miles above its entrance into the Indian Ocean. The location is the site of a large village headed by Kote Tzatzoe. Tzatzoe has finally fulfilled his father's decade-long desire for his son to return to the amaNtinde.[11]

Brownlee and Tzatzoe erect two huts in a location that offers *advantages of a very superior nature*. There is *both good ground for pasture and for agricultural purposes*, and the area might be *irrigated to an extent far exceeding any thing of the kind* that Brownlee has *seen in Africa*.[12] The site sits on the crest of a low rise that runs north to south, parallel to the river. About a half a mile due north, the iQonce makes a gentle turn to the southeast, before gradually completing a semicircle, and resuming its southward direction. Irrigation ditches, yet to be dug, will siphon water from the river before it makes its turn and bring the stream straight down to the fields of wheat and potatoes, and gardens of corn, melons, and other vegetables. To the west the ground slopes down toward the river and the *thick bush* of its immediate valley. The opposing riverbank reaches higher than the mission's ridge, blocking the view in that direction along with the setting sun. To the east lies another ridge and yet another in this undulating landscape. Thirty miles to the northwest, the striking mountain fortress of the Amathole range, with its sweeping, vegetation-laden walls, and exposed, stony parapets, rises from the striated plains. The redoubt, with the Chumie mission nestled at its base, does not dominate the landscape at the iQonce River. But it is a constant presence, like a squadron of ships seen from the shore, sailing just above the horizon.[13]

For all the travels he has undertaken and all the journeys yet to come, it is this view and these rolling ridges that will be the one constant for the remainder of Jan Tzatzoe's years: the center of the web to which he will constantly return, the complicated inheritance he will bequeath to his descendants, and the foundation upon which he will fashion the rest of his life. In so much as any one human life may be said to lay claim to a single location—to a place that resounds with meaning and through which it may be defined—Jan Tzatzoe is home.

Yet, even beneath the calming solidity of the Amathole mountains, Jan Tzatzoe is continually on the move. He is at Bethelsdorp, 165 miles from the iQonce, on 7 June 1826, for the first anniversary meeting of the Auxiliary Missionary Society. The society serves to bring the various missionary societies together and to allow the people of the many missionary stations to contribute funds toward the initiation and support of additional institutions. After the evening sermon, Tzatzoe speaks to the gathering, referring to the *spread of the Gospel as the grand means of Civilizing mankind*. If he *understands right*, he says, *there was a time when the English were a barbarous people*. He hesitates for *some time before he compares* the *ancestors* of the British to *any of the African tribes*, but, *at last*, he urges, *perhaps they were almost as barbarous as the Caffres*.[14]

The Reverend George Barker, Tzatzoe's companion from his days at Theopolis and the meeting's secretary, assures him that he *might compare the ancient Britons to the Bushmen*. Tzatzoe then gives this idea *a fine turn*. He asks: *If the Bible has affected such an amazing change as we now behold in Englishmen, if its effects on mankind are so great as to produce such a difference as we behold between the Bushmen and Englishmen, what can a knowledge of the Bible not do for us poor ignorant Africans?*

Tzatzoe argues that Christian belief and the assumption of Christian practices will raise Africans to a level of civilization equal to that of the British. At this time civilization carries a host of connotations from the use of superior technology, to new ways of dressing, farming, and interacting with the wider world through various media.[15] During the 1820s and early 1830s in South Africa, the idea that Africans are capable of this achievement reaches its heights. But the notion conceals a paradox.

Once the African adherents to the missionaries and the mission stations feel they have gained a sufficient knowledge of the Bible, have gained the level of the Englishmen in that respect (or have surpassed the level of most of the British and Dutch settlers), they will begin to ask why they remain below the level of the Europeans in South Africa's racial, economic, and social order. They will begin to come to terms with the underlying paternalism and European cultural chauvinism of the missionaries and their liberal supporters.[16] Held out as one of the missionaries' greatest successes in their civilizing and Christianizing project, Jan Tzatzoe will have ample opportunity to question why he is not being treated as an equal in the religious, political, and social realm.

The meeting continues with a report of the Auxiliary Society's work over its first year, a public recognition of its friends around the Cape Colony, and a listing of the activities of LMS missions *around the world*. The annual subscription is collected. Jan Tzatzoe, Reverend Barker, and Mr. Edwards each give 5 Rixdollars.

In April 1827 a Landdrost, or provincial governor, Major William Dundas, whose headquarters are in Graham's Town, visits *Mr. Brownley's Establishment.* He reports to his superior officer in Cape Town that Jan Tzatzoe is Kote Tzatzoe's *eldest son, having resided some time in the Colony speaks Dutch fluently, and has become a tolerable Mason and Carpenter—this person in consequence of his Father's advanced age is the principal of the Kraal, and does as much to forward improvement as his power and means will admit of.* Dundas does not report on Jan Tzatzoe's religious upbringing at Bethelsdorp, nor on his spiritual duties of itinerating, preaching, and interpreting. Instead, he sees him as a chief, returned from the colony to govern his father's people. Dundas, not Brownlee, is the first person to remark upon the civic and political role that Jan Tzatzoe has apparently assumed. Perhaps Dundas makes this observation based on his overly materialistic assessment of the Xhosa:

> The Kaffre is indeed the best possible material to work upon, for he is patient and enterprising in labours he is accustomed to, submissive under authority, generally honest in his dealings, at all times shews a desire to increase his Stock, and great activity in this his first object and to raise himself in the estimation of his Countrymen.[17]

Dundas may not have the capacity to admit that a Xhosa man like Tzatzoe can contribute to the spiritual and educational betterment of his people. Or maybe the military man views the iQonce River institution in a clear-eyed and practical manner, unclouded by humanitarian inclinations. At home among his people, Tzatzoe likely has assumed significant secular leadership responsibilities. Tzatzoe will later recall that upon his return to Xhosaland in 1826, he took the *reins of government* from his father. He was not a *teacher under the missionaries*, but an *assistant to the mission at my station* where his father's *people looked up* to him for *advice*.[18]

One of the main responsibilities of a Xhosa leader is to ensure the spiritual and material welfare of his people. These realms are intricately linked, and the leader must protect his followers from witchcraft, disease, and drought. Having returned to the amaNtinde with claims to a new spiritual power, Tzatzoe soon finds himself in direct conflict with the individuals in whom his father and the majority of the amaNtinde place their faith to access spiritual power and ensure worldly prosperity.[19]

One Sunday Jan Tzatzoe becomes aware that all the *adults of Tzatzoe's Kraals* have been compelled to attend at the *Rain Maker's*. In addition to witchfinding, or divining, and seeing to the health of individuals and the wider community, many Xhosa healers are employed to ensure the land's fertility through gifts of rain. Tzatzoe asks his father to explain the *nature of the meeting*. Kote Tzatzoe replies that the people are gathered to visit a sick man. Jan Tzatzoe answers that the sight of so many people engaged in such complicated dances is a *strange way of administering comfort*. He issues a *solemn, & faithful reproof, pointing out the aggravated nature of their sin, particularly their contempt of the word and day of God*, and condemns the *superstitious assembly as being in direct opposition to his word*. Tzatzoe could mean the word of God, but he might also mean his word as a chief.[20]

While the crowd seems assured that the *judgements of God will not be inflicted*, Jan Tzatzoe assures them that God is *just and holy, and an all powerful being, and would perform all his threatenings*. The image of one true and powerful God whose arrival is imminent and who promises swift judgment is one that Tzatzoe and Williams had employed at the Kat River. It echoes the coming of Christ in the Gospel of Mark: *John did . . . preach the baptism of repentance for the remission of sins . . . And preached, saying, There cometh one mightier than I after me* (Mark 1:5,7). It also speaks to the vengeful rider on the *white horse* of Revelations, who *in righteousness doth judge and make war* (Revelations 19:11–20). It is a trope to which Tzatzoe, Brownlee and future missionaries at the iQonce will return.

The rainmaker fails to procure rain that day, and he slaughters an ox on the next. But again no rain falls, and the rainmaker tells the people that Jan Tzatzoe has *blown it away*. Rainmakers often accuse individuals of polluting areas of land with witchcraft (the process often involves urination) so that the rain will not fall thereupon. The rainmaker cannot sleep, and *his God* has told him that there will be no more rain and that the people will perish from *drought and heat*. There is much consternation following the rainmaker's pronouncements, and a *great deal of discussion during the week*. The following Sabbath, there is a large congregation at the mission, and after the afternoon service, it begins to rain and continues on through the night. *Now the people say,* Brownlee concludes his telling of the story, that *God has given the rain*. But keeping in mind the fact that the rainmaker has accused Jan Tzatzoe of dispersing the rain clouds with his interruption at the rainmaking ceremony, is it God, or Tzatzoe as his intermediary, who obtains the people's credit for the rain arriving after the Christian ceremony?

A little over a year after their arrival, Brownlee has largely completed the irrigation channels from the iQonce to the station's fields and *erected temporary buildings* for the staff of the institution. Tzatzoe, his wife, and at least one daughter, Mary, are housed in a solid stone building, one of four at the station.[21] The others belong to European missionaries, with a similar structure reserved for services. All four houses are equidistant and sit atop the ridge that runs parallel to the river. Tzatzoe's house is closest to the chapel, and also to the large *open air bell* that hangs below a *trellis structure* and calls the people to their prayers. Sixteen acres of fields and gardens stretch from the ridge down to the river, growing mostly maize, also sorghum, millet, French beans, pumpkins and watermelons. There are fenced enclosures for twenty horses, sixty oxen, two hundred cows and calves, three hundred sheep, and one hundred and eighty goats. There is an orchard with one hundred and fifty fruit trees: apricot, peach, fig, almond, lemon, apple, and pear, arranged in four orderly rows. Above the stone houses stand several Xhosa kraals with their beehive-shaped, grass-walled homes and thorn-tree cattle enclosures. Jan Tzatzoe owns the station's only *waggon* and *plough*, and he is the first Xhosa man in Xhosaland to do so.[22]

Only a few Xhosa families have moved to live at the station. The small and stagnating flock comprises less than fifty adults, with none sufficiently pious to be judged ready for baptism. The mission adheres to a rigid schedule of worship. There are morning and evening services at which a *portion of Scripture* is read and explicated in the *plainest manner*, along with *prayer and singing* in Xhosa and sometimes in Dutch. In the evenings the missionaries catechize the listeners on the content of the morning's lessons, and the *hearers* demonstrate *evidence of a retentive memory, and often a very correct application of subject in all its bearings*. In addition there are two extra services on Sundays and also a weekday and Sunday school. Brownlee teaches from *Watt's Catechism*, a primer for school-age children that is around one hundred years old.

The missionaries engage in *a good deal of religious discussion* with their audience, whose ranks swell on Sundays to include *strangers*, new visitors to the station. They try to answer the *objections* that the Xhosa voice against the *reception of Christianity*. Understanding that adopting Christianity means acting *contrary* to Xhosa *customs*, the Xhosa worry, in part, that doing so will expose them to *hatred and violence from the more powerful tribes, that continue to live in their heathenish customs*.

To counteract this assertion, the missionaries use the example of Ngqika's people and the Kat River mission. Many of Ngqika's councilors, *Caffres of respectability* to Brownlee, had resisted the mission and predicted that the Xhosa who joined the institution would become sick or die of some *calamity of war*. But, during Makana's war in 1818, all of these councilors were killed. Not a single person from the station was injured, *although exposed in the same manner as the other Caffres*, and they retained all of their cattle. Although likely apocryphal, the message of the story is powerful, but also troubling: what if God fails to protect his converts in the future?[23]

Brownlee is anxious to undertake more evangelizing excursions. But he cannot itinerate by himself or with any assistant or interpreter besides Jan Tzatzoe. He informs London that a successful encounter requires someone who after the delivery of a *short discourse* on an aspect of the Gospel, is *qualified to meet all* the *objections* presented to the missionaries by their audience. Tzatzoe is *the only person on the Institution qualified so to act*. These *visits have not been so frequent or over that extent of the country* as Brownlee would wish for. For now the blame is laid at the feet of Tzatzoe's material responsibilities—as a carpenter, wagonwright, farmer, and pastoralist. Tzatzoe is also spending a substantial amount of time assisting the missionaries in their attempts to learn Xhosa, to produce a guide to the language, and to translate various works of the word of God.[24]

While committed to the *outward establishment* of the mission, Brownlee is focusing on learning Xhosa and translating the Gospel. With Tzatzoe's *valuable* assistance, Brownlee translates almost the whole of the Gospel of Mark. In doing so, the pair may have completed the first translation of a Gospel into a sub-Saharan African language.[25] There is an insidious aspect, however, to the endeavor. *The possession of a full manuscript of one of the Gospels* will, Brownlee reports to London, *be of service in enabling us to communicate more direct religious instruction to the Caffres, without the means of an interpreter*. Clearly, interpreters do not fall under Brownlee's "us" category. They are useful only in making themselves redundant.[26]

In December 1827 a life-threatening illness strikes Jan Tzatzoe's half-brother Soko. In Xhosa society, disease, along with other misfortune, is not attributed to chance or accident, but is understood to be the result of malevolent individuals, or a variety of supernatural beings, operating in the unseen world.[27] Four *Prophets*, ritual specialists also called Doctors by the Europeans, are hired to heal Soko and discover the source of his illness. They do so by conducting a smelling-out, or witchfinding ceremony. Entering a trance-like state, they dance to clapping hands and the beat of an ox-hide drum, pausing to speak or sing, and resuming the dance. By the morning of 16 December, after two days of activity, they have discovered four bundles of *bewitching matter*, also referred to as poison. One has been dug up from the floor of the house in which the patient is resting, and another *parcel* has been pulled from the thorn-tree hedge that encircles the kraal.[28]

The end result of the vast majority of witchfinding ceremonies is that the *prophet* accuses an individual of poisoning or attempting to poison the afflicted person. The suspected witch is seized and tortured into a confession—at which point their property is confiscated by the chief under whom they live. Because witchcraft is thought to operate at close quarters (the bundle under Soko's bed), accusations are most frequently leveled at a sick individual's close relatives and friends. Suspicion often falls upon the elderly or on individuals who appear to have accumulated significant wealth outside of the strictures of chiefly control.[29]

Jan Tzatzoe, Brownlee, and another recently arrived LMS missionary, a German, Friedrich Gottlob Kayser, journey across the iQonce to visit Soko. They arrive at a temporary respite during the ceremony. Soko is actively discouraging further investigation because he fears that the *persons who have been endeavouring to murder him by such means, would, by the discovery of their plans, be more enraged, and would certainly destroy him.* The missionaries talk to the assembled Xhosa about the *things of God*. They condemn the ceremony; they are present to *detect the impositions*.

Ever since he began accompanying European missionaries into Xhosaland in his youth, such critical confrontations over spiritual efficacy have been a key component of Tzatzoe's evangelism and his work as a translator. Tzatzoe's mediation is central to the cultural exchanges embedded within the conversations. To European missionaries, Tzatzoe has explained Xhosa concepts of healing and sorcery, of the ways that illness and misfortune enter the world and how individuals and communities can protect themselves against such evil; he has also mined these concepts for ways to express the tenets of Christianity.

If the healers are imposters, how are they deceiving the people? The missionaries feel that the diviners are making false claims to spiritual power. Finding the witchcraft bundles has nothing to do with Soko's illness. They say this not because they disavow supernatural causes for illness, but because, in their minds, the *Prophets* are appealing to the wrong power. *They point out to them that sin is the greatest sorcery, having bewitched all mankind.* It will *destroy all who* continue *under its dominion.* Activities described as sinful include pretending to be a Doctor or Prophet (false prophecy), ignoring the word of God, lying, stealing, cheating, whoring, and adultery.[30]

Ten years earlier, at the Kat River, Tzatzoe and Williams confronted a Xhosa *Prophet* in similar circumstances. At that time, they employed comparable language to convey the power of the spiritual presence they claimed to represent. Echoing the trope of the vengeful God of Mark and Revelations, they told the Xhosa assembled for the ceremony: *All the poison is not yet found but the great Prophet Christ is on his way to find it woe the man who has it hid when he cometh.*[31]

In both cases, Tzatzoe and the missionaries turn to the language of sorcery and countersorcery to convey the concepts of Christianity, allowing their listeners to internalize and respond to their message.[32] But while they likely intend for their listeners to understand the Xhosa terms they are using as metaphors, conveying a likeness only, the Xhosa may instead be taking terms like *great Prophet Christ*, or sin as *poison*, literally.[33] It is perhaps because of this literal understanding of the language they are using that the missionaries represent a minor insurgency into the ideology of the people to whom they are preaching. The few adherents of the Christian missions in Xhosaland tend to be the powerless and the weak within Xhosa society. Those with successful lives have scant need to contemplate the intervention of a new spiritual power as presented by mission Christianity.[34]

A month after the initial consultation in Soko's case, an *old woman* is accused, captured, and tortured. Jan Tzatzoe and Brownlee confront Kote Tzatzoe, his sons, and his councilors who, at first, deny the torture that consisted of scorching the woman's breasts, and then immobilizing her on top of a nest of biting, black ants. Kote Tzatzoe finally admits that he had approved the ants, but not the fire.[35] The missionaries press their case, arguing that the woman has a right to face her accusers, and have them prove the accusation. This is the legal procedure in Xhosaland for all those accused of crimes other than witchcraft, and extending its benevolence is a plausible idea.[36]

But some of the councilors argue fervently against the proposition. Their main political function is to protect their community from witches, and if they fail at this task, they will be *oppressed and destroyed by the more powerful chiefs*. Tzatzoe and Kayser respond that *although they should destroy the old woman, and every old woman in the tribe, Soko would obtain no relief from his sickness, nor would they have any security from the attacks of the other* Xhosa. In arguing against witchcraft trials, Tzatzoe and his fellow Christians appear to want to transfer this political burden to themselves. Tzatzoe, in particular, appears to be staking his reputation and future political prospects in a direct attack on the Xhosa healers. To protect the amaNtinde, he can call on the Christian God, and on the missionaries and the political power in the colony to which they have access. The argument lasts for over two hours but does nothing to shake the councilors' belief in the power of witchcraft or the rectitude of their fight against it.

After the meeting the missionaries return to the woman who is being tortured. Her binds have been loosened. She can clear the ants from her mouth and face, but the burns are more severe than Brownlee first observed. She speaks without *uttering a single groan*. Tzatzoe and Brownlee *converse* with her, and *endeavour to point out the way of salvation*. They *are unable to afford her any assistance*, so they *urge* her *to seek deliverance for soul and body from God*, to confess. In reply, the woman stresses her innocence from the charge of witchcraft. *Her thoughts are toward God*, she tells them.

A sense of impotence mounts among the missionary party. When the woman dies overnight, purportedly from strangulation, they once again seek out Kote Tzatzoe to argue for the burial of the remains instead of allowing them to be consumed by wild animals.[37] Kote Tzatzoe does not grant them permission. To a frustrated Brownlee, the chief speaks to them *with that fulsome compliment* which the Xhosa are so *lavish in bestowing on those they pretend to respect*. Kote asserts that an evil spirit possessed the woman and that her body's consumption by wild animals will release the evil leading to Soko's recovery. If buried, the spirit will remain with the body.

The witchcraft trials do not end with the woman's death. Soko grows more ill (although he will shortly recover), and by April 1828 four more individuals, including the man who has been caring for Soko for the previous five months, are accused. Jan Tzatzoe and Brownlee arrive too late to save him. His back is burnt severely, and he is being taken into his hut in order that he might produce the *bewitching matter*. The *most horrid screaming* tears the air open. The missionaries run to the hut where the man is yelling that his guards are burning his genitals. Looking inside they see a large fire with red-hot stones among its embers. The suspect is tied to the ground, and as the observers set foot in the hut, they see that one *stone is laid under him. It has been removed a little* upon their entrance.[38]

From 1828 to 1832 Jan Tzatzoe forms an extraordinary working relationship with Friedrich Gottlob Kayser, who arrived at the iQonce in September 1827. Kayser will prove to be among the most compassionate of the Europeans with whom Jan Tzatzoe will interact and one of Tzatzoe's greatest supporters and advocates. The four years that Kayser and Tzatzoe will spend together will be a high point in Tzatzoe's work as a translator and missionary. In an unprecedented fashion, Kayser will give credit to the man he calls John Tz. or John Tshatshu for his contributions to their joint efforts in evangelizing, and particularly in translation. Unfortunately, the actual translated texts from Dutch and English into Xhosa are not available, but the record of daily life in Kayser's journals and letters that speaks to their production provides a welcome window into the work in which Tzatzoe and Europeans like Brownlee have been engaged for years, and into the innovative work to which Tzatzoe has been a key contributor.[39]

Kayser accepts Tzatzoe's invitation, early in 1828, to accompany him to meet with a *great secret minister* of Ngqika. At the councilor's village, Kayser has Tzatzoe translate Romans 1:18–32 and Revelation 21:8. Both biblical passages describe a formidable Christian God, immanent like the figure of the Gospel of Mark, and vengeful: *But the fearful, and unbelieving, and the abominable, and murderers, and whoremongers, and sorcerers, and idolators, and all liars, shall have their part in the lake which burneth with fire and brimstone: which is the second death* (Revelation 21:8).[40]

Upon their return Tzatzoe tells Kayser about another *secret minister* who had been *one of the worst* in condemning God's word, saying *I am too strong, God has no power of me*. Echoing the language of Revelation, Tzatzoe had replied: *You shall yet see, that God has power of you, and then shall you weep*. Now, the *councilor* urges his people to hear and obey God's word. His people *are like the yellow of an egg* in Jesus Christ's *hands*.[41]

Kayser and Tzatzoe continue to confront *rainmakers* and *prophets* who live near the station. After a lengthy discussion of death and heaven, in which they speak of the true Lord and the all-wise Lord from whom forgiveness from sins can be gained, the healer tells them: *I am a prophet and my Lord told me, when I should die*. The missionaries use 2 *Kings* 18 and *Jeremiah* 27:9–10 to elaborate on the notion of *false prophets*: *Therefore hearken not ye to your prophets, not to your diviners, nor to your dreamers, nor to your enchanters, nor to your sorcerers* (Jeremiah 27:9). Tzatzoe and Kayser speak to another healer from Romans 3:10–18 and Jeremiah 23:23–32. Their biblical verses dovetail with both the investigative and punitive nature of Christ as metaphorically understood as a witchfinder: *Can any hide himself in secret places that I shall not see him?* (Jeremiah 23:24)

A Xhosa chief, Botman, who often visits the Kat River mission, camps near the station in July 1828. Tzatzoe and Kayser call on him at dinnertime in order to hold a service. Tzatzoe translates for Kayser the prayer offered by the chief: *Dear Father, who art in heaven you have prepared this meat for us, bless it. You have brought us in safety hither—we are blind and sinners—we thank you. We are on the road to meet an enemy, grant us success, and bring us safely back by Jes. Christ. Amen.*

By June 1829 Kayser has been at work learning Xhosa for two years. *During one session in the occupation of the Kaffer language*, Kayser mentioned to Tzatzoe that he thought that the Xhosa nation was *come from the north side down the sea to here*. Tzatzoe concurred. The *oldest of his nation* say they were *come from the north, and they speak much, of a large terrifying animal in the river* and a *large terrifying serpent*.[42]

Kayser can read from the few printed pamphlets in an intelligible fashion, and he can speak in *very short sentences*. But he is having trouble speaking fluently in long sentences, because to do so he must learn how to put *sometimes one sometimes more letters* in between every word. These letters relate nouns to verbs and come in many classes. Until now, he has not been able to acquire *a rule by John* for grammar, who has *only told* him: *You shall learn that by use, where you than shall feel it, what is the right letter*. Kayser and Tzatzoe have been working together, *seeking for words and for the radical word*, and *translating some little Kaffer-books* in order to gain a *knowledge of the syntax*. They are both *glad* that their *(sometimes troublesome) work has not been in vain*. Tzatzoe has told him that, through their work together, he has gained *more light and better knowledge of his language*.[43]

At the date of the 9th Nove [1829], Kayser decides *that in the new year (if it pleased my Lord b)* he will begin *with John Tz. a translation of the miracles of our Lord and Saviour Jesus Christ*. On the 9th Febr. [1830] *I began (in looking unto the Lord) with John, to translate His Miracles*. Within a week, Kayser reads his first *Miracle (John 4, 43–54)* to a crowd gathered at Soko's kraals for a feast:

So Jesus came again into Cana of Galilee, where he made the water wine. And there was a certain nobleman, whose son was sick at Capernaum.

When he heard that Jesus was come out of Judaea into Galilee, he went unto him, and besought him that he would come down, and heal his son: for he was at the point of death.
Then said Jesus unto him, Except ye see signs and wonders, ye will not believe.
The nobleman saith unto him, Sir, come down ere my child die.
Jesus saith unto him, Go thy way; thy son liveth.

In July 1830 alone, Kayser and Tzatzoe finish eight Miracles, *as: John 4, 43–54. Chapter 5, 1–47. Matth. 8, 1–4, Mrk 1, 40–45, Luk 5, 12–16. Mtth 8, 5–13. Luc 7, 1–10. Luc 4, 31–37. Mtth 8, 14–17. Mrk. 1, 29–34. Luc 4, 38–41. Mrs. 1, 21–28. Mtth 9, 1–9. Mrk. 5, 2–43. Luk. 8, 41–56 and Luke 16, 19–31.* Kayser and Tzatzoe also work on lists of Xhosa verbs in their active and passive forms, and some *prayers for children.* By the end of the year, Kayser promises to have *translated by John* the *Gospel of S. John* and to have started the *Acts of the Apostles.*

During the rest of 1830, Kayser engages in a series of interesting conversations with local Xhosa. The first is with Jan Tzatzoe's brother, who visits while Kayser and Tzatzoe are *busy in the Kaffer language.* The pair refuses to give him a gift of tobacco, arguing that he has left his own bagful in their safekeeping. The brother refers to Van der Kemp who *did not refuse the Captains* [chiefs] *anything; but did eat with them on one table and invited them to eat with him.* But *on the contrary* at the iQonce station, he suggests, speaking to the changing ideology of the British evangelical mission, the *Captains must sit down on the same place, where was the place for a common Kaffer; and if they get something to eat, it was given to them aside.*

Using the expression that he often draws upon to clarify their activities, Kayser writes that he *speaks again by John with* a man who tells them that his *wife in his sickness had called a Doctor.* But the man turned him away, saying: *I will not have anything to do with you. I shall see, what the Lord shall do with me by medicine.*[44] *I must be forlorn,* Jan Tzatzoe's daughter, Mary, tells Kayser on another occasion, *for I have not yet belief in Jesus Christ. I wish for it and for conversion to him.* Although later, he finds by *other conversations,* that the *good feeling was near gone to sleep again in her.*

Itinerating by himself at Kote Tzatzoe's kraals, Kayser speaks with more than 150 men. Some remember the *short catechism which I have translated by John.* At another kraal, Jan Tzatzoe translates John 3:16 for Kayser. *For God so loved the world, that he gave his only begotten Son, that whosoever believeth in him should not perish, but have everlasting life.* Kayser is upset by their reception. *Some were attentive at the explanation of that news; but some thoughtless and laughing as John prays in their language,* Kayser reports. *After it, John spoke earnestly with them—and they became quite silent; and some of the old declared, that it was true, what John says about their laughing.*

Kayser and Tzatzoe finish the translation of the Miracles of our Lord and Saviour Jesus Christ, *which I thought the most proper for this nation* on 6 December 1830. *They compose ten sheets in small octavo, and every number is concluded with a short hymn.*[45] What had set Tzatzoe and Kayser on the path of completing the novel translation project? According to Kayser's journal, his inspiration came *when in [a] conversation with the Kaffirs I had the opportunity to represent Christ to them as the greatest physician. I played on their great admiration for medical science. In this way I made a deep impression on some of the listeners.* But, sometime in 1830, in a letter written to friends in Germany, Kayser confesses that he had not represented Christ as the greatest physician to the Xhosa. It was Jan Tzatzoe who had made the breakthrough.

Of late I have had occasion to be reminded again of the words you spoke to us in lectures; "that a missionary should come to know what the heathens regard as their greatest or highest and then show Jesus Christ to be such," Kayser writes. *One circumstance of it was as follows: John Tshatshu, known to you from previous reports, had used a healing story from the gospel to show the big difference there is between a witchdoctor and Christ, the greatest physician of all.*[46] The phrase had a sudden impact. One of Tzatzoe's listeners exclaimed: *I am on the side of Christ, the great physician.* Kayser realized that he could apply *all the miracles and parables of the gospel* in a similar fashion, interpreting them in terms that relate to the *old practices* of the Xhosa. Jan Tzatzoe agreed, telling Kayser that this *incident has taught* him to *always keep that point in mind.*[47]

The healing stories that unfold in the Miracles of the Gospels of Matthew, Mark, Luke, and John, resonate particularly effectively in an African milieu. In them, Christ as *Physician* heals with merely a touch or with only a few words, and without recourse to material cause, human, witch, or other. He is powerful, fully capable of intervening in the material realm. This Christ is not judgmental or suspicious. He does not threaten torture. And instead of the confession of sins or changes in behavior, he asks simply for a declaration of faith, or in some cases, for nothing at all. In the raising of Lazarus in the Gospel of John, as well as the final miracle of the resurrection, Christ as *Physician* claims the power over life and death: *I am the resurrection, and the life; he that believeth in me, though he were dead, yet shall he live; and whosoever liveth and believeth in me shall never die.* This power has a specific resonance with the Xhosa, whose cosmology is particularly concerned with the nature of death (as aberrant and vile) and with the connections between the world of the living and that of the ancestors.[48] Finally, Christ as healer also draws upon an emerging legacy of Western-style medicine that is beginning to find its way to Xhosaland, is proving to be quite effective in combating basic diseases, and to which missionaries like Kayser and Tzatzoe attribute the power of their God.[49]

By 1832 Jan Tzatzoe is home among his father's people on the iQonce River. He is a preacher, an assistant to Kayser and Brownlee, an administrator, and adjudicator. He appears to be passing on the legacy of British civilization and Christianity to his children—his daughter Mary teaches at the Sunday school and is trying to start an infant school. The missionary station has thirty-six students at its day school and sixty at the Sunday school. There are ninety-one members of the institution: twenty men, thirty-two women, twenty-one boys, and eighteen girls.

About thirty miles, or a day or so ride from Tzatzoe's station on the banks of the iQonce, in the upper Kat River valley, the colonial government has settled scattered groups of mostly Khoisan settlers on some of the most fertile and well-watered land in the colony. The thousands of Kat River settlers have arrived from mission stations throughout the colony and have established gardens, homes, and small businesses cutting wood or hauling freight with their ox-wagons. The government intends to buy their loyalty as colonial soldiers with its beneficence (although not with official deeds to the land), but it has placed them on ground dear to the Xhosa, in particular to Maqoma, who had been forced from the region in 1828. The new residents of the Kat River Settlement specifically petition for James Read to serve as their minister.[50]

Kayser and Tzatzoe continue to work together fruitfully, itinerating, and translating more passages of the Gospel, including Acts and the first Epistle of Timothy. The Tract Society of the Cape will publish the translated *miracles of Christ*.[51] The interaction between Kayser and Tzatzoe is a highpoint in the appreciation of European missionaries and settlers of the contributions of Tzatzoe and his fellow African translators and intermediaries. The British will flex their military and political muscle in the coming decades, reflecting an increasing cultural chauvinism that will also infuse the personal power dynamics in which translation takes place, rendering these relationships fundamentally unequal. Tzatzoe's role in this arena will diminish, as will the importance ascribed to it.[52]

In December 1832 one of Tzatzoe's brothers is discovered weeping at church one Sunday; he admits to a *vision in which he saw a long rope hanging down from heaven upon the earth. He had several times seized the rope in order to climb to heaven—but every time he did fall off again.* His brother's attempts at conversion are taken as another indication that Tzatzoe is a *very useful auxiliary to the Mission*, and the missionaries expect that *arrangements would soon be entered into, which will enable him to enter more fully upon the stated work of a Missionary*.[53]

A very useful auxiliary to the Mission! Like Africans wherever Christianity is spreading, Tzatzoe has, in fact, been central to the mission's establishment and success. Tzatzoe accommodated the missionaries on land that his father gave them. Putting his own reputation as a chief's son at risk, he has traveled among neighbors, councilors, and chiefs, introducing the missionaries and their message, taking responsibility for the impact of the spiritual power they purport to channel. Tzatzoe has confronted rainmakers and witchfinders, and he has challenged his own father and brother on the gravest issues of life, death, and control of the forces that govern sickness and misfortune. From the missionaries he has gained relative material well-being and support in his own itinerating efforts. He has helped them with their stumbling attempts at the language. Together, they have fixed the words of Mark, and John, and Matthew in his natal language, the language of these mountains and this river, the language of his people.[54]

BUFFALO RIVER

A Blessing to His Tribe

1833–1835

During the maturing years of the nineteenth century, life in the eastern Cape is much like life at sea: the deck below is seldom, if ever, at rest. In 1833, after a relative calm, Jan Tzatzoe will see ripples racing toward him on the unworried waters that surround him, will see them right before he feels the gust on his cheek. He must ask himself whether these winds will blow through as capriciously as a summer squall, or whether they are the leading edge of a frontal assault.[1]

After six years of residence at the Buffalo River, John Brownlee finally admits three people into Church Fellowship. Tzatzoe assists Brownlee with his chapel services and itinerating trips, but the vast majority of the local Xhosa remain uncommitted to the Christian message and its rituals. The skeptical Africans volley the evangelists with questions: *Where does the soul go after death? How can God be omnipresent? What is sin? How does God permit Satan to use an influence in tempting man? If God made one man and woman only at the beginning, how comes the great variety of the human race?*

In May 1833 Jan Tzatzoe's brother, Soko, who has recently moved to the mission station, falls ill again. The missionaries diagnose consumption, but Soko insists on moving across the river, outside of the boundaries of the station, so that the *Caffre customs* can be *practiced with impunity*.

Despite the missionaries' interventions, both Kote Tzatzoe and Soko grow stronger and more belligerent in their belief in a *docteress* who draws a purported witchcraft bundle out of Soko's breast. She identifies another bundle as directly responsible for Kote Tzatzoe having to *go now about so much crooked. This lie,* Jan Tzatzoe tells Reverend Kayser, *has made my old father very strong in his belief on witchcraft.* An aunt and uncle of Tzatzoe's are smelled out and tortured. Kote Tzatzoe confiscates their property. Soko dies in a *quiet senseless state* on 10 July 1833.

Reverend Kayser initiates a move from the Buffalo to the Keiskamma where he can minister to Maqoma and his people. Tzatzoe interprets for the missionaries as Kayser, along with Brownlee and James Read, who is visiting from the Kat River Settlement, dictate the terms of the mission to Maqoma: *in this circle of the station no person can . . . call a Kaffer doctor or Doctress to a sick person, or to perform a doctor dance, or to make a noise at night in the kraal after killing, or to play with their shields during the day, or any other great noise.*[2]

Beginning in early 1833 a series of letters with the byline J. TZATZOE, Native Assistant Missionary, or John Tzatzoe, Native Chief and Missionary, are published in Cape Town's *South African Commercial Advertiser*. The letters respond to attacks made on Tzatzoe in the *Graham's Town Journal*. Founded in 1831 the *Journal* is edited by a shrewd and articulate settler named Robert Godlonton, and it claims to speak for the rights of the European settlers that it asserts are being eroded by undue sympathy for the indigenous peoples of South Africa. The *Journal* crystallizes the sentiments of many of the British settlers in the eastern Cape border region, who have begun to demand greater access to land and African labor, and more overt protection from Xhosa attacks, real and imaginary. Godlonton embodies the agitated state of his audience, voicing their complaints in vituperative language that is freighted with racial overtones.

The *Advertiser*, by contrast, under its co-founder and editor, John Fairbairn (who is married to John Philip's daughter Eliza), has been the mouthpiece of humanitarian liberalism at the Cape since it printed its first issue in 1824. The humanitarians include many within the London Missionary Society, and their reach extends to the innermost halls of power in London. The movement had grown out of the evangelical revivals of the mid- to late eighteenth century, with their emphasis on a personal relationship with God. During the nineteenth century it had acquired a complicated ideology built on a crusading activism that sought to extend social, political, and economic freedoms to the lower classes in Britain, as well as to the inhabitants of the British colonies, most notably through the abolition of the slave trade and of slavery itself. Humanitarianism made no distinction between the secular and Christian spheres (or between civilized and Christian behavior).[3]

The newspapers themselves represent an important development in the history of the Cape Colony. As in Britain and the United States during this period, the emergence of print as a widely disseminated medium (along with the spread of literacy) has created a profound new civic space for an emerging middle class. The pages of the newspapers contain unprecedented expressions of public opinion. They are also places where identities—such as settler or humanitarian—can coalesce and harden. What role are Africans to play in the new discourse? Certainly, their images will be mobilized to support the policies or ideologies of one side or the other. But what if they chose to represent themselves within this new space? Will an African, or any colonial subject, be able to create a convincing public persona for him or herself? Will they be free to speak and write for themselves?[4]

The attacks on Tzatzoe in the colonial press begin in letters to the *Journal* published on 10 January 1833 by a settler, William Southey, and an army officer, Lieut. W. Gilfillan, that take issue with Tzatzoe's testimony, printed in the *Advertiser* in October 1832, to a visiting colonial bureaucrat about the Fraser commando of 1818 and an incident involving the theft of four of Southey's horses. Shortly thereafter, letters signed by Tzatzoe rebut Southey and Gilfillan. The first reads:

THE CAFFER SYSTEM
January 23, 1833

To the Editor: Sir,—The remoteness of my situation prevents me from receiving early or regular intelligence of what is going on within the Colony, and had it not been for the kindness of a friend, I might have been months to come without any intelligence of the letters of Lieut. Gilfillan and Mr. Southey, in your number of the Graham's Town Journal which contains them. As I am personally implicated in both the letters in question, you will allow me to put a question, to Mr. Gilfillan, through the medium of your paper, which will bring the points at issue between us to a speedy termination.

Mr. Gilfillan asserts, that the cattle taken from the Caffers on commando described by Mr. Bruce, and on which he animadverts, were taken from Tslambi and not from Gaika's Caffers. I shall be much obliged to Mr. Gilfillan to mention the name of the place, and to inform me whether it was east or west of Fort Willshire, or east or west of Fort Beaufort? and at what distance from either of those places? As Mr. Gilfillan kept a journal by him, in which every thing connected with the [c]ommando is minutely recorded, he can be at no loss to answer the above questions. It is the opinion of some respectable persons who were present on the commando, that Mr. Gilfillan has confounded the commando in question with a subsequent commando, which these persons recollect Mr. Gilfillan to have been engaged in: and I want Mr. Gilfillan to have an opportunity of correcting the mistake into which he has fallen, before I bring forward the proofs I have at hand to establish Mr. Bruce's statement. Mr. Gilfillan's answer will decide whether the surmise I have ventured to express is correct or not

I am, &c, J. TZATZOE, Native Assistant Missionary[5]

The specifics of the debate between Tzatzoe and his detractors quickly deteriorate into arcane wrangling. But, more substantively, Tzatzoe's authorship of the letters is called into question. On 7 March 1833 Southey writes in the *Journal* that he read *with astonishment [a] letter signed "Jan Tjzatzoe": The writer of this letter I know not, nor do I care who he may be; I have to do with Jan Tzatzoe, whose name it bears and the abominable falsehoods it contains.*[6]

Throughout 1833 Southey and others continue to attack Tzatzoe's credibility. As they do so, Tzatzoe's letters grow more baroque in their style, and deviate from the specifics of the Fraser commando and Southey incident to denounce the whole of the commando, or patrol, system, which has been the major source of conflict in the border region since Governor Henry Somerset initiated the *spoor law* in his frontier meeting of 1818.[7] *I shall not pay much attention to Mr. Southy's [sic] trifling and shuffling remarks, but shall endeavour to state my facts, and dispose of my arguments without descending to low scurrility*, begins one letter dated 13 April 1833. *Nothing which Mr. S has brought forward has in the least served to justify either his conduct toward the Caffers, or the evils which result from the Patrole System. The more he attempts to justify the System, the more he exhibits the evils that must necessarily result from a System so impolitic in its principles, and ruinous in its consequences.*[8]

Tzatzoe's critics respond angrily to his ongoing correspondence. To X. Y., *Tzatzoe, or rather his advisers, (for poor man perhaps he does not know what he signs), are the greatest enemies the Frontier and Caffers now have, in laboring to keep up a hostile feeling and plundering disposition, but persuading the Caffers they are oppressed. The London missionaries are a band of fanatics who complain because we do not quietly sit still until we are assegaaied and our cattle swept away.* Addressing the LMS members in the eastern Cape in all but name, X. Y. specifically accuses those at the Kat River (James Read):

> Would Tzatzoe employ himself in inculcating on his friends at the Buffalo River, and his countrymen generally, the duty of their obeying the sixth and eighth Commandments, he might do some good in his day and generation and be esteemed; but whilst he continues to lend himself to his prompter at the Kat River, he must expect to share the fate of the whole faction—contempt and scorn.

Vindicator dismisses the possibility of Tzatzoe having written the letters:

> Poor simple Jan Tzatzoe is well known on the Frontier, and who could for one instant suppose that this really simple honest creature either did or could have written this and other letters published under his name

And even the possibility of Tzatzoe's role as a diplomat:

> ... and much more that he could have summoned up sufficient assurance to talk to Colonel Fraser until he had nothing to say, and became ashamed of the treachery of his conduct.

To the settlers, Tzatzoe's speeches and actions are pantomimes, his lips and tongue and hand moving by the direction of the missionaries.[9]

As with so many other areas of this life, the letters reveal Tzatzoe's intimate connections with Europeans—his intentions are intertwined with the needs and demands and sympathy of others. At first Tzatzoe's letters reflect his precise first-hand knowledge and political agenda, and there is little reason to doubt his involvement. Certainly, their English diction is not his. Yet there are letters in the archival record that appear to be in the same hand with which Tzatzoe signs his name. Nonetheless, they do tend to be matter-of-fact, and certainly do not achieve the rhetorical heights of the correspondence in 1833.

In later years Tzatzoe will continue to insist that he wrote the letters. In 1836 he will claim that he did so in Dutch with only his wife's aid, and without the assistance of any missionaries. He then *employed* James Read Junior to translate them into English.[10] Yet, some years after this assertion, in 1850, James Read Junior will provide a different perspective. As a result of another controversy swirling in the press at that time, Read Junior will attempt to reassure his LMS superior, Reverend Freeman, that he can stand up to the certain deprecation he will face. *I have never yet broken down in any case*, Read Junior will write, *I am naturally curious—but never blink. When yet a boy and but newly returned from Cape Town I conducted an intricate correspondence between J. Tzatzoe, the present Secretary Mr. Southey, and Mr. Gelfellan on the Frontier System.*[11]

What does James Read Junior mean by *conducted an intricate correspondence*? The first letters, especially, seem to reflect Tzatzoe's political concerns, and Tzatzoe is able to write and dictate in Dutch to a greater extent than his detractors imagine. But once the letters begin to deviate from specific incidents to the broader screeds, to what extent is Tzatzoe their author? And what about the idea to write letters under his name? To project himself into the colonial consciousness as an advocate and an active opponent of settler interests? Read Junior clearly mobilizes Tzatzoe's image—his public persona—as a way to convey the policy prescriptions (or propaganda in the opinion of others) of the humanitarian movement into the popular press. Jan Tzatzoe is now associated in the colonial and metropolitan public sphere with controversial items whose authorship he cannot prove definitively. The authenticity of his public persona will be questioned throughout the rest of his life.[12]

While Jan Tzatzoe and James Read Junior are embroiled in the letter-writing campaign, the Directors of the LMS write to John Brownlee on the *importance of a Native Agency*. The idea of equipping and trusting Africans to perform evangelical duties comes less from a call for African empowerment than from pecuniary worries. Her husband *is at present very anxious to introduce and encourage a Native agency at all our Stations*, Philip's wife, Jane, writes to a friend, *we find that unless something of this kind can be done it will be impossible to carry on the Mission efficiently—the expence* [sic] *of always getting European Missionaries will be greater than the Churches of home can sustain*. Jane Philip worries, however, that educating too many *individuals very far in advance of their particular tribe*, only *serves to fill them with pride and becomes injurious to them*. Better, Jane Philip concludes, to *bring forward the whole body of the young, and if there are a few that can be kept a little ahead of the rest—it is well as they will do for Schoolmasters &c*.[13]

Jane Philip's comment speaks to the paternalism that lies at the heart of the humanitarian movement. Despite the humanitarians' lofty rhetoric and achievements of legal guarantees of equality for all peoples, their accomplishments will be harshly judged. They will be seen to have prepared the ground for colonial societies that will develop stratified racial hierarchies. This judgment will be made on the contention that the humanitarians seldom if ever elevate the subjects of their attention to full and equal status with themselves. When the subjects metaphorically claim their adult status from the humanitarians, the humanitarians will falter. It will not be long before Jan Tzatzoe will glimpse this rotten core in the humanitarian ideology.[14]

Brownlee replies to the Directors of the LMS in a defensive manner. Yes, he is aware that the other Missionary societies are training Africans to be schoolmasters or assistant missionaries, but Brownlee has not encountered any Africans he feels to be suitable for these occupations, not even Jan Tzatzoe, who is the only African given the title of *Native Assistant* to an LMS mission in the Society's 1835 Annual Report.[15] Brownlee concedes that Tzatzoe did well as an interpreter for Reverend Williams in *Caffreland*, being fluent in both Dutch and Xhosa. At the Buffalo, Tzatzoe continues in that capacity, and Brownlee gives him an *opportunity for the exercise of the talent* he showed when Brownlee heard him preach at Theopolis. But Brownlee feels that Tzatzoe is hindered by an *inability to read correctly in the Dutch language*. He deals best with the Gospels and less successfully with the rest of the Bible. While he can now read the hymns printed in Xhosa that are used during the services, Brownlee is disappointed in his progress. By *reading*, Brownlee means Tzatzoe's reciting ability and not his understanding of the written word. In fact Brownlee does not mention Tzatzoe's intensive work in the arena of translation, work that belies Tzatzoe's inability to understand the Gospel. Brownlee's dismissive comments dovetail with a consistent inability to credit Africans with progress or potential; they may be read as racially informed, or at the least indicative of a strong cultural bias.

Brownlee is even more concerned with Tzatzoe's lack of participation in one of the *most important parts of Missionary labours in this country*, itinerating at the different Xhosa homesteads surrounding the mission station. Ever since Brownlee became fluent enough in Xhosa to conduct these journeys on his own, Tzatzoe no longer accompanies him. Despite constant urging about *his duties as a professed disciple of Jesus and the claims that the perishing souls of his countrymen have on his sympathy*, and the expectations of him as an *agent of the Society*, Tzatzoe has *shewn an unwillingness hitherto amounting to almost an entire neglect of this important duty*.

Brownlee also complains about Tzatzoe's unwillingness to put his training in carpentry and the *common works required in house building* to use in assisting the mission with items of a *secular nature*, or *any thing that is required for the use of the station*. His letter concludes:

> I neither mean by what I write to despise humble instruments, or a day of small things. . . . Should I write and give my unqualified approbation, and say Brother Jan Tzatzoe was a man of deep piety, fervent zeal, and spiritually minded, well acquainted with the Scriptures, and possessing talents of a superior order, and that instead of being employed as an assistant Missionary, he ought to be ordained to the work of the ministry, that he might enter more fully on Missionary work—such a report might excite a pleasant sensation on the minds of the Directors, at the same time it would leave me with a guilty conscience, that while I was endeavouring to please men, I had been acting deceitfully for God. I would by no means say that Jan is not useful, and had not this letter been carried to a great length, I would have favoured you with a specimen of his manner of speaking.[16]

Brownlee invokes the biblical verse from the Book of Zechariah in order to praise Tzatzoe's contribution in building the iQonce mission to date: *The hands of Zerubbabel have laid the foundation of this house; his hands shall also finish it; and thou shalt know that the Lord of hosts hath sent me unto you. For who hath despised the day of small things?*[17] But Brownlee does not foresee increased responsibilities for Tzatzoe. He may simply feel that Tzatzoe's level of literacy will not enable him to undertake formal missionary training. But he also dismisses Tzatzoe's potential contributions to the mission. In time, he will grow increasingly disturbed by Tzatzoe's secular duties as a chief.

In the midst of turmoil, Reverend Kayser will soon paint a radically different portrait of Jan Tzatzoe, the Xhosa leader and missionary, from that of Brownlee, as an example of the redeeming power of Christianity and British civilization:

> As a preacher Jan Tzatzoe possesses considerable talent, his addresses are pointed & powerful, & always command the attention of his hearer. His perfect knowledge of the Caffre character, his acquaintance with their habits & customs give him an advantage which few Europeans can attain in preaching to caffres. But the haste which he displays in combating Caffre prejudices & superstitions is really surprising. I have often listened with delight and astonishment to his discourses which are so full so simple and yet so powerful. The ease with which he can effectually arrest the attention of his countrymen, is matter of admiration. Here is a specimen of the great power of God in reclaiming caffres. But it is not only as a preacher that Jan Tzatzoe is a blessing to his tribe, he has considerable influence in civil affairs, & although he is unable to restrain their vicious passions, he can prevent a great many wicked acts, witness his conduct on the present occasion, & he was of great service at the station by restraining their oppression and tyranny.[18]

Ten years earlier Tzatzoe had berated Ndlambe and other prominent Xhosa leaders for living in a pitiful state, *worse than cats and dogs*. Then, Tzatzoe had insisted that the missionaries had *no authority to command*. Now, Kayser describes a man who has embraced his secular duties, and done so, at least in part, in order to move beyond the strictures of the mission so that he might offer, but also compel, a new way of life.

On New Year's Eve 1834 shocking news reaches Cape Town from the eastern Cape. The Xhosa have invaded the colony. British and Dutch settlers have been killed, tens of thousands of head of livestock captured. Graham's Town prepares for an attack, and the Khoisan Kat River settlers, leaving their own homes in danger, turn out in force in defense of the colony. At the outbreak of hostilities, Jan Tzatzoe is on a visit to an ailing James Read and his family at the Kat River, having arrived there on 19 December 1834. Prompted by an urgent letter from Brownlee to Read—*the state of things is very alarming*—and Kote Tzatzoe asking for his return *without delay*, Tzatzoe proceeds home to the Buffalo River station. The inveterate Brownlee, stalwart almost to the point of imprudence, is on horseback traveling to meet his two young sons who are returning for the Christmas holiday from their boarding school. A distraught and tearful Kayser, meanwhile, is pleading with Maqoma not to enter the war. Maqoma's reply: *I am a bushbock, for we Captains are shot like those and are not more esteemed as Captains.*[19]

The immediate cause of the war is clear. An incident directly attributable to the commando system has sparked an undergrowth of resentment and humiliation in Xhosaland, which has been growing drier and more flammable, and produced a conflagration. In early December 1834 members of a commando seeking stolen colonial cattle in Xhosaland had confiscated some animals from an innocent homestead. When faced with resistance, they fired indiscriminately into the gathering crowd, severely wounding a junior member of Xhosa royalty, Xoxo, with two buckshot pellets in the head.[20]

Upon his return to the Buffalo River, partly at Brownlee's urging of Christian forbearance, Jan Tzatzoe tries to keep the amaNtinde neutral. After the war Kayser will report to the LMS that the chief Jan Tzatzoe (not the assistant missionary Jan Tzatzoe) *not only stood firm himself, but . . . exercised a salutary influence over his father's tribe and prevented their being implicated in the plundering of the colony.*[21] A few members of the amaNtinde, however, join the invasion of the colony. Tzatzoe stands to lose the respect of those Xhosa lineages that have challenged the British militarily. Unbeknownst to him and the LMS missionaries in the Cape, he has also risked the respect of the British humanitarians, who will come to view the Xhosa invasion as a legitimate response to political grievances. And by refusing to assist the British in their response to the invasion, he will, despite his neutrality, be attacked by the South African settler lobby as anti-British and ungrateful for the gifts of which he has partaken. Yet again this incident points out the fragility of Tzatzoe's political and social status.

Despite their refusal to be counted amongst the aggressors, the Buffalo River institution, as well as Tzatzoe's people, initially seem to be under no threat from the invading Xhosa armies that surround them — Brownlee remarks the Xhosa show no such *disposition although we were completely in their power* — and the settlement on the Buffalo comes to serve as a refuge for Europeans, including several traders.

As early as 1 January 1835 several of the Xhosa chiefs send letters to the colony stating their reasons for undertaking the war and asking for a ceasefire and negotiations. But colonial officials have already begun to plan a reprisal and to mount an expedition to invade Xhosaland. Lieutenant-Colonel Sir Harry Smith, the commanding officer, rides the six hundred miles from Cape Town to Graham's Town in six days. Governor Benjamin D'Urban soon follows Smith.[22]

Philip and the other humanitarians have anticipated this use of the Xhosa invasion as a pretext for the invasion of Xhosaland and the alienation of African land. The settlers are *intent on taking over the whole country*, Philip writes, but *we have in our possession a chain of facts that will pull down their fist and tie their hands so as to make it very difficult for them to convert Caffirland into Sheep heaths for themselves or their friends*. Philip and the others rejoice as the expedition led by Colonel Smith, Colonel England, and Major Somerset sits delayed at the Fish River for six days because of high water. Philip exults: *like Pharaoh's chariots in the Red Sea*.[23]

In early February, as the waters of the Fish recede, the invasion commences with trademark brutality: British soldiers burn Xhosa fields, grain stores, and homesteads. They shoot artillery rounds into dense vegetation where Xhosa women and children take refuge with their cattle. At the Buffalo, Tzatzoe and Brownlee receive daily updates of the situation in the border region. After colonial forces cross the Fish, they see a flood of captured cattle passing by their station, being driven east, deeper into Xhosaland for safekeeping. This flood, though, will ebb and the cattle will stream back under colonial guard.[24]

At this point in time, Charles Brownlee, the Reverend's son, will later recollect, *Tzatzoe constantly received messages from the Gaika chiefs, urging him to take part in the war, and threatening to attack him as an enemy if he did not turn out with his tribe to assist in repelling the colonial forces which were then entering Kaffraria*.[25] On the station itself, the daily threats of violence grow more and more real, and the station comes under direct threat from individuals seemingly unconnected from the main Xhosa armies who are intent on looting. Jan Tzatzoe decides that there is now *no alternative either they must now go and fight with the English or be destroyed by the other Caffres*:

> The war-cry resounded on the hills around the station, and it was said that the Gaikas were about to attack the Tindes (Tzatzoe's tribe). Then followed a scene of awful confusion. Soka, Tzatzoe's brother, declared his determination of joining the Gaikas; a portion of the tribe followed him, and turning out with shields, assegais, and war-plumes, threatened to attack those who adhered to Tzatzoe. Flocks of cattle were being driven furiously in different directions, women and children running about, hardly knowing to which party they belonged; Tzatzoe's adherents concentrating on the station, while Soka's party, who had previously been mixed up with the others, were flying in the opposite direction.
>
> In the midst of all this confusion and excitement, Tzatzoe came to my father and told him he could no longer hold his ground, but must leave and join Pato, and if my father would go, his family could be carried in Tzatzoe's wagon. . . . Tzatzoe's entreaties were in vain; the missionary had taken his

stand; he considered he was in the path of duty and nothing could induce him to turn from it. . . . With a sad heart Tzatzoe left, and the people with him, three men only remaining on the station with us.[26]

One night, the Brownlee family is interrupted by crashes at their front door. Young Charles flees out a window into the night and hides by a deep pool of the Buffalo. Fearing his family slaughtered, he returns to find them shaken but alive. They leave on a harried, thirty-mile trek to join Tzatzoe, and many other refugees, at Wesleyville in the territory of a chief named Pato, who has declared himself loyal to the English. Their journey across the thorny hills and deep valleys includes a night in the bush, near-misses, dead neighbors, almost deadly dehydration, and a faithful Newfoundland dog named Cadet who judiciously leads the way (he does not bark at the Xhosa dogs they encounter and often rises on two feet to scout for danger).

Arriving at Wesleyville—the younger children on the backs of others, the *weary each supported by two stalwart natives*—the Brownlee family reunites with Tzatzoe, but soon leaves to spend the remainder of the war at Beka, situated between the Fish and Keiskamma Rivers.[27] Yet, even as he now campaigns with Pato and other Xhosa chiefs allied with the British against their countrymen, the British settlers accuse Tzatzoe of deserting Brownlee, not only once at the Buffalo, but again at Wesleyville. According to the *Graham's Town Journal*, the *faithless Jan Tzatzoe was the first to fly from the scene of danger, leaving Mr. Brownlee and his helpless family to shift for themselves in the best manner they were able*.[28]

Settler scorn and suspicion turns toward James Read and John Philip. Who has pushed for the rights of the Khoisan with the rhetoric of liberation and deliverance from oppression? Who has been addressing large gatherings of Xhosa chiefs and promising them redress for their lands lost to colonial conquest, by appeals to the Governor, and ultimately, to the Colonial Office in London:

> The improved tactics of the Kafirs, their murdering every white man which has fallen into their hands, and sparing the Hottentots which they never did before, and endeavouring to gain them over,—the irruption taking place at the moment of emancipation,—a staunch Philistine here stating that the Kafirs only wanted the neutral ground and he supposed they would retire when they had got it; the message sent in by Tyali so much in unison with this,— these and other circumstances show that other heads besides the Kafirs are at work.[29]

The suspicion of treachery in the outbreak of the invasion will linger and will eventually draw Jan Tzatzoe into its web.[30] Read and Philip's reaction to the

Xhosa invasion as revealed in their personal letters, however, makes a mockery of the charges. They are shocked and horrified, and not in the least exultant. But clearly their evangelical message of emancipation and talk of the protection of civil rights has seeped across the border region as readily as the guns with which the Xhosa are now fighting.

The Xhosa have learned earlier lessons, in the war of 1818, about direct assaults on British defenses, and they adopt a guerrilla style of warfare aided by newly acquired horses and muskets.[31] Fighting that can best be described as skirmishing continues from February 1835. The opponents move back and forth near the Fish River boundary. The Xhosa armies retreat into the forests or take to the high ground, and then return to ambush the combined British and Boer forces when military discipline commands long convoys into tight spaces. *We were entirely surrounded by the Kaffirs, and when I heard the yelling and whistling of the Kaffirs as they came rushing on us, I could not believe that even one of us could get off safely*, writes a young Boer soldier named Coenraad Schoeman of an encounter in which he loses five friends. It was *a terrible and sad day for us*.[32]

The war is contained to these brief intense encounters and is approaching a stalemate when, in late April 1835, the British trick the Xhosa paramount chief, Hintza, into surrendering at a parlay. When he tries to escape after a week of being held against his will and being forced to sign a peace treaty, several British officers and local Cape soldiers shoot him and ravage his body.[33] With the test of military strength between the Xhosa and the British still largely unresolved, the various Xhosa chiefs sue for peace in August 1835, anxious to return to their villages. While tired of waging war, the chiefs and their people are far from defeated. At one peace meeting, D'Urban and Smith confront 4,000 warriors, many armed with guns, and a numerous cavalry.[34] *They rose in their pretences*, D'Urban indignantly reports, and *talked of rights and grievances*:

> The chiefs pointed to their warriors, who, in discordant and terrific yells, responded to the appeal. They did not appear to regard the conflict as unequal.

Jan Tzatzoe and many of his people have actively served on the side of the British during the conflict, gaining hundreds if not thousands of head of cattle. Tzatzoe has won the high commendation of Colonel Smith and has been rewarded with cattle for his service. But he has risked his status among the royal families of Xhosaland who fought the colony, and the respect of Brownlee, who judges his military service (even for the British) detrimental to his piety and considers his actions that of a plunderer.[35] And, Tzatzoe has lost much else besides.

On 23 May 1835 D'Urban and Smith had arrived at the abandoned station at the Buffalo. With its steady water supply and commanding position on the top of the bench paralleling the river, they recognized an ideal location for a military encampment. Here, they would establish the capital of the newly occupied territory they had conquered from Xhosaland:

> This River, from its Source in the Mountains of its name, to the Sea, will be the Central Line of occupation of the Province of Queen Adelaide, and here on the fertile banks of this clear, rapid, and beautiful Stream, upon ground admirably fitted by Nature for the purpose of a Provincial Town, the Commander in Chief has fixed the site of one and named it, by a General Order of this day, King William's Town, in Honour of His Most Gracious Majesty.

Smith would commandeer and rebuild Brownlee's residence as his headquarters. Jan Tzatzoe's stone house would serve as his stables.[36]

QUEEN ADELAIDE PROVINCE

Becoming His Majesty's subjects

1835–1836

Following the frontier war of 1835 Governor D'Urban extends the colonial boundary past the Fish and Keiskamma Rivers, eastward to the Kei. D'Urban blames the historic insecurity of the border region on the *tangled jungles, impervious woody ravines* of these river valleys, *made by nature for the preparatory lurking place of the savage, before he springs upon his prey, and for the retreat and concealment when he has secured.*[1] Access to these hideouts has led to *constantly recurring evils*, with the *hostile inroads of the most barbarous and desolating kinds, penetrating into the very vitals of the unprepared country* alternating with a *ruinous and vexatious system of successful cattle-stealing.*

The Governor seizes the large swath of Xhosa territory, unapologetically, under the *right of conquest, that right by which the British dominions have been extended to their present magnitude.* Conquest has *ejected the Aborigines from the vast territory of America, the West Indies, the ancient oriental world*; it is the *right by which the Caffres possess this province*, and more so, the *Holy Bible, or most ancient history, is replete with the expulsion and banishment of nations and tribes. Are the Caffres, the possessors of this soil by right of conquest, not to be ejected by the same right?*[2]

A reordering of Xhosa society will be central to a colonized Xhosaland. Military posts and army detachments will provide discipline. European magistrates will appoint Xhosa *subordinates* of their own choosing in order to reduce the chiefs' hold over their followers: *The system of clanship by this very arrangement will be at once broken up, and its spirit and feeling will be rapidly subdued and forgotten, as the power of the Chiefs shall be seen to have ceased and passed away; and the whole will be brought under the operation of the General Colonial Laws.* In return for their submission, the Chiefs will receive the military protection of the British and the promise of treatment as British subjects in matters of law; additionally, they will receive missionaries, schoolmasters, and a regulated system of trade. Overall, the *terms, in short, of becoming His Majesty's subjects, settled by His Royal grace and favour, in a portion of the Land conquered from them (of which large tracts are still left vacant for the occupation and speculations of Europeans).*[3]

And if the plan fails? *It would be vain for the future to talk of any other relation with these people than the bayonet's point,* D'Urban writes, *if such relations, which God forbid, should so, at length, be forced upon us, we shall at least have the consolation of feeling that no endeavour, which could be devised, will have been omitted on our part to avoid them.*[4]

While the plans for Queen Adelaide Province are being finalized in September and October 1835, Jan Tzatzoe remains in the colony. In the meantime, in London, events have been in motion that will dramatically alter D'Urban and Smith's plan. After *ten year's* [sic] *combat for the deliverance of the Negro,* the leader of the humanitarian movement in Great Britain, Sir Thomas Fowell Buxton, has been shifting his attention from the recently victorious abolitionist cause toward a crusade against the deleterious effects that British civilization appears to be having on the indigenous inhabitants and neighbors of its colonies.[5]

Buxton is a brewer, a long-term Member of Parliament from Weymouth, a member by marriage of a wealthy and prominent Quaker family known for its work in the area of social reform, and the heir to William Wilberforce as leader of the abolitionist movement. Buxton is well aware that his nation's children have been flung across the oceans like stars in the sky, scattered and distant. One star shines brighter than most. Buxton's friend, John Philip, has been assiduously documenting the plight of the Cape Colony's aboriginal peoples as the strengthening tide of British and Dutch settlement has coursed into the interior of the continent. Philip has sent back a constant stream of dispatches, letters, and reports to Buxton and to the Directors of the LMS.[6]

I hate shooting innocent savages worse than slavery itself, Buxton writes to a friend in 1833, months after the passage of the Slavery Abolition Act. At home for the Christmas holidays, in January 1834, Buxton begins a *meditation* on his *new undertaking:*

My attention has been drawn of late to the wickedness of our proceedings as a nation, toward the ignorant and barbarous natives of countries on which we seize. What have we Christians done for them? We have usurped their lands, kidnapped, enslaved, and murdered themselves [sic]. The greatest of their crimes is that they sometimes trespass into the lands of their forefathers; and the very greatest of their misfortunes is that they have become acquainted with Christians. Shame on such Christianity!

And in a letter written to Philip written shortly after his meditation, Buxton lays out specific recommendations:

> In order to do justice we must admit—1st. That the native have a right to their own lands. 2nd[ly] That as our settlements must be attended with some evils to them, it is our duty to give them compensation for those evils, by imparting the truths of Christianity and the arts of civilized life.

Buxton is not necessarily arguing for the return of conquered land to Africans and other colonial subjects and the removal of British settlers, so that the Africans might govern themselves independently of Europeans. His vision, in fact, is not drastically different from the one favored by D'Urban and Smith, relying as it does on the civilizing potential of Africans living under benevolent and paternalistic British rule. But within a colonial framework, Buxton favors the preservation of African land rights.[7]

Concerned that the *native inhabitants* of the British colonies appear to be melting away before British colonization, in May 1835 Buxton appoints a *Select Committee to Investigate the Treatment of the Aborigines in the Colonies*—Van Diemen's Land, Upper Canada, the many corners of India, South Africa most prominently—and to inquire into what *measures ought to be adopted to intervene between the native inhabitants and the British settlers of these lands, in order to secure to them their due observance of Justice and the protection of their Rights; to promote the spread of Civilization among them, and to lead them to the voluntary reception of the Christian Religion*. The committee hears from colonial officials, diplomats, settlers, merchants, and some of the leaders of the indigenous peoples themselves. But its members refuse to arrive at any conclusions based on the evidence they have compiled to that point. Buxton needs better witnesses. He requests the Colonial Office to call on the Treasury to fund a summons from the Committee to John Philip.[8]

I know how reluctant the Treasury will be to incur this expense and would not propose it if I thought there was any other mode of arriving at the Truth, Buxton writes to Undersecretary, Sir George Grey. It is hard to imagine the British Empire balking at the price of one passage from Cape Town to London, but this scenario comes to pass. The Colonial Office's reply: How can we be sure that another session of the Committee will be funded and Philip will have a chance to testify? *Treasury will not give Money on probabilities*.[9]

Buxton then asks the LMS to pay for Philip's journey. After the Society refuses, Buxton takes its Director, Reverend William Ellis, along with him in late September 1835 to meet the Colonial Office leadership in person, including Lords Glenelg and Grey and Undersecretary John Stephen.[10] The Colonial Office is located within a pair of dignified seventeenth-century houses at Numbers 13 and 14 Downing Street. These are small, cold buildings with one waiting room, offices for the Secretary of State, three undersecretaries, senior clerks in four geographical departments, and a library. Yet within these walls decision makers issue directives that guide the actions of thousands of colonists and have consequences for millions more in the colonies. To keep the empire running the Chief Clerk has only to supply a few essentials: paper, pens, ink, pins, coal, and oil for the lamps.[11]

Buxton and Ellis ask Glenelg for an inquiry into the causes and conduct of the recent frontier war, especially the killing of the Xhosa chief, Hintza. They also ask him to *restore the country to the Caffres, or, if it must be part of the Colony, not to give it to the Colonists, but preserve it for the Caffres, under the laws of the Colony.*[12] Ellis includes one last detail about the meeting with Glenelg in a letter to Philip: *I mentioned to Mr. Buxton this morning the desirableness of your bringing with you a sensible intelligent Caffre, should you come.* Buxton thought that *it would be an excellent thing. Think of this. It might be of the utmost benefit to his nation.*[13]

Buxton immediately sets his cousin and longtime collaborator, Anna Gurney, to work on an *epitome of Philip's letters* on affairs in South Africa. The *able digest* that he submits to the Colonial Office a month later lays the blame for the war on the commando system and the settlers' desire for territory. Stephen, in particular, is overcome. *I only knew that you were crackbrained about Aborigines*, he tells Buxton, *I have now dived into all this neglected correspondence. I have read every word of the evidence before the Committee and I am lost in astonishment, indignation, shame and repentance. . . . It is already agreed, that you shall have Protectors of Aborigines in every colony where we get into contact with them.*[14]

Glenelg sends a cursory letter to South Africa suggesting that his inclination is to rescind the annexation of Queen Adelaide Province. His communication crosses the path of D'Urban's report on the war (written in its immediate aftermath), which is received in London in November 1835. D'Urban exults at four thousand Xhosa warriors killed, sixty thousand head of captured cattle, and the decimation of Xhosa corn fields and gardens. His tone strikes the wrong note for a capital grown queasy over overseas conflicts.[15]

Glenelg issues a final dispatch on 26 December 1835 that contains revised policies for the eastern Cape. It will arrive in Cape Town in March 1836 and shake the political foundations of the Cape Colony to their core, augmenting the ongoing movement of Dutch settlers into the interior of Africa that will later be sanctified as the Great Trek. The Colonial Secretary expresses horror at Colonel Smith's war on the civilian population of Xhosaland: *In the civilized warfare of Europe, this desolation of an enemy's country. . . rarely occurs,* and is met with *universal reprobation.* The dispatch concludes that the *extension of His Majesty's dominions in that quarter of the globe, by conquest or cession, is diligently and anxiously to be avoided.* Glenelg will endeavor to return the land.[16]

Regardless of how long the Glenelg reforms will hold sway in South Africa, it is remarkable to reflect on the power that, even at this height of the humanitarians' influence in England, the few have to shape policy and events in lands thousands of miles away across a communication divide that stretches for months on end. The production of potent images is crucial to this process. Even in the early nineteenth century, political campaigns are fought with sound bites and facile depictions. *The image is rising of the hunted people restored to their land, of Macomo, now so dejected amazed with unlooked for relief,* Buxton writes to Gurney, *"Irreclaimable savages," "just and necessary war," "the assignation for ever of the rich and fertile province of Adelaide to His Majesty's dominions," These and a thousand other impudent and damnable lies, detected, repudiated, and exploded.*[17]

If D'Urban is to be impugned for calling the Xhosa *irreclaimable savages,* his political opponents need to mobilize a compelling counter-image and symbol. Thus, Ellis's suggestion to Philip (which arrives at the Cape in December 1835) that he bring a *sensible intelligent Caffre* with him to England. But where to locate such a man?

At the eastern Cape, almost a year after the Xhosa invasion of the colony, a relative calm has descended. In June, with the arrival of the seven sister stars called iSilimela (the Pleiades) in the night sky, the Xhosa turn again to their fields, with the hope that this year peace will enable them to reap an abundant harvest. The return of the stars marks the beginning of a new year, and the public emergence of mature young men who entered circumcision schools as initiates a month or so ago.[18] On an almost weekly basis from within the colony, the European missionaries of all denominations unsuccessfully petition Governor D'Urban to return to their mission stations in the new Queen Adelaide Province. In reply, the Governor points to the history of the Xhosaland missions. The missionaries could not *flatter themselves that they had ever made a lasting salutary impression upon one of the race of Caffres.* To D'Urban, the Xhosa are wolves (which in truth they resemble very much), which, if they be caught young, may be brought . . . to an appearance of tameness, but which invariably throw it off, and appear in all their native fierceness of the woods, as soon as the temptation of blood and ravage, which never fail to elicit their native ferocity, presents itself to their instinctive thirst for it.[19]

D'Urban has imbibed a harsh and strikingly racist view of the Xhosa. The shock, fear, and destruction of the latest frontier war have sharpened racial antipathy. A new ideology has taken root among most of the British settlers at the Cape.[20]

In October 1835 Jan Tzatzoe arrives back at the Buffalo. The fields are newly planted and Tzatzoe's fruit trees now shelter soldiers from the spring sun. Does the mission bell lie discarded in the maturing grass? Or does it hang proudly and call the infantry to their maneuvers? Governor D'Urban and Colonel Smith wish to reward Tzatzoe for his service, even as the British settlers and the *Graham's Town Journal* refuse to credit Tzatzoe as an active participant on their side. Tzatzoe and the amaNtinde are to reside near the Buffalo River, but several miles from their old mission station. Although favorable compared to the lot of other chiefs, the site is not of Tzatzoe's choosing. D'Urban maintains a personal interest in Tzatzoe's case. He asks Smith to redraw a map of the *location of Tsatzoe*, which *although quite satisfactory as far as his interests are provided for, is not quite formal to become a Record of office for reference hereafter, and to serve as a model for his Title deed.* Later, however, Tzatzoe will testify that the Governor did him *no justice* in the choice.[21]

Having joined the British in campaigns against those Xhosa lineages that invaded the Colony, Tzatzoe finds himself mistrusted by many within the Xhosa state. He is also on the wrong side of Brownlee, Read, Kayser, and the other European missionaries who counseled neutrality and Christian forbearance in military matters. To complicate matters, many British humanitarians now ask how Tzatzoe could have fought against his countrymen if their cause was in fact fully justified as Buxton and Ellis have argued to the Colonial Office. It is therefore far from evident that Jan Tzatzoe will be the Xhosa man that Philip will nominate for a journey to Great Britain.

One of Tzatzoe's first official duties as a Fieldcornet and representative of the British Crown is to pardon, with Smith's permission, those leaders of the amaNtinde who forsook him and joined in the war against the colony. On 13 October 1835 Smith takes Tzatzoe on a horseback tour of his assigned land. Despite the fact that he has been subjected to one of the first documented forced relocations in South African history, Smith reports to D'Urban that *John Tzatzoe is a reasonable, docile man.*[22]

Meanwhile, back in Cape Town, Dr. Philip has sprung into action with regard to Reverend Ellis's suggestion that he bring an African with him on his voyage to England. On 17 December 1835 Philip writes to James Read urging him, in great secrecy, to endeavor to get hold of Tzatzoe, without loss of time, by any means.[23] No documents suggest how Tzatzoe becomes Philip's choice. Indeed, the LMS leadership in London apparently favors Maqoma for his higher profile as a chief. Is Tzatzoe selected for the ease by which he might be removed from the eastern Cape? Does Philip prefer Tzatzoe because he believes in his ability to serve as a spokesman and ambassador? Or does Philip see in the amaNtinde leader a sympathetic and easily manipulated mouthpiece through which the missionaries' concerns might circulate?

On Christmas Eve 1835 Philip writes again to Read to invite the missionary to Cape Town: the *Sea voyage* to Cape Town might be *useful* and *you will perhaps return by sea, or even think of a voyage to England*. James Read's son, James Junior, has already committed to join Philip on his journey across the sea. Philip still needs Read's help in locating Tzatzoe and getting him to Cape Town: *I am anxious about Tzatzoe. . . . You know what effect the presence of an intelligent Caffre would have on London at this time strictly to show him as a specimen of irreclaimable savages would do wonders. . . . I think such an exhibition . . . will do more for the Caffre and Hottentot Character than volumes on their condition would do. It will I think settle many questions in London!*[24]

In his letter to Read, Philip evinces faith that an English audience will perceive Jan Tzatzoe as civilized, as reclaimed. Beyond his appearance, Philip appears to believe that Tzatzoe will demonstrate his intelligence. What does he mean by this phrase? Perhaps it will be enough for Tzatzoe to sign his name? To speak the Dutch of Bethelsdorp, the Kat River, and the Buffalo River missions? To preach? Perhaps, even, to provide political commentary? The words *specimen* and *exhibition* indicate that Philip foresees a public role for Tzatzoe in England akin to that of other African and colonial figures who have been paraded across metropolitan stages in support of populist and propagandizing abolitionist or humanitarian campaigns. Yet other Africans have been displayed as anatomical oddities or freaks. If Tzatzoe journeys to England, will one, or both, of these traditions be reflected in the nature of the exhibitions of which he will be a part? Or will he blaze his own trail as an articulate advocate for his people and for the redeeming power of British civilization and Christianity?[25]

At King William's Town, Colonel Smith is desperate to consolidate his newfound power—which he substantiates in fiery outbursts toward individual Xhosa leaders on a regular basis—with a demonstration of British hegemony:

The people of all Tribes look up to me as the Great Chief under Your Excellency. So pray, your Excellency, let me go on *play acting* and have my great *meeting* as soon as possible.²⁶

The assembly on Wednesday 6 January 1836 draws Jan Tzatzoe, the other Xhosa chiefs, and their councilors to King William's Town, along with European military men, journalists, and missionaries. The Xhosa come from the entire region between the old colonial boundary at the Fish River in the west to the Kei River in the east. The meeting will formally introduce the new regime, appoint the colonial Resident Agents who are to reside with the various chiefs, and install the chiefs as British Magistrates over their people.²⁷

Led by Maqoma and Tyalie, six hundred Xhosa men on horseback march down a hillside next to the town, followed by around fifteen hundred foot soldiers. The army arrives unarmed. *No British heart could remain unmoved at seeing so high a compliment paid our Nation by these savages casting themselves unarmed into the midst of a British force, and in the face of the Troops, against whom they had so long contended in mortal strife*, marvels a correspondent for the *Commercial Advertiser*. As the infantry reach the town, they form into a *close and compact body*, and *at a signal from their leader*, they *move on again, singing one of their war songs: It was the most savage sound I ever heard, interspersed with a whistle that might bear some resemblance to the chirruping of a flock of birds, but the sound was most wild. Their bass notes were as terrific and deep as possible for the human voice to give utterance to.*

At twelve noon the following day, Smith fires the signal gun. He marches out to his marquee in the center of the parade ground with his wife and his officers. Maqoma and Tyalie sit to Smith's right and left respectively. The chiefs wear suits of blue cloth and *black velvetine waistcoats*, on which they display the medals Smith has given them. Kama, Pato, Botma, and Jan Tzatzoe, dressed in hats and shooting dress, spread out on either side. Smith fires off three rounds each from his five artillery pieces, and then, removing his hat and waving it about, calls out: *Long live our good King William the fourth!* The Xhosa respond with *loud, long and deafening* shouts and *raise their hands high in the air, snapping their fingers as they yell, with singular effect*. Smith rejoices: *Such a roar I never heard, with soldiers and wild men.*

You are now the Subjects of the most powerful nation, whose laws, manners, customs, and institutions are the admiration of the world, Smith's speech begins, but the English were once *as naked as you, as ignorant as you, as cruel as you were in the late war*:

But the bright day which has opened to you dawned upon them; they first learned to believe in the omnipotent power of God Almighty, who judges every man according to his actions; worshipped, honoured, and obeyed him; they loved their neighbours as themselves; and respecting their property ceased to be thieves; they believed all that ministers of God told them; they sent their children to be taught to read and write; they learned the use of money, and carried on an honest trade with each other, selling their skins, &c. and buying clothes, as you see us all now dressed; some were labourers in the field, some tended the herds and flocks, some made implements of husbandry, built houses, made guns, and every thing you see your brother Englishmen possess, while others made laws to govern the whole, under the King, whom we all love. Thus civilization gradually advanced, while we became acquainted with the works of art, knowledge increased, we threw off the yoke of despotism and barbarism, cast away our vicious habits, and put to death and banished by the law every one who by sin, crime, and wickedness, was a pest and an enemy to society at large.

Smith then sets out his new laws. He proscribes eating up, or the power of chiefs to confiscate their subjects' property; murder; belief in witchcraft (*did not Eno's "rainmaker" desire you to go to war, and encourage you by telling you that you would beat the English, the greatest nation in the world, whose power exceeds yours as much as the waters of the Keiskamma do the pools of the Peula rivulet?*); perjury; setting houses on fire; rape; and, above all, treason, or *lifting up your assegais against the King*.

Lastly, the Colonel addresses the amapakati, or councilors, to the chiefs. He tells them they are to be responsible for *the good conduct of the people of their village*. If a crime is committed, the whole village will be held responsible. Smith also wants the Xhosa to start burying their dead and to revise their work habits:

You must see that your people are active and industrious, that they work in the gardens; it is the duty of the men to work in the fields—not of women, they ought to make and mend your clothes and their own, to keep their children clean, wash your clothes, cook your food, and take care of the milk. You well know from observation, what work the Englishmen do, and what their women, this you must imitate, and not sleep half your time, and pass the rest in drowsy inactivity.[28]

And here terminated the most extraordinary and novel General Assembly that was ever held in this part of the world, Smith writes to Governor D'Urban. Yet Smith, in casting himself as the Xhosa's great chief and they as his children, pays scant attention to one of the day's most auspicious events. In a land of aridity where successful rainmakers are elevated for their prowess to the level of chiefs, Smith is relieved that his day has remained dry. *We were fortunate in the day*, he concludes, *soon after the ceremony it came on to rain, and we have had for two days violent storms of hail, which broke some of my windows;—rain and wind unimaginable.*

To this new world arrives a letter from John Philip to D'Urban (forwarded by the Governor to Colonel Smith) requesting Jan Tzatzoe's leave of absence from Queen Adelaide Province. Smith must wonder why Tzatzoe would want to turn his back on the vision the Colonel has laid before him at his Great Meeting, but he never gets the chance to ask. By the time the request arrives in King William's Town, Tzatzoe has taken leave of Smith in the company of two LMS supporters, Reverend John Ayliff and Captain John Fawcett, the latter of whom D'Urban describes as a *terrier of the Doctor*, to journey to the Kat River.[29] Smith is left to reply to D'Urban on 19 January 1836 that Tzatzoe's departure for the Kat River (a trip Smith thinks is temporary) has *as yet prevented me telling him that your Excellency leaves it to his own option to proceed to England at the request of Dr. Philip*. Nevertheless, Smith feels that Tzatzoe would *not avail himself of this permission: He is a person of a very domestic, docile, plain, well-disposed, tho' unenergetic turn, much pleased with his new farm and garden, and highly gratified at his appointment as Fieldcornet.*

Smith's depiction of Jan Tzatzoe owes much to the incipient racism in the eastern Cape. It also fails to account for the fact that Tzatzoe is likely doing his utmost to appear placid and content in the military man's presence. Smith offers D'Urban his opinions with regard to Tzatzoe's journey to England. Tzatzoe's presence in England as one of only two Xhosa chiefs who have converted to Christianity would reveal the *tardiness* of the spread of Christianity. On the other hand, Smith credits Philip's assertion that the trip will improve *Tzatzoe's own condition*. Also, the *magnitude of the power of England* will convince Tzatzoe of the *folly of the Kafir nation attempting resistance*. *The moment I see him therefore*, Smith concludes, *I shall put the question fairly to him, and leave the choice entirely to his own free will, option, and decision.*[30]

In the following week, Smith is pleased to see the Xhosa following some of his *Great Meeting* instructions: the people, including rainmakers, are attending services and they have begun to *bury their dead everywhere*. These bodies, Smith can almost gleefully report, have been *rather numerous owing to the hot weather and the want of meal*. But the Tzatzoe issue is growing in complexity. The chief remains at the Kat River without returning to consult Smith. In the event he has decided to go to England, Smith wants him to return to his new capital so that

Smith might *take down his opinions, views, and remarks, and make him swear to them*, precluding the possibility of Philip manipulating Tzatzoe's testimony.[31]

On the same day that he demands that Jan Tzatzoe return to King William's Town, Smith grants permission for Sanna Oursen, Tzatzoe's wife, to leave the Buffalo mission in order to travel to the Kat River where her husband has asked her to visit him. Smith initially denies Oursen's request, but relents because the *poor body was in such a state of affliction* at the news.[32]

Sanna Oursen arrives far too infrequently in Jan Tzatzoe's story. Her farewell to Jan Tzatzoe at the Kat River is one of the few occasions that she (or her children) emerge into view from the archival record. Several years earlier the Reverend Kayser spoke of the Tzatzoes' daughter, Mary, who was struggling to believe fully in Jesus Christ and teaching at the Sunday school. At the early Kat River mission, where the Reverend Williams and Sanna Oursen came into direct conflict, Jan Tzatzoe most likely tested the monogamous nature of his marriage, to his wife's dismay and displeasure. There is nothing else to speak to the strength or weakness of the relationship between the man and woman who came of age together at Bethelsdorp.

So, too, there are exceedingly few records that reflect upon Jan Tzatzoe's emotional ties to the missionaries with whom he has worked, to his father-in-Christ, James Read, to his wife, to his father, to his family, to the amaNtinde. There is much to ponder in the fact that almost twenty years after their marital conflict at the Kat River Sanna Oursen is so distraught at the prospect of not being able to answer her husband's summons in person. Perhaps she wants to wish him well on his trip to England? Perhaps to dissuade him from embarking upon it? In either case, an emotional connection is apparent.[33]

In a book soon to be published, Captain Fawcett will provide an eyewitness account of Tzatzoe's decisions to undertake the journey to England, and to do so without returning to King William's Town to bid farewell to his father, the amaNtinde, and Colonel Smith. *Tzatzoe took three days to consider this proposal*, Fawcett will relate, *it was no small sacrifice he was called on to make, in leaving his wife, his children, and his tribe, and going to a strange land and a strange people*. On the third day of his deliberations, Tzatzoe explained his decision. *The trial was one he felt in all its severity, and one which really put his principles and professions to the test*, Fawcett will report, *the sacrifice was great, but he felt convinced it was his duty to make it, and that he should receive an equivalent to the sacrifice in the benefit he hoped to confer on his nation*. As for returning to explain his decision to the amaNtinde, Tzatzoe is distraught: *I shall never be able to persuade my people to let me go, as they can never understand how it is possible that I should advance their interest by absenting myself from them*.[34]

Without returning to consult with Colonel Smith (from the unfounded fear that he will be prevented from departing), Tzatzoe takes leave of his wife and James Read and begins his journey to England. He travels in the company of a Kat River settler, Andries Stoffels. Stoffels is a long-standing member of Reverend Read's congregation and his contemporary in the passage of years. A member of a Khoisan clan, he followed Read from the mission station at Bethelsdorp to the Kat River. In Cape Town the pair will reunite with James Read Junior and Philip.

To an increasingly solipsistic and paranoid Colonel Smith, Kote Tzatzoe and the *whole* of the councilors of the amaNtinde are in *indescribable distress at Tzatzoe's absence* and his apparent decision to travel to Britain: *It is totally impossible to describe the feelings of mortification these people suffer from the conduct of their Fieldcornet. They all say he must have been practiced on, or he would never have acted so toward me and themselves. We heard a whisper of the kind*, says one councilor, *but think that it cannot be the case, Jan knowing the fear we have of the sea*. The councilors beg Smith to prevent Tzatzoe's departure; they see no *advantages* to his trip. Maqoma reputedly disavows Tzatzoe's mission. When told that Tzatzoe has gone to England as *a Kafir Chief, to speak forth about the Kafir people*, Maqoma replies: *Then if Jan is going to England about me and my people, I do not know him.*[35] Kote Tzatzoe goes further:

> What is he going for? we pray you, in the name of the whole Tribe, to write to Jan, and not allow him to go. How long has he been mad? O, send him back to us; we speak in the name of the whole tribe.... What have I done to my son? he used to be obedient to me; he has now run away from me. Do the Missionaries teach children to desert their aged father, and those dependent on them, without ever seeing them, or making arrangements for their comfort? What would Jan go for?—we have all we wish here—his gardens are good—his cattle fat—and his people happy;—all they desire is, that Jan should come back to them and take care of them.[36]

Despite Smith's overdramatization, it is clear that Jan Tzatzoe's commitment to Philip's undertaking comes at a deep personal cost. And yet Jan Tzatzoe has been exposed to the colonial vision of D'Urban and Smith. His house and lands have been removed from him, his people relocated. Three years earlier Tzatzoe had attended a gathering of the Xhosa chiefs living in the border region. There, Botma had expressed to a visiting journalist that there were *three things* he *must ever regret*:

> The first is, that I cannot speak in a language that we mutually understand, and tell you all the wrongs inflicted on my people by the Colony. The second

is that I cannot write a book, and publish in it these wrongs; and the third and last is, that I cannot put myself on board a ship, and lay these wrongs before the King of England!³⁷

Now, Jan Tzatzoe has an opportunity to present the *wrongs* done to him and his people before the English public and their king.

Jan Tzatzoe arrives in Cape Town on 20 February 1836. Presenting a letter in person to Governor D'Urban, he requests permission to travel to England. Despite sharing Smith's suspicion that Tzatzoe's decision to leave his people had not been made of his own volition, and that his departure had been manipulated by the LMS, D'Urban is convinced of Tzatzoe's sincere desire to undertake the voyage. Even though he counsels Tzatzoe against it, he grants him permission to embark.³⁸ As they wait for their ship to sail, Jan Tzatzoe, Andries Stoffels, and James Read Junior spend time exploring Cape Town. They must be struck by the graceful reach of the bay arching northward, by the way the early-morning rays of the sun strike each cresting wave and shatter into shards of shimmering silver. Tzatzoe comments, in particular, on his trip to see Mr. Prince's steam mill and when asked what pleases him most, responds: *the Public Library!* James Junior has been in town for a few months, lodging with Philip, and roaming the streets with a fellow lodger, a young French missionary, Eugene Casalis, of the Paris Evangelical Mission Society. Casalis describes James Junior as an *excellent mulatto*, the *exception to the rule* of mixed marriages, which *both as regards offspring and in other respects has been the reverse of satisfactory.*³⁹

In the thirty odd years since Jan Tzatzoe visited Cape Town with James Read and Dr. Van der Kemp in 1805 it has grown into a cosmopolitan city. Casalis delights in the *joyous talk and badinage of French sailors on the jetty.* The *wearisome monotony* of the city center takes on an entirely different aspect when the *sun* shines *brightly* and the *heat* is *tempered by a perfumed and life-giving breeze. Everywhere nothing but displays of flowers, of fruits, of appetizing productions, in marvellous profusion, delicacies* previously only glimpsed *in certain shop-windows of the Palais-Royal. Odorous pine-apples, oranges, mandarines, bananas, and sweet potatoes as big as our heads.*⁴⁰

In the streets, men and women of every description: *Malays,* with *brilliant black almond-shaped eyes, flowing jet-black hair, and chin ornamented with a pointed beard;* Hottentots, with *lips forming almost a snout, flat-nosed, grotesquely clad in sheep-skins, nevertheless, the direct descendants of the first possessors of the soil;* slaves from the *Guinea Coast or the northern parts of Mozam-*

bique; Cape Boers, with the *solid build, the fine face, the blue eyes, the light hair, which painters of Holland have so faithfully reproduced for us, generally stout, a lack of expression in their features, mingled with this immobility a look of sternness, desperate smokers,* their women with an *antiquated appearance, muffling* themselves in a *linen cap, bordered by a little frill,* wearing dresses that hang *straight down,* speaking a *Dutch* that is *singularly corrupted, barbarisms and solecisms abounding in it.*

James Read remains at Bethelsdorp recovering from an illness and mourning the sudden death of his seventeen-year-old daughter, Sarah. He will follow the travelers in a few months. From his bed he writes a letter that introduces the party to the Directors of the LMS. James Junior has been a *sphere of great usefulness* to him. Fluent in Dutch and English and his mother's Khoisan tongue, he has attended the finest school in Cape Town. James is intelligent, articulate, well-mannered, devout, committed. Stoffels is *open and free and able to comment on all the affairs of the tribes in and bordering on the colony and perfectly acquainted with the history of his nation and the system that has been employed against them.* Jan Tzatzoe is *highly respected by all the Caffre chiefs and caffres in general, and the chiefs of every denomination consider him very clever, but he is reserved and unassuming, he wants more confidence in himself, he must be encouraged.*[41]

James Read's characterization of Tzatzoe as *reserved* and *unassuming* echoes earlier commentary that referred to him as *docile* and *unenergetic.* Clearly, this placidity is one element of his character, one that is present in his interactions with certain European officials and missionaries. Likely it is a persona that he adopts precisely for such encounters. But prior events have also shown a different aspect of Tzatzoe's character, enabling him to face down powerful individuals within Xhosa society, to confront colonial officials, to assume a significant position of leadership for the amaNtinde and within the Xhosa state, to serve as an intermediary between European and Xhosa culture, and to embark on this unpredictable and dangerous journey to Great Britain.

Once across the ocean, will Jan Tzatzoe need to be encouraged to speak before Buxton's Aborigines Committee? Will he need to be encouraged to speak of God's word and good work? Of the redeeming power of Christianity and British civilization? Tzatzoe has given flight to the words of others. Now his voice will be heard. And he starts with an address in Dutch (translated by a correspondent of the *Commercial Advertiser*) to a church congregation in Cape Town that is gathered to bid the voyagers farewell—his last words in public before the glaring metallic-white Western Cape coast slips from view behind his ship's wake, and he is released onto the roiling ocean:

My Christian Friends,—I am glad to see you.—I am happy to find myself this evening in the midst of a Church of God. Who would have thought some time ago that a Caffer, as I am, should stand up to address you and to tell you what God has done for his soul?. . .

I am glad to find myself among you this evening, and I hope you are glad to see me, for the children of God should love one another. We are all brothers and sisters when the grace of God enters our hearts. . . .

We see the goodness of God in permitting us to meet in this place to pray together. We should pray to God to enable us to persevere in the ways of the Lord, and not faint till Jesus Christ come. God is not satisfied with the world, for it is wicked; the people of God should be different from the world, and should pray to him, and if we pray to God he will enable us to serve him in spirit and in truth. We should pray to God that through his great might all men might be led to believe in him, that we may have all the praises of God sounding from the tops of the mountains, and men shouting "See what great things the Lord has done." If we pray fervently for the Caffers, the Hottentots, Bushmen, Bechuanas, and all the tribes in the interior, God will answer our prayers by converting them.

The men of the world say that the world will not be changed, but we know that it will; the prophets foretold it. My Christian Brothers and Sisters pray for us, that we may be enabled to rejoice together, to speak together concerning the things of God, that our love to one another may be greater, that our joy may increase, and that sorrow and anger may no longer be known to us. Then there will be no difference between black and white, but all shall be brothers and sisters in the Lord. Therefore, my Christian friends, pray for these things.[42]

Part Two

Charles Darwin in Cape Town

November, 2000

On a blustery afternoon in Sea Point, Cape Town's oldest coastal suburb, I walked southward toward Cape Point alongside a concrete seawall that separated one of the main roads heading in and out of the city from the effusive expanse of Table Bay. Through a miasma of sea spray, Lion's Head soared above the sun-bleached beachfront properties. A childish, albeit superhuman, hand appeared to have clawed several small basins, now half full of crumbly white beach sand, out of the charcoal black igneous rock upon which the seawall is built. In order to circumvent a parking lot—where rusting jalopies and sleek German sedans lingered in equal measure—the path turned back toward the heaving swells of the Atlantic Ocean. At the apex of the curve, set into the tan quartzite rock that strafes the igneous formation in this one location, I stopped, as I often did, at a small, tarnished brass plaque that informed me that this geologic aberration had drawn the attention of one of Cape Town's most noteworthy visitors in the nineteenth century.[1]

The auspicious guest so deserving of commemoration was Charles Darwin. Darwin sailed into Cape Town—*this great inn on the great highway of nations*, as he termed it—while on one of the most famous voyages in history. During the first two weeks of June 1836 Darwin took away a generally positive impression of the little town and the *great mass of stratified sandstone* (known then and now as Table Mountain) at its head. He could compare the Cape Colony favorably to other *fragments of the civilized world* that his ship had visited in the southern hemisphere. *Little embryo Englands are hatching in all parts*, he concluded.[2]

As I thought of Darwin walking the macadamized streets of the nascent city, or remarking upon the striated rocks of Sea Point, I was reminded of the extent to which the Cape Colony was imbricated in the international intellectual and political currents of its day. I reflected on a world that had yet to experience the monumental upheavals of Darwinism, the flowering of the theory of evolution, and its eventual noxious offspring, scientific racism. But more than this, looking out upon Table Bay and the seductive arc of Robben Island, I thought of the other men, in other ships, upon other journeys, on the same waters at the same time, men like Jan Tzatzoe, whose ship had sailed from Cape Town for London four months before the arrival of the *Beagle*, and whose story I was uncovering in the letters, newspapers, and missionary reports of the archival record.

I imagined Darwin standing next to me at the ocean's foaming seam, staring out toward the ocean that would soon take him home after five years at sea. And Jan Tzatzoe, who could return his gaze, having just arrived in England.

England

The spring that moves the world

1836

In 1836 London is one of the world's greatest and grandest cities. Like the rampantly industrializing centers of Manchester, Liverpool, Birmingham, Leeds, Sheffield, and Glasgow, it is growing at an astonishing pace, spreading rapidly and without restraint in every direction, creating a vast middle class and an overcrowded and appallingly impoverished laboring class, attracting unprecedented levels of capital investment.

To its almost two million inhabitants, it is in equal parts oppressive and enthralling, its air thick with triumph and despair. With dense, choking smoke from factories and home coal fires, dense enough at times (occasions known as "pea-soupers") to blacken out street-lamps and begrime newly washed undershirts. With cries and moans and wails and screams and bellows and hymns rising to heaven from market vendors, clattering carriages, street urchins, railroad locomotives, wayward livestock, steam furnaces, slaughterhouses, and hundreds of chapels. With the stench of thousands of open sewers and humans and animals and their feces underfoot; with the acrid assault of tanneries and of chemical, glue, and tar factories. With a River Thames that exhales the fetid odor of decomposing waste of every kind: animal, vegetable, and mineral. With the imminent threat of cholera, typhoid, scarlet fever, whooping cough, measles.

How can it possibly appear to its guests from South Africa? They will travel the commercial chaos of its main thoroughfares, from the pedestrian crush of the newly erected and pleasingly symmetrical London Bridge to the majestic store fronts of Oxford Street, to the recently burned Houses of Parliament, to the sensible, and church-rich, suburb of Hackney in which they will be living, to the fashionable townhouses of Portland Place where they will soon dine with Sir Thomas Fowell Buxton. It must, quite simply, be breathtaking.[1]

During the week of 20 June to 27 June Jan Tzatzoe testifies for two and a half days before Sir Thomas Fowell Buxton's House of Commons Select Committee. Tzatzoe declares himself the *chief of a tribe, subject to the great chiefs*, but independent enough to *fight against* them. He understands the war of 1835 to have been caused by an overwhelming popular uprising in response to the wounding of a chief named Xoxo, and not, as the British settlers in South Africa contend, by a conspiracy among the chiefs to invade the colony. Tzatzoe insists that he has a *voice in these matters* and would have been consulted on a planned invasion.[2]

Tzatzoe details his participation in the conflict as initially neutral, then later as a British ally. He also defends Read and Philip from accusations of inciting the Xhosa to war.[3] He gives examples of double-dealing by English traders and of the unprovoked and rapacious nature of the commando system, including the one led by Colonel Fraser in 1817 that had impacted him directly. He describes assorted items relating to life in the Cape border region, such as the value of trade buttons as currency. He addresses the letter-writing controversy of 1833.

Tzatzoe narrates his personal history—his attachment to Dr. Van der Kemp and Read, his education in Dutch and the carpentry trade, and his career with the LMS—*when Mr. Read comes into Cafferland, to the schools, then I always interpret for him*. He insists that he can *write in Dutch*. Buxton prompts him to prove this ability by writing *God save the King in Dutch* and *signing his name* to it, which he does.

On his third day of testimony in 1836 Tzatzoe faces a hard line of questioning from one of Buxton's and the other humanitarians' main opponents on the committee, Sir Rufane Donkin, a former Governor of the Cape Colony.

Are you not a missionary?
I assist the missionary.
Are you a missionary yourself?
I say what I do; I sometimes preach.
Do not the other Caffre chiefs mistrust you, from your having changed your religion, and become a missionary?
No; they have the greatest confidence in me.
Where do you preach; in the colony, or to the Caffres, or both?
I preach among the Caffres, and I preach to the Hottentots and boors, if I can find them.
Do you appear before the Committee here as a missionary, to advocate the cause of the Caffres?
I sit here as an assistant missionary, and a Caffre chief.

England, 1836 127

Tzatzoe positions himself as both a spiritual and secular leader among the Xhosa. As he frequently has, he assumes both the persona of an independent evangelist, or missionary, and an independent chief of the amaNtinde. Fulfilling his political role, Tzatzoe tells Donkin that he is in England to *complain* on the Xhosa chiefs' behalf about the indiscriminate thievery of the commando system and the iniquities of the last war. Tzatzoe specifically details Governor D'Urban's confiscation of the amaNtinde land on the Buffalo River upon which the British military are building King William's Town. Ever since the time of Dr. Van der Kemp, Tzatzoe concludes, the *missionaries used to tell us that the good people and right people were here [in England], and that justice was here. When I heard that Dr. Philip was going to England, I was anxious myself to go.*[4]

After Andries Stoffels, James Read Junior, and James Read complete their testimony, the London Missionary Society commissions a painting by the portraitist Henry Room to commemorate the occasion. All five members of the South African party poses in one of the side chambers of the House of Commons, but Jan Tzatzoe is unmistakably the center of attention of *The Caffre Chief's Examination Before the House of Commons' Committee.*[5]

Tzatzoe stands on the far left of the picture on a carpet with a pale-violet, square tile pattern. At the center of each tile is a large red flower. Behind him are bookshelves, lined with expensively bound volumes, whose glass paneling is framed by ash blue, almost slate, woodwork. Tzatzoe is dressed in a dark navy military style overcoat, with a gold-embroidered standing collar and sleeves, and matching tuxedo-style gold-striped pants. His white-gloved right hand holds a handkerchief (he is the only subject wearing a glove). His left arm points suggestively toward a table at his left.

The table is covered in a finely wrought, floral-patterned, emerald tablecloth. Upon it lie documents and letters in a haphazard heap that draws the eye down toward an open box that sits at the base of the table. The box itself is a clay-like orange-red, against which the white luminance of the letters contained within it and the pink of the binding ribbons (familiar to any reader in an archive) are especially striking. Scrolls and multiple volumes, including several Parliamentary Blue Books, erupt out of the box like a covey of birds before a flushing dog. As some land on the table above and others scurry toward the corner of the painting, the viewer is prompted to see this evidence of the perilous situation in South Africa flying directly toward him.

Tzatzoe is the only one of the five figures whose eyes address the viewer directly, doing so in a serene and wholly dignified manner. On the far right,

Dr. Philip sits composed in an armchair, and, like all of the others excepting Tzatzoe, he has on a suit of sober black with a white undershirt. Eyebrows cocked, ruddy-cheeked, puffy-lipped he gazes to the left of the viewer with a self-conscious turn of his head. The three Kat River settlers are arranged in the center of the picture, slightly behind and to the left of the table. Behind them a rich claret drape flows down from the top of the painting.

Andries Stoffels, eyes distinctly rheumy, sits drawn up to the left of the table, and he looks directly up at Jan Tzatzoe. James Read Junior, youthful, is painted in profile, also looking directly at Tzatzoe, his left hand demurely tucked into the breast pocket of his thick wool winter coat. James Read looks out of the painting and to the viewer's left, wearing an avuncular, almost distracted expression. Read may have least anticipated his presence here in Parliament, inconceivable when he paced the deck of the *Duff* in 1800, or fled north from the colony in disgrace in 1816.[6]

Largely out of the public's eye, Room's painting will hang in the headquarters of the LMS and its descendant organizations, testifying to the transformative power of the mission field, until South Africa will finally be free of European colonialism. But engravings by several artists of Room's image, particularly an individual portrait of Jan Tzatzoe, will circulate widely in the following decades and will serve as visual representations of the power of Christianity and European civilization to shape a self-possessed and capable Anglo-Atlantic black identity. These engravings, however, alter Tzatzoe's image from the Room painting, turning his hair into long soft curls, lengthening his forehead, slimming and compressing his cheekbones, and rounding his eyes.[7]

While the travelers have justified their journey to England to testify before the Aborigines Committee, they are at liberty to travel to long-forgotten (for some) haunts. James Read visits his childhood home in Essex. He addresses a *public meeting*, sees the *house and chamber that gave him birth*, and even runs into an *old playfellow or two*. Later, Read will recollect that he reunited with his only sister and five first cousins, all in their mid-seventies to mid-eighties, whom he feared he would never see again. He wept at the death of the London Missionary Society leaders who inspired him and sent him off on his missionary endeavors, but he was grateful that their *children had risen up to carry on the great work among the heathen*. He noticed in Essex, as everywhere in England, that where previously there was ignorance of the *true religion*, a *great change had been wrought in the place*. The country air does him good, and he does his best to rest up and conquer the severe case of intestinal disease that has kept

1.1 Cape Town and Table Bay, circa 1830s (W. J. Huggins. Seascape. Courtesy Cape Archives).

1.2 Wagon Travel in the Eastern Cape (Lithographs published as part of *Scenery and Events in South Africa* by Thomas Baines. London: Ackermann and Co. 1852. Courtesy Museum Africa).

1.3 Xhosa village life (Lithographs published as part of Scenery and Events in South Africa by Thomas Baines. London: Ackermann and Co. 1852. Courtesy Museum Africa).

1.4 Xhosaland mission station (Wood engraving in *The Missionary; or Christian's New Year's Gift*, ed. William Ellis, by

1.5 The landing of the 1820 British Settlers, Algoa Bay (Morrison Collection. Courtesy Cape Archives).

1.6 View along the Chumie (Tyumie) Valley (Watercolor. Arthur William Godfrey. Courtesy Museum Africa).

1.7 Xhosa healer (or ritual specialist) with women and children (Frederick Timpson I'Ons. Courtesy Museum Africa).

1.8 Maqoma, son of Ngqika (In Fritsch, Gustav, *Drei Jahre in Sud--Africka*, Breeslau, Ferdinand Hirt, 1968. Courtesy Museum Africa).

1.9 John Fairbairn, Editor of the *South African Commercial Advertiser* (AG Collection. Courtesy Cape Archives).

1.10 Robert Godlonton, Editor of the *Graham's Town Journal* (Elliot Collection. Courtesy Cape Archives).

1.11 Sir Harry Smith (Morrison Collection. Courtesy Cape Archives).

1.12 Sir Benjamin D'Urban (From a mezzotint by Payne, after Mogford. Morrison Collection. Courtesy Cape Archives).

1.13 "The Caffre Chief's Examination Before the House of Commons' Committee" by Henry Room, 1836. Left to right: Jan Tzatzoe, Andries Stoffels, James Read Junior, John Philip (Morrison Collection. Courtesy Cape Archives).

1.14 Hogsback and the Amathole Mountains (Signed T. Baines, Grahamstown, August 1851. Courtesy Museum Africa).

1.15 Warfare in the Eastern Cape (Colored engraving in Maarten's *Painting Illustrative of the [Xhosa] War*, engraved by J. Harris. Morrison Collection. Courtesy Cape Archives).

1.16 Parley between British military officials and Xhosa leaders, War of the Axe (Colored engraving in Maarten's *Painting Illustrative of the [Xhosa] War*, engraved by J. Harris. Morrison Collection. Courtesy Cape Archives).

1.17 Sandile (AG Collection. Courtesy Cape Archives).

1.18 Sarhili (AG Collection. Courtesy Cape Archives).

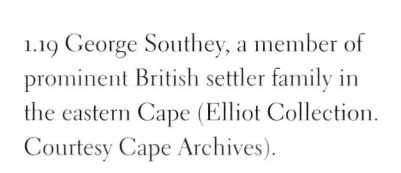

1.19 George Southey, a member of prominent British settler family in the eastern Cape (Elliot Collection. Courtesy Cape Archives).

1.20 King William's Town, circa 1860s (Lithograph from Bowler's *Kaffir Wars and British Settlers*. Morrison Collection. Courtesy Cape Archives).

him ragged and on a strict diet of *Rice water and Ships Biscuit for Breakfast, Tea and Supper. Sole fish and Biscuit for Dinner. This with all the luxeries about me is no small denial.*[8]

Soon, the party will undertake a series of meetings in London and the other great towns of England and across the countryside to proclaim their message of civilization and Christianity to the evangelical public and the merely curious. If funds are raised for books, clothes, agricultural implements, and printing presses for the South African missions, so much the better. If young men are moved to follow in their footsteps as missionaries to Tzatzoe's fellow chiefs, their work is doubly blessed. *'Tis likely we shall excite a great interest for Africa,* Read records. *We are every day out to dine, drink tea, or sup. We have scarcely an hour's time.*[9]

One dinner takes place at Sir Thomas Fowell Buxton's London home, which is set amidst the gracious Georgian elegance of Portland Place.[10] The Buxtons live toward the north end of the unusually wide street, close to where it opens up onto the formal gardens, lawns, and lakes of Regent's Park, in a world far removed from the slums of Whitechapel and the mercantile bustle that surrounds the African visitors' current lodging. On this mid-July day in 1836, Buxton's wife, Hannah, observes to herself that she will have to perform the main duties of host. Her husband is *sadly worn like a hackney coach horse.* The delegation from the Cape Colony enters a little after five o'clock in the evening. Among those awaiting the African party are Buxton's sisters, Sarah and Elizabeth, and Mrs. Upcher, an elderly American friend of the Buxtons.

Fanciful English attire, Elizabeth Buxton notes to herself upon regarding Tzatzoe.
Fine-looking and well-made, but with hair like a carpet.
Mrs. Upcher goes further, whispering in Sarah's ear:
What a fine head, and forehead and nose.
She pauses.
Of course I really shouldn't be fancying like this, but how his mouth caricatures a Negro's.
She sits back uperight, blushes; in the company of one of the men's champions, she shouldn't even allow herself to think such a thought.

The women have nothing but praise for James Junior. Yes, he looks more like a *Caffer than an Englishmen,* but he is pleasing and agreeable—he keeps the conversation going capitally. A *fat, fair, half ashamed, half amused English girl* takes Stoffels's arm and leads the guests to the table. There is nothing but praise for the visitors' table manners; they laugh frequently and seem genuinely at ease. After the tablecloth is removed, but before tea is served, the African men are questioned by the other guests.

What has struck Tzatzoe most about England? *The peace, he replies, everyone in the streets looks kind. No beggars, all look comfortable and happy, with their own business. No drunkards and fighting in the streets.*

What can he mention to the discredit of the British? Tzatzoe answers: *the British abuse their Sabbaths, carriages are about and people sell in the streets. The horses are admirable but what have the donkeys done to deserve such treatment? And as for the dogs, it is surely a wicked thing to make them work like Hottentots!*[11]

What would have happened to the sixty thousand inhabitants of Xhosaland if D'Urban's decision to annex seventy thousand square miles of Xhosa territory for Queen Adelaide Province had been allowed to stand? *They would surely have been entirely exterminated, but thanks to Mr. Buxton's hard work and his Committee all is well.* In 1836 extermination carries the primary meaning of banishment or extrusion, rather than utter destruction.[12] Tea is served, followed by hymns in Dutch sung by Tzatzoe, Stoffels, and James Junior. James and Tzatzoe sing another hymn in Xhosa, followed by a war song by Stoffels. The summer night is still hot, and maids bring iced desserts to the travelers. The surprise on the faces of the Africans reveals the novelty of the pucker-inducing embrace of the ice. Finally, speeches.

Stoffels begins; he is a skilled and passionate orator who is capable of reducing audiences of hundreds to tears when he preaches. The exotic click consonants of Khoisan please everyone in the audience. Tzatzoe stands next, but his time is cut short by Buxton, who expresses his joy at seeing the Cape contingent, and then with an increasingly belligerent and bellicose tone urges them to increase their and their peoples' knowledge of Christianity as the true path to peace, civilization, happiness, and heaven.

Dr. Philip closes with the 103rd Psalm (Psalm 103: 1, 3–6, 20) and a prayer:

> Bless the Lord, O my soul: and all that is within me, bless his holy name . . .
> Who forgiveth all thine inequities; who healeth all thy diseases.
> Who redeemeth thy life from destruction; who crowneth thee with loving kindness and tender mercies.
> Who satisfieth thy mouth with good things; so that thy youth is renewed like the eagle's.
> The Lord executeth righteousness and judgment for all that are oppressed . . .
> Bless the Lord, ye his angels, that excel in strength, that do his commandments hearkening unto the voice of his word.

Ending with a shared Amen, Philip gazes on the guests he has brought into Buxton's home. *So these are irreclaimable savages,* he exclaims to murmurs of agreement from the guests who are well aware of D'Urban's characterization of the Xhosa as *treacherous and irreclaimable savages.*

Monkeys, Mrs. Upcher adds, referring scornfully to another caricature, when she relates the evening's events to a friend. *How like some wonderful odd agreeable dream,* she recalls thinking to herself, invoking Psalm 68:31, *the wonder of witnessing Ethiopia stretch out her hands.*

On 2 August 1836, a Thursday evening, the African visitors attend a session of Parliament with seats below the gallery, as Sir Thomas Fowell Buxton's guests of honor. Tzatzoe and Stoffels *excite great interest* as they enter the hall. A new member from Newcastle is sworn in, a return of British marines killed and wounded under Lord John Hay in the attack on Fontarabia in Spain is read, and a committee is formed to inquire into the *state and management* of the British Museum. There are petitions from members of a Wesleyan Methodist Society in favor of a *Bill for removing the Civil Disabilities of the Jews,* and from the *well-known and scientific gentleman named Thomas Steele, praying that the House might have a monument of remembrance erected to Sir Isaac Newton.* The most keenly anticipated debate involves the Irish Church Bill. Sir Robert Peel, Lord John Russell, Hume, and others speak. The *Reformers gain the day.*

Leaving the debates, Tzatzoe is asked for his impressions. *I may forget the railroads, I may forget the Steam Engines, but I shall not forget what I have seen here tonight,* he replies. *I have seen a little company of men not taller than I am met here to touch the spring that moves the world.* To elucidate Tzatzoe's comments, Philip explains to Buxton and the others that the Xhosa chiefs *are without exception tall fine men.*[13]

Buxton chooses to record Tzatzoe's sentences in a letter for his wife and not for general publication, so their preservation is not a public relations exercise. Tzatzoe is soaking in the differences between the Cape and the thriving metropolis. He revels in London's modernity for which steam engines and railroads are leading symbols. Tzatzoe also understands that the power of the leaders in Parliament has a global reach. At this time, "spring" carries the meaning of an impelling agency or animating force. Tzatzoe is aware that the British leaders in Parliament have a great effect upon the forces that move the world, and that his corner of Africa is irrevocably, and with great immediacy, tied to the actions of the men in the room. And these men are literally and metaphorically of a similar stature to the Xhosa leaders with whom Tzatzoe interacts.[14]

After their visit to Parliament Tzatzoe and the others (with the exception of James Read, who embarks with his *carpet-bag, great coat etc.* on a quick evangelizing tour) prepare for a Special General Meeting of the LMS. The meeting is held on Wednesday 10 August 1836 in Exeter Hall for friends of the Society for the *purpose of receiving statements from the Rev. Dr. Philip, the Caffre Chief Tzatzoe, and Andries Stoffles, the Hottentot, in reference to the state and prospects of the Society's Missions in South Africa.*[15]

About five hundred yards east of Trafalgar Square and Charing Cross, Exeter Hall is set back from The Strand (a commercial thoroughfare that runs along the north bank of the Thames through London's bustling center). The Hall is the lodestone of the humanitarian and evangelical community of London and Great Britain. Its construction speaks to the massive popular appeal of the community, which had built on the mass political movement of the abolitionist era that had united and mobilized members of the lower and middle classes, women and men, for the first time.[16] Only five years old in 1836, it is a cavernous space expressly designed for charitable meetings and religious services. Jan Tzatzoe and his companions enter the building beneath a magnificent portico. Its twin columns rise from ten-foot-high, solid, square blocks that dwarf the visitors. The portico itself ascends for four stories, cresting in Corinthian capitals, and summits in a roof that bears the inscription in Greek letters "Philadelpheion," or Place of Brotherly Love. Once inside, Tzatzoe and the others climb a double staircase toward the Great Hall.

The Great Hall measures one hundred-thirty-six feet long, seventy-six feet wide, and forty-five feet high and is capable of holding in excess of three thousand people. Four large chandeliers hang from a high ceiling. Seats for a five-hundred-member choir surround an immense organ. At the instrument's base is a raised platform on which the speakers sit, rising to address the crowd below them, while an iron railing steadies their hand. It is from this magisterial setting that Tzatzoe and the others will address the thousands of predominantly middle- and upper-class male and female evangelicals who have come to hear them speak.[17]

Many eminent missionaries and clergymen address the crowd, but the night belongs to Tzatzoe, Stoffels, and Read Junior, *the long-benighted children of Ethiopia*, as they are described by the LMS's major periodical publication, the *Missionary Magazine*: upon our guests *although differing from ourselves in colour, every eye was fixed with hallowed and intense delight.* The Chairman of the Society, Reverend Ellis, extends his welcome and reads a short narrative of the lives of Tzatzoe and Stoffels. The narrative characterizes Tzatzoe as a *chief of the Caffre nation*, and *head of the Teenda tribe*, who became a *decided*

Christian at age twenty-four, and who has become an *able assistant missionary* and *faithful co-worker in the gospel*, working with Reverend Brownlee among his own people. Jan Tzatzoe then steps forward *to loud expressions of grateful joy* and addresses the assembly in Dutch, with Read Junior interpreting.[18]

Tzatzoe's address in the Great Hall is foundational. Its words will be widely reported and examined in the humanitarian and settler press, in good measure vilified as well as hallowed. This scrutiny assures that Read Junior's translation is faithfully recorded and reflective of Tzatzoe's Dutch. The speech itself is characteristic of many others Tzatzoe will give in Great Britain. Each speech will show variation on the themes he lays out in Exeter Hall, and they will reveal Tzatzoe's growing familiarity with Britain and with the expectations of his many and varied audiences.[19]

Tzatzoe begins by portraying a fallen South Africa in need of salvation. He then praises the British for sending missionaries to South Africa, for their consistent support of the extant missions, before asking them for more evangelists:

> I am surprised to see so many people assembled in the house of God. I am happy to have the opportunity of seeing those Christian friends who sent out Dr. Vanderkemp, Dr. Philip, Mr. Read, and all the other missionaries. I thank God that you sent out these devoted men, who came to South Africa, when we were shot with bullets, and when there was nothing but blood-shed in that ill-fated country. There was nothing to be seen but the bullet and assagai, the bow and the arrow; but the word of God has continued to this day. You must not be wearied in well-doing; the work is still great, and the work must be spread in the world. God might convert the world by his own power, but he employs instruments to bring men to himself. (Cheers.)
>
> You must send us school-masters and missionaries, elevate us and do us good, and raise subscriptions for the Missionary Society. We cannot allow you to be at rest till this great work is finished.

Now that they have *received the word of God*, Tzatzoe continues, his fellow Africans are ready, prepared, and eager to form their own missionary societies, to *send forth the word of God to others*. His statement reveals his own impulse as an assistant missionary and reflects the LMS's policy of encouraging its missions' inhabitants to contribute to evangelical societies. It exceeds such tutelage by its apparent insistence on Africans' ability to convey the message on their own, without European supervision, the supervision that is an unstated expectation of the European missionaries of the time.

Tzatzoe next remarks that Christianity has the potential to end fighting between Africans and, generally, to render the eastern Cape border region a peaceful place. Keeping in mind the fact that in Xhosa belief success attends rulers who can marshal spiritual forces to their side to deal with issues of evil (Tzatzoe calls these sin in his speech), Tzatzoe extends this logic to issues of political stability and security, an absence of misfortune, especially warfare. This state can be attained if a chief can provide his people with effective diviners who remove evildoers. The Christian God, as a new spiritual force in the border region, can cleanse the land of evil, of sin, and as a result the land will be healed. The warfare and disruption that arise because of evil in the land will be vanquished:

> God is great, who has promised it, and he will extend his word in the world. God is about to do away with blood-shed and war, and every thing that is sinful. War is bad, and other things have been bad, but good is come out of evil. Who knows, if these things had not taken place, whether missionaries would ever have gone out to that country? If we wish to serve God we must expect persecution; we must expect the wicked to oppose us: but God will surely finish his own work. . . . The word of God has turned us; the word of God has brought peace, has reconciled one man to another, and in us is fulfilled that text of Scripture, "The wolf shall dwell with the lamb." (Cheers.)

Tzatzoe then places himself and his African companions beneath English sovereignty, but in a way intended to make clear that the deference implies a sense of reciprocal obligations from those to whom the deference is granted.

> I thank the English nation for what we have received at their hands. You are our friends; we are your children. I am like one of your children. I have been brought up under the laws of England, and I have enjoyed all the privileges of your missions. When we signed the treaty with the British Government at the Buffalo River, a paper was read which told us that we then became the children of the King of England, and that we were now British subjects. If we are the children of England, and if one with yourselves, let us enjoy the privileges of Britons. (Loud cheers.)

Yet, Tzatzoe is aware that many will resist his call:

> Many Englishmen in the colonies are bad, (hear, hear,) but I will hardly believe that those Englishmen belong to you. (Laughter and applause.) You are a different race of men—they are South Africans, they are not Englishmen. (Cheers.)

In idiomatic language that his fellow Xhosa chiefs would understand, Tzatzoe reprises his trope of Africans as children, in order to signal his respect for the Englishmen he is addressing:

> I have now seen the English nation. I have travelled [sic] a little in this country. I have met with a friendly reception wherever I have gone; and I can say you are now my friends. I know my friends. (Applause.) Do not forget us. Our eyes are upon you. You are our parents. You sent us the word of God. I hope that you will still continue to send out that word.

Revealing a keen sense of the expectations of his audience, Tzatzoe shares a kind word for John Philip:

> I would thank you for ever having sent out Dr. Philip to our country. (Applause.) This gentleman never sleeps in Africa. (Laughter.)
> He is always doing good, he is always protecting us. He is our witness; he is a witness of the state of the colonies, and he is a witness of what God has done amongst us, He knows what we have suffered: he suffered with us. (Hear, hear, and applause.)

Finally, Tzatzoe reveals his concern for standing by one's word, for truth, that he has demonstrated in his diplomatic interactions with colonial officials and evangelical meetings with Xhosa spiritual leaders. Applying this personal conviction to the message he received from the missionaries, Tzatzoe seems to be saying that adhering to the truths of the word of God will result in a better world. Yet, is he not also questioning the veracity of the colonial administrators who have penned treaties similar to the one to which he has already referred?

> Very few people in the world love truth; they love darkness. Truth brings every thing to light; it reveals what is hidden. But there are very few people who will allow that they do not love the truth. They wish to take injustice and justice in one hand. Every man knows what is truth, but he wishes to mix the truth with falsehood. Some people are afraid to stand out for the truth; other people won't stand out for the truth; and others are ashamed of the truth. Take the truth. The truth is the most important thing in this world. It is honest. Where there is no truth, there is no true honour. (Applause.) We must all adore the truth—every man. The word of God is truth. The word of God tells us to do good; and the word of God tells us to stand on the truth. We ought to adhere to the truth, and to stand by the truth. I will not say more. (Loud applause.)

Tzatzoe ends his speech with two idiomatic phrases drawn from Xhosa oratory. Speakers often refer to "standing up" or "standing by" a worthwhile object, and they frequently end their speeches to public meetings with the expression: "I will not say more," or "I will say no more."[20]

Following Tzatzoe, Stoffels, Read Junior, and Dr. Philip each address the meeting. Stoffels praises the work of Dr. Philip and the missionaries in reaching out to the Khoisan community and in passing legal protection for them—the *charter of our liberties,* as he calls it—in the form of the 50th ordinance that guaranteed them fully equal rights under law. He concludes:

> The word of God has brought my nation so far, that if a Hottentot young lady and an English young lady were walking with their faces from me, I would take them both to be English ladies. Do instruct us—I say again, do instruct us! Do not leave us to ourselves. Hold us under your arm. We are coming on; we are improving; we will soon all be one.

In February 1838 James Read will offer a similar sentiment, describing to a missionary meeting in Cape Town how the *little Hottentot children* in his Kat River Infant Schools, who were thought to be *a sort of monkeys* when he and Dr. Van der Kemp began their labors, asked him not for *sugar-candy* or *clothing* when he told them he was traveling to England, but *for more maps to learn more geography* (indeed, traveling around England he realized they knew the towns and rivers of the region better than he did).[21] The meeting then hears Tzatzoe and Stoffels recite the Lord's Prayer in their *respective languages.*[22]

How does the audience react to the African men's speeches? These *beloved friends, natives of a distant land?* There are no focus groups or reporters standing at the ready for crowd reaction, but two speakers seem to capture the mood in the hall. The Reverend John Young, of Albion Chapel, is *deeply overcome by witnessing the spectacle that is before him*:

> We love these strangers for the sake of Christ, whom they and we love, and who, we trust, loves them and us. We welcome them as ransomed by the same precious blood, with which we trust we have been sprinkled; renewed by the same Holy Ghost which we trust has been shed upon us.

Young continues with evangelical rhetoric that is rich even by the florid standards of the time:

> We have here only the earnest and the pledge of that glorious inheritance which forms the burden of all promises, of the predictions of Scripture: "Ethiopia shall soon stretch out her hands to God!" The partition wall of China shall soon be broken down! The vast continent of Hindoostan shall soon be overrun by the armies of the living God! The temples of idolatry shall soon tumble into ruins! The delusions of the false prophet shall melt away before the effulgence of the Sun of Righteousness; anti-christ shall be destroyed by the breath of his nostrils and by the brightness of his coming!

Young concludes by offering a history of the Africa from which Tzatzoe, Stoffels, and Read have come.[23] He uses the declensionist tropes that will dominate Anglo-American attitudes toward Africa and Africans for centuries:

We cannot forget that these beloved brethren are natives from Africa. What a history is involved in that word! Time was, as we heard this morning, when Africa produced warriors, and legislators, and philosophers. Time was when Africa was the cradle of the arts, of literature, and of science. Africa was the scene of the labours of the apostles, and some of the earliest and most magnificent triumphs of Christianity. But her sun has long since gone down, and a long night of darkness and oppression has well-nigh obliterated all traces of her past history. Africa seems the compendium of all the sorrows and all the depravity of this world.

A sentence of outlawry seems to have been pronounced upon the fated sons of Africa, by common and universal consent, and they appear to have been doomed to perpetual and hopeless slavery. But that day has passed, and a brighter day has dawned.... Africa shall be free! She is beginning to be free! She is entering upon a course which shall know no change, no termination, until every one of her sable sons, holding up his outstretched arms to heaven, shall cry, "Behold! I am as free as you!"

Lastly, Edward Baines, Member of Parliament, gives his remarks to the Missionary Meeting on the recently completed proceedings of the Aborigines Committee, of which he is a member.[24] In his testimony to the committee, Baines relates, Tzatzoe displayed an *artlessness and dignity which proved that he was indeed a Chief, though an attempt had been made to deprive him of that character*. He clearly had the *interest of his nation at heart* when he came to England, and he taught the *British Senate* one *great lesson* in *political economy*:

> That by doing justice to the people of Africa, we should induce them to become our customers and friends—to take our wares and merchandise—that on visiting their coast, we might receive from them freight for our shipping, while they received from us articles that would advance their progress in comfort and civilization, and in all the useful arts; and that thus we might receive and render mutual benefits.

Finally, Baines asks the meeting to reflect on Tzatzoe and Stoffels *sitting a whole night in the House of Commons*:

> He was inquisitive to know what passed in their minds. He read in their expressive countenances the working of their hearts. A new world was floating before them—they were evidently contemplating the scene with profound attention, and with mingled sensations of wonder and admiration; reflecting that the interests and happiness of their own country were often involved in the deliberations of the assembly now before them.

A new world certainly is floating before Tzatzoe and Stoffels, a world that will continue to enlarge as they depart from London for an evangelizing and fundraising tour of England. This is a new world of economic and cultural trade, of political decisions being taken thousands of miles from the arena of their impact (but by people no taller than the African chiefs), of African demands for political reciprocity. Most of all, it is a new world marked by dramatic change, by expanding vistas and possibilities. *The Meeting might depend upon it, that this visit of Dr. Philip and his African converts would form a new era in our colonial history,* Baines concludes. Tzatzoe and the others are delayed from leaving the Missionary Meeting by a crowd of well-wishers: *scarcely one seemed willing to depart without first stretching forth the hand of welcome, and exchanging the look of Christian benevolence with those savage-born, but new-created men.*[25]

The *South African Commercial Advertiser*, *Graham's Town Journal*, and another South African newspaper, *Die Zuid-Afrikaan*, which serves the colony's Afrikaans population, all print extended transcripts of Jan Tzatzoe's testimony before the Aborigines Committee, along with many of his speeches in England; they cover James Read, Read Junior, and Stoffels to a lesser extent. The proceedings of the committee and Tzatzoe's journey to Great Britain are within plain view in the public imagination of South Africa during this time period. Tzatzoe continues to be a public symbol onto which the humanitarians and the British settlers in the Eastern Cape—the *different race of men*—can read their own agenda.

In his *Journal*, Robert Godlonton sneers at *Dr. Philip and his "Christian Trophies"*:

> It is proper that our friends at home [Godlonton means England] should understand who and what John T'Zatzoe is. Hence we sum up his character in a few words: He is the son of a petty Kafir chief, poor and of little or no influence. Jan was taken when a boy under the care of Dr. Van der Kemp, with whom he resided for some time at Bethelsdorp where he received what is called an education i.e. to scrawl his name and to read. He is considered by those who know him best to be a weak-minded, inoffensive man, who would have lived peaceably enough had he been permitted; but unfortunately he resided near the Kat River Settlement; hence poor Jan was made a convenient tool by our colonial agitators; calumnious letters were written and published respecting the colonists, which John was made to father, though we know he never wrote them, and of the exact tenor or which we believe him to be at this day entirely ignorant.[26]

The scurrilous and racist aspersions have followed Jan Tzatzoe, in his *splendid dress*, from the eastern Cape to England. Yet, crucially, neither the *Journal* nor the *Zuid-Afrikaan* suggest that Tzatzoe's speeches are being manipulated in the process of translation. As harshly as they judged Tzatzoe's authorship of his letters in 1833, the fact that they do not attack the authenticity of the speeches speaks reliably to the fact that Read Junior is not speaking for Tzatzoe in England.[27]

After the Missionary Meeting, the party splits up to spread their evangelical net more broadly over England. James Read misses Exeter Hall altogether, having embarked on a tour of *Yorkshire: York, Birmingham, Bath, Bristol*, and several other *great towns. Their meetings are at hand*, he explains to a friend, referring to the annual, nondenominational missionary meetings held to gather funds for overseas missions, and *they insist to have one of us down*. Read expects to meet up with his African compatriots in Birmingham.[28]

The tours continue throughout August. Read holds meetings at Hull, Cottingham, Swanland, Hornsea, Skipsea, Frodingham, and Driffield. In Burlington he speaks in a large Wesleyan chapel on the quay, then from Burlington to Muston, Scarborough to Malton. But Read is frustrated: *the people everywhere express such a desire to see one of the Africans*. The Africans are with Philip, attending meetings in the large towns that have attracted hundreds of people. In one night in Liverpool, they raise £1,600. The Africans are a potent public image, and the public relations campaign seems to be working.[29]

On the eleventh anniversary of the Central Yorkshire Auxiliary to the LMS, *friends of the mission* are admitted to the school-room of Lendal Chapel in York at nine o'clock on the morning of Monday 22 August 1836, for 1s 6d a piece. Over two hundred *ladies and gentleman* hear Reverend Ely, of Leeds, who comments on the *peculiar character* of the breakfast meal they are enjoying, in contrast to the *simpering tea-party or the uproarious dinner-party*. It is a *cheering reflection*, he continues, that the *Sabbath just passed had been solemnized all round the world, that the sun, on passing every meridian, had witnessed groups of Christians assembled for the purposes of devotion*.[30]

Next, the meeting hears from Jan Tzatzoe, who is introduced by Philip as the *Caffre chief*, a *chief by birth*. Philip relates that Tzatzoe has been a *humble and sincere Christian* for *fifteen years* who has *devoted his life to the cause of doing good*. Tzatzoe's speech is *received with the most marked attention*. Tzatzoe begins with another idiomatic phrase from Xhosa oratory:

> I will be very brief this morning. I have nothing to tell you this morning, but I would tell you — Rejoice, rejoice at what the gospel has done.

The negation that precedes the giving of news is characteristic of Xhosa diplomatic protocol.³¹ Tzatzoe praises the gospel for bringing the *children of Adam and Noah* together to the *feast*. The *Bible has done all for you; its general diffusion throughout this country has given you all the knowledge and wealth that you possess.* Tzatzoe thanks the British for sending the *word of God to the heathen*. He stands before them this day as a *monument of God's mercy*.

Read Junior asks the audience to pay attention to matters in Xhosaland and to be ready to petition in favor of the Africans in order to maintain their rights and to ensure the restoration of their land. Of immediate concern is the rise of the *patrol system* (commando system) which had led large numbers of Xhosa to renounce Christianity, on the grounds that the *British did not practice what they preached*.

Philip takes up Read Junior's themes. It is the *duty of Christians to become politicians as far as was necessary to protect them in the enjoyment of their rights*, he tells the audience. The *colonies of South Africa* are *as much an integral part of the British dominions*, as are the *counties of Yorkshire and Lancashire*, having *the same right to protection from the state*. Several members of the audience then echo the South African visitors' sentiments. Yes, Mr. Ford from the Society of Friends, insists, the *colonial history of Great Britain* is *one written in blood*.

A little late for breakfast, James Read enters the building and is *pronounced as the father of young Mr. Read, who had just done speaking*. There are *great cheers, stamping of the feet*. Read is overcome by emotion. Whether it is a father's pride in the growth of his son, or the recognition of his own thirty-six years of hard labor in the missionary field, Read cannot continue, his words temporarily choked back. When he can speak, he promises to return to South Africa, with *his zeal renewed, his faith quickened*.³²

In September Philip takes the Africans to visit Windsor Castle. While there, they make *an application for permission to enter the Royal presence*. The King respectfully declines *on account of severe indisposition*. But as his regrets are being delivered, the *Royal grandchildren* come down and present the *contents of a missionary box* to Philip before shaking hands with Jan Tzatzoe. The King's granddaughters add a box of clothes and money. Addressing a missionary meeting shortly after the visit, Tzatzoe will refer to the encounter in glowing terms:

I cannot resist speaking of a great wonder—that in the palace the King's grandchildren should take me by the hand—me, who am a black man; and they not only shook hands, but gave me money, and said, "That is for your infant schools." I am very much surprised that those children of royal blood should be concerned for my nation. That will be a great thing to tell the poor

Africans. I will make a box with a drawer for the money of the King's grandchildren, with a hole at the top, and I will say to the chiefs, "Now you must put some money over this."[33]

By the beginning of October the whole party is back in Hackney, a suburb of London. Read is finding the climate (or is it the attention and renown?) salubrious. But in a letter home to Bethelsdorp, he reports concern for the health of James Junior and Andries Stoffels, who are suffering in the cold and damp. The British government has agreed to fund their entire trip, Read continues, concluding with news from the British press: *The poor Wesleyans and their Society are lashed. They do not like the interest excited by our presence in England with Stoffels and Tzatzoe. I think all a wonderful providence.*[34]

The LMS has offered to provide twelve months of schooling to James Junior so that he might be ordained as a minister, but he is too sick to accept it. Instead he is ordained as an Evangelist on Tuesday evening, 25 October 1836, in Saint Thomas's Square Church in Hackney, a squat, angular structure, solidly built of dark red brick.[35] Read attests to his son's *decided Piety &c.* and, from his youth, the *very early progress of divine grace.* James Junior has superintended a dozen schools and begun *preaching with great acceptance to large congregations. . . . Few perhaps was ever the subject of more prayers not mere from his own family but of the Hottentot people and that from his birth.* Meanwhile, James has embarked on another calling while in England. *I believe he has something else in his head,* his father writes to friends in South Africa, *but I fear he will not succeed.* James Read Junior and Andries Stoffels sail for the Cape of Good Hope aboard the *Meg Merrilies* on 7 November 1836. And Jan Tzatzoe is left as the lone African member of the LMS delegation to Great Britain.[36]

GREAT BRITAIN

We Can Come to England and Get Justice
1836–1838

On 25 November 1836 Dr. John Philip *together with his interesting colleagues* are in Weymouth, a coastal town in southwestern England, which is the center of Thomas Fowell Buxton's parliamentary district. The visitors make a *very powerful impression* on the town. With his son having returned to the Cape, James Read will now serve as the primary translator for Tzatzoe, as the latter addresses his audiences in Dutch. The local chapel is crowded to excess—Buxton's friend reports an audience of 1,500—and Jan Tzatzoe, Philip, and Read are each presented with a portrait of Buxton himself. *The Chief told me he would shew it to all the Caffers*, the donor reports to the Member of Parliament.[1]

Tzatzoe and Read spend three days at Oxford. Both men speak at a public meeting, a Sunday service, and a public breakfast. We saw it all, Read enthuses, the *colleges, churches, libraries, printing establishments and, impossible as it may appear, 3 bibles printed in a minute by steam*. What does Tzatzoe make of the astonishing technology, the pewter-colored college walls, the manicured lawns, the vast accumulation of books?

Nottingham, Sheffield, Leeds, Manchester, Liverpool, Bath, Birmingham, Coventry, and *two or three towns of Somersetshire, Taunton, Yeovil and etc*. At a *most crowded meeting* in a little chapel in Read's hometown, a *young, most pious and zealous curate of the Church of England* presents Tzatzoe with a *very handsome compass*. The compass, the Reverend Sherwood tells Tzatzoe, *you will observe always points one way, it points to the north. The Bible also points one way, it points to Jesus Christ as the way to heaven*. Tzatzoe seizes on the metaphor, thanking the congregation, and adding that *he had come from Africa to England by the aid of the compass, without which he would have been lost on the great ocean; and had not the Bible and the Missionaries been sent to him he should never have found his way to heaven, nor would he be seen where he then was.* But, Tzatzoe continues, *my nation are, for the greater part, still without the Bible; they are bewildered and must be lost, unless England sends them that heavenly compass, and Missionaries explain it to them.*[2]

In a letter from Read to his friend James Kitchingman at Bethelsdorp, there is news that James Junior's plan has come to fruition:

> I hinted to you that it was not unlikely but James would get a wife in England. This is, I suppose, now settled. It is a young female he had seen at Bristol; 2 sisters, the youngest of the two, but the oldest intends to accompany her sister. . . . They have had a good education, but are plain and are not afraid of work.

Read wishes his own stay were at an end: *O, what a happy day it will be when it may please God to permit me to put my feet on board the ship with my face toward Africa.* And Jan Tzatzoe? There is no record anywhere, in personal or more public papers and letters, of the African leader expressing any discontent about his stay in Britain or his longing for home.[3]

At Nottingham, in the East Midlands, the *most wedged-in meetings*. Read is struck by the rapidly industrializing and urbanizing Yorkshire. Rotherham is *greatly increasing,* he tells Kitchingman (who grew up in the town) *and will soon join Sheffield, which is becoming immensely large.*[4] On to Mansfield and Chesterfield. On Christmas Eve 1836, Tzatzoe, a more flamboyant speaker after several months in England, is the main attraction, according to the *North Derbyshire Chronicle and Chesterfield Advertiser*:

> The chief stood up and bowed to the chairman, which produced a great sensation in the meeting, all wishing to gaze at him; and their curiosity was highly excited, to witness the great novelty of a Caffrarian orator. He is a well formed man, rather above the middle size, and was dressed in a blue uniform, trimmed with gold lace and gilt buttons. He spoke in Dutch with great animation, and very graceful action.

While Tzatzoe avoids politics in his speech, the newspaper is quick to editorialize about his plight as a supporter of the British government during the last war, whose land was, nevertheless, taken from him, and who is trying to win it back. *Every Christian, just, and humane mind must sympathise with him, and heartily wish him success.*[5]

The *Graham's Town Journal*, Read and Tzatzoe's old nemesis, disagrees. Printing a report of similar charges made against the colonial government at another provincial meeting, the *Journal* will comment:

It is proper that our readers should fully understand the astounding audacity with which these imposters carry on their system of deception. . . . Is it possible that the people of any enlightened town in Great Britain can suppose for a single moment that a British governor, and one especially of the disposition of Sir Benjamin D'Urban, could commit the gross injustice with which he is charged by the wretched tool of the party Tzatzoe. The fact is, that this chief was by his treaty with the colony placed in infinitely better circumstances than before the war.

The chief town of the new province being established in the very centre of the country alloted to him, was an advantage which would have raised this man at once to opulence and importance, had he had either common sense or industry to have availed himself of it. We say nothing of the value of British protection, or the importance of the means afforded him of rapid advance in the scale of civilization. The most abhorrent feature of the case, however, is not its falsehood, or its generally deceptive character, but the black ingratitude displayed in return for essential benefits—the viper stinging the hand held out to save it is a just simile of the whole case.[6]

On a Monday evening, the Queen-Street Chapel in Sheffield is the location for the *Annual Social Meeting of the Teachers and Friends* of the *Queen-Street Sunday Schools*. Read introduces Tzatzoe after a lengthy discussion of the history of *missionary labours in Southern Africa*. Tzatzoe is not only a *gifted preacher among his people*, Read continues, *he holds the situation of magistrate among certain tribes of his countrymen, who have the highest opinion of his judgement and disinterestedness*. Read discusses several cases where *Tzatzoe's tact and success in the judicial capacity* were evident. This is the only time in England that Read or Philip have spoken of Tzatzoe's duties as a chief and not as an assistant missionary, duties that are primarily judicial and administrative, and that have taken increasingly more time away from his evangelizing responsibilities. Read speaks of these duties as a Christian good, but in South Africa other missionaries have been, and will continue to be, less praiseworthy. Tzatzoe addresses his Sheffield audience in a *peculiarly earnest manner*. He asks for *books and teachers* to satisfy that *craving for general knowledge which exists among the various races beyond the Cape*.[7]

At a meeting the following day in the Nether Chapel, the issue of Tzatzoe's religious belief comes back to the fore. Tzatzoe is asked a direct question about his *personal religion* and whether he *is afraid to die*:

He hoped to live a little time, if it pleased God for the Sake of his people and country; but if he had had the disposal of himself, he would have been in Heaven years ago.

As he had before Buxton's committee when he asserted that he was both *an assistant missionary* and a *Caffre Chief*, Tzatzoe frames his response in a dual fashion. As a diplomat and leader in the Xhosa state, he is responsible to his people and the other Xhosa leaders, and he hopes that he might serve them for a *little time*. But he also has the pressing issue of a deep and personal belief in a Christianity that promises a perfect world in Heaven, as opposed to the imperfection of the earthbound world. A comforting home where Jesus will welcome the faithful with full acceptance and open, loving arms. This small exchange cuts to the core of Jan Tzatzoe's complex character. Upon his return to South Africa, as it had been before his journey, Tzatzoe's life will be dominated by the conflict between his secular duties and his profession of faith.[8]

The Sheffield meetings raise £72, much of it designated toward a printing press for the Kat River Settlement. Public awareness and indignation is raised even higher. In a letter to the *Sheffield Independent* printed after Read and Tzatzoe's visit, *Several Ladies of Sheffield* express their sentiments on the treatment of *the Natives of the British Settlements*. Their letter epitomizes Tzatzoe's reception by the British humanitarian public. In it the *Ladies* demonstrate a great deal of empathy for the Xhosa. They blame *colonial misrule* over Xhosa territory as the root cause of the 1834–1835 war, and they appear to endorse an unqualified return of African land and sovereignty:

> To the Editor of the Sheffield Independent
> Sir,—The presence of Chief Tzatzoe, of the Caffre nation, in Sheffield, reminds us of the iniquitous conduct of all the colonial governments of the British empire, in reference to the various aborigines, in whose land, by fraud or power, we have been enabled to colonize. It is a fact, that while our religious public has been making its houses of worship as fine, and its ministries as accomplished as possible; while our merchants have been in all the markets of the earth, and our tradesmen busy in keeping abreast with the new nations that have started into being during the past century; while our scholars have been enquiring into the origin and analogies of the fresh languages that have been discovered, and our philosophers have been haranguing each other about abstract rights, or genteel young senators have been flourishing with their maiden eloquence, the most infamous outrages on the natives have been proceeding, wherever the British colonial flag has waved, or the British sentinel been stationed, unregarded by the British public, and almost unknown, except to missionaries. . . .
> We are very glad to see the presence of the celebrated Tzatzoe in Sheffield, who, we understand, has come to this country to complain of the Colonial Government, which . . . deprived Tzatzoe, though in this war an ally

of the Government, of the command of land and property, which had for generations been possessed by his ancestors, to whom the charms of the natale solum are as strong as in any of the creatures of feeling and custom in England.

Sixty thousand of these Caffres have thus been badgered for colonial vengeance, 4,000 have been killed, and the nation driven from its towns and villages, and, in many cases, the exiles have had to see that severest of act of the victor's contempt—the change of the very names by which his town and home had been denominated. . . .

We remain, Sir,
Your obedient servants,
SEVERAL LADIES OF SHEFFIELD[9]

The Missionary Meeting in Sheffield in December 1836 raises such a clamor amongst the local citizens and businessmen that Tzatzoe and Read agree to address another public meeting on specifically mercantile and political topics: an *address on the nature of the late Caffre war, every fact of which is of the highest interest to those who are either looking to Africa for a market, or to its host of auxiliary churches*. Tzatzoe and Read will speak on the *connexion of the missionary and the commercial enterprize* and the *primary object of their visit to Europe*. As with the discussion of economic matters at Exeter Hall, the concern is how South Africa can serve as a market for British manufactured goods, to be exchanged for raw materials like gum, antelope skins, and agricultural products.[10]

Civilization follows missionary labour, as surely as the waggon follows the oxen, Read tells his audience at the specially designated mercantilist meeting in Cutler's Hall in Sheffield, *traders have penetrated twelve or fourteen hundred miles into the interior of Africa*, but always in the tracks of missionaries. In *Caffreland*, soon after the arrival of missionaries in 1816, a trade worth £30,000 a year sprung up between the Xhosa and the colony.[11]

Tzatzoe follows Read, speaking not to economic matters, but revealing a central concern of his journey to England:

He said he appeared before them as the representative of a nation, who had been for years chased before their enemies. The first white men they saw many years ago, had books, but did not communicate their contents to the Hottentots and Caffres. They only learnt what the books meant, and especially the Bible, where the missionaries went. Then they learnt what was right and wrong: and they said to one another, why do not the white men, who have the bible, act as it directs?

Tzatzoe's concern is with the books that the settlers brought with them, books that stand for the entire political, technological, and moral basis of the colonizers. The Bible is appealing in its morality, but the settlers who constantly refer to and take direction from their other written works—such as treaties, laws, even personal letters—do not seem to follow the letter of the law of their foundational text. He refers to several examples of colonial deviance, injustice, and untruthfulness. In response, Tzatzoe asks for equal treatment for Africans and colonists:

> A settler's cattle broke into a Caffre's garden, and remained the whole night, and destroyed every thing. The next day the Caffre took the cattle home, and asked to be paid for the injury. The Englishman offered him twenty buttons, and said that he must take them or nothing. Some time after, the Caffre's cattle got into the Englishman's garden, and the Englishman demanded three oxen for it. The Caffre refused it, and went to the Chief, who went for the settler. Having heard the case, the Chief said, the Caffre should pay three oxen for the damage to the settler's garden, when the settler paid three oxen for the damage to the Caffre's garden; otherwise the Caffre must pay, as the Englishman had paid, 20 buttons.

Tzatzoe refers to Smith and D'Urban's confiscation of his land during the formation of Queen Adelaide Province, despite his campaigning on the British side. *He could not understand this,* Tzatzoe says, *for other chiefs, who had done the same, had had additional territory given them, yet he had been the most faithful ally of the Government.* Worst of all, it seemed to be an entirely arbitrary decision:

> If the Governor had said, I am strong and you are weak, that would have been a reason for doing so, but no reason at all had been given.

Tzatzoe concludes his speech with another call for missionaries and schoolmasters, but his specific concern is evaluating the colonial mindset from a political point of view:

> Now he could say nothing to his people. They said to him he had told them not to do mischief, not to make war, and they had done as he had told them; yet they were punished, and they wanted to know what was right and wrong. He asked, therefore, for Missionaries and school-masters, that they might learn to read books, and know what was right and wrong.

After Sheffield, Read and Tzatzoe battle with wintry weather—*a great fall of snow, such as has not been known for years in England*—until they reach Bath, where both fall ill and return in haste to London.[12]

The winter months of 1837 proceed uneventfully for Read and Tzatzoe. Not so in Cape Town where the *Meg Merrilies* anchors in Table Bay on 12 January 1837. Jane Philip welcomes James Read Junior and Andries Stoffels ashore. Over the course of the next month, Stoffels grows increasingly ill, and when James departs from Cape Town for Algoa Bay, Stoffels remains behind on a farm in Green Point, a suburb of Cape Town. On his deathbed, he *expresses regret at not being spared to go and tell his people what he had seen and heard in England. He would go and tell his story in heaven, but he thought they knew more there than he could tell them.*[13]

As Stoffels lies dying in Green Point, in London there is cause for celebration. By December 1836 the revised policies of the Glenelg dispatch to D'Urban (which had arrived in the Cape in March 1836) have been put into effect in the eastern Cape. Queen Adelaide Province is no more. The British have officially withdrawn to the Fish River, some fifty miles due west of King William's Town, where they have fortified the new colonial boundary with border posts. All the chiefs residing west of the Kei River have signed lengthy treaties with the chief British administrator for the border region, Sir Andries Stockenstrom. While the treaties recognize Xhosa political sovereignty and land ownership, they also impose a series of conditions with regard to Xhosa interaction with the Colony. Governor D'Urban's European Resident Agents will remain at their stations as diplomatic agents, tasked with information gathering instead of administration.[14]

I have to tell you a piece of news, which has made me sing ever since I heard of it, Buxton writes to his collaborator Anna Gurney:

> Well, what is it? It is life, itself, and liberty, and lands and tenements to a whole nation. . . . It is nothing short of this—the hand of the proud oppressor in Africa has been, under Providence, arrested, and a whole nation, doomed to ruin, exile, and death, has been delivered and restored to its rights.
>
> On a given day the drum was beat in the front of Tzatzoe's house, and the troops were marched directly back again to the British territory, and the "fertile and beautiful Adelaide" was once more Cafferland. Only think how delighted must our savage friends be, and with what feelings must they have viewed our retreating army![15]

The *Graham's Town Journal* describes the turn of events in diametrically opposed terms:

> King William's Town was to be finally evacuated by the military yesterday. The buildings will revert to the people under Tzatzoe—and a gentleman has just informed us that when he left the Princess Tzatzoe, assisted by her Maids

of Honor, were busily employed in collecting glass bottles, pieces of rusty iron, and old rags, which lay scattered about in glorious confusion.[16]

Meanwhile, throughout March 1837, Buxton's Aborigines Committee has been hearing its third round of testimony. Tzatzoe, Read, and Philip return to observe the new session. Tzatzoe is a particularly controversial figure in the proceedings, which question, in part, three aspects of his testimony of June 1836. The first is his claim to have authored the letters published in his name in the colonial press. A new witness, a settler named W. G. Atherstone, reports a conversation with Tzatzoe in the eastern Cape in which Tzatzoe admitted to him that he *composed* the letters, *and got some one else to write them down*. Atherstone also questions Tzatzoe's account of a meeting at which both were present during which a Xhosa soldier accused Read of inciting the Xhosa to war. Lastly, Atherstone takes issue with Tzatzoe's claim in 1836 that Philip did not invite him on the voyage to England, but instead, that upon hearing that Philip was departing for England, Tzatzoe asked for permission to come along because the *people in England would listen to a case*. On 21 March 1837 Philip testifies in his own defense. *I beg to say that Tzatzoe is now present, if the Committee have any questions to ask him*, Philip concludes. The committee does not.[17]

The excitement of the new Aborigines Committee session comes among months of sustained travel for Tzatzoe and Read. *The fact is we generally have work cut out for us 3 weeks beforehand, letters from every part of the country*, Read complains, *so that we are just riding about from one place to the other without one day's rest*. In May the duo is back in London for the annual and highly anticipated May Meetings of the Evangelical movement. The Forty-third Annual Public Meeting of the LMS is held in the familiar confines of Exeter Hall on 11 May 1837.[18]

I suppose I must call myself a slave for I am the color of those of whom you made slaves. With this reference to a theme of central importance to his audience who pride themselves as the liberators of the slaves, Tzatzoe begins his speech to the Missionary Meeting. *But now Englishmen have made the slaves free, and have wiped the mark from my forehead*. Tzatzoe expresses his concerns in the abolitionist language that will appeal most strongly to his humanitarian supporters.[19] *And I take this opportunity of thanking the present Government of England, and thanking you who support it, which has given us our rights, and returned our country*. Flush with their victory over slavery, the audience members may well imagine in this moment of great optimism and idealism that they can improve the lot of Africans throughout the empire, free them from oppression and land alienation, and grant them rights as redeemed British citizens and subjects.[20]

But not everyone in the empire feels as warmly about the granting of rights and the redeeming of land as those in Exeter Hall do. When Tzatzoe comments that *it seems to me that you have great power in England, for you have the House of Commons, and the House of Lords in your hands*, the Graham's Town Journal is quick to add to their printed transcript of the speech: *Deafening cheers; and well there might be, for Jan, by accident, spoke here much more truth than is generally elicited from him*.

Tzatzoe continues by marking the highlights of his trip to England. His *very interesting* visit to the Houses of Parliament: *I find that whenever any thing happens to us in Africa, we can come to England and get justice*. His reception by the public: *I shall tell the people in Africa, that the people of England took as much care of me as though I were an hen's egg*. Does Tzatzoe recall this metaphor from his time at the iQonce when he had translated as one of Ngqika's councilors compared himself to the yolk of an egg in Christ's hands? His evangelical trips: *I have attended so many missionary meetings in England, that they appear like so many hillocks of stones placed upon the roadsides to mend them*. Is Tzatzoe referring metaphorically to the piles of stone alongside mid-nineteenth-century British roads, or to Xhosaland, where African and Khoisan travelers, in order to ensure good fortune, add to the pyramids of pebbles placed along trails and roads? Finally, his visit to Windsor Castle in September of the previous year: *It will be the greatest news that I shall have to tell them in Africa, that I found even from the King's Palace they are anxious to carry on God's work in Africa*. This incident revealed to him that everyone from the *King's Palace to the lowest of his subjects*, does not believe that there *is nothing to be done with the Kafirs and the Hottentots*, as the Dutch settlers of South Africa told the British missionaries when they first arrived at the Cape. In fact, Tzatzoe concludes (revisiting the power of the abolitionist rhetoric) *the Kafirs, the Hottentots, the Bushmen, the Griquas, owe their being to the English nation*:

> You have not only sought the welfare of their bodies, but likewise the salvation of their souls. I hope you will pray for them. Your prayers have broken off the shackles of the slaves. Therefore, I hope you will pray for them earnestly, for the prayer of a righteous man availeth much with God. I was a slave to sin before the missionaries came, but now, through the gospel I have been made free. I thank you for what you have done for me.

During the early summer months of 1837 Tzatzoe and Read travel throughout Scotland, raising over £2,000 for the missionary cause. Read reports to Ellis (who sent them north because the people of Scotland would *not be satisfied without a visit from the Africans*) that he feels the figure is respectable. Read *hopes* that the *impression* they have made is *not small*. Tzatzoe, though, is at times *downcast at there being no prospect of missionaries to take with him* back to the Xhosa. Perhaps this reciprocal arrangement is the one Jan Tzatzoe had in mind when he convinced himself that he could best serve the interests of his people and his fellow chiefs by traveling to England. It is another expectation that Tzatzoe will have to address upon his return to Xhosaland; another hope that may remain unfulfilled.[21]

Tzatzoe and Read's base while in Scotland is in Glasgow, where Dr. Philip's son is attending a seminary. In tender letters to his family (he imagines his sister, Eliza's, letter, *now speeding its way through the mighty Atlantic or flying along in the boot of the Glasgow mail*), Durant Philip describes his encounters with Read and Tzatzoe. Tzatzoe seems thrilled by his visit across the English border:

> The Scotch are in his estimation the *cleverest* people in the world because they have large mountains and because of the Caledonian Canal through which he passed. The Scenery quite enchanted him and with the Gaelic language he thought himself in Caffreland again, amongst his native hills & vallies. He was pleased also with the avidity with which the Highlanders heard the gospel preach so that the minister was obliged to go from the chapel & preach in the marketplace. He seems to have forgotten England amongst the beauties of Scotland and it is only brought to shew the superiority of Scotland.[22]

Durant also has a surprise for his sister: *At two meetings the Chief spoke in English, one of which speeches was a very good one*. Can this newly acquired ability be verified? In fact, upon Tzatzoe's return to Cape Town in 1838 Durant Philip's father will stun the audience of a Missionary Meeting held to celebrate the return of the travelers by announcing that Tzatzoe wishes to address them in English. *He knew but little English*, Tzatzoe will begin, *yet he wished as far as he was able, to tell the Meeting something of what he had heard and seen in England*. According to the news correspondent who will cover the meeting, Tzatzoe's English, *though broken*, is *perfectly intelligible*. Learning English and then having the confidence to speak in it before large crowds is startling evidence that Tzatzoe is making every effort to speak for himself, to let his voice be heard.[23]

Of the many meetings in Scotland, and the varied transcripts of Jan Tzatzoe's speeches, his address to a large public meeting in the Secession Church in Kelso on a Monday evening in early August 1837 is particularly noteworthy. The speech encompasses the ongoing evolution of Tzatzoe's thought and oratorical skill while in Britain (as seen in the Sheffield and Exeter Hall speeches), in addition to having several compelling and unique passages.[24]

A central town of the Scottish Borders Region, Kelso is located at the confluence of the Tweed and Teviot Rivers, and features (uniquely in Scotland) a cobblestone square that is fed by four cobbled avenues. Of Tzatzoe and Read's visit, the *Kelso Chronicle* editorializes: *we have never witnessed a meeting in Kelso where during so long a period the interest was so profound and unbroken, or the audience was so numerous.* The audience, *composed of all denominations*, hears Tzatzoe employ a biblical exegesis of the story of the man of Macedonia:

> He stood before them as the man of Macedonia stood before Paul, saying "Come over and help us, lest we perish." When the man of Macedonia appeared to Paul he appeared only in a vision, but (the Chief) stood before them a living man from Africa, crying unto them, "Come over and help us."

Tzatzoe takes on the role of spokesman or ambassador for his people and nation. Building on the biblical verse, Tzatzoe argues that he embodies the promise of Christianity and also the dire need of the Xhosa and of Africa as a whole. By identifying the difference between Paul's vision and his own physical presence in Kelso, Tzatzoe reinforces the reach of the empire in which his audience are enmeshed, and the new possibilities for the growth of Christianity that this far-flung web of trade and cultural contact now presents. For Tzatzoe to be present in front of them in person (replacing a mere vision) is to present a specific and distinct example of evangelical and colonial progress to his audience, and to encourage their continued support for this work.

Tzatzoe next reinforces that his message is far larger than himself, and that every member of the audience has a critical part to play. He uses religious language that surely allays any humanitarian or missionary concern that he might have left his Christian convictions behind in favor of a political agenda:

> When the man of Macedonian [sic] appeared to Paul he spoke only to himself. But what numbers were there here; and he now addressed each individual to come over and help them. When the man of Macedonia spoke to Paul, he did not say come over and help me—no, he wanted Paul to come over and help his people; and so it was with him, he wanted them to send missionaries to Africa to teach his people the way of salvation through a crucified redeemer.

Having spoken so confidently about the religious underpinnings of his belief, specifically of *salvation* through a *crucified redeemer*, Tzatzoe immediately confounds. *Those to whom he now solicited them to send the gospel were in a perishing condition, and they had this evening heard how destitute they were, and what need there was for missionaries*, Tzatzoe adds, using language that might equally refer to material discomfort or spiritual poverty.

> He was of opinion that the old people who first sent abroad the gospel wished that the Africans should be civilized as well as evangelized; and this opinion [was] confirmed [by the] frequency with which he was asked in England—"Were the ladies in his country beginning to wear bonnets?"
> He believed that they desired that the Africans should enjoy the comfort and improvement of civilized life; but before they can obtain these they must have the means to procure them. They wanted in Africa men to give them that knowledge which maketh wise unto salvation.

In addition to eternal salvation, Tzatzoe is concerned about material progress, the *comfort and improvement of civilized life*. He feels that Africans can gain this elevated material status if given the *means to procure* it, and interestingly, he calls these means *knowledge*, and specifically, knowledge that *maketh wise unto salvation*. It appears that this is a secular salvation, one that addresses the *perishing condition* of the people. This theme of a secular salvation that can be joined to a spiritual awakening is one that Tzatzoe will bring back to the Cape. He will explain, in English, to the Cape Town Missionary Meeting:

> That he then stood there, was owing to the Missionaries. But for them, he would be among the hundreds who had not heard the gospel, and who know of no other object in life but to hunt game, and bring home honey, and go after cattle. As soon as the gospel takes hold of the heart, then the people take the spade and work the ground, they take the axe and cut down the tree,—they begin to build the house. Before that they have not clothes, they rob and they kill.

In both Kelso and Cape Town Tzatzoe encapsulates the standard missionary and humanitarian rhetoric, the notion that Christianity and Western civilization in encountering native people bring with them new and better ways of working, of dressing, of building, of living.[25] Tzatzoe only mentions the positive consequences of the colonial encounter, but he does not limit himself to the fatuous pleasantries such an audience would expect to hear from him. He seizes on specific aspects of Western civilization that he wishes to introduce to his countrymen, such as more productive agricultural methods and sturdier homesteads. But for a man born, raised, and living in a festering border region, the child of a Khoisan mother whose people have faced hundreds of years of persecution from African and European colonizers, and a Xhosa father whose life was spent hopping from one insecure foothold to another, the most astounding aspect of his visit to Great Britain is the sense of peace on the island.

During his tour of England and Scotland, Tzatzoe tells those gathered in the Secession Church, he had seen castles and towers *mouldering into dust*. He realized that the British no longer *destroyed each other in war* as they had at *times* in their *history*, and hence had no use for the fortifications in this *present enlightened and civilized age*:

> Instead of fighting with guns and swords as formerly, the inhabitants of these countries now fight with pen and ink. The printing press and the newspaper have superseded the use of all other weapons of warfare. This was the happy style in which the people of England and Scotland were; and it was the warmest wish of his heart that his people should also be brought into the same happy condition.

Tzatzoe's manifests concern for his people's souls, but more importantly, for their earthly lives. Tzatzoe has spent eighteen months touring Great Britain, and more than the railroads, bursting halls, and churches, this peace is worthy of mention. He will be true to his word in carrying news of this *happy condition* home, and he will start at the Cape Town Missionary Meeting, upon his immediate return, when he will summarize the lessons of his time in Britain:

> He told the English that men should come and teach the Caffres, and make for them Colleges, and teach them Greek, and Latin, and Hebrew, and English, and then the Caffres would have a House of Commons, and a House of Lords, and then they would only fight like the English with a newspaper. . . . Then will come the time when the assagai will be put down, and nations will only fight with the book and newspaper.[26]

Jan Tzatzoe will attempt to propagate this new vision for the eastern Cape for the rest of his years, but it will dance before him like a mirage, shimmering and seductive in the summer air.

During Tzatzoe and Read's time in Great Britain, the Aborigines Committee has served as a window into the process of British colonization, and the public imagination has been fired. In 1837 a London newspaper, the *Sun*, summarizes the proceedings in terms that would make Exeter Hall cheer:

> Wherever our standard has been planted, and the land taken to form part of our dominion, the inhabitants have been hunted, ploughed, or starved out of existence, with much cruelty and wanton waste of human life. Instead of looking on the Aborigines as infants confided to our care, whom we are bound to protect and instruct in all our civilization, England has almost uniformly regarded them as wild beasts, of whom the land could not too soon be cleared.[27]

The Aborigines Committee's final report, which is published in late June 1837, harshly denounces British colonialism in South Africa and stands as a strident defense of the central beliefs of the humanitarian ideology, including the notion that the *native inhabitants of any land have an incontrovertible right to their own soil: a plain and sacred right, however, which does not seem to have been understood*. The report's final statement on the War of Hintza, as it terms the recent conflict, however, reveals a degree of excision, particularly with regard to the mass of evidence that it had accumulated about the Cape Colony: *While we purposely abstain from dwelling upon the circumstances which immediately produced it*, it concludes, *we, without hesitation, name its real, though perhaps remote cause—it was the systematic forgetfulness of the principles of justice in our treatment of the native possessors of the soil.*[28]

In fact, *after a great deal of poking at his conscience*, Buxton had agreed to the *censoring* of the report produced by himself and his co-authors, including Anna Gurney:

> I bore it well at first, but when I saw him [Sir George Grey] put his ugly scratch against our stinging morsels, I almost fainted with horror. Still, I think we shall retain almost all that is necessary—though the ornamental will surely perish. Such gashes and ghastly wounds as he has had the heart to make.[29]

Buxton is unduly concerned. His report's strident humanitarian rhetoric will not only live in posterity, it will survive as a symbol of the end of one epoch and the beginning of another.

For on the morning of Tuesday 20 June 1837 the British public learns that King William IV has died. His niece Victoria ascends to the throne. In the years prior to Victoria's ascension, Buxton, Philip, the LMS, and the humanitarian movement have gained their greatest victories and risen to a remarkable level of political and cultural influence in Britain. But this is their high-water mark. While they have pronounced and inquired, advised and even dictated policy changes, they have done so against an onrushing economic, social, and political tide of change. In the face of this tumult, they have erected barriers and dug trenches in order to divert the waters around small pieces of territory. In some few cases, they have built arks that have borne individuals and small groups to safety. These ships will ride the waves for a while before they too are submerged into its depths. As the tendrils of the tide begin to creep over the final report of the Aborigines Committee, what will Jan Tzatzoe, as a *native possessor of the soil of Africa*, of the red earth, and of the waters of the Buffalo River, do?[30]

Jan Tzatzoe and Read attend their last meeting in England on Tuesday 17 October 1837. The *Farewell Meeting* for the LMS is held at Exeter Hall.

More than 4,000 people, the *greater part consisting of elegantly-dressed ladies*, say good-bye to Philip, Read, and Tzatzoe, along with thirty or so missionaries and their wives destined for service in India, South Africa, and the South Sea Islands. Tzatzoe's speech is brief. He thanks the crowd in his usual manner for sending missionaries to Africa and promises *not to forget them. He will be constantly looking up to God for his blessing upon them.* He refers to the gifts of the King's grandchildren to him, and the clothes and other *articles* with which he is returning. These alone will serve to convince his countrymen that they have friends in England. Words will not be necessary.[31]

In an editorial written in January 1838 to celebrate Tzatzoe and Read's impending return to the eastern Cape, the *South African Commercial Advertiser* will reference Tzatzoe's statement to the Farewell Meeting. Tzatzoe had said that he would return to Xhosaland with *clothes and other things*, donated by the British, which would convince his people that they have friends in England:

> These gifts will not be confined to clothes. Teachers, artizans, implements of husbandry, will be furnished with liberality, with all the instruments by which society is raised into order and happiness.... Tzatzoe will speedily be among them and speak to their eyes as well as to their ears. We can assure them, he brings "News," which they will call "Good."[32]

How to greet loved ones? How to convey the new sights and sounds and ideas? Will Tzatzoe's fellow chiefs dismiss him or embrace him? Will he reform his partnership in mission with John Brownlee? After months spent as the object of veneration and appreciation, how will he endure the deprecations of the racial order on the frontier—from the petty calumny to the institutionalized land alienation? What news will Jan Tzatzoe bring home?

As the party prepares to leave England for their return voyage, they must convey the news ahead of them by mail that they are not bringing the one gift most keenly anticipated by James Read Junior. *The young person that was to come as wife for James is no more*, Read writes to the Cape, *her poor sister is distracted*. James is back at the Kat River Settlement awaiting his father's return. He will receive the news of his fiancée's death with the *resignation of a Christian*.[33]

Philip, Read, and Tzatzoe embark upon the *David Scott* on 25 November 1837. The Reverend G. Schreiner and his wife accompany them, along with *three young females, one for a school, a niece of Mrs. Philip and a young female as wife for Mr Blore*. The Schreiners intend to establish themselves among the Xhosa in the eastern Cape. A variety of circumstances will take them northwards instead, into the interior of the country, where their daughter, Olive (whose novel *A Story of an African Farm* will be hailed as one of South Africa's preeminent literary accomplishments and a major monument in the worldwide feminist movement), will be born in 1855. In latter years do Gottlieb and Rebecca Schreiner tell their daughter stories about their sea-voyage to the Cape? The evening prayers, the daily Dutch lessons during which the whole party, with the exception of Philip, read a portion of Scripture, and translate it into Dutch? Their fellow passengers who are *any thing but agreeable—Infidels* and *scorners* who speak with the *filthy conversation of the wicked*. Having anchored the previous evening in Table Bay, the travelers disembark in Cape Town on Wednesday, 7 February 1838.[34]

Part Three

Tzatzoe In Kuruman

I needed to find Jan Tzatzoe. Not only in microfilmed newspapers and leather-bound volumes yellowed by foxing, but in person. I needed a corporeal presence, a literal embodiment. I queried the Internet, followed leads dug up at conferences, spoke to the appropriate officials and received the requisite permissions. It took me two days to get from Johannesburg to the Kuruman mission station, stately with syringa trees. When I got there, no one seemed to know where Tzatzoe was.[1]

We looked in the old mission church, a beautiful spacious T-shaped structure, with carefully restored stone walls and thatching. In 1838 the original timber roof beams (long and strong enough to support the largest structure in the interior of Africa to that point) had been transported almost three hundred miles by ox-wagon from territory under Mzilikazi's control near the Witwatersrand. The impeccable mud and dung floor is remade in a "traditional" manner, every three months, from cattle dung and local red clay. We looked in the modern archive and classroom building, constructed with funding from a local asbestos-mining operation. We looked in the visitors' center. We looked in the outbuilding that housed the original mission printing press, the first to be carried into the interior of Africa. I wandered through the mission gardens, along the hand-hewn walls of the mile-long irrigation canal, pausing under the tree by which David Livingstone proposed to the daughter of Kuruman's most famous missionary, Robert Moffat.

Jan Tzatzoe ended up being in the last place we looked. He rested in a dark and well-shaded corner of the airy mission house, about four hundred miles from home. Backed by a coarse, whitewashed, stone wall, he stood next to an elderly James Read and James Read Junior. John Philip cocked one quizzical eye at his companions. Andries Stoffels was there, too, serious in a high-collared black coat. I couldn't quite believe my eyes. This was not the Tzatzoe I had come to know from a black-and-white engraving.

The magnificent oil painting, resplendent in a burnished gold frame, by Room of the London Missionary Society delegation from South Africa has been at Kuruman since 1990, when in a fit of good spirit, the current incarnation of the LMS—in whose London headquarters, Livingstone House, the picture had been hanging for one hundred and thirty years—decided to repatriate it to South Africa.[2] John Philip undoubtedly visited the Kuruman mission and, in disgrace, James Read lived nearby with his family.

But it seems like an abbreviated outcome for Jan Tzatzoe and Andries Stoffels to end up on the fringe of the Kalahari Desert, so far from the arcing Amathole Mountains. Appropriate that these African leaders are finally back in Africa, recognized for their contributions to mission work by featuring in the most famous LMS mission of them all. Unfortunate, that they are so far from home.

The room, though high-ceilinged, was dark, with no artificial lighting and windows sized appropriately for a hot climate and an age when glass was particularly dear. I didn't have a flash for my camera, but I took photographs of the portrait nonetheless. I had them developed in Rosebank, a bustling shopping center in Johannesburg, where the increasingly affluent and expanding black middle class meets the old white suburbs. I told the photography shop attendant that they were special, that I had taken a whole roll of just one individual in the hopes that a single picture would emerge out of the dark. He asked who he was and I told him that he was an African chief and missionary who lived in the eastern Cape. The assistant replied that his grandfather had also been a chief, but that I probably wouldn't have heard of him, since no one else around here had.

Who?
Albert Luthuli, he answered.
Of course, I know him, I replied. President of the ANC. Nobel Prize winner.
Fitting for one chief and leader to meet the grandson of another.
But who in this new country would care?

KING WILLIAM'S TOWN

The war of words is the best war

1838–1845

After landing in Cape Town in February 1838, Jan Tzatzoe meets with the newly appointed Governor of the Cape Colony, Sir George Napier, and receives a *handsome present as a mark of his esteem*. He suffers with James Read and the Schreiners through an unpleasant voyage back to Algoa Bay on a small, leaky ship. Upon learning that their first choice of vessel was *wrecked* before reaching the eastern Cape, Read sees the work of an *overruling providence*. News of their arrival at Algoa Bay in March 1838 travels quickly. Two of Tzatzoe's brothers and *several of his people* undertake the one hundred and fifty mile journey from King William's Town to Port Elizabeth to greet him. *Every Mountain, every valley, every inch of ground appeared precious in my sight*, Read writes to Reverend Ellis of the London Missionary Society, *it has required something to be convinced that all I have witnessed is reality and not a dream.* Tzatzoe must wait a little while longer to see the land of his birth. Does he join Read in exulting in their first night spent camping in the open air, a night that Read confesses to have *longed for when lying on the feather beds in England*?[1]

Maqoma meets the party near the Kat River Settlement, hosting them for a night of feasting at his kraals. Together they journey to Philipton, where they watch Read reunite with his family and his congregation. Maqoma sends *word to the other chiefs. They spent a few days together in talking of what I had seen in England*, Tzatzoe reports to the Directors of the LMS. Tzatzoe is anxious to share his experiences from across the ocean with the leading chiefs of Xhosaland. Despite their reputed protestations upon his departure that Tzatzoe's thoughts and feelings are of little relevance to them, the chiefs appear to be equally anxious to hear from him.[2]

Instead of the complete transcript of Jan Tzatzoe's reunion with his fellow chiefs (of all the discussions in Tzatzoe's life) with which posterity might be blessed, there is only this: *how kindly I had been received by the Christians of England and how greatly they had felt for the Caffers and other natives of the other parts of the world.* Yet Tzatzoe's descriptions of what he *had seen* in England will disperse widely. In 1839 an English traveler will spend a night at a Xhosa village east of the Kei River, where the inhabitants will have *heard of the vast population of England, and of traveling by steam upon railroads, and of various other incidents from their countryman, Jan Tzatzoe.*[3]

Tzatzoe cautions his audience that *they must maintain peace with the Colony*—this he was instructed to do by Lord Glenelg himself as well as by the *Advertiser* as a condition for the receipt of the *gifts* of British civilization—but he assures them that they have a sympathetic ear in Cape Town. Should the *colonists illtreat us we must complain to the Governor,* and *he would see that justice is done.*

Finally it is time for Jan Tzatzoe's homecoming. He rides to meet his family and people on the banks of the Buffalo River. If any ill feeling exists toward him for the manner in which he left in the early days of 1836, these concerns have evaporated as the seasons have passed:

> I found my wife and children quite well. It was a great day for my people who stood about me, gazed at me and said how stout you are. How well you look. We can see that you have been treated well by that nation. Have you really been over the great waters? And come back unharmed? Can you really now see that these people are our friends. Some said how often did you outspan? Where and how did you cook your victuals? To all these questions I had to give answers. I told them I was treated as kindly and tenderly as if I had been a little child in England and Scotland.

How can a dinner at the Buxtons be compared to an outspan—a night spent camping while on journey with ox-wagon and oxen? What does Tzatzoe recall for his family? The immensity of Exeter Hall? The sun setting over the Scottish heath? There are a thousand other questions to ponder.[4] To all these and other questions, there are no answers.

In the decades between the first meeting of Jan Tzatzoe and James Read at Algoa Bay in 1804 and their arrival in the Eastern Cape in the autumn of 1838 (with the occasional drought), Tzatzoe's name and actions and opinions appear in the historical record of the time—in missionary letters, colonial officers' reports, newspaper articles, even missives signed by the chief himself—with a frequency akin to the myriad small pools and vleis of rainwater that materialize in the veld after the soaking summer rains. But in the years following Tzatzoe's return home in 1838, a merciless sun will bake the mud of many of the vleis into ripples of rocky clay. Those that remain will become shallower and more widely dispersed. Historians must meet at them like wildlife converging around waterholes in the dry season.

The Forty-Fifth Report of the LMS for 1838 lists Jan Tzatzoe as a *Missionary* in the Buffalo River mission. Every other LMS mission in the colony lists only Europeans as Missionaries. Still the society displays an uneasy confidence in Tzatzoe (despite the *very pleasing letter* received from him in September 1838). *His attention appears to be considerably diverted by the secular duties devolving on him as head of his tribe*, the report regrets. Tzatzoe has not stopped believing or professing; he is, however, preoccupied.[5]

The demise of Governor D'Urban and Colonel Smith's Queen Adelaide Province has left the border region in an unsettled political and social state. Most troubled is the region closest to the British. While this territory, between the Fish and the Keiskamma, nominally belongs to the British, Xhosa chiefs have been allowed to resettle it. Jan Tzatzoe's amaNtinde and the amaGqunukhwebe of Pato are located closest to the colony. Settled next to Fort Peddie, Pato is keen to curry favor with the British.

Besides dealing with his people's location in an especially troubled region, Tzatzoe is faced with dangerous infighting within the Xhosa state. The trouble had begun in October 1836, when a *most unjustifiable aggression on certain kraals located on the location of Jan T'zatzoe* had occurred. On 19 October Tzatzoe's brother, Nolo, reported to Captain Charles Lennox Stretch, the British government's diplomatic agent for the region from the Chumie to King William's Town, that a *Patrole* (that Nolo felt had been sent by Maqoma) had taken over 200 hundred head of cattle from Jan Tzatzoe's village, had injured several men and killed one.

Within a day or two, however, the cattle had been remanded and compensation paid. Suthu, the great wife of Ngqika (who had died in 1829), and the mother of the active and ambitious Maqoma, had been the aggressor. Maqoma, now in his mid-thirties, and his brother, Tyalie, had restored peace. But a message had been sent. Without the protection of their chief, the amaNtinde were in a particularly vulnerable position. In 1837 members of the Ngqika lineages once again raided the amaNtinde kraals.[6]

In late August 1838 Tzatzoe must deal with another potentially explosive case. Jacob Baushe, described by Tzatzoe as a *Caffer of my tribe*, and his wife are returning to King William's Town after four years of service in Graham's

Town. Close to the new colonial boundary, two of Pato's men confiscate Jacob's cattle and other goods. According to the new treaties, Pato has the obligation to arrest any Xhosa passing past his kraals who have strayed from the main road onto bypaths, and who are in possession of cattle or goods that they cannot prove they have obtained legally by showing a written pass to that effect. Jacob immediately complains to Jan Tzatzoe, who sends him straight back to Fort Peddie to see Pato and the resident colonial official, John Mitford Bowker, the scion of a prominent British settler family. Bowker rejects Jacob's claim out of hand, while verbally abusing him.

A few days later Tzatzoe leaves to visit friends in the colony, and in his chief's absence, Jacob attacks Pato in order to exact retribution from the men who confiscated his cattle. Pato and Bowker accuse Tzatzoe of allowing *unjustifiable conduct* by his people. Pato promises his own reprisals. Tzatzoe demands that Pato apologize for the initial confiscation. During the next two months, minor skirmishes break out between the groups.

Although I was angry with them [Jacob and his brother] *for having in my absence helped themselves, I have nonetheless detained the twenty head of cattle until an investigation takes place,* Tzatzoe writes to Stretch, *and if any of my followers have given just cause for this breach of the Caffer laws, I shall be the first to say, punish them, but I cannot tolerate the robbery of my people and when inquiry is demanded from the proper authorities, it is refused.* Tzatzoe positions himself as a secular leader, demanding respect from his followers, and also due process and fully equal status from the colonial officials. As in his speeches in England, he appears to be asking the British to keep their word and to treat the Xhosa as full partners. Tzatzoe is acting under the impression that a colonial official such as Bowker bears no higher rank than himself in political matters, and in fact, should defer to his knowledge and expertise.

During this acme of humanitarian influence on the frontier, an investigation is, in fact, carried out. With regard to the initial confrontation, Pato's men testify that Jacob was sighted far from the main road, that he asked a young boy from their kraal how he could avoid Bowker's residence, and that he could not produce a pass to legitimate his cattle. In reply Jacob contends that he detoured off the main road in order to visit a friend who was to give him two more head of cattle, and that he had, indeed, produced a pass that had immediately been torn to shreds by his interrogators.

On Jacob's trip back to Pato, when he had asked Bowker for restitution, Bowker's translator, George Cyrus, testifies that Bowker told Jacob that, if their claim was just, they could simply return to the colony to get another pass. Jacob refused, claiming that his *orders* from his *Chief* were to *demand* that Bowker send his own messengers to Graham's Town to verify the pass. Bowker, in turn, blames Jacob for deviating from the main, or high, road. If he had not done this, he would have been able to show Bowker his pass directly, and been allowed to pass. Jacob replies: *What new thing is this, that we cannot go in our own country with cattle where we please?*

In late November 1838 Suthu's councilors, who represent the leadership of the Ngqika lineages, decide to act on behalf of Jan Tzatzoe. The councilors ask Bowker to initiate a meeting between Pato and Tzatzoe in Suthu's name. Under the direction of Suthu's councilors, both sides exchange cattle to resolve the matter. The incident with Pato reveals a shift in the relationship between the amaNtinde and the Ngqika lineages. Unexpected as it is may be given Tzatzoe's service with the British against the Ngqika in the war of 1834–1835, their suspicion of his trip to England, and their attacks on the amaNtinde while he was in Britain, Tzatzoe's newfound bond to Suthu, Maqoma, and the other major chiefs is welcomed by both sides. As the future leader of the Ngqika, Sandile, Suthu's son and Maqoma's half-brother, will be the ultimate beneficiary of Tzatzoe's knowledge, diplomatic skill, and colonial connections.[7]

An unlikely pair of visitors calls upon Jan Tzatzoe in King William's Town early in 1839. Englishmen James Backhouse, a botanist, and George Washington Walker are Quaker missionaries. They have spent six years working in Australia and Mauritius, and they are engaged in an extensive journey around South Africa. A fastidious observer, Backhouse records his impressions of many of the locations and landscapes central to Tzatzoe's forty-five or so years in the eastern Cape.

Bethelsdorp (upon their visit on 8 December 1838) is a *square of whitewashed, red-tiled, stone houses,* but *far from an improving* station, due to extensive droughts. Port Elizabeth reminds Backhouse of a *small English sea-port,* a *town* said to *have been chiefly raised by the sale of strong drink.* Heading east toward the Sundays River, Backhouse notices many different species of *Euphorbias*; at night, hyenas harass the camp. There appears to have been little change in the vegetation of the region over the course of the nineteenth century. Using scientifically precise and restrained language, Backhouse describes an open savanna dotted with anthills, acacia, and *caulescent* aloes, interspersed by ravines choked with dense forest (still the home of buffalo, rhinoceros, elephant, and lion).[8]

The appearance of *some Earth-worms of great size* (the longest measures 3 *feet 8 inches*) after a thunderstorm distinguishes the journey from Graham's Town—a large town of around *four thousand inhabitants,* but with only one *spacious* street, which serves as its *market-place*—to Philipton in the Kat River Settlement. On 22 February 1839 Backhouse proceeds over dry hills covered with yellow-flowered Doorn-boom acacias to reach King William's Town.

Jan Tzatzoe, living alongside the Brownlees, in a house built by Colonel Smith's now-withdrawn army, is a gracious host and interpreter. One night, Backhouse visits Tzatzoe's house where he meets Sanna Oursen. To Backhouse, Tzatzoe is *by far the most enlightened Caffer* that they have *met with. I was comforted while sitting a short time with him, in a very perceptible feeling of the love of our Heavenly Father, uniting our hearts in Gospel fellowship,* Backhouse recalls, *notwithstanding no words were spoken on the occasion.* Next door, however, inside another European house, Kote Tzatzoe and his brother do not show *much change from the ordinary habits* of the Xhosa. They are seated on a mud floor around a small fire, smoking tobacco.[9]

A better-known pair of travelers, Dr. John Philip and his wife, Jane, pay the Buffalo River station a visit in June 1839. The Philipses still trust Tzatzoe to translate their sermons and conduct their interactions with the local Africans. They praise him for the large amount of ground he has under cultivation and for his perseverance in assisting John Brownlee in building irrigation canals from the Buffalo (even after thirteen years the local terrain has prevented their completion and the mission fields can only grow maize and millet due to drought conditions). But they are shocked by his living conditions that strike them as squalid and hardly befitting a Christianized and civilized chief.

Yes, the *appearance of his dwelling* is superior to that of the other Xhosa chiefs, but it is also *disappointing*. The whitewash on the rooms of Tzatzoe's house is still wet. The dwelling reveals the *appearance of a cleaning up*, Jane Philip writes, *which made us to fear that it was not always so clean as could be wished.* The windows remain unglazed, even though the Philipses *knew Jan Tzatzoe had brought glass with him from England.*[10]

As with the glass, it appears to John and Jane Philip that Tzatzoe is not using the cultural, intellectual, and spiritual tools he has gained in South Africa and Great Britain to separate himself and his family from the environment of heathenism and barbarism that surround them. During his absence Tzatzoe's son underwent the Xhosa circumcision rites, and his wife and daughter contravened Brownlee's instructions by attending Xhosa ritual dances. Now a second son threatens to follow the path of his elder brother.

Jane Philip takes Tzatzoe's wife and daughter aside, *urging upon them repentance and an entire changing conduct.* Sanna Oursen seems *affected*, and she promises to *endeavour to return unto the hand against whom she acknowledges she has sinned.* Jane Philip also talks to Tzatzoe's daughter about her conduct of the Infant School, *pointing out some things which she might improve and advising her to study the lesson herself before she taught them to the children. She has a large supply of materials,* Philip complains, *but does not know how to turn them to use.*

Later that evening, John Philip remonstrates with Jan Tzatzoe, taking the occasion to talk *faithfully* with him *respecting the state of his family and what appeared to be his own deficiencies.* Philip *points out the necessity of more exertion on Tzatzoe's part as an agent of the Society particularly in itinerating as well as the necessity of general improvement in the government and discipline of his family. I heard he will be stirred up to greater exertion,* Jane Philip summarizes, *but much allowance must be made for the people with whom he is connected and the business he has to transact respecting his tribe.*

The more tolerant and pluralistic middle ground of Van der Kemp and James Read, of Friedrich Kayser and even Joseph Williams, a world that was made by both Tzatzoe and the missionaries with whom he worked, is no more. Humanitarians like the Philipses live in a world that has swept aside slavery and reversed colonial expansion; their expectations have been raised, as has their chauvinistic and paternalistic arrogance. They now expect to remake the colonial world, and they demand that their subjects meet the European standards of respectability that govern acceptance and assimilation into the ambit of British culture and civilization.[11] To see Jan Tzatzoe, the man whom they have spent years praising, and on whose behalf they have made countless promises of transformation, returned to circumstances that do not allow for this vision to be brought into effect—or worse, refusing to partake of it—must be deeply troubling. It appears that Tzatzoe can, or will, not be the man they have promised their followers in Britain, and perhaps, promised themselves he would be.

John Brownlee has quietly (and to his mind, reluctantly) been relaying a similar critique of Tzatzoe's behavior to his London Missionary Society superiors. A few months before the Philipses' visit, he questioned the chief's piety (he never saw him *seeking seasons of retirement* for prayer on his own) and his itinerating (for which he showed *no disposition, although often remonstrated with*).[12] In 1838 Brownlee had extended this critique to include Tzatzoe's leadership position within the Xhosa state. *The sphere in which he might most benefit cause of God might be by exerting his influence as a Christian chief, and by endeavouring to abolish some superstitious customs which are very injurious to the spiritual and temporal interest of the people,* Brownlee reported, but *I am sorry to say there is a great influence exerted against him not only by his own relations, but also by some of the superior chiefs.*[13]

Brownlee and the Philipses are hardly sympathetic to the difficulty of the choices placed before Jan Tzatzoe upon his return to the amaNtinde. Still, even as they condemn his behavior and rue his decisions, their comments acknowledge that this new humanitarian world to which they would like to see Tzatzoe wholly committed is not the only new world, or set of expectations, in which the African leader must live, or to which he feels himself beholden. Tzatzoe's secular duties as a political figure among the Xhosa have come to occupy a central place in his life. As Brownlee reports: *The constant intercourse he has at all times with the Kafirs when awake must have a paralizing effect on his mind.* He must ensure the political and material prosperity of the amaNtinde within the Xhosa state, the more powerful leaders of which appear to value his counsel, but also likely maintain a suspicion of his vacillating behavior in the last war (and as a curse of his status as an intermediary) his proximity to the British. In addition Tzatzoe faces an increasingly hostile, racist, and vocal population of British settlers who are encroaching on Xhosa land, and testing the possibilities of their brute power. He must reestablish relationships within his family after two years' absence, and steer through the rapids of his own expectations and disappointments after a journey in which he saw unimaginable worlds and in which he was feted and celebrated and praised at every turn. *He looks back to England with very kindly feelings and would I am persuaded be glad to return if he could do it,* Jane Philip allows.

Years later, Tzatzoe will claim that he refused to itinerate in 1838 and 1839 because, unbeknownst to the LMS, John Brownlee had begun to withhold Tzatzoe's salary as an assistant missionary.[14] In addition to his concern over his pay, the incident suggests that a clash of personalities emerges during this period between Tzatzoe and an increasingly bombastic and censorious Brownlee, who (while he doesn't decry it in his letters and reports) is surely frustrated with his lack of success in converting the people of the mission to an appropriate level of Christian piety. Tzatzoe finds himself, a man who has commanded the respect of thousands in England and who has spoken with Lords and British royalty, being forced into a position of subservience, and his hesitance to itinerate may be a quiet refusal to bow before any of Brownlee's demands.

Speaking of Tzatzoe's family's decision to turn their back on Christian practices, Brownlee accuses Tzatzoe of *want of principle and decision* in his inability to impose the requisite demonstration of his continued Christian belief and British mores of civilization on his people, and even on his family. Yet Tzatzoe's actions can be understood as a series of wrenching decisions that result from complex personal and political calculations (and, yes, competing principles) of how to locate himself and his followers amidst the influences in his new life in the border region. Tzatzoe is struggling against an increasingly powerful strand of paternalism in the ideology of the missionaries with whom he is working. He can gain respect from his African followers and fellow chiefs. Little wonder that he turns toward them.

The smallest pool of sources relating to Jan Tzatzoe's life upon his return to the eastern Cape border region is, perhaps, also the deepest and most reflective. In December 1840 the Governor of the Cape Colony, Sir George Napier, calls the Xhosa chiefs to a grand meeting to revise and strengthen the colonial treaties under which they have been living since 1837. The ongoing concern is cattle raiding across the border region (or the *constant plundering of our farmers*, as Napier writes to Lord Russell, head of the Colonial Office in London), and the chiefs continue to maintain that while they have little direct control over their subjects, they are doing their best to bring the thieves to justice. Jan Tzatzoe, seated amongst the chiefs, delivers a speech that reiterates the language and political understandings he had expressed in London, throughout Great Britain, and upon his return to Cape Town. Here is a leader who still seeks truthfulness behind British intention and action, who wishes to engage diplomatically with the British to further both their and the Xhosa state's interests, and to do so in a less destructive manner. His statement to Napier and the chiefs reiterates his commitment to fighting for justice with the pen and ink, the book and the newspaper:

> We thank you that you came to see the children of the Amakosa; we thank you that you came to see the sons of Gaika, and that every Kafir will be able to say, that you are their father—they will now consider you as their father! The war of words is the best war—unlike the war of weapons.

Unfortunately, for Jan Tzatzoe, and for South Africa, the time for a war of words is eroding; wars of weapons loom on the horizon.[15]

Between 1840 and 1844 British settlers, encouraged by a growing export market in wool, and with the colonial government increasingly on their side, expropriate more and more African land. Reverend Brownlee increasingly monopolizes the church, though he converts few Africans. The Commando system once again rears its head as the colonial government (blaming the chiefs for failing to recover stolen colonial cattle and punish cattle thieves) abrogates the treaties that Stockenstrom, at the height of the humanitarian influence in the Cape Colony, put in place to supervise cattle thieving in the region. One night Tzatzoe and Stretch together observe the settlers of Fort Beaufort celebrating the reversal of the treaties with riotous rejoicing, drunkenness, and the burning, in effigy, of both Philip and Stockenstrom. *The clamour was triumphant*, Stretch will later remember, and a *novel sight* for Tzatzoe and several other Xhosa leaders.[16]

Stretch places the blame for the breakdown of the détente squarely on the colonial side. In a memorandum reviewing the so-called Treaty system, Stretch notes that the colonial government didn't commit enough forces to ensure a secure border. Worse, the chiefs felt that they were subject to a double-standard, whereby the colonial government could monitor and arbitrarily punish a chief's subjects while the former were in the colony, but the chiefs were not allowed, in a reciprocal fashion, to police European settlers in their domains. The chiefs also felt insufficiently informed by the colony on changes in political arrangements, and felt a lack of respect regarding the importance of their opinions on these matters.[17]

Acting as a senior diplomat, Jan Tzatzoe brings these feelings to Stretch's attention. This diplomatic work has been at the center of Tzatzoe's chieftainship, along with his mission work, during this period of shifting circumstance. Relying on Tzatzoe's testimony, Stretch notes that the *Gaika chiefs were not even treated with common civility*, and uses as his central example a visit to the border region by a new Governor of the Cape, Sir Peregrine Maitland, in 1844. According to Tzatzoe, Maitland did not *condescend to consult the Heads of the Nations, but commenced at the Tail with the little chiefs at Fort Peddie* (these were Pato and his brothers, who had caused trouble before). Tzatzoe had informed the Governor: *It was not good to get the little dogs barking at the big dogs.*

Stretch further reflects that with the revocation of the treaties, the chiefs and other members of the Xhosa state became suspicious of the Christian missionaries (especially those associated with the Wesleyan churches) amongst them, sensing an imperial agenda lurking behind a Christian façade:

> The chiefs complained that the Governor had been induced by the missionaries to make the change in the country to obtain by force what they could not accomplish by a moral influence, to rule over their people, "to steal their people, and be magistrates and chiefs themselves." They demanded the names of the missionaries and observed Williams and Van der Kemp did not act this way with God's word. . . . The whole country was roused against the Gospel, and the churches and schools were from that day deserted.

Perhaps not incorrectly, the chiefs sense that the missionaries, in their frustration at their lack of evangelical or worldly success, have abandoned their moral underpinnings in a quest for raw, secular power. Having observed in the first half of the decade just passed that the missionaries were able to change colonial policy, and even to replace unsatisfactory officials with more sympathetic ones, it is logical to think that the missionaries might still be able to compel colonial policy, and, at this time, do so in the direction of more coercive policies. In fact, after the repudiations of the Treaties, many of the newly arrived missionaries in the eastern Cape have pushed for provisions in colonial policy that allow for the colonial punishment of any Xhosa who mistreat (in the eyes of the missionaries) those Xhosa who remain on the stations. These provisions also allow for punitive treatment by the missionaries of the subjects living on their stations.

Where do these developments leave Jan Tzatzoe as a representative of the time of Williams and Van der Kemp, a Christian in a country roused against the Gospel, a Xhosa leader whose secular power and diplomatic alliances are being called into question? A few days after Christmas 1844, at the end of a lengthy silence, comes a dire pronouncement. *I think it is very desirable that the Directors should know his true character*, John Brownlee writes of Tzatzoe, *so that no unreasonable expectations may be cherished by having a wrong estimate of him as a Missionary agent*. Brownlee reports negatively on Tzatzoe's potential to work as a native agent, or African missionary, and he does so in a work of revisionist history.[18]

The 1840s are an historical era in which competing visions of South Africa are first being written, histories that often depend on documentary evidence and biographical narratives. Crucial to the liberal humanitarian ideology of John Philip and James Read is the presentation through a biographical lens of a redeemed African, whose character is remade by the evangelical vision, who is *savage-born* but *new-created*.[19] Brownlee needs to explain why Tzatzoe has seemingly rejected the abolitionist-humanitarian vision, of which he had been such a prominent exemplar. Of course Brownlee does not point to his own authoritarian behavior or domineering personality, or to the increasing chauvinism and paternalism of the missionary ideology. He rejects any claim that Tzatzoe and other Africans might make to ownership of Christian ideology and practices.

Rather Brownlee discredits the notion that Tzatzoe had ever been truly remade. In doing so, the missionary adopts the increasingly racialized rhetoric that British settler interests, and even many missionaries, are using to describe the Xhosa—a rhetoric that paints them as inherently aggressive, ungrateful, and irredeemable. With hindsight Brownlee claims to have seen early warning signs of Tzatzoe's rejection of the mission life. During his career with Joseph and Elizabeth Williams, Brownlee says, Tzatzoe revealed *a propensity to those idle habits so common among this people*, but Williams gave *a short account of his real character*. The situation worsened when Tzatzoe joined him at the Buffalo. There he was *again thrown in the midst of his friends. His house was a place of common resort at all times, as a place of lounge and gossip*. Tzatzoe's family came under the *influence of idle retainers* and was constantly instructed in heathenish customs. The worst of these were the initiation ceremonies, where young men and women painted their bodies and went around naked, showing the *mark of heathenism*, where they danced all night and *gross wickedness* was *commonly practiced*. Tzatzoe's return to the Xhosa led to his final downfall: *At the same time, we must make more allowances for him, considering his former character, and the very unfavourable position he is placed in for cultivation of duty. Instead of being supported by any of his family or friends, they lay as a dead weight upon him*.

Brownlee's letter denies Jan Tzatzoe's crucial contributions to the border region—his assistance to the missions, his diplomacy, his evangelical aid in the form of translation—and it reinforces the caricature that the British settler lobby has favored: a weak, petty, dimwitted tool of the humanitarians, whose true nature is ultimately revealed as his humanitarian luster is rubbed away by African superstition and savagery. After the 1840s, in the contest of historical memory, Tzatzoe (and the few European allies he has left, including the Reads) will not be able to re-present this slanderous biography in the European public arena.[20]

But the public presentation falls far from the reality of Jan Tzatzoe's life at the mission, and of Tzatzoe's own sense of himself during this period. Yes, Tzatzoe is increasingly involved in the affairs of the amaNtinde (and the Xhosa as whole) during the time. But his actions perhaps speak less to a withdrawal from the mission and more to his deepening commitment to Xhosa culture and the Xhosa state. In so doing, he seems to have remained true to the vision of peace and *fighting with the pen* that he acquired while in Britain.

Tzatzoe also maintains a connection to the LMS and its Christian teachings, and even to British humanitarian ideals, during this period. In 1849 Tzatzoe will insist that he continues to spread Christianity on his own terms during this period. And in 1845 he will petition the Directors of the LMS for funds to educate his *younger children out of the Colony in some Good School*. His eldest sons have *adopted the Customs of our heathen ancestry*, Tzatzoe will write, which have *done great injury to the cause of God*.[21]

Jan Tzatzoe (despite Brownlee's polarizing picture) is still moving from one world to another, and contributing to both. But in the shifting and dramatic circumstances of the 1840s, in which walls are closing, in which tolerance and pluralism are increasingly hard to find, the LMS appears to be distancing itself from African Christians like him. Where will he turn when the tumultuous waves of war yet again break over the eastern Cape border region in 1846?

BRITISH KAFFRARIA

Our perilous condition and our duties as subjects

1845–1868

In September 1845, more than twenty years after he helped John Brownlee establish the Chumie Mission Station, Jan Tzatzoe stands once more beneath the serrated crags that adorn the ridges of the Amathole mountains. Tzatzoe has joined the other Xhosa chiefs living in the eastern Cape border region for a meeting with Sir Peregrine Maitland, the Governor of the Cape, near Diplomatic Agent Charles Lennox Stretch's Chumie Valley station. The abrogation in 1844 of the so-called Stockenstrom treaties has led to widespread tension. The Xhosa correctly surmise that the British settlers and their government abettors intend to capture more land for themselves. Racial tension polarizes all interactions. Stretch reports that, even among the amaNtinde, there *exists a sullen reckless determination to try their strength with the Colony.*

Brownlee is far more optimistic. In a move that reveals the complex and seemingly contradictory nature of his relationship with Jan Tzatzoe, Brownlee requests one hundred stand of arms from a local British military officer to arm five hundred warriors under Tzatzoe's control. Brownlee assures Captain Maclean that the amaNtinde *will all to a man act with the Government.* While he no longer values Tzatzoe as a Missionary agent, Brownlee does see him as a capable Xhosa leader who has not turned against the British colonial presence, and with whom he still has a meaningful relationship. Brownlee wishes to call on Tzatzoe as a result of a threatening diplomatic crisis, as Joseph Williams did many years before. The missionary faces embarrassment, or worse, if the situation does not unfold as he foresees.[1]

At the Chumie, Maitland's speech addresses *foolish words of defiance* and war-mongering by Sandile (who has now assumed the regency of the Ngqika lineages) and the *young men* under his control:

They [Sandile and his men] ought to know that they can gain nothing by war. England can send an army sufficient to eat up the whole Kafir nation, if necessary, without difficulty. Is the chief Tzatzoe blind, that he does not know this? Or dumb, that he does not tell it to you? Or are you deaf and foolish that you do not hear and understand it?

Maitland expresses himself in a new language of imperial power and control, one that no longer veils its racial and chauvinistic underpinnings. It is a language of frustration and arrogance, and it presages brutal and pitiless action.[2]

Maitland and his subordinate officials in charge of diplomatic relations recognize Jan Tzatzoe as a key Xhosa political figure and intermediary, one through whom they might convey a sense of the power and possibility of the British Empire. In negatively assessing Tzatzoe's contributions to the Buffalo River Mission, John Brownlee has not only underestimated Tzatzoe's continuing commitment to Christianity, but also drastically misunderstood the chief's standing among the Xhosa. In the tense atmosphere of the border region, the *idle gossip* (in Brownlee's words) that has prevented Tzatzoe from itinerating near the mission station is, in fact, high-level diplomatic and political discussion reaching all the way to Sandile. As an example, attempting to locate Sandile in September 1845, Stretch is told: *Sandilla was gone to see Tzatzoe*. Indeed, these newly strengthened ties to the Xhosa state might be strong enough to overwhelm the loyalty on which Brownlee is counting.

When the colonial authorities declare their intentions in March 1846 to invade Xhosaland — ostensibly to redress the emancipation from police custody of a Xhosa man held captive for stealing an axe from a border canteen — Sandile chooses Jan Tzatzoe to ride the fifty miles to Fort Beaufort to make a last-minute plea for peace to Lieutenant-Governor John Hare. Hare insists that Sandile communicate directly to Stretch. Facing a preemptive British invasion, the Xhosa abandon Sandile's Great Place, avoiding a direct confrontation with superior British firepower.[3]

Tzatzoe returns to the burning capital before retreating to King William's Town. Here, he hears news that the *wagons* have *been burnt*. Employing horses and guns the Xhosa armies (led by Maqoma) have been ambushing the British forces as the red coats meander around Xhosaland employing search-and-destroy tactics. In one spectacular success the Xhosa have decimated the British army's long supply train, capturing many wagons filled with china, ammunition, food, and clothing and burning the rest. The victory panics the European inhabitants of the region, including missionaries like Brownlee. They retreat with their families behind the walls of Fort Peddie, which sits, exposed, among *undulating hills*. But the Xhosa are emboldened. They decide to press their attack on Peddie, and from thence to Graham's Town. They will push the English back to the sea.[4]

The tide of war floods through King William's Town. In response to a general muster, Jan Tzatzoe and the amaNtinde regiments join Sandile and the vast majority of the other Xhosa chiefs who have aligned themselves amidst the scattered mimosa in front of Fort Peddie. This momentous decision will shock Tzatzoe's humanitarian supporters when they learn of it. Tzatzoe will need to explain and justify it, and it will be alternately condoned and condemned.

The attack on Peddie on 28 May 1846 is impressive, but of little consequence. The British army and the European settlers retreat into the fort and barricade the doors, leaving their African allies to defend droves of cattle bellowing near the fort's walls. Between five and ten thousand Xhosa warriors (the largest army marshaled since Makana's attack on Graham's Town in 1818) surround the position, forming into four large phalanxes, in martial regalia with their bodies painted red with clay. They sing war songs, whistle, and stamp.

Were it not that life and death were concerned in it, I should have pronounced it a most beautiful sight, one eyewitness will remember. *The Kaffir commanders sent their aides-de-camp from one party to another, just as you would see it done on a field-day with European troops. The main bodies were continually increasing with horse and foot-men, and soon after eleven the array was terrific.* As the battle progresses the waves of Xhosa warriors are dispelled by artillery and rocket fire from within the fort. Only the African allies of the British engage in direct combat. But the Xhosa chiefs secure victory on their own terms by capturing the *greater part* of the colonial cattle.[5]

Several days after the siege, in June 1846, a devastating colonial cavalry charge upon a Xhosa army—caught by chance on an open plain and out of the natural fortresses from which they launch their successful ambushes—ends any hope of a continued invasion of the colony, but the war drags on. During the months of deprivation and military stalemate, Tzatzoe does not join many of the other Xhosa chiefs in outright warfare in the mountains. Instead, he retreats from King William's Town to a secluded location near the coast, in order, he will later recall, *to get out of the way altogether*. Here, he safeguards both his own cattle and those belonging to John Brownlee, which Tzatzoe had driven with him from the war-zone, and continues to keep *worship for the people*.[6] In choosing a path of neutrality, Tzatzoe, in fact, improves his ability to intervene as an intermediary and diplomat. His efforts confer an elevated status upon him from his fellow chiefs and from the British.

A few examples of this diplomacy must suffice. On 2 November 1846, accompanied by *several followers* and acting on information from John Brownlee that the *Governor had sent for him*, Tzatzoe visits a British official, Captain

John Maclean, at a border post. Tzatzoe carries himself like a powerful Xhosa leader, with the *coolest effrontery imaginable*. He accuses the British of *think*ing and *speak*ing for him, *when he had not done so himself*. Befitting this posture, Tzatzoe plays a leading role in the ongoing crisis. A British observer in November 1846 notes that:

> The Gaikas are busy in returning cattle, horses, & guns, and in fact bid fair to come up to something like the mark. . . . The murderers of the Hottentot & those who fell on the Escort, have been given up in whole or in part. All this moreover is attributed to Jan Tshatshu's exertions.[7]

Tzatzoe is Sandile's primary emissary in diplomatic dealings with the colony. In one instance, the British Lieutenant-Governor for the eastern Cape reports to the Governor that *Sandilli had charged me with unjustly attacking him and had declared to Captain Maclean (through Jan Tatzoe) that he did not know what I wanted of him or words to that effect*. Sandile depends on Tzatzoe's diplomatic ability to the extent that he refuses to surrender if Tzatzoe is not permitted to accompany him to the parley.[8]

In referring to Tzatzoe and his participation in the attack on Fort Peddie, John Brownlee writes to the London Missionary Society in December 1846, *I am unable to give a good testimony. There was a general muster of all the Kafir force, yet there was no particular or urgent necessity for him to have gone there.* Once again Brownlee underestimates Tzatzoe's standing within the Xhosa state, and the complicated personal and political dilemmas with which he is confronted. *In inducing some of the Church members to go with him, he not only used every argument, but even threatening,* Brownlee continues, *it appears his design seemed more a desire to advance his chieftainship than from personal danger, as the heathen part of the population could have gone out without him.*

Without giving Tzatzoe a chance to defend himself, Brownlee expels him from the church in whose founding the Xhosa chief had played the foundational role, and onto the mercy of the new regime: *As the country will now be under English rule, probably a number of chiefs may be employed as head men over certain tracks of country*, Brownlee writes. *He is likely to be employed in that way.*[9]

Almost immediately after receiving Brownlee's letter, John Philip and the LMS examine Jan Tzatzoe's wartime actions, along with the other adherents of its mission stations in Xhosaland. By January 1847 Philip has a report in hand from a *most respectable* missionary, Mr. Robert Niven, which finds *nothing* in Tzatzoe's *conduct inconsistent with the Christian character*. Philip initiates his own investigation.

The war staggers to a conclusion by late December 1847. The British annex to the Cape Colony all the Xhosa land from the Keiskamma to the Kei, henceforth to be known as British Kaffraria. Upon his return to King William's Town, Jan Tzatzoe is removed from the land he had held since his return from England and ordered to a location about four miles from Brownlee's residence. *The plan was that no caffres should remain within 2 miles of the Town*, Tzatzoe will remember. His house is commandeered, as it had been in 1835. This time it will serve as King William's Town's new jail.[10]

Tzatzoe has not only lost his home of twenty years. When he retreated from King William's Town, he had to convey his entire family with one wagon. He abandoned items that were subsequently stolen by Dutch and British soldiers and settlers: *an Iron Mill he received as a present in England; his Plough, Do; Five bags of nails, Do; Two globes; the Greater part of his valuable Books also which his friends gave him; A four Post Bedstead with mattress made at Cape Town.* One book in particular reputedly drew the ire of the troops, a humanitarian tract published in the wake of Tzatzoe's visit to England, entitled *The Wrongs of the Caffre Nation*.[11]

These household items represent a world of possibilities, where the best of two cultures might be married, where books and globes can reveal new worlds. Within the walls of Tzatzoe's house, these items would have nestled alongside the compasses, the portrait of Buxton, and the looking glasses that Tzatzoe brought back from England. The items and the hopes they embodied have been evicted. The same walls now enclose those who have no hope: the defeated and dispirited subjects of an imperial state.

An old figure, now knighted, returns to the region as the Governor of the Cape Colony. Sir Harry Smith (the title earned for service in India against the Sikhs) will fulfill the plans that he and Governor D'Urban hatched in 1835 to govern the Xhosa in Queen Adelaide Province. There will be no Xhosa settlement allowed between the Great Fish River and the Keiskamma River, and the country between the Keiskamma and the Kei will be divided into districts, each administered by a colonial representative who will supervise a *head man* for each district (chosen from amongst the chiefs). Each *head man* will then appoint a *head man* for each village. The Xhosa are promised the *same privileges as white men* under the colonial government, and they will owe it absolute obedience. The chiefs who are chosen, or choose to become, head men will have to turn in people identified as *thieves* and obey the colonial *commissioners without question*. They will no longer be able to *eat up* (or confiscate the property of) other Xhosa individuals, and they will not be able to conduct witchhunts or punish suspected witches.[12]

Declaring himself the Xhosa's Supreme Chief, Smith convenes a Great Meeting in King William's Town on 1 January 1848. Taking note of the fact that he is speaking on the eleventh anniversary of the Great Meeting in which he introduced himself as the Governor of the soon-to-be repealed Queen Adelaide Province, Smith begins: *I left you learning to be English—rich—your people protected—all of you happy.* But after your *wicked and unprovoked war against the colony, look now at yourselves. Where are the large herds of cattle I left in your possession? Fools!!! Now you are submissive at my feet.*

Smith lays out the new political dispensation before turning to material concerns. He will survey the land, so that each man might have his own plot. You must *build houses, not huts, such as dogs live in,* he instructs. *Has Jan Tzatzoe not told you of the houses* [in which] *the English live?* As other colonial officials have done, Smith invokes Jan Tzatzoe as a symbol of cultural mediation through which to convey the power of British imperialism and civilization. After the chiefs declare their allegiance to him, he directs their attention to a wagon in a nearby field: *You dare to make war! You dare to attack our wagons! See what I will do if you dare to touch a wagon or oxen with it again. Fire!* A large explosion rocks the wagon. *You will be blown up along with it.*[13]

That this humiliation takes place on the banks of the Buffalo River, where Jan Tzatzoe had reunited with his father's people, speaks to the degree of change in the area, where Xhosa and European settlement zones once came together to form a border region. Tzatzoe's personal fate mirrors that of his country and countrymen. The British have yet to break the back of African resistance to their rule, but they now hold the land on their own terms, and any uncertainty in their intentions has been removed.

Responding to John Brownlee's accusations of Tzatzoe's participation in the siege of Fort Peddie, and after fourteen *anxious* months of the *most careful investigation*, Philip exonerates Tzatzoe in a final report to London in January 1848. He has heard personal testimony from those involved. Contrary to Brownlee's claims that there was no *urgent necessity* for Tzatzoe's choice, and that he *induced* reluctant members of the amaNtinde to action in order to *advance his chieftainship*, Tzatzoe *himself stated* to Philip that he was at Fort Peddie *by accident and by constraint, that he was not actually engaged in the fight, and that no one saw him carrying arms or has attempted to disprove his statement.*

While *defensive warfare* is *defensible in a Christian*, Philip concludes that Tzatzoe demonstrated the correct approach by fleeing *the scenes of war* in an attempt to maintain his neutrality.[14] In the war of Hintza in 1835 Tzatzoe's humanitarian supporters had been shocked by his decision to engage in violence, albeit on the side of the British. Now, by remaining on the sidelines, Tzatzoe appears to be responding as they have urged, and Philip has rewarded this narrative with his continued support of Tzatzoe. Indeed, in his cooperation with Philip's inquiry, Tzatzoe carefully maintains a colonial public persona that he has cultivated through the years with the assistance of Philip, the Reads, and other humanitarians.

In a letter (marked as *not sent*) and a *Declaration* written to Philip in 1849 (likely September or October), however, Jan Tzatzoe directly defends his decision to engage the British forces at Fort Peddie. The letters reveal a fully vested Xhosa leader who blames the colonial government for the recent war. Tzatzoe argues that the British made a mockery of the frontier treaties before finally revoking them. They humiliated several chiefs and constructed Fort Hare in Xhosa territory without the requisite permission. He describes the *ill advised proposition of certain parties* to make *religious Caffre customs matters of treaty*, and the *rash and unbending character* of certain British officials. He is indignant that while the *Caffers were styled irreclaimable savages and faithless men*, in fact, he, along with chiefs like Pato and Kama, had been *faithful in executing the treaties. If any of these were drawn into the war*, Tzatzoe explains, *it was owing to the indecision and tardiness of the Government*. These reasoned expressions of political opposition are consistent with Tzatzoe's statements in Great Britain. There he declared he was on the side of truth and wished that the Englishmen would behave likewise, keeping their word as they had not done. There, he stated he was willing to accept British rule, but he wished to be treated as an equal subject of the King.

Indeed, the authoritative tone of the letters is reminiscent of a confrontation between Tzatzoe and Smith that occurred about a year before they were composed. In October 1848, against a backdrop of disappointment and dispossession, Smith met once more with the Ngqika chiefs to introduce the *Lord Bishop* from Cape Town, *who rode ninety miles yesterday on purpose to be at this meeting*. Then, the Governor turned to Jan Tzatzoe:

> Have you nothing to say? You, who have been in England, seen the great world there, and you saw that no man there eats the bread of idleness? and yet, fool! you dared join with the Kafirs against the power of the Queen. Have you nothing to say to the Lord Bishop for the furtherance of education among your countrymen?

The Lord Bishop is a great and wise man, and the Great Chief has already remarked that I am a fool. How, therefore, can I give any advice upon this subject? Tzatzoe retorted. *But we certainly require teaching to remove our ignorance. The Lord Bishop will best know how to accomplish this.*[15]

In the letters, Tzatzoe continues by casting himself as the central intermediary between Sandile and the Government in 1846—*just before the war broke out Sandilla sent me to confer with Govt and to explain matters but Col. Hare would not receive my message and said everything was to come through Captain Stretch*—before, it would seem, developing the explanation upon which Philip's exoneration was based:

> Sandilla then sent a message to order all the Chiefs and their people to arms. I then called all the members of the Church together and consulted with them as to the course we should take in such emergency—it was resolved that considering our perilous condition and our duties as subjects to the Caffre Govt we should obey the order—but I at the same time told them that they need not actually fight as from the irregularity of Caffers warfare they might shun it altogether.[16]

In response to Sandile's call for a general muster, Tzatzoe explains his decision to join the battle against the British. He positions himself as the leader of a collective body responsible for decision making, which reflects the reality of Xhosa politics. Indeed, it is only once the collective decision has been made that Tzatzoe claims to have spoken from an individual perspective, advocating a measured degree of participation in any actual conflict. This is a position he claims to have maintained throughout the actual battle. There is no compelling evidence that speaks to whether or not Tzatzoe actively joined in the battle. His claim to have *shun*ned the actual fighting may be factual, or it may reflect his efforts to maintain his colonial persona. Tellingly, Tzatzoe ends his letter with a passage that implies a more active participation.

Many people have blamed me for this [the decision to join the attack], Tzatzoe continues, *and wondered how I could have acted so instead of standing on the high principle of the quakers that Christians should not fight.* In reply, Tzatzoe focuses on the hypocrisy of the humanitarian rhetoric. He asks why he is being excoriated now for fighting in support of the Xhosa state, when during his time in England the British humanitarians who believed that the Xhosa in the war of 1835 were legitimately defending their territory against the aggressions of the British condemned his *position in fighting against my own Countrymen* as *unnatural.*[17] Also, in 1846, missionaries in Xhosaland were urging their Xhosa congregations to ally with the British against their Xhosa countrymen and in some cases were themselves leading the men into action. If Mr. Calderwood and Joseph Read (James Read's son) *considered it their duty to aid their Govt* in 1846, and their decision had not *affected* their *Christian standing*, Tzatzoe now *trusts* that a *righteous sentence will be given in* his *case.*

Tzatzoe adopts a brave position in arguing against the LMS leaders who brought him into the church, helped establish the Buffalo River mission, and facilitated his trip to England. Circumstances have changed. Tzatzoe allies himself with his *countrymen*, as a *subject to the Caffre Government.*[18] The LMS and its European missionaries are part of the new British colonial world with its harsher racial ideology and authoritarian policies. Tzatzoe's critique is grounded in the historical situation he now faces and the historical experiences through which he has lived. He seeks after truth; he wishes to fight with the pen and the ink. But the British have abrogated their word.

Where Tzatzoe's letter to Philip articulates the political reasoning behind his service in the war, his *Declaration (respecting his money concerns and joining in the war)* downplays that service while expressing an intensely personal distress. The LMS has not kept its promise to compensate him for his work with Reverend Brownlee:

1 That when leaving England as we all know the Directors agreed and resolved that his Salary in future should be L60 a year—for his Services as Native Teacher and assistant to Mr Brownlee
2 That at the same opportunity he expressed a wish to recieve [sic] his money through Mr Read, which he for a time did—and got it regularly—but the late Mrs Philip writing to Mr Read that as Tzatzoe recieving [sic] his money through him Mr Read would be offensive to Mr Brownlee and advising him rather to draw through him Mr B Mr Read desisted drawing again
3 That from the time he ceased to recieve [sic] his money through Mr Read—he has never recieved [sic] any at all nor any regular accounts of what money was drawn or what paid out, he believes Mr Brownlee paid some debts for him but he does not know how much or to whom. that from the time Mr Moffat came from England and visited Cafferland viz in the month of July 1843 he has heard nothing whatever of Salary and does not know why it was withdrawn or kept back
4 That with respect to his Services as teacher he always continued their itinerating to the kraals on the Sabbath and taking his turns at the Chapel when requested by Mr Brownlee or taking the whole of the duties when Mr Brownlee was from home

Taken together, the letter and *Declaration* of 1849 are weighted toward an open declaration of resistance to the new colonial order. Having encountered so many disappointments, Jan Tzatzoe seems to declare his sympathy for the Xhosa armies in the war, if not his outright support. Yet, Tzatzoe's words also carefully parse his actions in order to preserve his colonial persona. This key contradiction between loyalty to and participation in the Xhosa state (and an accompanying sense of grievance toward British colonial policies), and an ongoing justification of his actions to his humanitarian supporters in order to maintain himself as a Christian in their eyes is one that has shaped Tzatzoe's engagement with the eastern Cape border region. The tension born of the contradiction will continue to have deep political and personal consequences.

Since the last war, the British settler presence in the eastern Cape has intensified. In 1849, a visitor describes Port Elizabeth as a *rising and important town* whose population has increased steadily in the last twelve years, with many new *immigrants from England and Scotland*. Surrounded by *cheerless and uninviting sandstone hills*, Graham's Town *has little beauty and no antiquity to boast of*. British Kaffraria, commonly called *Kaffirland*, with its *dreary plains, glens*, and *wooded hills*, however, holds *great interest*, as it contains an *immense body of aborigines, brought into close contact with the colonists, the effect of which remains* to be seen. Views of the *highly picturesque Amatola range* distinguish the *fair and beautiful scenery* of the road from the Kat River Settlement to King William's Town, which is dominated by the British military and colonial officials.[19]

In October 1850 Jan Tzatzoe reports to Captain Maclean that *evil talk* is sweeping the land. Another prophetic figure, Umlanjeni, who is cut from the mold of Makana (and whom many claim is his actual reincarnation) is promising to *cause all the white population to die*. Tzatzoe expresses incredulity to the colonial official. Do the Xhosa not know what became of Makana and his prophecies, he asks rhetorically?[20] Nonetheless, the most bitter, devastating, and prolonged of the wars in the eastern Cape to date begins on Christmas Day 1850.

In the initial days of the conflict, Tzatzoe attempts to reign in his followers, most of whom join the rebellion.[21] Reinforced by a number of Khoisan, including many of the Kat River settlers, the Xhosa fight with unprecedented sophistication, ferocity, and resolve. We *have now a far different enemy to deal with than the bush fellows with only Assegais*, Governor Smith (besieged near the Kat River in the early days of the war) writes to Robert Godlonton, *the fellows now come out and on*. Far from being defeated or even cowed in the war of 1846–1847, the Xhosa choose this war to stage their last fully fledged resistance to the imposition of a new colonial dispensation. *Arise, clans of the Kafir nation!*

the white man has wearied us; let us fight for our country: they are depriving us of the rights we inherit from our forefathers, Sandile exhorts his followers.[22]

Despite the apparent military difficulties, the British settlers are delighted with the chance to finally impose their will on the eastern Cape. *Everything depends upon unity among us,* Reverend Calderwood writes to Godlonton, *a great crisis has come, but with Gods blessing and unity we are equal to it. An opportunity is now opened for a permanent settlement, united and firm.* A land speculator and wool farmer named William Southey goes even further than Calderwood: *All Kafirs, even to Natal, must be subdued, their Lands conquered from them and they themselves made Servants. . . . Stockenstrom ought to have been hung in 1837. Urge the active people to arms; there is nothing now for it but an attempt at extermination,* Smith adds. *I care not what the people in England think of my fiery proclamation.*[23]

James Read, having spent over fifty years in the colony, despairs of a *general war between the races*. As a colonial commando heads for the Kat River bearing a *red flag* with a single word—*Extermination*—written upon it, Read articulates the central dilemma at the heart of his humanitarian leanings, an unsolvable paradox that will outlive its author (who will die on 8 May 1852) influencing events in South Africa for scores of years to come:

> I would go tomorrow into the blacksmith's shop to help to beat the swords and guns to pieces and the spears, the bayonets and assegais into pruning hooks and sickles. All violence to get redress is contrary to my principles. . . . But my principles are that every man should enjoy equal civil rights the one with the other, and it has been my practice of upwards of 50 years to help those who could not help themselves and had no one else to help them to the enjoyment of them.[24]

At the British military's request, Jan Tzatzoe relocates three miles from King William's Town toward Fort Murray in order to provide critical security for the road that links King William's Town with the coast.[25] Several other chiefs—Pato most prominently and successfully—provide a similar service. But, as in the war of 1846, Tzatzoe's efforts to maintain a colonial persona are directly contradicted by his loyalty to the Xhosa state. While none other than Governor Smith defends him as *truly loyal*, other colonial officials (and the settler public) accuse him of spying, distributing weapons, and concealing Xhosa soldiers.[26]

In 1855 a colonial government inquiry will conclude that Jan Tzatzoe and the amaNtinde were substantially involved in the conflict on the Xhosa side. Most of the men of fighting age joined the Xhosa forces. Many others would journey back and forth between the warring sides, some even attacking colonial patrols while claiming to be living peaceably near King William's Town. One eyewitness will claim that while they remained with Tzatzoe, Tzatzoe's younger brother led one raid, and that his chief councilor headed another. No one will offer a direct and verifiable accusation of Tzatzoe himself (who will deny the accusations made of him), but the balance of the testimony and Tzatzoe's actions point toward his embrace of the rebellion.[27]

Tzatzoe maintains a liminal (and highly dangerous) position between the Xhosa and the British in his new location, enabling him to serve as a key ambassador and the main diplomatic intermediary between Sandile, Maqoma, and the colonial government. Seeking peace, or at least parley, Sandile and the other chiefs repeatedly send their envoys directly to Tzatzoe, who then accompanies them to see the colonial officials at King William's Town. In just one example, in December 1851 Charles Brownlee (now a colonial official himself) reports that *Sandile has sent Mkebe, one of his councilors, into Jan Tzatzoe's location to endeavour to assertain the views of His Excellency the Governor respecting the granting of peace to the Kaffers.*[28]

Despite his diplomatic value Tzatzoe clearly feels his own vulnerability as an intermediary. After a meeting with Maclean in March 1851, in which the colonial official berates him for failing to maintain the security of the Kei Road and accuses him of *acting a double part*, Tzatzoe confronts Pato (who has been attracted by the shouting between the amaNtinde chief and the colonial official). *Why do you people stay here*, he asks, *the English will kill you.*[29]

In June 1851, Maclean receives information from Xhosa informants that Tzatzoe is providing the rebels with tactical information on *every movement the British troops are mak*ing. And a year later Maclean becomes convinced that Tzatzoe is supplying Maqoma with gunpowder.[30] Upon receiving Maclean's report, the new Governor of the Cape (a Waterloo veteran and former aide-de-camp to the Duke of Wellington), Sir George Cathcart, goes so far as to issue Lieutenant-Colonel George Mackinnon, the Chief Commissioner of British Kaffraria, with an official authorization allowing Tzatzoe's arrest: *I should have no hesitation in ordering his arrest on the ground of the suspicion of his guilt—which is sufficiently warranted by our present information—and without making any specific charge, except that of being a false friend and therefore an enemy.* Cathcart is not only suspicious of Tzatzoe, but of all the people under his control. *His tribe are I believe in open hostility with the exception of about perhaps 100, who are doubtful friends & spies & agents of mischief*, he adds to Maclean. *It would be better to have them declared enemies.*

Tzatzoe is never arrested on suspicion of spying, but the suspicion itself traps him behind colonial walls. Still, he continues to enjoy an elevated status amongst the British. Upon issuing the permission for Tzatzoe's arrest, Cathcart is quick to qualify his instructions:

> Should Tzatzoe be arrested I wish him to be lodged well—in either the kitchen or some one of the outhouses of what was my Quarter with a guard— but well fed & allowed to walk with an escort & to have his wife &c with him if he desires it.[31]

The war officially ends on 2 March 1853, and seven days later Cathcart introduces Maclean to the Xhosa chiefs as Chief Commissioner for British Kaffraria. Deeply suspicious of Tzatzoe's service during the war, Cathcart also confiscates a large section of Tzatzoe's prewar land holdings on the *right of the Buffalo River*, including some acreage in a Royal Reserve and divides the rest between two loyalist chiefs.[32] As a subject of the colonial state Tzatzoe repeatedly appeals to return to his prewar holdings, and is repeatedly denied. He is a stranger, barely noticed in this new world. No more journeys, and his pleas, the *Graham's Town Journal* gleefully elucidates for its readers, come from a time that has now passed:

> Jan Tzatzoe was speaking . . . about getting back his land, which is within five or six miles of this place. We told him it could not be granted, as it interfered with the Governor's arrangements about the settling of the country. "I don't care (says Tzatzoe) I will ask for it at any rate, and if it is not granted I will go to the Queen and ask for it there—I have plenty of money." Ah, Jan, the London Missionary Society have not the power now as when they had you in a general officer's uniform speaking for them in Exeter Hall.[33]

In the ensuing years Tzatzoe continues to petition for his lost land and houses while eking out a living as a farmer and cattle herder. He continues to profess Christianity, but he remains estranged from the Buffalo River mission. His new location is half as large as before, and *this most barren*, in Tzatzoe's words. The government does officially recognize the amaNtinde's land rights in this inferior location, issuing an official deed of sale after purchasing a section of the land adjoining King William's Town known as Grand Stand Farm.[34]

In 1855, in a plaintive letter (which appears to be written in Xhosa in Tzatzoe's own hand) to another new Governor of the Cape, the celebrated and historically controversial Sir George Grey, Tzatzoe attempts to refute the charges by the government's inquiry into his supposed participation on the Xhosa side in the war:

> I therefore pray you Chief that these false things which are heaped upon me may be taken off me that I may be clean before the Government, before my Teacher and before my people, and that I may be permitted to return to my

land, of which I was deprived . . . and that I may be placed by you upon the same footing as Pato, Kama, Siwani, and Umkai and those other chiefs who did not enter the war.[35]

Tzatzoe's letter to Grey insists that only *tens* of his followers broke his word during the war, which was to *lie still! do not fight!*[36] His pleading tone might be the result of the grim material exigencies of the land on which he is now living. It might also result from his recognition that power in the border region has swung irrevocably toward a harsh British colonialism, and that his primary identity is now that of a colonial subject. His future in the eastern Cape lies with the British. He will emphasize his affiliation with British missionaries and colonial officials throughout the rest of his life, while he attempts to rehabilitate his loyalist colonial persona. Despite all that has passed between them, and the arrogant and insulting manner in which he has been treated, Tzatzoe offers John Brownlee as a character witness. *Ask of my missionary*, he concludes, *he has known me and my character for thirty years.*[37]

But in 1855 it is Brownlee's son, Charles—who has known Tzatzoe all his life, and who will go on to a career as a leading colonial administrator of African people and land—who emerges as Tzatzoe's staunchest defender. Brownlee insists that Tzatzoe *remained at peace* during the war, assisting the British by escorting wagons from Butterworth, driving cattle back from the Kei to feed the British troops, and *providing messengers to convey letters to Fort Cox (losing two men* and having *four severely wounded* in the process). Brownlee concludes by reminding the colonial authorities that Tzatzoe had built a *European house* and planted *two orchards* on the land taken from him by Cathcart. One of the orchards, he adds, is *still to be seen at or around Colonel Somerset's quarters.*[38]

Beginning in 1856 the prophecies of several Xhosa preachers (most prominently a man named Umhlakaza) sweep through Xhosaland. If the Xhosa slaughter their cattle (which are said to be tainted or bewitched), destroy their grain stores, and refuse to cultivate, their ancestors will return from the dead. New cattle will arrive and grain pits will fill up. The Europeans will be driven into the sea. Many of the leading chiefs in Xhosaland lend their support to the prophets. They are driven, in part, by an epidemic of lungsickness that is destroying their cattle.[39]

When *three messengers from Umhala arrive* at his village on 11 October 1856, Tzatzoe reports to his local colonial magistrate, Colonel Fielding, that he feels obliged to *assemble his Tribe to hear the news sent by the Prophet Umhlakaza.*

Tzatzoe engages with the messengers, asking them *when the new people would come with the Cattle*, since his *people* are *dying of hunger, their Cattle having all died of the Lung-Sickness*. But Tzatzoe appears to be speaking out of desperation, or perhaps with an ironic or satiric bent.

In fact, Tzatzoe does not remain to hear the messengers elaborate on the necessity of *kill[ing] all the cattle, throw[ing] away bewitching matter, and destroy[ing] the Kaffir Corn*. He impresses on his people the necessity of *cultivating their gardens*. Then, accompanied by several of his *immediate followers*, he takes leave of the assembly to plough his fields.

The enduring image of Tzatzoe respectfully allowing his fellow Xhosa leaders' messengers to address his people—while he cultivates his fields against their wishes—is emblematic of the central tension between his association with the Xhosa state and his efforts to maintain a colonial persona. While he refuses to join the millenarian movement, placing him directly at odds with powerful chiefs like Sarhili, Sandile, Umhala, and Suthu, he continues to interact with the Believers (those who slaughter and refuse to cultivate) and their followers. This affiliation enables him to serve as one of the main conduits through which intelligence on the cattle killing passes to the colonial officials.[40] By late 1857, while Unbelievers, like Tzatzoe, *collect together* in an attempt to protect their crops and animals, tens of thousands of Xhosa starve to death or enter the colony seeking relief. In lieu of food Sir George Grey offers the survivors a term of service on settler farms or in settler homes.[41]

Despite his cattle herds and continued cultivation, Jan Tzatzoe struggles to stave off starvation. He is incensed that the land taken from him in 1852 sits idle, neither occupied nor ploughed. And in an additional insult, in 1857 the government confiscates 8,000 acres of his *best arable land* in order to settle immigrants from the German Legion in the villages of Breidbach and Hanover. On 7 June 1857 Tzatzoe pens a last (and unsuccessful) Memorial on the subject of his, and the amaNtinde's, lost lands:

To His Excellency
Sir George Grey, G.C.B.
Governor, Commander in Chief
&c &c &c

The humble Memorial of Jan Tzatzoe Gaika Chief
Respectfully Sheweth

That Memorialist removed to his Land at the other side of the Buffalo River and on the breaking out of the War of 1850 Sir Harry Smith told Memorialist that all the Kaffirs who were not fighting against the English must for the present remove to the other side of the road. . . .

Memorialist removed again according to this order. And when the War was over Memorialist asked Col. Maclean permission to return to his gardens and land but Col. Maclean said "No" You cannot go back you have given gunpowder to Macomo"

Memorialist demanded a trial but there could no man be found to prove the slander. . . .

Memorialist & his people are compelled to reside on a Barren hill and the land of his forefathers given to another

Memorialist would respectfully submit that now when the lung sickness has reduced his people to poverty that Your Excellency would order that the Memorialist be allowed to cultivate his land again and to raise food for himself and people

Memorialist during the last Wars found Messengers to bring Cattle for the Troops from the Country beyond the Kei And in every way to the best of his ability Memorialist shewed himself faithful to the British and a friend of Peace

Memorialist had the honor of an interview with Your Excellency. . . . it was then ordered by Your Excellency that Memorialist's land should be restored to him but Your Excellencys order has not as yet been complied with

Trusting your Excellency will direct that Memorialist be reinstated in the land of his forefathers. Memorialist as in duty bound will ever pray.[42]

Unnoticed, Jan Tzatzoe lives out his days near King William's Town. He has been expelled, or withdrawn, from the embrace of the London Missionary Society; his role as an intermediary, a man between worlds, has come and gone; the eastern Cape border region is now under colonial domination. Tzatzoe has been rendered just another colonial subject, and his presence in the historical record fades.

On 13 August 1860 Prince Alfred, the teenage son of Queen Victoria, rides through the Amathole Mountains on his way to the provincial capital that is now the third largest town in the Cape Colony.[43] A chronicler of Alfred's South African journey delights in the symbolic weight of the royal visit: *But ten years have passed, and where General Smith fled for dear life through hordes of infuriated savages, the young Prince galloped as securely as he might have done at Windsor or Balmoral followed indeed by crowds of shouting Kafirs too, but shouting only in excess of enthusiastic joy. Now the site of the hostile Gaikas had been scattered and peeled.*[44] A deputation of Christian Kafirs greets Alfred in King William's Town. *We, the Christian natives of King William's Town and*

Peelton, are glad to-day because we see with our eyes the son of our great Queen, they tell the young Prince. We have been taught by the Word of God to love our Queen.[45]

As Queen Victoria's son journeys through the eastern Cape, two Xhosa princes reciprocate the royal visit. Jan Tzatzoe's son, Boy Henry Duke Tshatshu, and Maqoma's son, George Mandydi Macomo, are in England for schooling.[46] In letters to the Governor of the Cape Colony, the young men ask how their families are *getting on* and about plots of land he has promised them. They report that there is a white Christmas with snow on the ground for weeks, and they can *stand it as well as the English people*. Their education is proceeding capitally. They are learning English and have reached the 48th Proposition in Euclid— Latin as well, and a Bible class, whose lessons about *Christ and his suffering for sinners* they hope to teach their people. They ask for God's blessing for Grey's rule, quoting for his benefit the first verse of the fifth chapter of the Gospel of St. Matthew: *Blessed are they which do hunger and thirst after righteouness [sic] for they shall be filled*. They are hopeful that preachers will return with them to their people, and that God will *rise up that dark country* to help the Missionaries teach the people to *know their Saviour and save their souls*.[47]

In 1832, four years after British forces exiled him from his Kat River home, Maqoma told a visiting journalist. *We were once men—were once alive—now we are dead. We are without lands—Men without lands, what are they? They can do nothing; they are wanderers, and have no rest.*[48]

In 1857 the British settlers of King William's Town invited the Reverend Tiyo Soga to consecrate their new Wesleyan Chapel. Soga's father was a councilor of Ntsikana, and he was a recently ordained minister having returned from Scotland to the land of his fathers. Soga's topic: *the desire of the Patriarchs for a better land*.[49]

Jan Tzatzoe, a wanderer, still searching for a better land, dies near King William's Town on 28 February 1868.[50]

Epilogue

Although a bronzed plaque in the main square of King William's Town canonizes John Brownlee as town father, there is no public mention of Jan Tzatzoe in the town he helped found. Indeed, Jan Tzatzoe's life has left only a few vestiges.[1]

Besides the Room painting now hanging in Kuruman, there are profiles and engravings in several books published during his lifetime. A *Tribute for the Negro: Being a Vindication of the Moral, Intellectual, and Religious Capabilities of the Coloured Portion of Mankind*, self-published in 1848 in Manchester, England, by Wilson Armistead, a free man of African descent, displays the engraving of Room's group portrait next to its title page. Armistead intended his book to demonstrate *from facts and testimonies, that the white and dark coloured races of man are alike the children of one heavenly father, and in all respects equally endowed by him.*[2] Alongside biographical portraits of Phillis Wheatley, Toussaint L'Ouverture, and Olaudah Equiano is a prominent biographical portrait of Jan Tzatzoe. All serve to confirm that the

> [s]able inhabitants of Africa are capable of occupying a position in society very superior to that which has been generally assigned to them. . . . [T]hey are possessed of intelligent and reflecting minds.[3]

Tzatzoe (and his engraving) also feature as the preeminent example of a *Kafir of the Amakosa* tribe of the *Great South African Race* in Dr. J. C. Prichard's 1855 *Natural History of Man*. Beginning in 1803 Prichard, who likely heard Jan Tzatzoe talk while he was in England—he lived in Bristol, the site of several Missionary Meetings at which Tzatzoe spoke, and moved in humanitarian circles—published a series of volumes in an attempt to classify the world's (or more correctly the British colonial world's) peoples, placing them into distinct groups or *races of men*. Prichard undertook his life's work to establish a unity among human beings. He posited that there were many different *tribes of the human family*, in order to counteract the dominant scientific notion of his age that humanity had, in fact, split into several species.[4] Scholars have seen in Prichard's work the first glimmer of nineteenth-century anthropology, or ethnology, as it was called at the time.[5]

There is also the unfulfilled promise of a remarkable letter I found in the early months of 2001. While the majority of my archival research passed in front of me atop the pale-varnished school-like desks of the Cape State Archives, I was also trying to systematically scan the extensive manuscript collection of the South African Library for any trace of Jan Tzatzoe and those who entered his life. So it was among the scrawled accounts of various adventurers and travelers into the interior who may have passed through the Buffalo River, or multiple descriptions of the sea voyage to the Cape, in a place where I had no compelling reason to be looking, that I happened upon a letter from a woman named Anna.[6]

A widowed mother of seven children, Anna writes to ask an important man for a favor. Her elderly aunt has died, and she has to clean up the family home. Her grandfather was a controversial, but important, man, who left many papers relating to his work in South Africa. Can she send the box containing these documents to Cape Town to be examined under strict confidence? The implication is that she thinks there might be some money in it for her. No copy exists of any reply.

And there the matter should end, except for this. Anna Louisa Jones was born Anna Louisa Read, the youngest daughter of James Read Junior. Her spinster aunt, dead at eighty-five, was her father's younger sister, Martha Matilda Read. The family home in which both her aunt and her grandfather had lived was located in the Kat River Settlement, and the grandfather whose box of papers needed to be surveyed was the Reverend James Read.

The expert in Cape Town to whom Anna Jones wishes to send the box is William Philip Schreiner, brother of Olive, and son of Gottlieb Schreiner and Rebecca Lyndell, who voyaged to the Cape in 1838 with James Read and Jan Tzatzoe. But it is not familial connections that prompt Anna's letter. Schreiner is an ex–Prime Minister of the Cape and a leading humanitarian political figure of the time, and it is a busy time at that. In 1912, when he reads Anna's letter, South Africa has just been created as a union; the Cape Colony, now transformed into a province, must fight to keep its humanitarian tradition alive. Will

Schreiner is so busy, in fact, that he forwards Anna's letter to his brother, Theo, with the brief addendum: *Please read and return. . . . No time to read.*

To the best of my knowledge, James Read's box of documents has never been found. Read's box could be buried in an attic in Adelaide in the eastern Cape, where Anna Jones died in November 1925, or in Adelaide, Australia, or Adelaide Street, London. Anna's letter sent me sailing back up the hill to search for her descendents in the Birth and Death Registers of the Cape Province, but the trail ended in the 1960s. If James Read's letters and diaries should ever be found, would a starkly different Jan Tzatzoe emerge from their pages?

There is the old Buffalo River mission station itself—its stone walls restored, white shutters and trim repainted, roof rethatched. In 2003, when I first visited, the mission had been taken over by Maritz Ngobe, a self-proclaimed guardian of local history and memory, albeit with an eccentric twist. As Ngobe rose to greet us from beneath a leafless tree whose trunk served as his backrest and against which he had stacked books like small buttresses supporting a cathedral, he apologized for the length of the grass surrounding the house. Letting it grow was an intentional and not a negligent act, he told us, an ingredient in his mission to claim this small plot of land for the amaNtinde and turn it into a spiritual center, the *fundamental centre of Isintu*. The amaNtinde, however, disavowed his kinship.

Ngobe's occupancy of Tzatzoe and Brownlee's old mission station had brought him into conflict with the South African government's Cultural Heritage Commission. The bureaucrats wished to evict him in order to conserve the building as a National Heritage monument (neither of us knew at the time that the cold forces of historical preservation would prevail). In response, he had declared his intentions for the site with large white block letters painted on wooden signs and the granite boulders that surrounded the residence. One read: *Isaih 28 14–21*:

> Wherefore hear the word of the Lord, ye scornful men, that rule this people which is in Jerusalem. . . .
> Behold, I lay in Zion for a foundation a stone, a tried stone, a precious corner stone, a sure foundation. . . .
> For the Lord shall rise up . . . that he may do his work, his strange work. . . .

We talked in the midwinter sunshine beneath soaring eucalyptus trees, the smell of dried grass pungent in the air. A century-old, sixty-foot-high, flaming aloe tree rose above the mission house's western wall. Ngobe's discourse was wide-ranging, impressive and impressionistic, and inflected with arcane knowledge garnered from books and, possibly, from stories told by the elders. Because

Tzatzoe had come to resent and resist the English presence, Ngobe insisted, his papers and belongings were burned along with his home upon his death. To Ngobe, Tzatzoe had served as a radio beacon, broadcasting the Christian message across the hills.[7]

Finally, there is a sparse graveyard, located just across the brushy and trash-filled Buffalo River from the mission house, on ground where Jan Tzatzoe once walked. One of the many well-tended graves with their burnished granite slabs for gravestones and offerings of plastic flowers holds the body of Steve Bantu Biko. Biko was born in King William's Town on 18 December 1946 and he rose to prominence during the 1970s in the struggle against apartheid as the leader of the Black Consciousness movement. Before he was beaten and tortured to death by the South African Security Police in Pretoria in 1977, many believed him to be a likely future president of South Africa. His highly politicized funeral in King William's Town marked a key moment in the resistance to apartheid. Raised in mission schools like the great majority of the other anti-apartheid resistance leaders including Nelson Mandela, Biko preached a doctrine of black self-worth and self-definition that drew upon his Christian upbringing and education.[8]

At Biko's grave, in 2003, I felt the spirit of Jan Tzatzoe, who settled on the overlooking ridge, who built a home for himself with the stones that lay about, who cultivated the local fields in all senses of that word. And Tzatzoe also lives for me in his conversation with the men who greet him and Reverend Williams at the Kat River; in the heated confrontation with Colonel Fraser; in the eureka moment when Jesus becomes a great physician; in the gaze from the stage of Exeter Hall upon an adoring crowd; in the courage to remind his fellow chiefs and the representatives of a threatening colonial power that fighting can be done with the pen and the ink; in the calm and knowing eyes that look back at me from Room's painting.

I linger with a living man from Africa.

NOTES

PREFACE

1. Noël Mostert, *Frontiers*.
2. With all due apologies and gratitude to John Demos, see his *The Unredeemed Captive*.

INTRODUCTION

1. At Tzatzoe's baptism in October 1814, his age was listed as twenty-two, KAB A559 Bethelsdorp vol. 4. I am employing the term "eastern Cape" because Tzatzoe's story takes place in the contemporary Eastern Cape Province of South Africa. From the early nineteenth century until 1994 various borders splintered the region, and different parts of the Eastern Cape were called by different names. The term "South Africa" is not the anachronism that it might appear to be; in some contemporary documents it was used to refer to the Cape Colony and the African territory beyond it. For my use of the terms "amaNtinde," "lineage," and "state," and for my preference for "Tzatzoe" over "Tshatshu," please see the relevant footnotes in the chapter entitled Xhosaland, 1810, below.
2. Tzatzoe's story is unique in southern African history in both the multiple roles he played and the fact that his life was lived and recorded in the multiple arenas of the eastern Cape, Cape Town, and Great Britain. Tzatzoe's life has barely featured in extant South African historiography. He is given sole attention in D. Crafford, "Jan Tshatshu," in *Trail-Blazers of the Gospel*, 15–19, and P. J. Jonas, "Jan Tshatshu and the eastern Cape Mission—A Contextual Analysis," 277–92. Both accounts are drawn from secondary sources. James Read, prominently, and Tzatzoe to a lesser degree feature in Elizabeth Elbourne, *Blood Ground*. Zoë Laidlaw uses Tzatzoe and his comments on seeing the British Parliament in action to begin her *Colonial Connections*. Tzatzoe is mentioned in passing in: Noël Mostert, *Frontiers*; Jeffrey Peires, *The House of Phalo*; Timothy Keegan, *Colonial South Africa*; and Alan Lester, *Imperial Networks*.

3. With Tzatzoe's story, we witness the arrival of colonialism from an African point of view, echoing the recent call by Norman Etherington, a prominent historian of South Africa and of missions and empire: "The period 1815 to 1854 can fairly claim to be a turning point in history. . . . That is one reason why so many historians have tried to tell its story. . . . We need histories which are less determined, more aware of multiple possibilities, histories which suggest life beyond the struggle against apartheid. [We need] compelling stories [that imaginatively locate the historian and his reader in a] place where the agents of colonialism appear first as specks on a distant horizon. [This task may be best accomplished with the use of] significant anecdotes [to bring the lives of individuals] sharply into focus." See Norman Etherington, *The Great Treks*, Preface, 1, 5. For an example of Etherington's approach (in survey form) drawn from North America, see Daniel K. Richter, *Facing East from Indian Country*.

4. Tzatzoe speaks as a witness to colonialism's potentials and perils. In this way, my presentation of Tzatzoe's life responds to the ongoing debate between John and Jean Comaroff and their many interlocutors about colonialism colonizing the "consciousness" of Africans. In Jan Tzatzoe's life, we can see an African consciousness assimilating the colonial presence, shaping and assisting in its dissemination, resisting and embracing its messages, discussing it in narrative and historical terms. In his later life, Tzatzoe chafes under the raw and hegemonic power of the colonial state, but never stops challenging the power and questioning its hegemonic signs. Tzatzoe "speaks" to and about these issues. At every stage of his life, Tzatzoe breaks down the dialectical-Hegelian model for which the Comaroffs, especially in volume 1, have been critiqued. See, most notably, Jean and John L. Comaroff, *Of Revelation and Revolution*, vols. 1 and 2; Paul Landau, *The Realm of the Word*; Elizabeth Elbourne, *Blood Ground*, and idem, "Word Made Flesh: Christianity, Modernity, and Cultural Colonialism in the Work of Jean and John Comaroff"; and Sally Engle Merry, "Hegemony and Culture in Historical Anthropology: A Review Essay on Jean and John L. Comaroff's *Of Revelation and Revolution*"; J.D.Y. Peel, "For Who Hath Despised the Day of Small Things? Missionary Narratives and Historical Anthropology." My hope is that Tzatzoe's life speaks to the possibility of recovering a "subaltern consciousness" from the colonial archive; see Premesh Lalu, "The Grammar of Domination and the Subjection of Agency: Colonial Texts and Modes of Evidence," 45–68.

5. A case might easily be made that no other period or location in southern African history has enjoyed such extensive and repeated scrutiny from historians. This maxim holds especially true for the last two decades or so, which have witnessed a profusion of academic work. The historical body of work is built upon the pioneering efforts of George McCall Theal, *History of South Africa from 1795 to 1872*, and G. E. Cory, *The Rise of South Africa*. For a brief selection of the more recent work with particular relevance to Tzatzoe's story, that of the Xhosa, and of South Africa's eastern Cape region more generally, see Clifton Crais, *White Supremacy and Black Resistance in Pre-industrial South Africa* and *The Politics of Evil*; Elizabeth Elbourne, *Blood Ground*; Timothy Keegan, *Colonial South Africa*; Alan Lester, *Imperial Networks*; Noël Mostert, *Frontiers*; Jeffrey Peires, *The Dead Will Arise* and *The House of Phalo*; Les Switzer, *Power*

and Resistance in an African Society; Monica Hunter Wilson, *Reaction to Conquest*; Richard Price, *Making Empire*; Andrew Bank, "Liberals and Their Enemies: Racial Ideology at the Cape of Good Hope, 1820–1850"; Natasha Erlank, "Re-examining initial encounters between Christian missionaries and the Xhosa, 1820–1850: the Scottish case."

6. For "missionised region," see Robert Ross, *A Concise History of South Africa*, 36. Scholars have suggested that the eastern Cape and its neighbor, the Natal Province, saw the first attempts in Africa of the form of indirect rule that would be infamously adopted under Lugard in Nigeria. Thus, the system of colonialism put in place in the Cape had ramifications throughout the British imperial world, and influenced regions under the control of other European countries such as Rwanda. See additional notes in QAP, Price, *Making Empire*, 192–98, Keegan, *Colonial South Africa*, and Mahmood Mamdani, *Citizen and Subject*, esp. chap. 3.

7. Jill Lepore, "Historians Who Love Too Much: Reflections on Microhistory and Biography," 133. I have been inspired by work that calls itself microhistory, new narrative history, new biography, experimental history, and creative nonfiction.

8. For interaction, see Monica Wilson and Leonard Thompson, eds., *The Oxford History of South Africa: vol. 1: South Africa to 1870*, 1. "This work derives from our belief that the central theme of South African history is interaction between peoples of diverse origins, languages, ideologies, and social systems, meeting on South African soil." The theme of interaction was reassessed and challenged in fruitful ways by a later generation of historians, who I feel too easily caricatured it as a hollow effort to suggest that British civilization would "interact" with African savagery and barbarism, lifting Africans out of their traditional ways into a more enlightened existence. Worse, critics claimed that emphasizing "interaction" was a way of covering up and ameliorating as somehow equal a deeply unequal relationship, in which Europeans extended social, political, economic, and cultural dominance over Africans. Last, interaction between diverse peoples carried a patina of essentialism, of placing Africans, Europeans, and others into hermetic boxes. As such, population groups interacted, but they did not merge, or meld, or change: "modern" British settlers interacted with "traditional" Africans, neither side being influenced by this interaction. I feel that this book might suggest renewed attention to the idea that South Africa's exceptional history lies in its uniquely long and detailed history of a reinvigorated sense of interaction.

9. For scholarly attention being directed toward intermediaries in colonial Africa, see Benjamin N. Lawrance, Emily Lynn Osborn, and Richard L. Roberts, eds., *Intermediaries, Interpreters and Clerks*, esp. the Introduction. Also see the comprehensive discussion of the literature surrounding such figures in Emily Lynn Osborn, "'Circle of Iron': African Colonial Employees and the Interpretation of Colonial Rule in French West Africa," 33–34. A recent account of the activity of intermediaries in a colonial setting (Oaxaca in colonial Mexico) provides a compelling model for the eastern Cape: see Yanna Yannakakis, *The Art of Being In-between*. See also Louise A. Breen, "Praying with the enemy: Daniel Gookin, King Philip's War and the dangers of intercultural mediatorship," in Martin Daunton and Rick Halpern, eds., *Empire and Others*. In the

1970s South African scholar Monica Wilson presciently called for historians to elaborate on the role in South African history played by individuals who participated in the translation of language, but who also "mediate[d] ideas, law, custom, symbolism . . . [who] listen[ed] as much as [they taught]." These were men who sought to "reconcile men, to achieve mutual understanding": Monica Wilson, "The Interpreters," 17–20. Wilson, following Clifford Geertz, himself drawing on a term fashioned by Eric Wolf, called these individuals "cultural brokers"; thanks to Andrew Bank for this point on the origins of Wilson's phrase. In addition to Frances Karttunen's *Between Worlds: Interpreters, Guides, and Survivors*, I have turned to the vast literature on the American "West" for assistance with thinking through intermediaries; in particular see Margaret Connell Szasz, ed., *Between Indian and White Worlds: The Cultural Broker*; James H. Merrell, *Into the American Woods: Negotiators on the Pennsylvania Frontier*; Richard White, *The Middle Ground*; and James Axtell, *The Invasion Within: The Contest of Cultures in Colonial North America*.

10. There have been no monograph-length studies of intermediaries in colonial South African historiography. Many of the issues raised by Tzatzoe's life (and the roles he played) resonate in that of Hermanus Matroos: see Robert Ross, "Hermans Matroos aka Ngxukumeshe: A Life on the Border," 47–69. For the early years of Dutch settlement at Cape Town and intermediaries, see V. C. Malherbe, "Krotoa, called 'Eva': A Woman Between." Ursala Trüper has unearthed the fascinating case of a Nama woman named Zara Schmelen who married a London Missionary Society German missionary and assisted him in translating parts of the Bible into Nama: see Ursala Trüper, *The Invisible Woman*. For Christianity and intermediaries, see Stephen C. Volz, "From the Mouths of our Countrymen: The Careers and Communities of Tswana Evangelists in the Nineteenth Century." Sol Plaatje was a translator and much more: see Brian Willan, ed., *Sol Plaatje: Selected Writings*, and *Sol Plaatje: South African Nationalist, 1876–1932*. Shula Marks evokes the world of three South African women, each in between in her own way, in *Not Either an Experimental Doll*.

11. A cultural intermediary may well be defined by their position of marginality, or, essentially, of loneliness, or so I infer from the stimulating book by Leo Spitzer, *Lives in Between*; my thanks to Julie Wiese for this timely reference. For conversations on the margins, see C. A. Bayly, *Empire and Information*, 341, and Yannakakis, *The Art of Being In-between*, xiv. For lives on the margin, the fashioning of selves (see next note) and a microhistorical approach, see Natalie Zemon Davis, *Women on the Margins*.

12. See Jo Burr Margadant, "Introduction: Constructing Selves in Historical Perspective," in Margadant, ed., *The New Biography*, 9. My thanks to Andrea Mansker for this reference. In writing about Hermanus Matroos, Robert Ross echoes this intervention, noting that "after Mlanjeni's war [1850–1853]" there was a dramatic reduction in the number of "occupations on which major black careers could be built": see Ross, "Hermanus Matroos," 69. Another South African example of the fashioning of multiple selves in a highly contingent historical moment is Charles Van Onselen's work on Kas Maine, *The Seed Is Mine*. A recent collection of essays about the Cape Colony and its connections to the Indian Ocean world deals, in part, with this question of the

creation of identity: see Nigel Worden, ed., *Contingent Lives*. See also the essays in Ronald Hoffman, Mechal Sobel, and Fredrika Teute, eds., *Through a Glass Darkly: Reflections on Personal Identity in Early America*.

13. For hybridity and the overturning of dualities, see Frederick Cooper and Ann Laura Stoler, "Between Metropole and Colony," esp. 4–11, 34, and Homi Bhabha, "Of Mimicry and Man: The Ambivalence of Colonial Discourse," in Cooper and Stoler, *Tensions of Empire*, and Comaroff and Comaroff, *Of Revelation*, 2:410.

14. Increasingly, scholars have come to view agency as a concept with limited use, one whose time has run its course. Environmental historians have asked whether trees, or the influenza virus, or free-range cattle can be said to have the agency to act on humans or on other aspects of the natural world. According to Walter Johnson ("On Agency," 113–24), social historians, who developed the concept or "trope" of agency with reference to "giving slaves back their agency," need to rethink the concept because it relies on the "categories of nineteenth-century liberalism . . . of a liberal notion of selfhood, with its emphasis on independence and choice." As such, it can hardly be responsibly applied to describing the conditions of slavery, or of most African societies—or colonial frontiers, for that matter—conveying as it does the whiff of the free economic actor of nineteenth-century social theory, who is capable of rational, equal, and unlimited choice in his transactions. Indeed, one of the central dilemmas in trying to make sense of Jan Tzatzoe's life lies precisely in this antiquated understanding of agency. His contemporaries, especially the missionaries with whom he works, often expect him to operate as a free agent but he cannot because the very idea of the liberal self does not fit his sociocultural position in Xhosa society. Thanks to Mart Stewart and Richard White for prompting my thoughts on this matter. In addition to evaluating the question of "free will" in "agency," Pamela Scully and Clifton Crais raise the issue that discussing whether an African subject (Sara Baartman) "either possessed agency or did not presents a binary of power or victimization that forecloses our ability to grapple with the complexities of her life": see Pamela Scully and Clifton Crais, "Race and Erasure: Sara Baartman and Hendrik Cesars in Cape Town and London," 303. Andrew Apter defines "sociopolitical agency" as "the capacity for effective social action that . . . for Ahearn . . . is 'the socioculturally mediated capacity to act,'": see Andrew Apter, *Beyond Word*.

15. This formulation echoes Margadant's "invention of selves." See Scully and Crais, "Race and Erasure," 304. Gilmour adopts a similar approach to the study of language as part of a contested encounter. She sees new linguistic opportunities giving "possibilities and strategies for self-determination to African people," as opposed to a previous sense that African "lives and world-views" were "in various senses determined by their experiences of colonization and their inculcation into colonial discourse": see Rachael Gilmour, "Missionaries, Colonialism and Language in Nineteenth-Century South Africa."

16. Nelson Mandela, *Long Walk To Freedom*. For a particularly well-received biography of Mandela, see Anthony Sampson, *Mandela: The Authorized Biography*. Recently Mark Gevisser's life of Thabo Mbeki captured the public imagination: *Thabo Mbeki: The Dream Deferred*. For recent academic works, see, for example, Andile Mngxitama,

Amanda Alexander, and Nigel C. Gibson, eds., *Biko Lives!: Contesting the Legacies of Steve Biko*, and Diana Wylie, *Art and Revolution: The Life and Death of Thami Mnyele*. Clifton Crais and Pamela Scully address the biographical approach to those "people whose lives traversed so many geographies and different cultural worlds" in *Sara Baartman and the Hottentot Venus*, in particular 5–6. During the mid-nineties, Charles Van Onselen enjoyed popular and critical success with his presentation of a non-elite African life, *The Seed Is Mine*. Ciraj Rassool focuses on biography, the production of history, and biographical representation in "The Individual, Auto/Biography and History in South Africa."

17. Some key studies of African political leaders are Timothy J. Stapleton, *Faku: Rulership and Colonialism in the Mpondo Kingdom (c. 1780–1867)*, and idem, *Maqoma: Xhosa Resistance to Colonial Advance, 1798–1873*, and Leonard Thompson, *Survival in Two Worlds : Moshoeshoe of Lesotho, 1786–1870*. The biographies of literate Africans examine lives lived after the establishment of colonial rule in South Africa and expand greatly with the advent of the twentieth century. The best-known individuals are Tiyo Soga and Sol Plaatje, the former of whom merits a new treatment. See above for Plaatje; for Soga, see Donovan Williams, *Umfundisi: a Biography of Tiyo Soga, 1829–1871*. For a cogent introduction to "African intellectuals" such as Soga, Jabavu, and Rubusana during the late mid- to late nineteenth century, see Mcebisi Ndletyana, ed., *African Intellectuals in 19th- and Early 20th-Century South Africa*. There are also studies of Zulu amakholwa Christians: for example, Paul La Hausse, *Restless Identities: Signatures of Nationalism, Zulu Ethnicity, and History in the Lives of Petros Lamula (c. 1881–1948) and Lymon Maling (1889–c. 1936)*.

18. For example, the life and ideology of Steve Biko, born in the town that Jan Tzatzoe founded, might profit from a renewed understanding of the almost one hundred and fifty years of intellectual exchange in the eastern Cape.

19. See David Cannadine, *Ornamentalism*, preface.

20. See Cooper and Stoler, "Between Metropole and Colony"; Catherine Hall and Sonya O. Rose, eds., *At Home with Empire*, and Martin Daunton and Rick Halpern, eds., *Empire and Others*. For South Africa and Great Britain, see in particular Lester, *Imperial Networks*, Elbourne, *Blood Ground*, and Price, *Making Empire*. Maya Jasanoff reiterates the centrality of this historiographical thread (and the pleasure and necessity of "just telling stories . . . that reflect back many features of the larger world in which they are set") in her work on collecting and empire. Her collectors are intermediaries in their own right: see Maya Jasanoff, *Edge of Empires*, in particular 3–13. Both Ashis Nandy, *The Intimate Enemy*, and Yannakakis, *Art of Being In-Between*, xiv, are useful in thinking through the ideological and sociopolitical consequences of colonizer and colonized being included in one frame. Yannakakis posits that native intermediaries create a "colonial hegemony" or "common symbolic framework" through which they mediate colonial power. Jan Tzatzoe allows for a discussion of the worlds of the colonizer and colonized in South Africa in one unified field. The literature on the early contact between American Indians and Europeans in North America has been especially helpful. See Andrew R. L. Cayton, *Frontier Indiana*, Colin G. Calloway,

New Worlds For All, James H. Merrell, *The Indians' New World*, and Joel W. Martin, *Sacred Revolt*.

21. In the abolitionist context, questions of literacy, authenticity, the making of new selves, and auto/biographical presentations by Africans in the eighteenth and nineteenth centuries have crystallized around the life of Olaudah Equiano, or Gustavus Vassa: see Vincent Carretta, *Equiano, the African*, and Paul Edwards, "Unreconciled Strivings and Ironic Strategies: Three Afro-British Authors of the Late Georgian Period (Sancho, Equiano, Wedderburn)," in David Killingray, ed., *Africans in Britain*. Equiano represented himself in person and in print as a man who embodied the "redemptive passage" from slavery to freedom. He allowed his "own life story" to stand as the "most powerful argument against slavery": see Adam Hochschild, *Bury the Chains*, 172–73. In this way, Equiano "gave the abolitionist cause the African voice it needed": Carretta, *Equiano*, 367. Jan Tzatzoe likewise "fashioned" his life story to greater ends, coming to serve as an "African voice" for the redeeming power of evangelical humanitarianism.

22. Howard Lamar and Leonard Thompson, eds., *The Frontier in History*, 7: "We regard a frontier not as a boundary or line, but as a territory or zone of interpenetration between two previously distinct societies.... [T]he zone closes when a single political authority has established hegemony over the zone." It is interesting to note that this definition, while dated, is still the one most frequently mobilized by historians of regions around the globe. See, for example, Gregory Nobles, *American Frontiers*. For a discussion of the frontier paradigm in South African historiography, see Nigel Penn, *The Forgotten Frontier*, esp. 9–14. Richard Price addresses the creation of colonial knowledge in this particular border region in *Making Empire*. I am using "border region" instead of "frontier" to refer to the shifting and indistinct boundary region between the Cape Colony and its African neighbors because the latter implies one (more "advanced") society inexorably extending its dominance over the other (devaluing the dynamic quality of both societies), and also includes a teleological framework in which the frontier opens and inevitably closes. Historians are employing the term "borderland" to describe the northern and southern border regions of the United States: see Alan Taylor, *The Divided Ground*, and Beth LaDow, *The Medicine Line*. For a brief introduction to the eastern Cape frontier, see John Milton, *The Edges of War*.

23. Contingency is critical to my story of Jan Tzatzoe. His story and its time are interesting precisely to the extent that they were contingent. On contingency in history, see Stephen Jay Gould, *Wonderful Life*.

24. For outstanding examples, see Comaroff and Comaroff, *Of Revelation and Revolution*, vols. 1 and 2; Paul Landau, *The Realm of the Word*; Lamin Sanneh, *Translating the Message*; Elbourne, *Blood Ground*. Also see unpublished dissertations by Stephen Volz, Fiona Vernal, and Sara Jorgensen. For a good introduction to the more recent work, see Derek Peterson and Jean Allman, "Introduction: New Directions in the History of Missions in Africa," 1–7.

25. William Worger, "Parsing God: Conversations about the Meaning of Words and Metaphors in Nineteenth-Century South Africa," 419. For a concise overview of the

literature and debates over colonialism and language in the South African context, see Gilmour, "Missionaries, Colonialism, and Language."
26. On translation in a South African context, see Isabel Hofmeyr, *The Portable Bunyan*, and Rachael Gilmour, *Grammars of Colonialism*. For an example of identity formation, mission Christianity, translation, and the predicament of an intermediary, see Jill Lepore, *The Name of War*. Tzatzoe's life answers many of the "challenges"—surrounding issues of South African Christianity, colonialism, subaltern history, and the colonial encounter as seen through the lens of translation—identified by Richard Elphick in "Writing Religion into History: The Case of South African Christianity," in Henry Bredekamp and Robert Ross, eds., *Missions and Christianity in South African History*.
27. Paul Landau, "'Religion' and Christian Conversion in African History: A New Model," 8–30; Derek Peterson, "Translating the Word: Dialogism and Debate in Two Gikuyu Dictionaries," 31–50; William Worger, "Parsing God," 417–47.
28. The literature dealing with African Christianity is immense. Since the publication of the Comaroffs' two-volume *Of Revelation and Revolution* the field has been rent by a debate over whether the Western missionaries colonized the Africans' consciousness or provided them with, among other benefits, written vernaculars and the ideology with which to resist colonial rule; see the discussion in previous notes. For the latest synthesis on missions, see Norman Etherington, ed., *Missions and Empire*. For South African Christianity, see esp.: Elbourne, *Blood Ground*; Richard Elphick and Rodney Davenport, eds., *Christianity in South Africa*; David Chidester, *Savage Systems*; and Bredekamp and Ross, eds., *Missions and Christianity in South African History*. For African Christianity, see esp.: Richard Gray, *Black Christians and White Missionaries*; Steven Kaplan, ed., *Indigenous Responses to Western Christianity*; Thomas Spear and Isaria N. Kimambo, eds., *East African Expressions of Christianity*; and M. Louise Pirouet, *Black Evangelists*.
29. I am indebted to Paul Landau for this formulation.
30. For South Africa, inspiring recent works that unfold the possibilities of imaginative history in the coming years are Crais and Scully, *Sara Baartman*, and Wylie, *Art and Revolution*. For a literary precedent, see Charles Van Onselen, *The Seed Is Mine*. Shula Marks engages with the possibilities of microhistory in *The Ambiguities of Dependence in South Africa*. A controversial and extremely popular life history that has elements of history and fiction is Elsa Joubert, *Poppie Nongena*. For a scholarly response, see Anne McClintock, "The Scandal of Hybridity: Black Women's Resistance and Narrative Ambiguity," in *Imperial Leather*. Southern African historians have written successful scholarly books that take narrative seriously: see, for example, Tim Couzens, *Murder at Morija* and idem, *Tramp Royal: The True Story of Trader Horn*; Jeff Guy, *The View Across the River*; Neil Parsons, *King Khama, Emperor Joe, and the Great White Queen*. For Africa, see: Robert W. Harms, *The Diligent*; John K. Thornton, *Kongolese Saint Anthony*; and Landeg White, *Magomero: Portrait of an African Village*. In addition to the works listed in the notes below, other "narrative" or "micro" histories that I found particularly helpful are: Edward Muir and Guido Ruggiero, eds., *Microhistory and the Lost Peoples of Europe*; James Goodman, *Stories of*

Scottsboro; Emilia Viotti da Costa, *Crowns of Glory, Tears of Blood*; and Aaron Sachs, *The Humboldt Current*.

31. Following from John Clive: "Historians, unlike poets and novelists, must try to get their facts right. But fact alone . . . will never be sufficient to cast that spell that lingers in the memory and is conducive not just to reading, but to rereading": see John Clive, *Not By Fact Alone*, xiv. I also follow Greg Denning on the use of historical imagination: "Imagination is not necessarily fantasy. Imagination is restoring to the past all the possibilities of its future." See Greg Denning, "Texts of Self," in Hoffman et al., *Through a Glass Darkly*, 161–62. It is interesting, and perhaps not coincidental, how many students of narrative and contingency in history are also lifelong baseball fans.

32. The critic James Wood praises authors who can animate their characters, "getting [them] up and running": James Wood, *How Fiction Works*, 96.

33. I have drawn on several key works for inspiration in literary, thematic, structural, and mechanical innovation. For a constant reminder that history is always personal and that description can be magical, see Julia Blackburn, *Daisy Bates in the Desert*. For inspiration in allowing the story to show and to tell, see John Demos, *The Unredeemed Captive*, which also italicizes quoted text, and Jonathan Spence, *The Question of Hu*, which is told in the present tense. For the use of the historical imagination (and the present tense and italicizing quoted text), see Richard A. Rosenstone, *Mirror in the Shrine*. For exceptional characterization and the present tense in African fiction, see Yvonne Vera, *The Stone Virgins*. For the use of the present tense and a narrative schema that I found helpful, see Donna Merwick, *Death of a Notary*. For a recent work in what the author terms "experimental history" that has found a wide popular audience and a welcoming scholarly reception (and also employs italicized text), see Martha Hodes, *The Sea Captain's Wife*.

KELSO, SCOTLAND, 1837

1. Information and quotations from the meeting are taken from BL *Kelso Chronicle*, 4 August 1837. Excerpt of newspaper account for last paragraph: "[The chief] stood before them as the man of Macedonia stood before Paul, saying 'Come over and help us, lest we perish.'" When the man of Macedonia appeared to Paul he appeared only in a vision, but (the Chief) stood before them a living man from Africa, crying unto them, "Come over and help us." For Tzatzoe's impressions of Scotland, WITS Philip Papers Cc (3) Durant Philip to Eliza Philip, Glasgow, 28 June 1837, and Philip Papers 1.2 Letters to Miss Wells, Durant Philip to "My very dear Friend," Glasgow, 19 July 1837.

2. Clothing description is taken from Room's portrait of Tzatzoe and the other members of the LMS delegation to England, based upon personal observation and photographs, Moffat Mission Trust, Kuruman, South Africa, December 2006. The physical description is derived from images, both written and pictorial, of Tzatzoe. I do not know with historical certainty that Tzatzoe wore his dark blue suit in Kelso, but I do have evidence of many other missionary meetings in Great Britain in which this was

the case. For example, BL *The Bristol Mercury, Monmouthshire, South Wales, and West of England Advertiser*, Saturday, 24 September 1836.

XHOSALAND, 1810

1. The description of the journey into Xhosaland to Tzatzoe in 1810 is taken from LMS, South Africa Incoming, H-2130, Box 4, Folder 2, A, Read to Directors, Bethelsdorp, 5 February 1810. I have employed a fair amount of historical imagination in this scene, although it is all, with the exception of Read rubbing his arms, which seems like a universal human response, based on direct source material: i.e., Read discourses in a nostalgic manner about England and the resemblance of it to Xhosaland, but he does not discuss this revelation while he describes his accident. Later in the trip, he refers to the red earth adhering to his pants. No monograph to date has dealt with the life of James Read. I am using Xhosaland geographically to describe the region from Algoa Bay east to the Kei River and beyond it to the land of the amaPondo.
2. The London Missionary Society (LMS) was formed by Congregationalists in the late eighteenth century in London. Elizabeth Elbourne offers the clearest and most current discussion of the ideology behind the LMS and the evangelical movement and its impact on South African missions and South African history: see Elbourne, *Blood Ground*. See, also, Richard Lovett, *The History of the London Missionary Society*, and John de Gruchy, ed., *The London Missionary Society in Southern Africa*. A recent "narrative" or popular history dealing with the LMS and the trip of two of its directors around the globe between 1821 and 1823 is Tom Hiney, *On the Missionary Trail*.
3. The young son of the chief Tzatzoe was baptized as Jan, or John, in 1815 at Bethelsdorp. Several sources from James Read suggest that Tzatzoe was known as Jan prior to the baptism, likely as early as 1804. Several historical accounts give Tzatzoe the Xhosa first name Dyani, but I have been unable to locate this usage in archival materials. It is possible that the name Jan was an attempt to Europeanize Dyani, but it is more likely that Dyani was a later attempt to pronounce Jan in Xhosa. I employ Jan or John because that is the usage in the archive. I have chosen to employ the usage "Tzatzoe" to refer to the chief and his son. The vast majority of the colonial-era documents have this spelling, and Jan Tzatzoe signed his name as such. The usage stands in for Tshatshu, which is the modern orthography for this Xhosa surname. Jan Tzatzoe's descendants have Tshatshu as a surname. In part, I do not adopt the name Tshatshu because I wish to keep my discussion to the historical figure, Jan Tzatzoe, found in the archive. A few contemporary accounts do refer to Jan Tzatzoe as Jan Tshatshu.
4. These hills are the site of present-day Port Elizabeth. People who self-identified as amaXhosa were Nguni-speakers who spoke an intelligible language and attributed their descent to an ancestral chief, Tshawe. Anthropologists and historians have long debated over how to refer to the small Xhosa communities that were known as "tribes" at the time. I am employing the term "lineage" in order to emphasize that these groupings centered around loyalty to, and claims of descent from, a chief, or a chief's ancestor. Chiefs passed their leadership to their sons. Often, sons broke

away to form their own lineages. However, these designations and loyalties were fluid. The amaNtinde, headed by Kote Tzatzoe's father, were at the small end of the spectrum. Ntinde broke away from the line of descent after Tshawe but before Phalo, to whom the vast majority of the Xhosa traced their ancestry. In consequence, while the amaNtinde were at the small end of the spectrum in terms of Xhosa clans, they were one of the most venerable. Robert Balfour Noyi, who grew up during the period of my account, gave the name Tshiwo, son of Gconde, as the primary ancestor; he was presumed to be a descendant of Tshawe: Robert Balfour Noyi, "The Kafirs and their Country," in Bokwe, *Ntsikana: The Story of an African Convert*, 36–40. See also Jeff Peires, *The House of Phalo*, chap. 2. A Xhosa intellectual of the early twentieth century, John Henderson Soga, perhaps in deference to his Scottish heritage, employed the term "clan": John Henderson Soga, *The Ama-Xosa: Life and Customs*. The British colonial administration also adopted this designation: "This tract of country . . . is inhabited by clans of a remarkable race called kafirs, each clan having a chief who is assisted in governing by a council, and owning a certain portion of territory within defined limits." Imperial Blue Books of South Africa OPB 1/13, *Correspondence with the Governor of the Cape of Good Hope relative to the state of the Kafir Tribes*, 2, Cathcart to Pakington, Fort Beaufort, 20 May 1852, 107. Even though amaXhosa society was decentralized, I employ the term "state" to describe their political arrangement. I prefer this less-freighted term to "tribe," "nation," "people," "Xhosa-speakers," or "ethnic group." I follow from Joseph C. Miller's insightful comments to the H-Africa online forum that African languages have "no word for a concept cognate to 'tribe.'" In the same discussion thread, John Thornton advocates the use of the term "state" for "the majority of African societies outside of the regions of widespread nomadism like the Sahara." Thornton bases this usage on the existence of a court system that has "final authority and the power to enforce its decisions." He also attributes to African "states" the "right and power to collect revenue (including service) from the [*sic*] members, clear cut boundaries defined by jurisdiction (not necessarily by geography), and a permanent governing structure. While stratification is not theoretically necessary, I believe that all of these polities are, in fact, stratified." Thornton response to "The term 'Tribal,'" 3 April 2007, and Miller response, 8 April 2007, from Discussion Logs (April 2007) www.h-net.org/~Africa, accessed on 30 August 2008.

5. The initial meeting between Jan Tzatzoe, Read, and Van der Kemp and Kote Tzatzoe's decision to leave his son at Algoa Bay were subject to revision and retelling throughout Tzatzoe's life. See my further discussion of this key moment in "Makana's Kraal." For Kote Tzatzoe, see A. W. Burton, *Sparks from the Border Anvil*. Burton was one of the most comprehensive antiquarians of the Eastern Cape. Cory Library, Burton Papers, notebooks, 14, 604 (2). See also *The Progress of His Royal Highness Prince Alfred Ernest Albert*, 50.

6. Cuyler was born and raised in Albany, New York. He was a Loyalist in the American Revolution who fled to Canada. He embarked from Cork harbor, thinking he was destined for service in India. It is unclear whether it was in America that he learned Dutch, the language in which he wrote much of his South African correspondence. See Ben Maclennan, *A Proper Degree of Terror*, 48–49.

7. I reluctantly use the terms "European" and "Xhosa" for these zones. The designations simplify the population movements that were involved, but they are preferred to the more generic, and confusing, "Western" and "Eastern" zones. For the use of "zones" and "border region" instead of "frontier" or "frontiers," see the Introduction.
8. For an introduction to the history of the Cape Colony and its northern and eastern frontier in the eighteenth and nineteenth centuries, see Richard Elphick and Hermann Giliomee, eds., *The Shaping of South African Society*.
9. Read and Van der Kemp had been recalled to Cape Town by a reinstalled Dutch government (the British held the Cape from 1795–1803). Officials in Cape Town were upset about mission stations sheltering Khoisan who might work on colonial farms, and on the refusal of the mission Khoi to serve on commandos. In Read's account of their stay in Cape Town, we can see the militaristic and radical evangelism of the time: "At the very moment that the Devil was ready to shout Victory! behold the Lord appeared! as King of Zion! and showed that Floats and Armies are at his command for the Protection of his Servants and Cause." LMS South Africa Incoming, Box 3, Folder 1, D, Read to Directors, Cape of Good Hope, 7 October 1805 and Box 3, Folder 2, B, Read to Directors, Cape of Good Hope, 13 January 1806. In the nineteenth century, evangelicalism began to focus on merging Christianity with the cultural mores of European civilization. See Elbourne, *Blood Ground*, and Boyd Hilton, *The Age of Atonement*.
10. See Peires, *House of Phalo*, 3, for a discussion of population estimates. The Dutch and British colonizers referred to the amaXhosa with variations of the Arabic word kafir, and, occasionally, as Kosas. The term Caffre, or Kaffre, in the nineteenth century had not acquired the extremely negative connotation of the twentieth century. I therefore have not elided it from the primary source accounts that I quote. I do not employ the term in my text, and when speaking, use the pronunciation "Caff-ri" no matter which version on paper, in order not to verbalize "Kaffer." Thompson suggests that proto-Xhosa were living east of the Kei by 1,000 A.D. and had reached the Great Fish River by the sixteenth century. A line running roughly along the Great Fish, where the average annual rainfall decreased to twenty inches or less and rain-fed agriculture was no longer feasible, halted Xhosa expansion to the west. See Leonard M. Thompson, *A History of South Africa*, 4–5, 12.
11. These sounds are written as q, c, and x, respectively. Thus, the name "Xhosa" itself incorporates a click.
12. I employ the term "Khoisan" to refer to all those Africans known as "Hottentots" or "Bushmen" in the early to mid-nineteenth century. A large and vigorous scholarly debate exists over the identity of the Khoi, or Khoekhoe and San, and whether they were distinct ethnic groups. By the time of this story, the Khoisan of the colony were no longer living in independent polities and were laborers within the Cape Colony. The eastern Cape had few-to-no San groups. For recent discussions of terminology, see Elbourne, *Blood Ground*, and Penn, *The Forgotten Frontier*. For Khoisan society and its breakdown, see Richard Elphick, *Kraal and Castle*, and Susan Newton-King, *Masters and Servants on the Cape Eastern Frontier, 1760–1803*. For the dispersal of Christianity in the European zone, particularly among the Khoisan, and the develop-

Notes to Pages 14–16

ment of mission stations, see Elbourne, *Blood Ground*, and Jane Sales, *Mission Stations and the Coloured Communities of the Eastern Cape, 1800–1852*.

13. LMS, South Africa Incoming, H-2130, Box 4, Folder 2, A, Read to Directors, Bethelsdorp, 5 February 1810. Read's letter is the main source (unless otherwise noted) for the journey to Kote Tzatzoe.
14. For Read's departure from England and the *Duff*, BL *Sheffield Independent*, 24 December 1836.
15. I am choosing to employ the term "village" instead of "homestead," following my discussion of "tribe" versus "state," in order to reduce the exotic, and possibly pejorative, connotations of the language used to describe Xhosa society and history in English. Xhosa hymn-writer, journalist, and minister John Knox Bokwe employs the word "village" to describe Xhosa settlements in his *Ntsikana: The Story of an African Hymn*, Cory Library, Pamphlet Box 70, Bokwe, *Ntsikana: The Story of an African Hymn*, 15.
16. Cowper Rose, *Four Years in Southern Africa*, 70. Rose provides the italicized descriptive language in the following two paragraphs. My description also relies upon KAB CO 163, Brownlee to Bird, Chumie, 20 August 1822, although Brownlee's account focuses on the geology and hydrology of the region. Rose emphasizes the romance of the African setting, including lurid descriptions of local women and classical references to African male figures.
17. As in other semiarid grassland regions around the world, humans helped to maintain grassland through burning regimens. See Stephen J. Pyne, *Fire: A Brief History*. My landscape and flora descriptions are informed by personal visits to the region; see also Mostert, *Frontiers*, xxii. Mostert notes the intermingling of old and young vegetation, of desert with rainforest, and the Atlantic and Indian Oceans.
18. Alberti, journeying through the region from 1803 to 1806, noticed similar fauna and flora to Rose. Alberti described an abundance of mimosa and other "bushy trees" between the Great Fish and the Keiskamma, with fewer trees and bushes on the plains heading toward the Kei but a greater abundance of Aloes and Euphorbia: see Ludwig Alberti, *Account of the Tribal Life & Customs of the Xhosa*. On trees, KAB CO 184 Thomson to Bird, Chumie, 20 December 1822. Fire and cattle references are from Rose, *Four Years*, 125.
19. In addition to information drawn from the specific sources cited in the text, my information on Xhosa life and cosmology are informed by Jeff Peires (a Xhosa-speaker), in *House of Phalo* and *The Dead Will Arise*, whose books on these subjects remain the gold standard; John Henderson Soga, *The Ama-Xosa*, and Alberti, *Account of the Tribal Life*. The italicized phrases in this and the following two paragraphs are from LMS Read to Directors, 5 February 1810. I have restricted myself in this chapter to developing those dimensions of Xhosa society that emerge from the narrative itself. I will discuss religious and cultural dimensions as they insert themselves into Tzatzoe's story.
20. For construction and interior description, Bokwe, *Hymn*, 9.
21. For sunrise, Rose, *Four Years*, 83. On 111, with a sentiment known to many visitors, he adds: "That moment, when an African sun wakes a world to life, is well worth the rest of the day." For elephant's tail, 77.

22. For clothing, decoration, animal fat, and "polished bronze," Bokwe, *Hymn*, 8. Bokwe's use of the term "bronze" resonates with similar, classically inspired descriptions of the Xhosa by early travelers to South Africa like Alberti.
23. I have described an imagined Xhosa village based on Peires, *Phalo*, 3; Alberti, *Tribal Life*; and Mostert, *Frontiers*. Read's letter includes the details in italics.
24. For oxen used in battle and warfare among the Xhosa, see Mostert, *Frontiers*.
25. For military training and hunting, see Roger S. Levine, "'African Warfare in all its ferocity': changing military landscapes and the study of precolonial and colonial conflict in southern Africa," in Richard Tucker and Ed Russell, eds., *Natural Ally, Natural Enemy*. For hunting, Rose, *Four Years*, 126, and warriors, 78, in addition to Read and aforementioned secondary sources.
26. Rose, *Four Years*, 146, and Bokwe, *Hymn*, 15, also note contemporary traditions.
27. For the expansive nature of sub-Saharan African societies, see Igor Kopytoff, *The African Frontier*, and Emmanuel Kreike, *Re-Creating Eden*.
28. "The chief, assisted by his councilors, consults on every public act. [He has] little independent power, and few privileges. When war is resolved on, he leads; in hunting, his share of the spoil is large, the breast of the hippopotamus and one of the tusks of the elephant. . . . [His] house [is] not distinguished. . . . [He] can't compel personal service without paying for it." Rose, *Four Years*, 77.
29. For background on Van der Kemp, see Elbourne, *Blood Ground*, 92–102. For his time in Xhosaland, see Ido. H. Enklaar, *Life and Work of Dr J. Th. van der Kemp, 1747–1811*, 86–109. I will use Jank'hanna through the text because it is the name historians have offered to date. Bokwe offers, I think, a more convincing Xhosa rendition of Van der Kemp's name and its meaning: Nyengana, "meaning one who had appeared as if by accident": Bokwe, *Hymn*, 14. Later, in his 1914 *Ntsikana: The Story of an African Convert*, 5, Bokwe adds "one who had appeared sneakingly, as if by accident." Bokwe based his text on extensive oral interviews of Xhosa informants who knew Ntsikana, Van der Kemp, Read, et cetera.
30. On Ngcongolo, Bokwe, *Ntsikana: Convert*, 7.

BETHELSDORP, 1811–1815

1. Basil le Cordeur and Christopher Saunders, eds., *The Kitchingman Papers*, 21.
2. For a further discussion of the intimacy of the early relationship between Read and Tzatzoe, see "Makana's Kraal." References to Tzatzoe's mother's ethnicity are scattered in the secondary literature, but I could not find direct archival evidence to support the contention.
3. le Cordeur and Saunders, *Kitchingman Papers*, 22.
4. For the war, Colonel Graham, and Grahamstown, see Ben Maclennan, *A Proper Degree of Terror*. I am employing the historical usage, Graham's Town, instead of the current Grahamstown. The land conquered from the Xhosa, known as the Zuurveld (or Sourveld), in which the new town was located, was named the District of Albany in honor of Colonel Cuyler's birthplace: see Mostert, *Frontiers*, 391–92

5. BL *Sheffield Mercury and Hallamshire Advertiser*, 31 December 1836; description from the *North Derbyshire Chronicle and Chesterfield Advertiser*, 24 December 1836. This description of Jan upon his arrival with the missionaries is tinted with metaphoric language and intended to reveal the progress he has made by the time the sentence is written in 1836. Read, in fact, refers to Tzatzoe as "totally naked." But he is likely differentiating between the antelope and animal skin karosses worn by the Xhosa and the sheepskin clothing of the Khoisan.
6. BL *North Derbyshire Chronicle*, 24 December 1836.
7. KAB CO 2606 Report upon lands in the District of Graaff Reinet, 18 August 1815.
8. For an account of revival and the specific quote on Tzatzoe, SOAS, Annual reports, *Twenty-first Report of the Missionary Society*, 1815. On British evangelism in the early nineteenth century, see Elbourne, *Blood Ground*, chap. 1, and "British Beginnings," in Jean and John Comaroff, *Of Revelation and Revolution*, vol. 1, and Boyd Hilton, *The Age of Atonement*.
9. KAB A559 Bethelsdorp, vol. 4.
10. Elbourne, *Blood Ground*; Sales, *Mission Stations*. For a recent and comprehensive geographic treatment of these issues, see Elphick and Davenport, *Christianity in South Africa*. For an in-depth discussion of the relevant literature on conversion, see "Smeared with Chalk: Tswana Conversion to Christianity," in Volz, "From the Mouths." On the last point I am referring to scholars working within the church tradition who take as given the truth of Christian revelation.
11. Physical description and figures are taken from LMS, SA Incoming, Box 6, Folder 2, D, Short account of the state of the missionary Institution at Bethelsdorp, James Read, 22 November 1815.
12. For singing, LMS, SA Incoming, Box 6, Folder 2, C, Evans to LMS, 30 October 1815. For rest of quotes in paragraph, SOAS, Annual reports, *Twenty-first Report*, 1815.
13. LMS, SA Incoming, Box 6, Folder 2, C, Extract of letter from Rev. J. Evans, Bethelsdorp, to Rev. Peter and others at Carmarthem, 30 October 1815.
14. LMS, SA Incoming, Box 6, Folder 2, E, James Read and Messer, *Report of the Mission at Bethelsdorp for 1815*. As with other speeches given by Tzatzoe, Read's account is not direct. It is his recollection (if not transcription) of a speech given in Dutch. Still, the presence of quotation marks in the text indicate it is a more authoritative account than the recall of conversations (such as that between Kote and his son) previously cited.
15. I am citing all Biblical verse in the text not the notes. Throughout my text, the verse is taken from an 1823 King James version of the *Holy Bible*.
16. The missionaries exult in their report to London: "the Lord is abundantly blessing our Labours, and showering down grace upon the poor Hottentots (to use their expressions) in torrents." LMS, SA Incoming, Box 6, Folder 2, E, James Read and Messer to Directors, Bethelsdorp, 31 December 1815.
17. Material for preceding two paragraphs from LMS, SA Incoming, Box 6, Folder 2, C, Extract of letter from Rev. J. Evans, Bethelsdorp, to Rev. Peter and others at Carmarthem, 30 October 1815.

18. Block quote and material in paragraph from LMS, SA Incoming Box 6, Folder 2, E, James Read and Messer, Report of the Mission at Bethelsdorp for 1815. On Jager, John 6:53, "I say unto you, except ye eat the flesh of the Son of man, and drink his blood, ye have no life in you."
19. For adultery, LMS, SA Incoming, Box 6, Folder 2, E, James Read and Messer to Directors, Bethelsdorp, 31 December 1815.
20. On the woman and kraal, SOAS, Annual reports, *Twenty-second report of the Missionary Society*, 1816. On the officer, LMS, South Africa Incoming, H-2130, Box 5, Folder 3, A, Read to Campbell, Bethelsdorp, 8 January 1814.
21. Makana-Nxele has attracted the attention of many scholars writing about the eastern frontier during the early nineteenth century. See Peires, *House of Phalo*, chap. 5; Janet Hodgson, "A Battle for Sacred Power: Christian Beginnings among the Xhosa," in Elphick and Davenport, *Christianity*, and idem, "A Study of the Xhosa Prophet, Nxele." For Makana (section ending in "true God"), SOAS, Annual reports, *Twenty-second report of the Missionary Society*, 1816. For section ending in "literally fulfilled," LMS, SA Incoming, Box 6, Folder 2, C, Extract of letter from James Read to Directors, Bethelsdorp, 11 November 1815.
22. For the harsher reality of Xhosaland and the material life of the Xhosa, see Peires, *House of Phalo*. For the construction of Africa and its landscape, see "Africa Observed," in Jean and John Comaroff, *Of Revelation and Revolution*, vol. 1.
23. For Read on Makana, LMS, SA Incoming, Box 6, Folder 2, B, Extract of letter from James Read to Directors, Bethelsdorp, 24 August 1815. Another letter from Bethelsdorp describes Makana as the Xhosa man who "came to us some time ago to ask for a Missionary": see LMS, SA Incoming, Box 6, Folder 2, D, Mrs. Smith to Burder, Cape Town, 21 December 1815.
24. For "qualifications," LMS, SA Incoming, Box 6, Folder 2, B, Extract of letter from James Read to Directors, Bethelsdorp, 24 August 1815. For "curiosities," KAB CO 67 Read to Alexander, Colonial Secretary, Bethelsdorp, 22 September 1815. For "Caffre chief," SOAS, Annual reports, *Twenty-second report of the Missionary Society*, 1816.
25. KAB CO 2599 Read to Cuyler, Bethelsdorp, 29 August 1815.
26. LMS, SA Incoming, Box 6, Folder 2, D, Williams to "Revd Sir" probably Burder, Bethelsdorp, 11 December 1815.
27. KAB CO 2599 Cuyler to Colonial Secretary, Uitenhage, 1 September 1815.
28. For Read's letter, KAB, CO 74, Read to Alexander, Colonial Secretary, Bethelsdorp, 19 January 1816.
29. LMS, SA Incoming, Box 6, Folder 3, A Translation of a Letter written by the young Caffra chief to Mr Bresler one of the Gentlemen of the court of circuit, Bethelsdorp, 20 January 1816. As this letter is drawn from the LMS archive, the original Dutch version was not included. It is unclear if the translation was by Read or another South African missionary, or by an LMS clerk in London. The archival copy has a postscript: "Mr Bresler has promised to lay the Letter before the Governor in Jan's own hand writing." It is certainly possible that Read attempted to exaggerate Tzatzoe's literacy by having him transcribe a text, or even, passing off his own handwriting (or that of another mission member) as Tzatzoe's.

MAKANA'S KRAAL, 1816

1. For Bird, KAB CO 4838 Bird to Read, Cape Town, 14 February 1816. For Read, LMS, SA Incoming, Box 6, Folder 3, B Read to LMS, Bethelsdorp, 31 March 1816.
2. Read on Tzatzoe, LMS, SA Incoming, Box 6, Folder 3, B Read to LMS, Bethelsdorp, 31 March 1816. For Joseph's story, Genesis 37:3.
3. For communication to Cuyler, KAB CO 2603 Joseph Williams to Lieut. Col. Cuyler, Bethelsdorp 26 March 1816; KAB CO 2603 J. Read to Lieut Col. Cuyler, Landrost, Bethelsdorp 26 March 1816. For communication from Cuyler, KAB CO 2603 Lieut. Col. Cuyler to Read, Uitenhage, 26 March 1816. For gunpowder, LMS, SA Incoming, Box 6, Folder 4, D Report of the Missionaries at Bethelsdorp, for the year 1816.
4. For ceremony, including Messer, Read, and Tzatzoe sermons, LMS, SA Incoming, Box 6, Folder 4, D Report of the Missionaries at Bethelsdorp, for the year 1816. For weeping, LMS, SA Incoming, Box 6, Folder 3, B Read to LMS, Bethelsdorp, 31 March 1816.
5. BL the *Sheffield Independent*, 24 December 1836.
6. Elbourne drew upon Van der Kemp's journal in a Netherlands archive to describe the decision as one where Tzatzoe was "left at Bethelsdorp for education by his father": see Elbourne, *Blood Ground*, 281. Personal communication, Elizabeth Elbourne, April 2010. This moment represents an instance in which Tzatzoe and those around him begin to produce or construct the narrative of his life differently and for differing purposes. See Rassool, "The Individual."
7. Read sends his pages to the Directors of the LMS, who print the entire twenty-page letter in their periodical, *Transactions of the London Missionary Society*: James Read, "Narrative of the journey of Mr. Read and others to Caffraria," *Transactions* 4, no. 29 (1818): 279–93. Also LMS, SA Incoming, Box 6, Folder 3, C, Read to LMS, Conga's kraal, Caffre Land 18 April 1816 and LMS, SA Incoming, Box 6, Folder 3, D Read to LMS, Bethelsdorp, 31 May 1816. Read also produces a substantial report submitted to Colonel Cuyler for the colonial government, KAB CO 2603 J. Read to Lieut Col. Cuyler, Landrost, Bethelsdorp, 18 May 1816. It is by comparing these accounts that an understanding of what transpired on the trip may be reached. Care must be taken to strip down Read's hyperbolic language—composed to inspire his British readers—and to account for the tendency of parts of the narrative to rely on the emerging tropes of evangelical writing (missionaries being surrounded by natives who become pacified by the preached word or the lone African who responds to the missionaries despite the resistance of her companions.) But as Read's narrative progresses, it acquires a momentum all of its own, and he seems to forget to add the formulaic elements of the story in favor of striking detail. For emerging tropes in travel writing in this period, see Mary Louise Pratt, *Imperial Eyes*. Unless otherwise cited, information about the journey on the following pages is from Read's letter of May 31 1816, which is unpaginated.
8. Honey, or honey-guide, birds lead large mammals, particularly honey badgers and humans, to beehives. They eat the beeswax, larvae, and honey that remains after the hive is opened for its honey. In local folklore, the birds are reputed to lead people

toward dangerous animals if they have previous experience with people not sharing the honey. My thanks to Nancy Jacobs for this information. Personal communication, Nancy Jacobs, March 2009.

9. Bokwe calls such a tree an Umqonci tree, Cory, Bokwe, *Ntsikana: African Convert*, 27.
10. The roots of vegetation are a metaphor for strength in belief in the Word in the Bible, for example Mark 4:17. Makana may be employing this connotation, or the usage may come from his own imaginative attempts to convey meaning to his audience who are familiar with livestock. LMS, SA Incoming, Box 6, Folder 3, D Williams to LMS, 15 June 1816 to 7 August 1817.
11. For Read's impressions of Makana, Enklaar, *van der Kemp*, 109, 131, 141 and LMS, SA Incoming Box 6, Folder 3, C Read to LMS, Conga's Kraal, Caffre Land, 18 April 1816. For Makana's time with Van der Lingen, Thomas Pringle, *African Sketches*, 428–29 and Peires, *House of Phalo*, 69–72.
12. Bokwe, *Ntsikana: African Convert*, 1–13. Bokwe employs a delightful phrase, drawn from isiXhosa, to describe Ntsikana's detached state while immersed in the aftermath of his vision: "He looked a little put out. His features, betraying a disposition to what some people call 'dwelling in the me,' appeared even more reserved than usual." According to one account, his prophecies began immediately: "Something had commanded him to wash off his red ochre; this thing also said that there is coming from the West another people, whose hair resembles the brushes of cows. This people brings with it the word of life. I see this country full of white homes. I see upon it a network of waggon roads. All its brows are entirely denuded of their grass by sheep." Bokwe notes that Ntsikana also first heard the Bible preached during Van der Kemp's visit to Xhosaland in 1799: Bokwe, *Ntsikana: African Hymn*, 14. Information on Ntsikana's biography also taken from Cory Library, MS 9063, N. Falati, "The Story of Ntsikana: A Gaika Xhosa," 1895. Falati claims that the rays of light concentrated on Ntsikana himself, not on the side of his ox; this version more closely resembles the visions of other Christian prophets.

For the hymns, see Janet Hodgson, *Ntsikana's Great Hymn*, and Philip, *Researches*, 2:188. The Great Hymn reads in part, "He who is our mantle of comfort, The giver of life, ancient, on high, He is the creator of the heavens. . . . He alone is a trusty shield, He alone is our bush of refuge." In addition to Xhosa idiom, Ntsikana's hymn incorporates biblical references to the notion that the "Lord alone will save us," and to God as a mantle, cover, cloak of righteousness, and shield of faith—see, for example, Ephesians 6:16. Personal communication, Tina Campomizzi, July 2008.
13. There had been multiple shipwrecks along the coast, most notably that of the *Grosvenor* in 1782. For a narrative account of the "white" descendants of the survivors of another shipwreck in 1737, see Hazel Crampton, *The Sunburnt Queen*. For a discussion of Xhosa understandings of water, the ocean, and the arrival of Europeans during this period, see David Chidester, *Savage Systems*, 78–84. In the nineteenth century many of the Xhosa military and spiritual leaders would talk about driving the Europeans back into or across the sea.

14. The specific reference to Adam and Eve is from KAB CO 2603 Read to Cuyler, Bethelsdorp, 18 May 1816.
15. For Xhosa understandings of spirit, or umoya, see Mongameli Mabona, *Diviners and Prophets among the Xhosa*, 348–50. For breath, or umpefumlo, see Peires, *Dead Will Arise*, 104–5. For a discussion of witchcraft, sorcery, and the identification or "smelling-out" of witches, see "iQonce." In the Bible, God is often seen to work through the agency of the wind. Personal communication, Tina Campomizzi, June 2008.
16. The amaRharhabe Xhosa form one half of Phalo's succession, the other half, who live east of the Kei, are called the amaGcaleka (after two founding chiefs respectively), see Peires, *House of Phalo*, 45–63.
17. KAB CO 2603 Read to Cuyler, Bethelsdorp, 18 May 1816. The specific term "cats and dogs" is taken from Read's report to Cuyler. In general, the report, while considerably abbreviated, mirrors Read's letters to the LMS in great detail.
18. Although Read names the river, the archival record suggests that it had already acquired the moniker of the Buffalo River by the time of Read's visit. There is no further mention of the Somerset.
19. KAB CO 2603 Read to Cuyler, Bethelsdorp, 18 May 1816.
20. Ibid.
21. The literature on raiding and militaristic behavior in southern Africa is underdeveloped, especially compared to the extensive literature on similar activities among American Indians. Scholars are beginning to explore this aspect of African societies and its continued legacy in faction fights, beer-drink conflicts, and urban gangs. See Gary Kynoch, *We Are Fighting the World* and Clive Glaser, *Bo-Tsotsi: The Youth Gangs of Soweto*. Also, unpublished African Studies Association paper (2005) by Sean Redding.
22. Christianity spread ahead of the missionaries through Khoisan and other agents, and recent research into people like the Lemba suggests that direct Semitic influence (monotheism and ritual practice) arrived in southeastern Africa from the Middle East perhaps as long as 1,500 years ago, see "Lost Tribes of Israel," Cicada Films for NOVA, 2000.
23. LMS, SA Incoming, Box 6, Folder 4, D Report of the Missionaries at Bethelsdorp, for the year 1816.
24. In a parting letter written about a month after the travelers' return from Xhosaland, Read muses that while the spiritual labors of Van der Kemp had "seemed not much blessed in Caffre land," the old pioneer had made the "name of a Missionary reliable, by his disinterested behaviour. The Caffres were no more afraid of us than of one another." LMS, SA Incoming, Box 6, Folder 3, D Read to LMS, Bethelsdorp, 31 May 1816.
25. For specifics of Read's adultery and flight north, and the change in LMS ideology that it reflects, see "iQonce," and Elbourne, *Blood Ground*, 221–22. Read does not comment on his emotions, and the paragraph from "Flee to seek" to "effusion of flies" is imaginative on my part.
26. For specific verses from the sermons of Read and Williams, LMS, SA Incoming, Box 6, Folder 4, D Report of the Missionaries at Bethelsdorp.

27. Final section from LMS, SA Incoming, Box 6, Folder 3, D Read to LMS, Bethelsdorp, 9 June 1816, unless otherwise noted.

KAT RIVER, 1816–1818

1. For a separate account of Tzatzoe's work at the Kat River, see Roger S. Levine, "An Interpreter Will Arise: Resurrecting Jan Tzatzoe's Diplomatic and Evangelical Contributions as a Cultural Intermediary on South Africa's Eastern Cape Frontier, 1816–1818," in Lawrance, Osborn, Roberts, eds., *Intermediaries, Interpreters and Clerks*.
2. Basil Holt, *Joseph Williams*, 40–44.
3. For seedlings and food supply, Holt, *Williams*, 43; for missionary training, 1–10. Holt draws on the records of the LMS's Committee of Examination. Holt cannot confirm these familial relationships, but the coincidence seems fairly persuasive. George Barker definitely married a Sarah Williams, who was working with Elizabeth Rogers (soon-to-be Williams) in the household of a Reverend Waters: Holt, *Williams*, 11.
4. Elizabeth's letters to which I am referring were published in John Philip, *Researches in South Africa*, and referred to by Holt. There is no way to authenticate to whom they were sent and how Philip acquired them, but there seems little reason to doubt their actual composition by Elizabeth Williams. I relied on comparing the letters written by Elizabeth during Joseph's life and after his death and their similarity suggests a continuity of authorship. Here, I refer to those letters I found in the archive that had not been transcribed. The biographer of Maqoma, Timothy Stapleton, dismisses Williams's letters as being "of little value as historical sources" because they are "semi-literate": see Timothy Stapleton, *Maqoma*, 29.
5. Unless otherwise noted, information on the settlement of the Kat River Mission in the rest of this chapter is taken from LMS, SA Incoming, Box 6, Folder 3, D, Williams to LMS, 15 June 1816 to 7 August 1817, which is unpaginated. For son Joseph, Holt, *Joseph Williams*, 139. For names and families of Bethelsdorp men, KAB, CO 2603, Frontier Orders from Cuyler, Uitenhage, 11 June 1816.
6. For "powder and ball," Philips, *Researches*, 165, quoting Elizabeth Williams to unknown friend in London.
7. This description is drawn from my visit to the site, July 2003. I followed the Kat River down from its heights and followed the directions of Williams's biographer, Holt, who describes his efforts to locate the grave in *Joseph Williams*. The old mission and Williams's grave are now lost in the bush that has grown up on the location. The surrounding hills are about five hundred feet in height.
8. For social relationships among the Xhosa, see Peires, *House of Phalo*.
9. For background on Xhosa adjudication, see Soga, *Ama-Xosa*; Peires, *House of Phalo*. For "recompense," KAB Cape Archives CO 2603 Williams to Fraser Kat River 13 November 1816.
10. For Bird's letter, KAB CO 4838 Bird to Read 23 August 1816. For Williams reply, KAB CO 2607 Williams to Fraser 7 October 1816.
11. See the introduction for discussion of Hermanus Matroos.

12. Makana insists that his adherents follow his "word." If an audience does not listen to his preaching, Tzatzoe appears to follow the biblical injunction to "shake off the dust under your feet," see Matthew 10:14, Mark 6:11, and Luke 9:5.
13. For house and fields, Holt, *Williams*, 42.
14. For "lessons," AB *Report of the House of Commons Select Committee on Aborigines (British Settlements)*, 1:572. In his testimony, Tzatzoe refers to "my school" at the Kat River. Williams does not mention his assistance.
15. See "iQonce" for a discussion of the literature on witchcraft and possession.
16. For "better men," AB, 1:572.
17. See Sanneh, *Translating the Message* and the discussion of missionaries and translation in the introduction.
18. For an interesting analysis of the process by which African polities split, propagated themselves, and, especially, incorporated new members or smaller polities, see Kopytoff, *The African Frontier*.
19. Stapleton, *Maqoma*, 24.
20. Williams says that the news was conveyed with "the Idea of its being religious news. My reply was I had no such news in Gods word."
21. The list of requests is fascinating in its detail (only very small beads) and in the fact that Ngqika is in control of the exchange. To this end, it is interesting that he requests looking glasses, or mirrors, which are so critical to the analysis of the Comaroffs (as gifts or "colonizing instruments" from missionaries to Africans that would reflect back new colonial selves). At least in this one anecdote, Africans do not appear to be "bothered by [the mirror's] arresting gaze": see Jean and John Comaroff, *Of Revelation*, 1:170–97, 334n37.
22. For more on translation see, especially, "iQonce." The equality of the relationship speaks to the "micro-politics of power" in the realm of translation: see Andrew Bank, *Bushmen in a Victorian World*.
23. Philips, *Researches*, 166–67, quoting Elizabeth Williams to unknown friend in London.
24. The great abundance of rumor in a border region or frontier can in some ways be used to characterize such a locale. Luise White begins to provide a historical analysis of rumor in an African colonial setting in *Speaking with Vampires*. On crisis with Ngqika, Williams writes: "I am now inclined to think that if they [the Xhosa] know that I keep a constant correspondence with you for the sake of informing you and complaining against them they will very soon be weary of me & take means to get me out of the way—From this I doubt not but you see what an unpleasant situation I stand in and also an unsafe one I hope and desire that God will ride among them with the sword of truth," KAB CO 2603, Williams to Fraser, Kat River, 18 November 1816. For "hands of English," and other information on the mission unless differently cited, LMS SA Incoming, Box 6, Folder 3, D, Williams to London Missionary Society, 15 June 1816 to 7 August 1817. The mission was beset by rumors and threats of imminent destruction by local African chiefs from its founding; for further examples of these crises and Tzatzoe's role in diffusing them, see Levine, "An Interpreter Will Arise," in Lawrance et al., eds., *Intermediaries, Interpreters, and Clerks*.

25. Eloquence was highly prized at these local political gatherings, or meetings, which have counterparts in most precolonial African societies. The isiXhosa version was likely called an "imbizo," although Gerhart and others suggest the seSotho word for such a meeting, pitso, came to acquire this meaning (in isiXhosa) in the twentieth century: see Gerhart, *Black Power*, 125. For the workings of a similar institution, the Tswana kgotla, see Landau, *The Realm of the Word*. For the role of speech in the "beer-drink," see Patrick A. McAllister, *Xhosa Beer Drinking Rituals*. I have no direct evidentiary basis to claim that Tzatzoe was concerned for the amaNtinde at this time. However, based on his father's expectations for his son and Jan Tzatzoe's latter position as chief of the amaNtinde, I feel confident saying that the status of his father's people would have been a consideration for him. For a different discussion of this stage in Tzatzoe's life, see Levine, "An Interpreter Will Arise."

26. This formalizing of allegiances can be read as an attempt by the colonial state to make the Xhosa "legible," following James C. Scott, *Seeing Like a State*. It might also be seen as one of the first steps toward indirect rule, and it anticipated the type of colonial control and information gathering that would be imposed in the region beginning with the ill-fated Queen Adelaide's Province: see Lester, *Imperial Networks*, 78–105, and Price, *Making Empire*.

27. Bird recalls the task in a letter to Williams: "You will remember that when His Excellency [Somerset] was at the Kat River, I was extremely anxious to learn from you, the names of the Chiefs who adhered to Gaika [Ngqika] and that with the aid of Jan Tzatchou [Tzatzoe] you furnished me with a List of the supposed subordinate Chiefs and of Gaika's Heemraden or Council," KAB CO 4841 Bird to Williams, at Kat River, Colonial office, 8 September 1818.

28. Evidence for conference from George McCall Theal, *Records of the Cape Colony: from February 1793 to April 1831* (Cape Town: Government of the Cape Colony, 1897–1905), 11, 310–16; Philip, *Researches*, 2:170–79, checked against original in LMS by Williams, and AB, 1:569; Mostert, *Frontiers*, 449–56; Stapleton, *Maqoma*, 26; "Distress and dread" and dragoons, Philip, *Researches*, 2:172; "First chief," Theal, *Records*, 11, 313; "Intercourse," Philip, *Researches*, 2:174. "Countenance" and "This Ngqika," Theal, "Records," 311–13.

29. AB, 1:569. Jan Tzatzoe will tell the story in England in 1836 when he will testify before a House of Commons subcommittee investigating colonialism in the British colonies. His testimony seeks to establish the coercive nature of British rule in the border region. The incident described above serves to foreground his narration of the intervening twenty years, and it is possible his choice of locating himself in the narrative may have been influenced by his treatment during that time by the British colonial authorities and the LMS, and the light he wishes to cast on both parties. For more on the meeting, see Philip, *Researches*, 2:176. I checked this version of Williams's letter against his original in the LMS archive.

30. For the diplomatic background and Tzatzoe's recollection of these events, see Mostert, *Frontiers*, 457–61 and AB, 1:569; for a further discussion of the events, see Stapleton, *Maqoma*, 27, who relies on the *Cape Frontier Gazette* and Peires, *House of Phalo*, 63.

31. In fact, the cattle were restored to Ngqika and his followers when the government realized a mistake had been made.
32. The conversation is taken from AB, 1:569–70, and the previous note describing the production of this testimony (in 1836) applies. The original orthography of the Aborigines Committee Report has "Gaika" and "T'Slambee" for Ngqika and Ndlambe. For "chastened," in 1832 Tzatzoe will recall that the Colonel had "nothing to say in his defence, but appeared ashamed of the duplicity of the transaction," SACA *South African Commercial Advertiser* 17 November 1832. The distance in years between event and description speaks to changes in the border region and to Tzatzoe's ability (in the 1830s) to cast colonial officials in a critical light. Yet, I feel confident that given the diplomatic complexity of the situation in 1818, the terminology reflects Tzatzoe's understanding of the interaction at that time.
33. Previous historians, including Mostert, have argued that the departures from the station were the direct result of fear of the wrath of Ngqika for the diplomatic snafu. But neither the Williams's rhetoric nor Tzatzoe's actions seem driven by fear of Ngqika—quite the opposite, in fact. Ngqika's reluctance to attack the station may have stemmed from his fear of a confrontation with the colony or its representatives. The section on the departure, with the exception of directly footnoted citations, is from LMS, SA Incoming, Box 7, Folder 4 C Williams to Burder, Kat River, 14 April 1818.
34. I would like to thank Andrew Bank for pointing out the importance of intimacy in Tzatzoe's story; unfortunately, the evidence that speaks to this sphere is extremely piecemeal. For gender relations in Xhosa society, see Natasha Erlank, "Gendered Reactions to Social Dislocation and Missionary Activity in Xhosaland."
35. For permission and delay, KAB CO 2613 Williams to Fraser, Kat River, 16 April 1818.
36. The illness, a rapid fever that Williams contracted while building in the hot sun, struck on 23 August 1818: see Holt, *Joseph Williams*, 84. For "decent burial," LMS, SA Incoming, Box 7, Folder 5 A Barker to Burder, Theopolis, 28 August 1818. For Elizabeth's journal, see Philip, *Researches*, 2:181–82.
37. For Barker and Tzatzoe's journey, see LMS, SA Incoming, Box 7, Folder 5 A Barker to Burder, Theopolis, 28 August 1818. For Elizabeth's conversations and reactions, see Philip, *Researches*, 2:183–85. The image of the dust and the glances is imaginative, with no direct evidence in Williams's letter.

FISH RIVER VALLEY, 1822

1. Bokwe, *African Convert*, and idem, *African Hymn*. Ntsikana adhered to a mission-inspired Christianity, although he referred to the eventual reign on earth of Sifuba-Sibanzi, the Broad-Breast, or Broad-Chested, One. Bokwe compares this appellation to Bunyan's "Great-heart": *Hymn*, 13–24. Some of Ntsikana's leading followers were members of the Soga family, whose son, Tiyo, would be the first officially ordained Xhosa minister. AB, 1:572. Tzatzoe testified that most of the members of the Glasgow missions such as Lovedale were originally with Williams at the Kat River.
Title quotation taken from William Shaw, *The Story of My Mission in South-Eastern Africa*, 315. The term reflects Shaw's desire for a mission in "eastern Africa." A letter

from Philip to the LMS states that Tzatzoe was at Theopolis until the start of the Buffalo mission in 1825, but Tzatzoe itinerated and also helped John Brownlee found the Chumie mission station in 1820: see "iQonce." Philip visited Tzatzoe in Theopolis in 1821 and 1823, BRWN Philip to Burder, Graaff Reinet, 5 August 1825. There is also a record of Tzatzoe preaching at Bethelsdorp from Hebrew 11, on 3 September 1819 (or possibly 1820), LMS, South Africa Journals, Box 3, Barker, Bethelsdorp, January 1820. This chapter is based on Shaw, *The Story*, and Stephen Kay, *Travels and Researches in Caffraria*. The accounts are extremely similar. Most likely, Shaw, writing decades after the publication of Kay's volume, took Kay's account and only changed it subtly. Shaw does not take direct credit for the "memoranda" in his text, but excerpts it, embellishing in differing areas significantly enough to merit reading both texts.

2. Their sheer numbers, however, bring about a seismic shift to the old institutions in the border region, and in the coming years they will grow more belligerent in their demands for the expropriation of African land and the protection of their holdings by imperial might. On the 1820 settlers, see Mostert, *Frontiers*, 520–34.
3. Shaw, *Story*, 1–20, 325–26.
4. For "marauders" through "comrades," Kay, *Travels*, 28–29.
5. Makana was no longer the same figure with whom Read and Tzatzoe had interacted in 1816. Following the Fraser commando, he had assumed the mantle of a warrior prophet, encouraging his followers to adopt the customs against which he had once inveighed (such as the wearing of red clay on the body). His theology had shifted as well. Now he preached an apocalyptic vision of a final battle between the god of the Europeans, Thixo (the name by which he had previously called God in his preaching in Xhosaland), and the god of the Xhosa, Mdalidiphu (a name of his own invention). Mdalidiphu would help the Xhosa to drive the Europeans back to the ocean from which they had come and onto which they had been cast because they had once murdered Thixo's son. Makana had anticipated the attack and prepared Ndlambe's battle plan. He would draw Ngqika's far smaller force into the open and encircle them with his larger army. Despite an explicit warning from Ntsikana to Ngqika that the chief was leading his people into a trap—Ntsikana saw the "heads of the Gaika being devoured by ants"—Ngqika committed to the attack. Legend holds that fires were lit so that survivors of the battle might be killed and that this action was an unprecedented escalation in the lethality of Xhosa warfare. See Bokwe, *African Convert*, 20, for the prophecy. The Xhosa writer, Bokwe, quotes the English colonial historian Theal on the savagery of the victory. Given recent work on the Mfecane, it seems likely that the genocidal nature of Amalinde has been overstated, and while Ndlambe certainly won a convincing victory, we might try to understand the language of annihilation metaphorically: see Caroline Hamilton, *The Mfecane Aftermath*. Indeed, Falati's alternate account simply states, "The Gaikas experienced a severe defeat" N. Falati, "The Story of Ntsikana". For the events from 1818 to 1822, see Peires, *House of Phalo*, 59–71, and Mostert, *Frontiers*, 446–516.
6. For the trip up the Fish River valley, Kay, *Travels*, 28–30. The description is based on Shaw and Kay, and on personal observation from July 2003 and January 2006, as is the description of the occasionally hot winter's day.

7. On the opening of trade between the colony and the Xhosa, the existence of trade fairs, and the volume of trade, Roger Beck, "The legalization and development of trade on the Cape Frontier, 1817–1830," Ph.D. thesis, Indiana University, 1987.
8. Shaw, *Story*, 329; Kay, *Travels*, 34.
9. The preceding two comments are the only section of the narrative of the evening session taken from Shaw; the rest is from Kay.
10. Except where noted, the evening interchange is taken from Kay, *Travels*, 35–38.
11. For "finest river," Shaw, *Story*, 331–32. For meeting at Tzatzoe's kraal, Kay, *Travels*, 38–40.
12. Shaw, *Story*, 332. For "breast of man," 333. For "oriental," Kay, *Travels*, 42.
13. Both Shaw, *Story*, 333–35, and Kay, *Travels*, 42–46.
14. On Tzatzoe's diplomacy, Shaw, *Story*, 335. For rest of the paragraph, Kay, *Travels*, 47.
15. Shaw, *Story*, 336. Soga, *Ama-Xosa*, has a discussion of African hunting practices.
16. For game pits, see Kay, *Travels*, 51, and Cory notebooks MS 109, Conversation with Somana and Tanco, Jan 22 1910. The men, both born in the 1820s, mention that they did "catch game by way of pits, about five feet deep," with a "large sneezewood pole sharpened at one end, also smaller ones." This game included bush buck, wild pigs, bluebuck, and hippo.

IQONCE, 1825–1832

1. The current motto of King William's Town is E'Qonce Malicume ("At the Buffalo River may there be prosperity"). As mentioned, the Xhosa name for the river that was named the Buffalo River by colonial officials (and now flows through the heart of East London and King William's Town) appears to have been iQonci, which refers to a local tree that some speculate is a boerboom: Cory Burton papers 14,610 (2). Burton says of the iQonce "What does that mean? Will anyone ever know?" I employ the contemporary "Chumie" of the British archive; the river and valley were also known as the Tyhumie or Tyumie. The Amathole (sometimes spelled amaThola) were referred to by British settlers as Hogsback. Basil Holt, *Greatheart of the Border*, 19, says the Xhosa call the mountains Belekazana, or woman with child on her back. Local legend and tourist brochures claim that the Amathole inspired the landscapes of J.R.R. Tolkien's *The Hobbit*, but the timing of Tolkien's birth in South Africa and departure for England at age three does not support these contentions; nonetheless, guidebooks insist on this fact. It is fair to say, however, that Hogsback does resemble Tolkien's Middle Earth. The description of the mountains as dolphins is my own, taken from personal observation, July 2003. The group of missionaries led by Tzatzoe in 1822 visited Brownlee at the Chumie. They noted the "Abundance of Timber," and a well-ordered mission station: Kay, *Travels*, 32–33. Additional information on the physical setting is from KAB CO 142, W. R. Thomson to Bird, Thumie, 24 November 1821. For Chumie in the only published monograph on Brownlee (and Tzatzoe by implication), Holt, *Greatheart*, 40.
2. For details on Brownlee's split from the LMS, BRWN, letters 1–21. These letters mostly concern the LMS's refusal to expel James Read for his adultery, and the refusal of the

LMS's board to cede control of the South African mission to the local missionaries. The LMS also found itself (especially in the wake of the 1820 settlers) in competition with even more socially conservative churches and mission organizations. For Read's case and the shift in ideology, Elbourne, *Blood Ground*, 197–232, esp. 220–32. For Read and Moffat at Lattakoo, Volz, "From the Mouths," 48–66. For respectability at the Cape, see Robert Ross, *Status and Respectability*. Today, Lattakoo is known as Dithakong. It is located near Mafeking. Thanks to Nancy Jacobs and Paul Landau for clarification.

3. For the founding, Holt, *Greatheart*, 10–24. Tzatzoe was at Chumie with Brownlee at the station's founding, but the preponderance of evidence points to him being at Theopolis in subsequent years. For the subsequent visits, 48–50. For the printing press and publications, Robert Young, *African Wastes Reclaimed*, 12–14.

4. Description drawn from portrait on the cover page of Andrew Ross, *John Philip (1775–1851)*, and several engravings in Basil le Cordeur and Christopher Saunders, eds., *The Kitchingman Papers*, as well as the Room portrait in Moffat Mission Trust, Kuruman, and an individual portrait of Philip that hangs next to Room, personal visit, December 2005. Ross's biography is the only monograph on Philip. *The Kitchingman Papers* are an irreplaceable resource for historians studying the LMS in the early nineteenth century; they contain letters from Tzatzoe, the Reads, and Philip among others. I checked the original handwritten Kitchingman letters in the Brenthurst Library for accuracy, and for relevant evidence in the sections that the editors elided from the published texts. There was no more substantial information on Tzatzoe.

5. Information on the Philip and Campbell report from CO 102, Philip and Campbell, Memorial to the Directors of the London Missionary Society, &c &c &c December 1819. For Philip, and the "deeply ambiguous" and conflicted nature of the "humanitarian liberalism" that he embodied, Andrew Bank, "Liberals and their Enemies," esp. 82–140.

6. Philip, *Researches*, 2:196–97.

7. BRWN Brownlee to Philip, Chumie, 3 July 1825.

8. This paragraph and rest of section dealing with justification for mission is from BRWN Philip to Burder, Graaf Reinet, 5 August 1825.

9. See "Introduction" for the roles of similar intermediaries in the border region.

10. Philip's letter of 5 August 1825 enclosed Brownlee's of 3 July 1825 to him on the subject of the mission. There is no reason to doubt that Philip had genuinely been looking for a companion for Jan Tzatzoe for a while. The letters do not suggest that Philip suddenly appropriated the idea from Brownlee, but that momentum had been building for a while and that the mutual expression of interest was, if not preordained, fortuitous.

11. Brownlee reconnoitered in the springtime, KAB CO 234 Brownlee to Henry Somerset, Commanding on the Frontier, Chumie, 18 November 1825, traveling with orders from the government to gather and report political information on the Xhosa and to return to the colony when called, KAB CO 4854 Plasket to Somerset, Commandant on the frontier, 8 December 1825. There is no record of whether Jan Tzatzoe was pres-

ent on the trip, or played a part (surely he did) in the final decision. As one example of many of the erasure of Jan Tzatzoe from historical narratives, Burton (a leading chronicler of the eastern frontier) says the following of the move: "When Brownlee left [Chumie] in 1825, among those who followed him to the Buffalo mission was 'Old Tshadchoo' Kote Tshatshu, father of the notorious Jan Tshatshu who went to England in 1836. . . ," Cory, Burton papers 14,610 (18)

12. LMS, SA Incoming, Box 10, Folder 1 B Miles to Hankey, Cape Town, 31 March 1826.
13. The foregoing description is taken from Chris Hummel, ed., *Rev. F. G. Kayser: Journal and Letters*, 55. Kayser notes the fields, irrigation ditches, bushy banks, and orientation. I also draw on observations and photographs taken during visits to the original site in King William's Town, July 2003 and January 2006.
14. The account of the missionary meeting is from LMS, SA Incoming, Box 10, Folder 1, D, Barker to Burder, Theopolis, 8 July 1826.
15. For the understandings of "civilization," see Jean and John Comaroff, *Of Revelation and Revolution*, esp. vol. 2, Gail Bederman, *Manliness and Civilization*, George W. Stocking, *Victorian Anthropology*.
16. For a discussion of liberalism, see *Buffalo River*. For paternalism and cultural chauvinism, see Elbourne's analysis of the missionized Khoisan in *Blood Ground*, esp. 293–344, and Andrew Bank, "Losing faith in the civilizing mission: the premature decline of humanitarian liberalism at the Cape, 1840–1860," in Daunton and Halpern, eds., *Empire and Others*.
17. KAB CO 2692 Dundas to Bourke, Graham's Town, 3 April 1827. For Dundas, see Mostert, *Frontiers*, 576. Dundas describes Brownlee as a "quiet, unassuming, painstaking, man."
18. The assertive self-description of Tzatzoe as an integral part of the mission and leader of the amaNtinde is from his testimony before the Aborigines Committee in which he was trying to emphasize his secular credentials as a witness to the spread of British colonialism in the eastern Cape, AB, 1:563–83.
19. A discussion of Xhosa ritual specialists, and the terminology I employ to describe them, follows in this chapter.
20. The scenes describing the rainmaker confrontation are taken from a letter from Miles, quoting a letter from Brownlee to Miles, LMS, SA Incoming, Box 10, Folder 2 A Miles to Burder, Cape Town, 13 February 1827. For rainmaking, see Mbiti, *African Religions*, 174–77. Rain is also to be understood metaphorically. Can a chief secure the peace, security, and fertility of his community? If he does, the rain will fall. See Steven Feierman, *Peasant Intellectuals* and Lan, *Guns and Rain*. Tzatzoe's case (with Brownlee present to report the conversation) echoes the Comaroffs' discussion of an encounter between David Livingstone and a rainmaker, in which they stress how the healer is "seduced into the modes of rational debate, positivist knowledge, and empirical reason at the core of bourgeois culture" by participating in an argument over who was the "legitimate" rainmaker, see Jean and John Comaroff, *Of Revelation*, 1:206–11. Here, an African intermediary prompts a similar discussion with a rainmaker.

The rainmaker insistence on an idea of "his God" who is opposed to the Christian God and the Comaroffs' notion of rationality is echoed by a similar discussion in 1817 between Tzatzoe and Williams and a female healer. The healer insists she can "smell-out" sorcery with the help of a lion (an animal used as a synonym or praise for a chief) who comes to her in a dream. When asked how the lion "knows these things," she answers logically, "perhaps he [the lion] has a fellowship with God & he [God] has thought proper to make known these things to us by a Lion," LMS, SA Incoming, Box 6, Folder 3, D, Williams to LMS, 15 June 1816 to 7 August 1817. My thanks to Paul Landau for elucidating the lion reference. Clifton Crais also analyzes the 1817 confrontation: see *Politics of Evil*, 125–29.

21. Mary Tzatzoe is the only child of Sanna Oursen and Jan Tzatzoe that I have found named in the archive, until the 1860s when Boy Henry Duke Tshatshu is mentioned.

22. Hummel, *Kayser*, 75–76, 198: also BRWN Brownlee and Kayser to Miles, Buffalo River, 26 December, 1828.

23. BRWN Brownlee to Miles, Buffalo River, 21 September 1827.

24. For "so to act," BRWN Brownlee and Kayser to Miles, Buffalo River, 26 December 1828. For "country" and rest of paragraph, Buffalo River Mission published in SOAS, Annual Report of the London Missionary Society for 1828.

25. BRWN Brownlee to Burder, Buffalo River, 3 August 1827. Robert Moffat's Gospel of Mark (of 1828–1829) is currently considered by scholars to be the first translation of a Gospel into a Sub-Saharan African language, personal communication, Paul S. Landau, 19 July 2009. Brownlee's letter does not further elaborate on his claim. Writing in 1902 Robert Young mentions that Brownlee had undertaken a translation of the Gospel of Matthew as early as 1825. Young adds that the "utmost caution was exercised before these Gospels were committed to the press," Young, *African Wastes*, 13–14. By far the most comprehensive listing of early translation work in Xhosa is found in the Reverend Appleyard's 1867 *Apology for the Kafir Bible*. Appleyard has this tantalizing description of "Translations not Printed" by the London Missionary Society: "Mark, And First Epistle of St. John, by the Rev. J. Brownlee. The venerable translator of these books is perhaps not aware that these early productions of his are still in existence. They were saved . . . out of a general burning of papers, the accumulation of years, left behind by the Rev. W. Shaw on returning to England in 1856. In their present form they have been copied by another hand, and the latter contains here and there proposed alterations by the Rev. W. Shaw. . . . Probable date of copy, 1828" John W. Appleyard, *An Apology for the Kafir Bible*. This evidence suggests that Brownlee's original may well have been completed in 1827, as stated in his letters. It also speaks poignantly to the fate of so much valuable archival material.

The first printed Xhosa scriptural material (date unknown) was likely Luke's Gospel, printed in the 1833 by Boyce and Show on the Methodist Press in Graham's Town: Gerard, *Four African Literatures*, 29, and Clement Doke, "Scripture Translation into Bantu Languages."

26. Without the specific Xhosa texts produced by Tzatzoe and Brownlee (and later by Tzatzoe and Kayser) to which to refer, it is difficult to undertake an exact study of

Tzatzoe's work as a translator. In my understandings of the work, I have been aided by Walter Benjamin: "The task of the translator consists in finding that intended effect upon the language into which he is translating which produces in it the echo of the original." Benjamin concludes his meditation by discussing how the Scripture like all great texts contains its "translation between the lines." See Walter Benjamin, "The Task of the Translator," in *Illuminations*, 76–82. Also, see Mary Snell-Hornby, *Translation Studies*. Thanks to Paul Landau for referring me to Snell-Hornby.

27. Information for Soko witchcraft scenes (that continues below): BRWN, Buffalo River, 26 December 1827, 12 February 1828, 11 April 1828. In this description of the Xhosa religious worldview, I am relying upon Peires, *House of Phalo*, 67, John S. Mbiti, *African Religions*, 162–74, and Comaroff and Comaroff, *Of Revelation*, 1:153–60. I am sympathetic, however, to Paul Landau's argument about the difficulties surrounding the very notion of "African religion." Landau points out that it was during the colonial period, with its attempts at Christian conversion, that certain African ideas and practices were conceptually and linguistically placed under the rubric of the term "religion." "'Religion' and Christian Conversion in African History: A New Model," 8–9. Peires seems to agree: "Religious practice [was] an inseparable part of secular activity. . . . It was a technique for getting things done and its practitioners . . . were not metaphysicians but technicians who understood the mechanics of the unseen world." I can reference only in the most cursory manner the vast literature on African religion and medicine. For background on African religion, see Thomas D. Blakely, Walter E. A. van Beek, Dennis Thomson, eds., *Religion in Africa: Experience and Expression*; T. O. Ranger and I. N. Kimambo, eds., *The Historical Study of African Religion*; J. Matthew Schoffeleers, *River of Blood*; W. C. Willoughby, *The Soul of the Bantu*; Janet Hodgson, *The God of the Xhosa*; Geoffrey Parrinder, *African Traditional Religion*. On evil, colonialism, and Christianity, see Gray, *Black Christians & White Missionaries*, chaps. 4–5.

28. Authors on the subject (see above) universally agree on the difficulty of assigning names to the category of individuals subsumed under the terms "prophet" or "doctor," in large part because they took on so many different roles. The task becomes even more complicated when an author attempts to recover usage in an African language, particularly in an exclusively archival setting such as that involving Jan Tzatzoe where the isiXhosa terms, or proper nouns, being employed have not been preserved. These ritual specialists have been pejoratively referred to as "witch-doctors," but one might also employ the terms: medicine-man, diviner, medium, healer, physician, wardoctor, rainmaker, or shaman, to list the most common. I have chosen to use the terms "healer" and "diviner" interchangeably, unless the specialist I am describing is engaged in a specific act (for example rainmaking), in which case I can employ a more specific name. Contemporary sources suggest the isiXhosa term "igqira" for a diviner. Backhouse divides the "Caffer doctors, or Amagqigha, into three classes. 1. The Smelling-doctors, who pretend to detect the operations of witchcraft in calamity, disease, &c. 2. The Handling-doctors, who administer medicine, but connect it with dancing, drumming, interrogations, and responses. . . . 3. Doctors of medicine, who

trust to pharmacy alone for the cure of disease. . . . [Also], persons who profess to be makers of rain . . . [those] who practice augury by burning certain roots [usually as regards success in war]," Backhouse, *Narrative of a Visit*, 1844, 230–31. The individual is called to her profession (a process known as ukuthwasa) when the ancestors or other spirits possess her (often in a process in which she removes herself from society). This possession manifests itself with physical illness, lethargy, seizures, and mystical visions. A diviner consults on her case. If he finds that her experiences are not the work of sorcery, but are the signs of a calling, the igqira undergoes an extensive initiation process that cures her mental and physical symptoms.

29. There is an extensive and expanding literature on witchcraft in Africa. For a contemporary discussion in an African setting of sorcery and counter-sorcery as a discourse and language through which to understand and challenge the use of power and change in society, see West, *Kupilikula*. For a fresh and well-argued approach to the subject that argues that witchcraft is a continuation of political expression, see Peter Geschiere, *The Modernity of Witchcraft*. Other works that have been particularly helpful to me are: Isak Niehaus with Eliazaar Mohlala and Kally Shokane, *Witchcraft, Power and Politics*; Henrietta L. Moore and Todd Sanders, eds., *Magical Interpretations, Material Realities*; and Adam Ashforth, *Witchcraft, Violence, and Democracy in South Africa*. For a particularly compelling account of witchcraft aimed at a popular audience, see Adam Ashforth, *Madumo: A Man Bewitched*. Clifton Crais addresses the relationship between chiefly power, magic, and the "smelling-out" of witches: see *The Politics of Evil*, 41–55.

30. To Kayser, to sin was to "lie, cheat, envy, steal, whore and commit adultery and injustice of injustice," LMS, SA Incoming, Box 11, Folder 1 B Kayser to fathers and brethren, buffels river, 15 May 1828. Hodgson traces a shift from a Xhosa conception of sin as actions that transgress the norms of the community, a "social infraction," to the "idea of a moral relationship with God and a sense of personal responsibility to him, to sense of personal inadequacy to be recognized and outgrown by grace," Hodgson, *Great Hymn*, 63–67. To compare sin to sorcery would be to emphasize the idea of sin as social transgression, as witchcraft was quintessentially antisocial.

31. For the confrontation between Tzatzoe, Williams, and the female diviner at the Kat River, LMS, SA Incoming, Box 6, Folder 3, D, Williams to LMS, 15 June 1816 to 7 August 1817. The context of Williams's language is important. The passage in which this quote is embedded makes clear that he (and by implication Tzatzoe as interpreter) are invoking a direct comparison between a diviner and the "great Prophet Christ" (although the arrival of this Christ is not imminent, a key point that may not have been understood by their audience): [I have kept the archival punctuation in these passages] "it was my firm belief that it was so and that it was through her falsehood so many were poisoned and sick & that the great prophet Christ who knew all things without being instructed by any would know when he came if what she had said to me and to the people were true and also how many persons she had poisoned while she pretended to throw the poison away and that the punishment which he would inflict on such liars as she was would be much greater than what was inflicted on

the Caffres whom she pretended to point out as guilty to be punished and who at the same time were innocent. . . . I also exhorted her to confess that she was a deceiver before all the Caffrees and to seek forgiveness of sin and the friendship of the great prophet Christ before he came to chastise her for her falsehood—She asked where Christ was? I replied he is in his house over our heads but he sees every action we do and hears every word we speak and knows every thought we think and all this will be brought forward by him when he comes and every individual must answer at his call." The missionaries who are recording Tzatzoe's translations are likely communicating with him in Dutch, which complicates an analysis of the linguistic shifts involved. In this case, there are direct correlations between the English word "prophet" and the Dutch "profeet," between "poison" and "vergiftigen," and between "witchcraft" or "sorcery" and "toverij." For Dutch translations, see http://www.freedict.co/onldict/dut. html, accessed on 29 May 2009. Unfortunately, the accounts of these conversations do not speak directly to the Xhosa words involved, but a close reading of the English texts reveals some interesting possibilities. By the mid- to late nineteenth century, isiXhosa incorporated English loanwords to convey the ideas of Christianity: "umprofeti" for "prophet," for example. As Paul Landau has pointed out, words in an oral culture are freer than those in a literate culture, and a literal rendering of the term that was employed might have cut off its multiple meanings. "Spoken words seem magical from the point of view of literacy. . . . [S]poken words . . . are part of the world they fleetingly exist in" (Paul Landau, "'Religion' and Christian Conversion," 8–9). At the iQonce mission, unlike the Kat River mission, Tzatzoe contributed to the fixing of words to paper. On the Xhosa vocabulary for "bewitching matter," "sin," "poison," "diviner," et cetera, I employed Rev. Albert Kropf, A *Kaffir-English Dictionary*, and Rev. W. J. Davis, rev. by Rev. William Hunter, *An English-Kaffir Dictionary*. A Xhosa anthropologist uses the term "igqirha" to apply to individuals he describes jointly as "diviners and prophets" throughout Xhosa history: see Mabona, *Diviners and Prophets*. An igqira often sucks the bewitching matter out of a person who is ill. Kropf identifies "witchcraft" as "ubugqi" or "ubutakato." The word for "poison" (in the sense of "bewitching matter") might have been "ubuhlungu." Peires identifies "bewitching matter" as "ubuthi" (a contemporary term), but the dictionaries suggest that this was a usage among the eastern Nguni (i.e., Zulu) that was popularized in Xhosaland by Mlanjeni in 1850. Kropf uses "uku mbulula" to describe the work of investigating sorcery through "isanuse," or "smelling out." He calls healers who divine the future "igqira lokuvumisa" and healers who deal with sorcery and the poison that witches use "igqira lokumbulula." To attest to the widespread discourse of the language and signs of magic and witchcraft, one episode of a documentary on the Mek "tribe" of New Guinea in 2008 showed a witchfinder literally sucking out iron filings from the bodies of individuals in the community: "Living With the Mek," Travel Channel, February 2008.

32. The language of sorcery has often been used to translate Christian concepts. For one example, a contemporary African scholar and clergyman noted a similar translation in Malawi, when his choir sang the following lines: "What will it profit you, my friend /

With all the witchcraft of this world/If you do not have the witchcraft of Jesus." He explains: "Those who practice witchcraft (*Mfiti*, sing.) are regarded as antisocial and anti-life. It is the *sing'anga*, (healer, medical practitioner) who provides medicines that can protect one from those who practice witchcraft. . . . Jesus is *sing'anga*, but not *mfiti*, even though the *afiti* can often also be *asing'anga* (healers)." The singers later agreed that by "witchcraft of Jesus" they were seeking to invoke the "power of Jesus"—in this case, the power of counter-sorcery: see A. C. Musopole, "Witchcraft Terminology, the Bible, and African Christian Theology." The process also worked in reverse. When Jan Tzatzoe's brothers returned from the Kat River Mission to the amaNtinde in 1817, they demonstrated unusual symptoms of Christian conversion like washing off the red ochre from their bodies. Williams described their activities as a "state of derangement, powerfully affected by the Word of God." The amaNtinde rejected them for "fear that they should fall into the same snare" as the brothers. Here, the amaNtinde are likely referring to symptoms of sorcery, LMS, SA Incoming, Box 6, Folder 3, D, Williams to LMS, 15 June 1816 to 7 August 1817. Similarly, in 1817, Ndlambe accused Tzatzoe and Williams of "corrupting" the mind of Ngqika when the latter's behavior began to change after contact with the mission, KAB, CO 2603 Williams to Fraser Kat River 22 (November) 1816 original just has 22nd.

33. For example, in 1817, after their itinerating, an adherent at the Kat River mission had described his spiritual state to Tzatzoe and Williams thusly: "I am rotten and stink and liable to fall. My hope is in God who has given his son for such sinners as stink and who has appointed his blood to cleanse them." LMS, SA Incoming, Box 6, Folder 3, D, Williams to LMS, 15 June 1816 to 7 August 1817. The language of the response suggests that the listener had understood himself as a person either bewitched by sin, or guilty of harboring sin as a witch might harbor the potential for witchcraft, and by implication, the *Prophet* Christ as akin to a diviner. An igqira who can educe witchcraft, and thereby diagnose and heal cases of illness or misfortune is an "igqira," is "anuse," or simply an "isanuse." The word "anuse" derives from the Xhosa word "ukunuka," which means "to smell" or "to stink" (meat can smell in this way). It also describes how a diviner smells-out sorcery in a witchfinding ceremony. Burton distinguishes an "Isanuse," who finds "ubuti" and is used in cases of lightning strikes, outbreaks of cattle diseases, or other calamities, from an "igqira," who addresses individuals who have suffered sickness or accidents, although an igqira can also smell out witchcraft. He also describes "itolas," or "war doctors," and herbalists who are "ixwheles," or "inyanga": Cory Burton 14, 619 (1). With regard to Tzatzoe's usage in 1817, Christ seems to have been literally understood as a witchfinder, and one whose arrival was imminent, not one who was anticipated to arrive in the distant future. This understanding supports Paul Landau's contention that Africans actually most often understood the terms employed by missionaries on an absolutely literal level (Personal communication, November 2002). Worger, however, argues that words assigned to "God" in the colonial encounter during the process of translation by missionaries (and I suggest native assistants), either took into account, or were forced to interact with, the outstanding degree to which African languages relied on metaphor. See

William Worger, "Parsing God," esp. 419–20, and Derek Peterson, "Translating the Word: Dialogism and Debate in Two Gikuyu Dictionaries," 31–50. Hodgson suggests that Ntsikana (who heard Tzatzoe and Williams preaching at the original Kat River mission) used metaphorical language to name Christ. These included the "Lamb of God" (Imvana kaTixo) and "Sifuba-sibanzi," which she translates as "Broad chested" or "Broad breast." Hodgson links this term to Van der Kemp's possible portrayal of Christ as Bunyan's "Great-heart," a warrior Christ armed with sword and shield. She adds that Ntsikana referenced Christ as a conqueror. There also appears to have been a heroic character in Xhosa myth in the form of a young prince named Broad Breast, whose chest was formed of an iron plate: Hodgson, *Ntsikana's Great Hymn*, 15, 41–42.

34. There were Xhosa individuals, like Makana and Ntsikana, who incorporated the new Christian spiritual power. Their large followings indicate a degree of syncretism with Xhosa beliefs to which the missionaries were unable, or unwilling, to commit. But they also were initially outside of the mainstream of Xhosa society.
35. These black ants nest in trees and are called "isiApompolo": see Kropf, *Dictionary*.
36. For the torture case, BRWN Buffalo River, 26 December 1827, 12 February 1828, 11 April 1828.
37. Peires argues that abandoning the dead to wild animals was a relatively new custom among the Xhosa, driven by smallpox epidemics of the late eighteenth century, when the "fatally ill were not allowed to die in their homes, but were chased out into the bush": see Peires, *House of Phalo*, 68. For practices around the abandoning of the dead and dying outside of the space of the community, see also Andreas Sagner, "The Abandoned Mother." Crais suggests that, along with consumption by wild animals, burning bodies destroyed the evil or evil spirit housed within: see Crais, *Evil*, 130.
38. These vivid accounts of torture belie the notion that violence directed against accused witches grew in the twentieth century: see Crais, *Politics*, 129–30, and Niehaus et al., *Witchcraft, Power*. Historians must be careful, however, when describing African practices of torture and cruelty because missionaries and white settlers were apt to exaggerate their descriptions in order to demonstrate the "barbarism" or "heathenism" of their intended converts and subjects: see, for example, Lepore, *Name of War*. However, mission stations came to serve as places where the victims of such torture could find refuge, and there are a multitude of missionary accounts whose very specificity speaks to their accuracy. The multiple accounts suggest a historical depth to the violence directed as punishment toward suspected witches For one of many examples I offer the following from an eastern cape missionary, John Ross: "One of these was a middle aged woman who was burned for Witchcraft. The flesh of the feet, legs, thighs and the middle of the back was literally roasted. The bones of the heels and legs halfway up the latter were laid bare such likewise was the case with the hands and arms. When discovered she had lain two weeks in this state without any dressing of the wounds. These were infested with worms. She was lying under a bush against which two of the people of the Kraal had placed a few branches and thrown some grass on them. She was laid out to die. Her daughter, a girl of about eight years of age, was her only attendant. All she could do was to bring her Mother water, and hold it to her mouth

to drink, beat off the dogs that were attracted by the stench and keep the fire alive that the wolves might not attack her by night." KAB CO 323 John Ross to Thomson, Lovedale, January 1827.

39. The biblical translations produced by Brownlee or Kayser in partnership with Tzatzoe do not appear to be housed in any archival collection in South Africa or Great Britain. One possible explanation is that translations produced by Tzatzoe, Brownlee, and Kayser in the 1820s and early 1830s would have needed to be revised in light of the discovery by W. B. Boyce in the early 1830s of the so-called Euphonic Concord, or alliterative concord, upon which was built the underlying grammar of isiXhosa and other Bantu languages. Boyce printed his St. Luke's Gospel in 1833 and his "Grammar of the Kafir Language" in 1834 on the Graham's Town press: W. G. Mears, foreword to Boyce, *Notes on South African Affairs*. Kayser noted after the outbreak of the frontier war of 1834–1835 that he was glad not to have lost his "translations of John [and] the acts. They are still in my hands. . . [But] nothing had been done in regard of printing them with the orther [sic] translations." These particular texts were supposed to be printed in Graham's Town in 1834, but no evidence exists to suggest they ever were. Hummel adds that Kayser, along with Tzatzoe, had translated Matthew and all the Miracles by 1830, and most of the New Testament by 1832: Hummel, *Rev. F. G. Kayser*, 121, 125n15. Shepherd describes a meeting at the Buffalo River Mission in 1831 of representatives of the "London, Wesleyan and Glasgow Societies" in which the participants agreed to pool their efforts, specifically collecting the "books of the Bible which various missionaries had translated." This effort would explain how Appleyard in 1867 (as mentioned in an above note) would list Brownlee's Mark among the items left behind by William Shaw. It is interesting, therefore, that Appleyard does not list any text by Kayser among the extant printed or unprinted translations available in 1867: R.H.W. Shepherd, *Bantu Life and Literature*, 30–32, and Appleyard, *Apology*, 7–10. According to Hodgson, "mission teams from diverse societies" published the Old and New Testaments in Xhosa in 1857 and 1846, respectively: Hodgson, "Christian Beginnings," in *Christianity in South Africa*, 77, 414n51. Likely, Tzatzoe, Brownlee, and Kayser's translations were subsumed into later versions. While it would be interesting to see how the texts to which Tzatzoe contributed translated the biblical term "prophet" on the page, they would likely not fully illuminate the discussion in this chapter, since, on the page, Christ would have been rendered by his name and not by the metaphorical associations assigned to him in the speeches. On the translatability of the Bible and Christianity, see Lamin Sanneh, *Translating the Message*. Comaroff and Comaroff, *Revelation*, 1:213–30, has a discussion of translation, arguing for a "linguistic colonialism" (219) of the seTswana by missionaries. I would contend that Tzatzoe's example offers a counter-example. Comaroff and Comaroff, *Revelation*, 2:63–118, offers a discussion of native agency and the work of Christianity among Africans. Elizabeth Elbourne calls attention to issues within the Comaroffs' work, in particular their under-appreciation of the role of African intermediaries such as Jan Tzatzoe in the colonial encounter: see Elbourne, "Word made flesh." Appleyard, who completed a translation of the Bible into Xhosa in the 1840s and 1850s, does not men-

tion receiving or requesting any help from African intermediaries. He was assisted by several other Europeans. Clearly, the ground on which the missionaries stood shifted between the 1820s and 1850s, as African intermediaries were deemed disposable. Of course, Appleyard also spoke of the "wonderful changes" brought about by the famine that resulted from the Xhosa Cattle Killing of 1856–1857: see Appleyard, *The War of the Axe*, 133.

40. Unless otherwise indicated, the following paragraphs are drawn from LMS, South Africa, Journals, Box 4, number 99, Kayser, Buffalo River, and Hummel, *Rev. F.G. Kayser*, 54–72.

41. This interesting metaphor for leadership of an egg in one's hand was repeated by Tzatzoe in England. It appears to derive from the well of Xhosa proverbs.

42. These water spirits, or i-Canti, are well known elements of Xhosa cosmology: see Soga, *The Ama-Xosa*, 193–96.

43. As noted above, W. B. Boyce "discovered" the Euphonic concord underlying isiXhosa syntax in the early 1830s. LMS, SA Incoming, Box 11, Folder 3, C, Kayser to Directors, buffels river, 4 June 1829.

44. LMS, SA Incoming, Box 12, Folder 1, C Kayser to Directors, Buffelsrivir, Kaffraria, 14 July 1830.

45. LMS, SA Incoming, Box 12, Folder 1, C Kayser to Directors, Buffelsrivir, Kaffraria, 13 December 1830. On 3 July 1832, Kayser wrote to a friend that the "Cape Society [for promoting Christian Knowledge]" was to publish the Miracles, but as described in the notes above, I am not aware of an extant copy. The editor of Kayser's journal and letters, Rev. Hummel, notes that "the matter of Xhosa translations done by Kayser requires further research," suggesting only that he might be associated with a book of hymns published in Lovedale in 1864. Hummel, *Rev. F.G. Kayser*, 88, 90n13.

46. As with Christ as "Great Prophet," it is unclear how Tzatzoe translates the phrase "Great Physician" (and, by implication, the word his Xhosa listener would have used in reply). A possibility is that Tzatzoe was basing his comparison on the specific activities of one set of ritual specialists, emphasizing their supernatural work in the realms of healing and counter-sorcery versus the realm of diviners. In this case, he likely would have used the word "igqira." For example, Musopole translates the chiChewa word "sing'anga wa mkulu," which substitutes for isiXhosa's "igqira," for Jesus as the "great Physician." But for Kayser, the phrase "Great Physician" may have been a more acceptable way of comparing Christ in English to a Xhosa ritual specialist than were "Great Witchdoctor" or "Great Magician." I think the evidence (particularly Kayser's statement that Tzatzoe used "Great Physician" to mark Christ's difference from a "witchdoctor") suggests the possibility of the Xhosa words "inyanga" or "ixwhele," which some contemporary linguists associate with healers who employed herbs and the application of charms to cure sick individuals. These individuals were thus distinguished from those described as (singular) "igqira." It might also follow that the verb "umpiliso," which derives from the verb "pila" ("to be well"), would have been used. But, clearly, the biblical Great Physician heals through supernatural forces, which argues against a shift toward the name for herbalist. As follows in the text, the most

important aspect of the shift for this work is in the use of the miracles themselves as evangelizing tools.

47. The discussion is taken from Hummel, *Rev F. G. Kayser*, 70–71. Sources are both an extract from his personal diary dated 9 November [1829], and a letter written to Germany, dated 1830, that Hummel attributes to the Leipzig Missionary Archive. Tzatzoe had not invented the association of Christ with the term "Great Physician," which not only has biblical resonance (particularly in the Gospel of Luke, who is, himself, described as a physician), but also features in biblical scholarship and commentary: for instance, Cotton Mather's *The great physician, inviting them that are sensible of their internal maladies, to repair unto him for his heavenly remedy*, 1700; or John Gardner, *The Great Physician; the connection of diseases and remedies with the truth of revelation*, 1843. It is interesting to note that the great expansion of Christianity across Africa would await the introduction in the early twentieth century of Pentecostal ideologies that emphasize the church as a site of healing. Tzatzoe's efforts anticipate this development, but cannot be linked to it in a causal sense: see, for example, Allan A. Anderson and Gerald J. Pillay, "The Segregated Spirit: The Pentecostals," in Elphick and Davenport, *Christianity in South Africa*.

48. For a discussion of Xhosa attitudes to death as "evil and unnatural" and the ancestors "constantly manifest[ing] [themselves] in the lives of the living, see Peires, *Dead Will Arise*, 31–32 and 128–32. There are over thirty "healing stories" from the Gospels. Mark tends to stress their importance, and John contains several that are not found in the other three Gospels. For the quote on resurrection, see John 11:25–26.

49. In 1832 Kayser describes a vaccination campaign against a smallpox epidemic in the region. The missionaries successfully vaccinate their followers, whereas large numbers of unbelievers die. In this case, church attendance skyrockets. Kayser says that he and John Tzatzoe notice a "strong impact on the heathens" from "God's mercy": see Hummel, *Rev. F. G. Kayser*, 74. For the emerging connections between missionaries and Western medicine (what Megan Vaughan calls "biomedical" practice), see Paul S. Landau, "Explaining Surgical Evangelism in Southern Africa," 261–81, and Vaughan, *Curing their Ills*. See, also, Comaroff and Comaroff, *Revelation*, 2:323–64. For a further discussion of healing, colonialism, and "medicalization," see Nancy Rose Hunt, *A Colonial Lexicon of Birth Ritual, Medicalization, and Mobility in the Congo*. Especially in the nineteenth century (before the germ theory emerged), it would be hard to disaggregate belief in the efficacy of Western medicines with belief in the "medicine" of herbalists, or even diviners. Both witchfinders and surgeons claimed to extract disease-causing agents from ill bodies. The use of the terms "doctor" or "witchdoctor" for Xhosa religious specialists brings to mind the "Big Medicine" and "medicine men" of the American West. If "medicine" was the English term adopted in North America to describe activities similar to those that were considered witchcraft or magic in southern Africa, it is interesting to note that "Christ as healer" returns to a medical tradition. In a study of the northern border between the United States and Canada, Beth LaDow argues that local Indians called the region the "medicine line" as a "thing with magical political power": see LaDow, *The Medicine Line*, 40–41.

50. A civil servant, A. F. Bruce, mentions 4,000 Hottentot settlers in a letter to the *South African Commercial Advertiser*, SACA 31 October 1832. For Kat River Settlement, see Elbourne, *Blood Ground*, and Robert Ross, forthcoming.
51. Buffalo Station in 1832: SOAS, Annual Reports, Thirty-Ninth Report of the Missionary Society, 1833. Again, I was unable to locate this publication in the South African or British archives.
52. European missionaries will take on African languages for themselves, and the first generation of 1820 British settlers (and missionary children) will grow up with a native knowledge of African languages. In addition, the new chauvinism will downplay the importance of African contributions to the new South African world.
53. For "fall off again," LMS, SA Incoming, Box 13, Folder 2, A Kayser to Directors, Buffelsrivier, Kaffraria, 3 December 1832. For "Missionary," LMS, SA Incoming, Box 13, Folder 2, A Report of the Cape Town Auxiliary Missionary Society in connection with the LMS, 1832.
54. For Tzatzoe helping with the translation of the various Gospels listed, as well as catechisms and children's books, BRWN Buffalo River, 26 December, 1828 and Brownlee and Kayser to LMS, Tzatzoe's Kraal, Buffalo River, 1 January 1830. The larger point to be made is that Tzatzoe can serve as an illustration of the work, of the roles, that countless other Africans undertook at mission stations throughout Africa, and later, in the establishment of colonial rule.

BUFFALO RIVER, 1833–1835

1. In a literal and symbolic sense in this chapter, Tzatzoe and Brownlee's mission station (and its historical setting) become more European during this period, thus the shift from iQonce to Buffalo River in my narrative.
2. For Soko and Kote incident, Tzatzoe's quote and Maqoma, LMS, SA Incoming, Box 13, Folder 3, C Kayser to Directors, Buffelsrivier, Kaffraria, 12 July 1833, including extracts from Kayser's journal. For death of Soko, Hummel, *Rev. F.G. Kayser*, 93. For "variety of the human race," BRWN, Brownlee to Ellis, Buffalo River, 16 December 1833.
3. For humanitarian liberalism and the British settler response, at the Cape and in Great Britain, see Keegan, *Colonial South Africa*, 75–128; Bank, "Liberals and their Enemies"; Lester, *Imperial Networks*; Elbourne, *Blood Ground*; and Mostert, *Frontiers*.
4. Bank discusses these two pivotal newspapers in relation to Benedict Anderson's formative work on "imagined communities" in "Liberals and their Enemies," 19–22. See also Kirsten McKenzie, *Scandal in the Colonies*.
5. SACA 9 February 1833, excerpted from GTJ.
6. GTJ *Graham's Town Journal*, 7 March 1833. The question of authorship, and the sense of authenticity in Tzatzoe's speeches and the writings attributed to him, was a theme throughout his time in the public arena. The suspicion derived in large part from the popular appeal of the abolitionist movement, and its use of propaganda, often in the form of the life story, or literal presence, of a "redeemed" African. Opponents

of reform immediately questioned whether Africans were speaking for themselves, parroting abolitionist or humanitarian rhetoric, or simply serving as public fronts for their benefactors' words. Thus when Tzatzoe traveled to Britain his detractors did not question the transcripts of his speeches, but insisted that the words he was speaking had been scripted for him. Some went so far as to insist that Tzatzoe's Dutch was not being faithfully translated by James Read and James Read Junior: see the chapters "England" and "Great Britain."

In an attempt to question the authenticity of the letters and other public statements of 1833, Eastern cape settlers would testify before the Aborigines Committee that Tzatzoe was barely literate. But this approach represented a narrow view of literacy, and even if he didn't (as will become obvious) write the letters word for word, I argue below that Tzatzoe clearly had some degree of authorship over them.

The comparison of Tzatzoe's personal letters, or even signatures, with his opus of public letters was also the case in the attribution of 1789's *The Interesting Narrative of the Life of Olaudah Equiano*, to Equiano, or Gustavus Vassa, as the purported author generally referred to himself. Such textual analysis more quickly dismissed Ottobah Cugoano as the primary author of *Thoughts and Sentiments on the Evil and Wicked Traffic of Slavery* in 1787 than it was able to disqualify Vassa. Recent scholarship does suggest that Vassa's account of his birth in Africa and journey through the Middle Passage is fictional, which in some ways adds to his consideration as a literary figure: see Paul Edwards, ed., *Equiano's Travels*, and Carretta, *Equiano*. Carretta makes a strong case (citing Ira Berlin) that Vassa was an "Atlantic creole," a man who was able to create a new self among the meetings of worlds along the Atlantic littoral. Part of this self involved the invention of a life story that appropriated key narrative elements from all sectors of the emerging Atlantic world: an African homeland, the Middle Passage, North America, and Britain. As we will see, Tzatzoe embraced the abolitionist rhetoric and narrative, but it doesn't appear he fabricated his life story.

It is interesting in light of Equiano to note that Tzatzoe and his supporters never produced a work that fit into the autobiographical genre, and this fact may speak to Tzatzoe's inability to write in a sustained manner. It is also possible that such a project would have been initiated if the humanitarians (and Tzatzoe himself) had not fallen out of favor in the 1840s and 1850s. James Read did write a laudatory evangelical biography of Andries Stoffels, but only after the latter's death: see James Read Senior, *The African Witness: or, a Short Account of the Life of Andries Stoffles; Published with Josiah Basset, The Life of a Vagrant, or the Testimony of an Outcast*, (London: 1850.) I analyze the specifics of the 1833 letter writing campaign later in this chapter.

7. For commando or patrol system, see Mostert, *Frontiers*, 627–31, and Lester, *Networks*, 21, 42–43.
8. *South African Commercial Advertiser* (SACA), 13 April 1833.
9. These four letters are from GTJ, 11 April 1833.
10. AB, 1:563–83.

11. LMS, South Africa, Incoming, Box 25, Folder 4, D, Read Junior to Freeman, Philipton, 4 July 1850. Read may have the wrong Southey. Mostert indicates that it was another brother, Richard, who became Secretary of Lesotho. A third brother, George, was reported to have killed the chief Hintza in 1835.
12. Unless specifically indicated, the section on the newspaper correspondence draws on SACA, 7 November 1832; 17 November 1832; 8 December 1832; 9 February 1833; 13 February 1833; 20 March 1833; 13 April, 1833; and GTJ, 10 January 1833; 31 January 1833; 14 February 1833; 7 March 1833; 21 March 1833; 4 April 1833; 11 April 1833; 9 May 1833; 16 May 1833; 27 June 1833; 15 August 1833; 3 October 1833.
13. For John and Jane Philip (Jane administered the LMS in South Africa while Philip was away), see Natasha Erlank, "Jane & John Philip: Partnership, Usefulness & Sexuality in the Service of God." WITS Philips Papers, Jane Philip to Miss Alice Wills, Cape Town, 28 March 1834. Wills appears to be a friend of Jane, not her daughter: "Guide to the Archives Housed at Historical Papers." On Native Agency, see Elbourne, *Blood Ground*, 336–40, although Elbourne deals with a later period, and Comaroff and Comaroff, *Of Revelation*, 2:87–88.
14. See Bank, "Losing Faith," in *Empire and Others*, and Keegan, *Colonial Order*.
15. SOAS, Annual Reports, Forty-First Report of the Missionary Society, 1835. Other Africans were called "native teachers" or simply not identified by either name or position.
16. BRWN Brownlee to Ellis, Caffraria, 29 July 1834.
17. Zechariah 4: 9–10. My thanks to Lamin Sanneh for emphasizing this biblical usage. Sanneh adds that a nineteenth-century missionary working in West Africa cited the text in a similar mission context. Personal communication, April 2004.
18. LMS, South Africa, Incoming, Box 14, Folder 4, B, Kayser to Director, Theopolis, 10 June 1835.
19. For outbreak of hostilities, SACA 31 December 1834. For "without delay," Brownlee letter to Read, undated and contained in LMS South Africa Incoming, Box 14, Folder 3, A, Philip to Ellis, Cape Town, 9 January 1835. For "bushbuck," LMS, South Africa, Incoming, Box 14, Folder 3, D, Kayser to Directors, 17 March 1835.
20. On Tzatzoe, the Reads, and the outbreak of war, LMS South Africa Incoming, Box 14, Folder 2, C, Read senior to Philip, Philipton, 23 December 1834 and Read, Junior to Philip, Philipton, 30 December 1834. On Brownlee, BRWN Brownlee to Ellis, Caffraria, 14 March 1835.
21. LMS, South Africa, Incoming, Box 14, Folder 4, B, Kayser to Director, Theopolis, 10 June 1835.
22. Mostert, *Frontiers*, 677–79.
23. For "Sheep heaths," BRENT Brenthurst Library, Kitchingman Papers, MS. 183/2, Philip to Kitchingman, Cape Town, 20 January 1835. For "Red Sea," Bodleian library, Rhodes House, Philip Papers MSS Afr. s. 217, Philip papers 4, 1834–1835, unpaginated.
24. Mostert, *Frontiers*, 686–90.
25. Information on Brownlee and Tzatzoe in war: BRWN Brownlee to Ellis, Beka, 14 March 1835; Brownlee to Ellis, Somerset, 19 January 1836.

26. Charles Brownlee's "reminiscence" was written in 1873; the frontier had been settled. His account is tinged with nostalgia, but the detail of his description is compelling. Soka was dead at this point, so either Brownlee conflated his name with another of Jan Tzatzoe's brothers or there was another brother named Soka: Charles Brownlee "The Old Peach Tree Stump: A Reminiscence of the War of 1835," 231–48.
27. Charles Brownlee's account ends with a wistful recollection of the original Buffalo River station. "On the banks of the Buffalo, where . . . in the midst of gross darkness, lived a solitary missionary, now stands King William's Town, the third largest town in the Colony, with seven European churches and two Native chapels," Brownlee, "The Old Peach Tree Stump."
28. KAB, A519, D'Urban, 37 GTJ, 27 February 1835.
29. Ibid., 6 February 1835.
30. GTJ, 22 September 1836. The charges will be the subject of testimony before Buxton's Aborigines Committee: see "Queen Adelaide Province," "England," and "Great Britain."
31. For tactical and strategic changes, see Roger Levine, "African Warfare," in Richard Tucker and Ed Russell, eds., *Natural Ally, Natural Enemy*.
32. KAB A835 Schoeman letter home, 10 March 1835.
33. On Hintza, see Mostert, *Frontiers*. For an examination of the death of Hintza and its reverberations through history, see Premesh Lalu, *The Deaths of Hintsa*. Lalu interrogates the construction of the colonial archive, and demonstrates how, in the case of the killing and beheading of Hintza, or more broadly, the search for an objective truth of the past (or even a "subaltern consciousness") might give way to an examination of the processes of colonial domination of Africans as reflected in the archival record. I hope that my narration of Tzatzoe's life provides a fruitful case study for historians, including Lalu, with regard to such questions of subaltern agency, representation, domination, and difference. See also Lalu, "The Grammar of Domination."
34. On the peace meeting, KAB OPB 1/9 1 D'Urban dispatch and enclosures to Earl of Aberdeen, 19 June 1835.
35. BRWN Brownlee to Ellis, Somerset, 19 January 1836. Brownlee says: "My advice from the commencement of the war was to Tzatzoe's people . . . to abstain as far as possible from war, but the love of plunder was a strong excitement. . . . [A] time of war is not favourable for the growth of piety, and all who have engaged have suffered temporal loss."
36. For King William's Town, see Mostert, *Frontiers*, 732. The colonial correspondence that describes the founding of the town (included the cited text) is excerpted in Robert Godlonton, *A Narrative of the Irruption*, 2:183. Godlonton has an appendix that prints the General Order establishing the town, dated Head-Quarters on the Buffalo, 24 May 1835: "the ground on both banks of this clear, rapid, and beautiful river, along an arc crossed by four fords, to which corresponding roads from all parts of the country converge (near the Mission House destroyed by the savages) is hereby appropriated," Godlonton, *Irruption*, 2:256–57. For Brownlee's house and the use of Tzatzoe's house as a stables, see AB, 1:580.

QUEEN ADELAIDE PROVINCE, 1835–1836

1. D'Urban frequently employs this naturalistic language to dehumanize the Xhosa and render them more animal-like. Later in this chapter, he will compare the Xhosa to wolves who can not be "tamed." For the use of such language, see Levine, "African Warfare."
2. D'Urban defends his and Smith's actions in OPB 1/9 1 D'Urban dispatch and enclosures to Earl of Aberdeen, 19 June 1835.
3. (QAP) Records of the Province of Queen Adelaide, consisting chiefly of the private and confidential correspondence between Governor Sir Benjamin D'Urban, Colonel H. G. Smith, Lieutenant-Colonel H. Somerset, and other high officials; copied and arranged by George McCall Theal, 1913, Articles of a Treaty of Peace, granted the Kafir Family of Gaika, 387–92. Historians have called this plan grandiose and full of hubris, but it anticipated British colonial policies, both in Natal, and also in the eastern Cape, following the annexation of British Kaffraria in 1848, and certainly after the Cattle Killing disaster of 1857. Some historians have argued that Smith and D'Urban's vision was the first example of what would be called "indirect rule" in Africa, stressing Smith's direct influence on Theophilus Shepstone, for whom the latter worked during this period: see Thomas McClendon, "The Man Who Would Be Inkosi." Other historians analyze the plans of both individuals as a "direct rule" approach. For different understandings of these issues, see Lester, *Imperial Networks*, esp. 78–104. For a materialist perspective, see Keegan, *Colonial South Africa*; for a postmodern perspective, see Crais, *White Supremacy*.
4. QAP, D'Urban to Bell, Graham's Town, 25 September 1835, 5–8. Also verbatim in KAB GH 19/4 D'Urban, confidential notes on Treaties of 17 September 1835.
5. Buxton, *Memoirs*, 1st edition, 1849, 306–7. For the humanitarian movement, see "Buffalo River." Buxton, Philip, and other humanitarians had formed a network between metropole and colony that resulted in the passage and ratification of Ordinance 50 in 1828, an act that granted Khoisan and other free blacks in the Cape Colony full legal rights. After 1834 slaves entered a four-year apprenticeship period before fully gaining their freedom in 1838. For evangelical and political networks, see Lester, *Imperial Networks*. Michael A. Rutz examines the interconnections of politics and mission organizations in the early to mid-nineteenth century, stressing the emergence of public opinion. He analyzes the careers of James Read and John Philip, specifically, in "'Meddling with Politics': The Political Role of Foreign Missions in the Early Nineteenth Century." My thanks to Nancy Jacobs for alerting me to Rutz's work.

Alan Lester and David Lambert defend the practice of biography with which this work is engaged and speak to the interconnections between metropole and colony, and the networks that sustained both, in David Lambert and Alan Lester, eds., *Colonial Lives Across the British Empire*. Philip, Buxton, Smith, and D'Urban all engaged in "imperial careering," in Lester and Lambert's phrase.
6. For Buxton, TFB Buxton to Pringle, Volume 12, 145. Buxton, *Memoirs*, and Priscilla Johnston, *Extracts from Priscilla Johnston's Journal and Letters*, and R. H. Mottram, *Buxton the Liberator*.

7. Buxton, *Memoirs*, 1849, 306–7. Buxton's fireside journal entries makes for great reading and is as complete a rendering of the evangelical humanitarian ideology as I have found. In the interests of narrative continuity, I could only employ these brief selections. Buxton is clear that his granting of land rights to Africans will come only under a system of British sovereignty.
8. AB, I, iii and 1. Mostert calls the *Select Committee* the "apogee of the philanthropic crusade in the nineteenth century, the high point of their post-emancipation power and influence, and of their political impact upon South African affairs." To Mostert, the committee grappled with how to brake the "inner momentum of overseas settlements heading recklessly toward disastrously expensive confrontations with indigenous peoples." The committee remains "one of the most striking and impressive examples of public inquiry in nineteenth-century Britain, its massive report one of the most absorbing public documents of that century": see Mostert, *Frontiers*, 739, 801–2. For scholarly work on the Aborigines Report, see C. A. Bayly, "The British and Indigenous Peoples, 1760–1860," in *Empires and Others*; Laidlaw, *Colonial Connections* and "'Aunt Anna's Report': the Buxton Women and the Aborigines Select Committee, 1835–1837," 1–27; Elbourne, *Blood Ground*, 288–92; and Lester, *Imperial Networks*.
9. TFB Volume 14, 98–100, Buxton to Grey, 6 September 1835; TFB Volume 14, 100, Grey to Buxton, 20 September 1835.
10. Of Stephen a historian has written: "[He] relentlessly tortured himself, somewhat masochistically delighting in the physical and mental anguish brought about by the mountain of detail in which he deliberately immersed himself . . . and thus . . . attempted to make himself indispensable," John Winston Cell, *British Colonial Administration*, 11.
11. Cell, Colonial Administration, 3–5.
12. LMS Home Personal Box 5. Folder 1 #7, Ellis to Philip, London, 26 September 1835. As noted above, the second half of the request echoes D'Urban's vision for Queen Adelaide Province. Keegan makes a strong case that humanitarian thinking contained within it the seeds of the white supremacist order that emerged in the Cape, and, he argues, spread to the Witwatersrand. He is reacting to the body of work that suggests that white supremacy in South Africa emerged either on the frontier or during the industrialization process following the mineral revolution. He writes: "The contradictions inherent in the whole liberal humanitarian project of the first half of the nineteenth century are a theme running through my study. Early nineteenth century liberalism was profoundly ambiguous. Its rhetorical commitment to the legal forms of equality and freedom was in sharp contrast to its fundamental compatibility with cultural imperialism, class domination and, ultimately, racial subjugation. And it could be argued that these were not just failings, but were a function, direct or indirect, of the role of liberal ideology in sustaining the hegemony of class and culture in the rapidly developing economic order of free-trade capitalism," Keegan, *Colonial Order*, 13.
13. LMS Home Personal Box 5. Folder 1 #7, Ellis to Philip, London, 26 September 1835.

14. For the working relationship of Gurney and Buxton, Levine, "Sable Son of Africa," Ph.D. Thesis, Yale University, 2004, and Laidlaw, "'Aunt Anna's Report'." For "epitome," Buxton, *Memoirs*, 312–13. Buxton describes the meeting in which Stephen responds to Gurney's "able digest" in a letter to Gurney in November 1835. It continues: "You remember how cold used to be my reception at the Colonial Office when I talked about South Africa, Caffres, and Aborigines. I went there yesterday saw Glenelg, Grey, and Stephen and found the Attitude of these changed to blood-almost to fever heat. They talked of Hintza, Southey, Philip, Somerset, D'Urban, with absolute familiarity, knew more about it, spoke more indignantly against commandos than you or I ever did, intimated that they would revoke D'Urban, restore the country to its owners, acknowledge the error and the national disgrace . . . prohibit the entrance of an armed man into Caffreland. In short, take the most audacious of our suggestions and the most extravagant of our whimsies and they talked of them as sober sensible justice and the least which could be done for a race whom we have so grievously oppressed," TFB collection, vol. 14, 162–66, Buxton to A. Gurney, 24 November 1835.
15. Buxton *Memoirs*, 311, and Mostert, *Frontiers*, 755–56.
16. KAB OPB 1/9 1, Glenelg dispatch to D'Urban, 26 December 1835. For the Glenelg dispatch, D'Urban's rebuttal, and the controversy's connections to the "Great Trek," see Joseph H. Lehmann, *Remember You are an Englishman*, 195; Etherington, *Great Treks*; and the classic and still definitive work in this area, W. W. Macmillan, *Bantu, Boer, and Briton*.
17. TFB, vol. 14, 162–66, Buxton to A. Gurney, 24 November 1835.
18. For iSilimela and the agricultural cycle (see next paragraph), see Peires, *House of Phalo*, 7, 195n45–46. Hodgson notes that the stars derived their name from ukulima (to hoe . . . dig . . . plough), they were the "digging-for" stars. Their appearance represented the Xhosa New Year, as well as the coming-out ceremony of the initiation or circumcision schools; therefore, men marked their years of maturity as izilimela, or, literally, a certain number of isilimela(s): see Hodgson, *Great Hymn*, 36.
19. KAB OPB 1/9 1 D'Urban dispatch and enclosures to Earl of Aberdeen, 19 June 1835. For a study of the wolf, its image in human society, and what this relationship reveals about culture, see Jon T. Coleman, *Vicious: Wolves and Men in America*.
20. These processes have parallels in societies undergoing slave revolts: see, for example, da Costa, *Crowns of Glory*. Relevant here, too, are Euro-American encounters with American Indians: see, for example, Lepore, *Name of War*. For the eastern Cape, see, in particular, Crais, *White Supremacy*; Bank, "Liberals and their enemies," esp. 189–236; and Mostert, *Frontiers*.
21. QAP D'Urban to Smith, Port Elizabeth, 23 November 1835, and Smith to D'Urban, King William's Town, 22 September 1835. The tract of land was granted to the "Tribe of John Tzatzoe" and it lay "upon the Right Bank of the Buffalo River from the confluence of the Quaguebe up the Ford on the road to Fort Beresford"; also, KAB LG 604 Smith to D'Urban, KWT, 15 October 1835. Unfortunately for Tzatzoe's descendants, only land confiscated by the state since the early twentieth century is eligible in the post-apartheid Land Claims process. Tzatzoe's testimony to the Aborigines Commit-

tee in 1836 was as follows: "Did the governor know of the wrong that had been done to you? [the confiscation of Tzatzoe's land to establish King William's Town and his removal from the town center] I do not know that; but he knew that he had taken my country. . . Why did the governor wish you not to live so near town? I do not know. Did he state any reason? No." AB 1:581.

22. QAP Smith to D'Urban, KWT, 12 October 1835; QAP Smith to D'Urban, KWT, 13 October 1835.
23. Rhodes House, Philip papers, MSS Afr. s. 217, Philip papers, vol. 4, 1834–1835, unpaginated.
24. KAB A1487 Philip to Read, Cape Town, 24 December 1835.
25. See the notes in the chapter "England" for further discussion of the exhibition of Africans and other colonial peoples in Great Britain. Philip's use of the term "specimen" suggests that the visitors were displayed as part of the focus on collection within the imperial imagination: see Jasanoff, *Edge of Empires*.
26. QAP Smith to D'Urban, King William's Town, 30 November 1835.
27. "Great meeting" description from QAP, Smith to D'Urban, King William's Town, 10 January 1836; SACA, 27 January, 1836; W. B. Boyce, *Notes on South African Affairs, from 1834 to 1838*, quoting Greig, 33–59; also, KAB A519, Smith speech to assembled chiefs, 7 January 1836.
28. As a colonial official, Smith presents the vision of civilization that many scholars have attributed to Christian missionaries: see Comaroff and Comaroff, *Of Revelation and Revolution*.
29. On terrier remark only, QAP, D'Urban to Smith, Cape Town, 29 January 1836.
30. QAP, Smith to D'Urban, King William's Town, 19 January 1836.
31. Ibid., 26 January 1836.
32. Ibid.
33. My thanks to Andrew Bank for suggesting that I more fully explore Tzatzoe's intimate life.
34. AB, 2:28. In 1837 Wade reads excerpts of Fawcett's book into evidence in an attempt to discredit Tzatzoe's original testimony before the committee. Fawcett's account is used to discredit Philip's testimony that Tzatzoe traveled to Britain as a political figure and not as a representative of the LMS. Theal cites Fawcett's book as John Fawcett, "Account of an eighteen months' residence at the Cape of Good Hope in 1835–1836," an "octavo volume of ninety-eight pages, published at Capetown in 1836": George McCall Theal, *History of South Africa, 1795–1834*, 442 (accessed through books.google .com on September 2008).
35. QAP, Smith to D'Urban, King William's Town, 14 February 1836, and Smith to D'Urban, King William's Town, 21 February 1836.
36. The testimonies of the chiefs and councilors were given as affidavits and printed in the *Zuid-Afrikaan* of 12 May, GTJ, 25 May 1837.
37. SACA, 7 November 1832.
38. For letter to D'Urban, KAB, GH 22/1 Jan Tzatzoe to D'Urban, Church Square, Cape Town, 20 February 1836. D'Urban summarized his decision thusly: "Concluding how-

ever that although I thought his determination to go was a very unwise one for his own sake and theirs, that I would now oppose no obstacle to his going, and so ended the matter. It was not worth while to stop him now, and it would only have been distorted into an apprehension of suffering evidence chosen by the Dr. to appear in England. These people must have stratagem and deception to work with, or they could not exist. It is their atmosphere, the breath of their nostrils," QAP, D'Urban to Smith, Cape Town, 12 February 1836.

39. For library, SACA, 2 March 1836. On Casalis and Read Junior in Cape Town in 1836, see Eugene Casalis, *My Life in Basutoland*, 267–75. Casalis added that Read Junior had "the fine figure of his father; his hair was rather curly than woolly [sic], while those of his features he had inherited from his mother were not repulsive. He was a true Christian, having as his great desire to aid his father in his evangelical labours, and to succeed him later on. He was, in addition, a very intelligent young fellow, well educated, and overflowing with spirits. He had studied at the Cape Town College, and was going to England to complete his theological preparation."

40. Quoted text in the description of Cape Town is from Casalis, *My Life*, 265–86. Casalis also describes his excursions into the Cape countryside.

41. For Sarah Read, SOAS, Annual Reports, Forty-Second Report of the Missionary Society, 1836. For comments on Read Junior, Tzatzoe, and Stoffels, see LMS, South Africa, Home Office Papers, Incoming to Committee, H-2115, Box 6, Folder 11, A, Read to Ellis, Hackney, 21 August 1836.

42. For the report of the church meeting, see SACA, 2 March 1836.

CHARLES DARWIN IN CAPE TOWN

1. On my recent visits to Cape Town in 2006 and 2007, the plaque has been removed, and has yet to be replaced. The lawn between the boulevard and the seawall was featured in ESPN's advertisement for the 2006 World Cup.

2. Charles Darwin, *Charles Darwin's Diary of the Voyage of H.M.S. "Beagle,"* 405–6. Darwin remained interested in South Africa and the other "embryo Englands." In his 1872 *The Expression of the Emotions in Man and Animals*, Darwin drew attention to the one reply by a "native" he had received to a questionnaire about emotion that he sent out across the globe. The answers were penned by Christian Gaika, a son of Ngqika and half-brother of Sandile, a headman under indirect rule who worked as a constable, and a recipient of a mission education: see Robert Shanafelt, "How Charles Darwin Got Emotional Expression out of South Africa," 815–42. My thanks to Nancy Jacobs for this reference.

ENGLAND, 1836

1. James Read arrived in early June 1836 and was met by his son at London Bridge, KITCH, Read to Kitchingman, Hackney, 22 June 1836. My description is drawn from, especially, Tristam Hunt, *Building Jerusalem*; Roy Porter, *London: A Social History*,

185–305; Boyd Hilton, *A Mad, Bad, & Dangerous People?*; and Liza Picard, *Victorian London*. Africans, and their descendents, living in Britain at this time occupied various roles from street beggars to a "scattering" of respectable or even eminent positions as nurses or ministers. Men worked as seamen, dealers or merhants, and semi-skilled artisans, women as domestic servants, with almost no presence in rural occupations: see Ian Duffield, "Skilled Workers or Marginalized Poor?: The African Population of the United Kingdom, 1812–52," and Norma Myers, *Reconstructing the Black Past*.

2. In order to maintain my focus on Tzatzoe's life, I have had to de-emphasize the Aborigines Committee and its report in my story. For the committee and its impact, see Laidlaw, "'Aunt Anna's Report'"; Elbourne, "The Sin of the Settler: The 1835–36 Select Committee on Aborigines"; *Blood Ground*, 287–92; Mostert, *Frontiers*; and Lester, *Imperial Networks*, 105–37.

3. A committee member confronted Tzatzoe over the claims of Read's involvement in the war, which stemmed from an affidavit by a British settler. The written testimony claims that the settler and Tzatzoe had been riding together when a shot drew their attention. The Xhosa soldier who fired the shot then insisted that the English had begun the war: "Isongolo [Read] had told us, 'Don't you see that the English are taking away all the country? Why do you sit still?'" Tzatzoe insists that he does not remember hearing the shot, and that the Xhosa man had instead said: "Where is the good governor that was coming, that Gongola told us of?" Three times, Lushington asks if Tzatzoe heard the shot. Finally, Tzatzoe replies that the man "must have had powder that one would not hear the noise of." It is quite possible that this retort is more than a literal answer, but, in fact, reveals Tzatzoe's wit on full display, as it will be in later incidents throughout his life.

4. The summary of Tzatzoe's testimony is taken from AB, 1:563–83.

5. Henry Room, of the Birmingham school, was a portrait painter, whose work often featured in the *Evangelical Magazine*. His portrait of Jan Tzatzoe et al. was a work with which he was closely associated. *Evangelical Magazine and Missionary Chronicle*, 28 1850, 532–35.

6. This description is based on a personal inspection of the painting, now hanging in the Moffat Mission Trust, Kuruman, December 2005. Read notes in a letter of 22 June 1836 that the weather is still "raw and cold. I can bear a good great-coat altho' summer," BRENT Read to Kitchingman, Hackney 22 June 1836.

7. My description of the engravings is from a photograph made of an original of Tzatzoe in the School of Oriental and African Studies, London, and a similar reproduction courtesy of Museum Africa. There is also an engraving of the Room drawing; this was reproduced by the Cape Archives. See "British Kaffraria" for a discussion of the dispersal of these images.

8. For "great change," SACA 21 February 1838. In a letter to his friend, James Kitchingman, Read notes that "his bowels are in a bad state," adding that according to his doctor, who is "very young," "adherence to Diet is every thing." "But I must look to a higher hand," he closes. For above, "playfellow," and "denial," BRENT 183/4/15 Read Senior to Kitchingman, Hackney, 22 June 1836.

Notes to Pages 129–130 243

9. Read to Kitchingman, 2 August 1836, from Hackney, near London, in le Cordeur and Saunders, eds., *Kitchingman Papers*, 163–64. Tzatzoe's visit to England can be understood with reference to a large literature on the interrelationship between the British Empire and its colonial possessions. For a general history of Britain during this period, see Linda Colley, *Britons*. For the importance of missions, and a discussion of the weight of the "influence of the Empire brought home" by the missionary movement, see Susan Thorne, "Religion and Empire at home." See also Susan Thorne, "'The Conversion of Englishmen and the Conversion of the World Inseparable.'" Catherine Hall developed the notion that "colony and metropole are terms that can only be understood in relation to each other, and that the identity of colonizer is a constitutive part of Englishness" in her *Civilizing Subjects*. For a similar though later journey, see Neil Parsons, *King Khama, Emperor Joe, and the great white queen*. Please see later notes in this chapter and the notes of "Queen Adelaide Province" for a discussion of Tzatzoe's visit in the context of other African and colonial visitors to Britain.

10. The dinner party took place on 16 July 1836. Information for this section when not identified separately is taken from letters describing the dinner: see E. N Buxton to Northrepps, no date, in Charles Buxton, *Memoirs of Sir Thomas Fowell Buxton*, 312–13; G. Upcher to Anna Gurney, 7/19/36, vol. 14, 71–74, and Hannah Buxton to Miss. G. and Miss. B, 7/7/36, 70, in *Thomas Fowell Buxton Collection*, (TFB). Hannah's letter mentions that she comments on her husband's health to herself. Mrs. Upcher's letter to Anna Gurney discusses her observations of Tzatzoe: "The Caffre chief a fine personable man—handsomely dressed in a military coat blue & gold, he has a good forehead & more—I will go no lower, lest I should affront you as I have affronted myself for fancying (I will just whisper in Sarah's ear [Sarah Maria Buxton, Gurney's companion]) that his mouth caricatured a Negro's! Oh! For shame to breathe it especially as their champion protests there is *nothing African* in his countenance."

11. It is unclear if Tzatzoe intends the last line to be humorous or satirical. Dogs in London at the time were put to work as guard dogs, but not used as beasts of burden (if Tzatzoe is referring to the countryside then he would likely have seen working dogs). It appears Tzatzoe may be joking about the pampered house and lap dogs of the time. If so, the line is quite revealing. Despite the wealth of information on Tzatzoe in contemporary documents, there are extremely few instances, such as the dinner party, where the give and take of conversation is revealed, where Tzatzoe's voice comes to the fore in a private setting. For dogs in London during this decade, I rely upon a personal communication with Dr. Charles R. Perry, September 2008.

12. Lester gives a figure of ninety thousand Xhosa temporarily becoming colonial subjects. Lester stresses the importance of the type of evangelical and imperial networks that were precisely the ones that resulted in Tzatzoe's trip to England: see Lester, *Imperial Networks*, 80–81. Both Philip and Buxton used the term in correspondence. Likely it referred to expulsion of the Xhosa rather than genocidal activity; according to the Oxford Educational Dictionary, both meanings were available at the time. For

genocide, see Crais, *White Supremacy*; for extrusion, see Bank, "Liberals and their Enemies."

13. For the trip to Parliament, Read to Kitchingman, 2 August 1836, from Hackney, near London, in le Cordeur and Saunders, eds., *Kitchingman Papers*, 163–64, letter includes postscript dated 5 August and *Morning Chronicle*, 3 August 1836. The quotation is from TFB, vol. 14, Buxton and L. Buxton to E.N.B., 1 January 1837, 171–74. Tzatzoe's comment is reminiscent of Sebele's on meeting Queen Victoria in 1895: "I had no idea she was so small." Parsons does not elaborate on potential meanings: see Parsons, *King Khama*, 229.

14. Laidlaw opens *Colonial Connections*, 1, with this scene, and implies that Tzatzoe means "spring" to refer to Parliament as a colonial hub. Tzatzoe's evocative and metaphoric language in this exchange permits a brief but important and revelatory examination of the mechanics of the translation through which almost all of Tzatzoe's words and meanings are being constructed. What does Tzatzoe mean by the phrase *touch the spring that moves the world*? Is he using the term to refer to an upwelling of water, to a specific mechanical object, or metaphorically, to an animating force? He is using a Dutch word that is translated (likely by one of the Reads) into the English word "spring." In Dutch, *geest* means "vital principle" or "animating force in living things." *Veer* or *springveer* means "metal object that returns to its original shape." *Opwellen* would connote an upwelling of water. For the verb "touch," Tzatzoe could have employed *aanslag* to mean the tactile sense of touch, or *aandoen*, to mean "to have an effect upon," as in "it touches me." Given the context of the translation, Tzatzoe likely uses the words *aandoen* and *geest*. The difficulty of parsing this phrase speaks to the power of translators in such situations, and the micropolitical climate in which such translation takes place. Finally, it reveals the difficulty of recovering exact meaning from historical sources in translation. See "iQonce" for a discussion of translation. For the usage of "spring" in 1836, see Oxford English Dictionary online, def. 1, number 23: "That by which action is produced, inspired, or instigated; a moving, actuating, or impelling agency, cause, or force; a motive. Frequent from 1700," accessed on July 2008. For the Dutch words for "spring" and "touch," http://www.freedict.com/onldict/dut.html and http://lookwayup.com/free/EnglishDutchDictionary.html, accessed on July 2008.

15. For Read, see le Cordeur and Saunders, eds., *Kitchingman Papers*, Read to Kitchingman, Hackney, 2 August 1836 with postscript 5 August, 167. For the Meeting, the *Missionary Magazine and Chronicle*, September 1836, 54. As noted in the chapter "Queen Adelaide Province," Tzatzoe's visit to England correlated with a lengthy history of the display of foreign peoples in Britain. As previously discussed, some of these visits corresponded with abolitionist or evangelical propaganda events in which Africans in particular were revealed as newly formed, but they may not have been as common as historians have assumed, especially prior to the 1850s. Thorne notes: "Great excitement was also incited by the presence on the missionary podium of the occasional native convert to Christianity." Her examples postdate Tzatzoe's visit: Thorne, *Missions*, 64. Especially in the early 1830s, as the campaign for emancipation built to

a frenzy, humanitarian audiences were exposed to missionaries returning from the colonies to rail against slavery. In 1832 William Knibb and others "traveled the country on speaking tours": Hochschild, *Bury the Chains*, 344–45. The visits of Africans also occurred in the context of what Bernth Lindfors calls "ethnographic showbusiness": see Bernth Lindfors, ed., *Africans on Stage*. See also Roslyn Poignant, *Professional Savages*. Both books deal mostly with post-1880s Great Britain and with paid exhibitions. Pamela Scully and Clifton Crais analyze "Sara Baartman's 1810 exhibition in London" as embodying the "transition between the older tradition of freak shows and the emerging nineteenth-century desire for evidence of the ethnographic 'real' and the rise of a bourgeois consumer culture of the exotic": see Scully and Crais, "Race and Erasure: Sara Baartman and Hendrik Cesars in Cape Town and London," 304–5. See also Crais and Scully, *Sara Baartman*, esp. 71–80. Equiano and Sarah Baartman are the African visitors most frequently discussed until the "Zulu" visitors of 1853: see David Killingray, "Africans in the United Kingdom: An Introduction," 14–17. In his work on a group of Zulu performers in England in the 1850s, Lindfors demonstrates this perception by noting that prior exhibitions were "not uncommon": "Africans and other so-called 'primitive peoples' were still a relatively rare sight in even the most cosmopolitan European capitals, and it was not uncommon for exhibitions to be held to display such peoples to audiences": see Lindfors, "Charles Dickens and the Zulus," 63. See also Zine Magubane, *Bringing the Empire Home*. In my work with British sources, I found few other exhibitions or visitors. I think it might be conjectured that Tzatzoe's visit to Britain was a relatively unprecedented event, which only heightens its importance. There were also similar visits to Washington, D.C., by American Indians during this period.

16. As Michael Rutz points out, the "first decades of the 19th century saw the rise of petition campaigns, and the influence of public opinion in British politics." James Read and John Philip, and by proxy, Jan Tzatzoe, "made full use of the press, of the anti-slavery movement, and of their connections to important political figures" (Rutz, "'Meddling with Politics'," 117). For a thorough introduction to abolitionism and the mass mobilization it represented, see Adam Hochschild, *Bury the Chains*.

17. Description of Exeter Hall is based upon Michael Alpert, *London 1849*, 126–27, and www.victorianlondon.org/buildings/exeterhall, accessed August 2007. I am hypothesizing that the meeting took place in the Great Hall and not in the smaller meeting room on the first floor. I tried to locate Exeter Hall in London in July 2002; the Strand Palace Hotel stands on the site. For the audience at the Exeter Hall Missionary Meetings, see Susan Thorne, *Congregational Missions and the Making of an Imperial Culture in Nineteenth-Century England*. Thorne argues, in part, that missionary institutions were a constitutive part of the formation of a British middle-class identity in this period.

18. The introduction to the meeting is taken from the *Missionary Magazine and Chronicle*, September 1836. Tzatzoe may have been given an unusual amount of recognition and fame as a visitor to Great Britain because of his aristocratic status, or "rank," in the eyes of the British public whose relationship to the colonized was mediated by

status, or class, in addition to race. In this view, Tzatzoe's purported presence at the head of a hierarchical society would have been reassuringly familiar: see Cannadine, *Ornamentalism*, esp. 122–25. Certainly, he was most often referred to as a "chief" and the LMS took pains to present him as such.

19. All of the excerpts of the speech are from Rhodes House Library, Oxford University, Mss. British Empire S.44, vol. 41, *Patriot*, London, 17 August, 1836. The *Patriot* transcript includes all the material from the meeting published by the *Missionary Magazine*, but also includes the crowd's interjections, and a fair amount of text that was elided in the *Magazine*.

20. Elbourne analyzes this paragraph of the speech with reference to these "characteristic expressions" of the time in Xhosa and Khoisan oratory. I also saw them frequently employed in the primary accounts: see Elbourne, *Blood Ground*, 434n112.

21. SACA 21 February 1838.

22. *Missionary Magazine and Chronicle*, September 1836.

23. The notion of an Africa whose suffering "sons of Africa" or "sable sons" needed to be helped had a long resonance in abolitionist rhetoric: see Carretta, *Equiano*, 257–58. Reverend Young's speech taken from Rhodes House Library, Oxford University, Mss. British Empire S.44, vol. 41, *Patriot*, London, 17 August 1836. Interestingly, the *Missionary Magazine*, as the official mouthpiece of the LMS, did not report a majority of Young's testimony, including his discussion of Africa.

24. While Tzatzoe and the others wrapped up their testimony in late June, the committee officially closed on 3 August 1836, and on 5 August, the House of Commons ordered the *Report from the Select Committee on Aborigines (British Settlements;) Together with minutes of evidence, Appendix and Index* to be printed. The volume ran to 841 folio pages. AB, vol. 1. But the *Report* did not contain a summation or recommendations, which were to follow in 1837.

25. The quote on handshakes is from the *Missionary Magazine and Chronicle*, September 1836, 54; on Baines, 67.

26. For "trophies," GTJ 3 November 1836. For the block quote, GTJ 10 March 1836. In the 10 March edition, Tzatzoe gets off lightly in comparison to the vitriol directed at Stoffels. "The most peculiar characteristic of Andries is loquacity, mingled with a large share of low cunning. When he has not a part to act he is a perfect buffoon, vociferously noisy, vulgar, and overbearing, and as full of mischief as an ape. But when on his guard he can be as demure as possible, and display a most perfect Spaniel-like subserviency to the wants and wishes of his acknowledged patrons." And of Read Junior: He "possesses a good deal of activity and some natural shrewdness. An opinion may be formed of him by his publicly declaring himself proud of his Hottentot origin, whereas it is apparent to every one who knows him, that he is vain to a degree of those shades which his European parentage have given to his complexion." The editorial concludes on the trip itself: "Such are the persons whom Dr. Philip is about to take home, in order to establish his charges against the government and the inhabitants of this frontier, and in respect to which we can only remark, that they are most suitable for the work in which he is about to employ them."

27. For "splendid dress," GTJ 27 September 1836.

28. Read to Kitchingman, 8/2/36, from Hackney, near London, in le Cordeur and Saunders, eds., *Kitchingman Papers*, 163–64.
29. Information on Read's travels, the request to Arundel, and the Liverpool meetings from LMS, Box 6, Folder 11, A, Read to Arundel, 18 August 1836. I spent two weeks in London in June 2002 going through the British Library's Newspaper Collection. Almost every town mentioned in Read and Philip's correspondence as the site of a meeting had a weekly paper of its own, and the larger towns had several. Looking through this proliferation of newspapers (approximately forty all together) for the dates when I knew that the African visitors were holding meetings, I found seventeen articles reporting Missionary Meetings in which Tzatzoe spoke. Philip "400 to 800 people a night," Rhodes house, MSS Afr. s. 217 Philip papers 1834–1842, Philip papers 5, 1836–1838, unpaginated.
30. Account of York meetings is taken from the *Yorkshire Gazette*, June–August 1836 and the *Yorkshireman*, 27 August 1836.
31. See note 20 on Xhosa oratorical practice at this time; see also the chapter "Kat River."
32. Read's appearance is from le Cordeur and Saunders, eds., *Kitchingman Papers*, Read Senior to Kitchingman, Hackney, 4 September 1836, 167–69.
33. For the visit to Windsor, GTJ 9 February 1837. Tzatzoe's speech reiterates the theme that Africans are just as capable of propagating missions. Indeed, the Xhosa chiefs' money could reinforce and add to a King's! Tzatzoe will repeat the story of the visit to Windsor, the children's missionary box, and his desire to make one for the Xhosa to a Cape Town Missionary Meeting of 1838.
34. le Cordeur and Saunders, eds., *Kitchingman Papers*, Read Senior to Kitchingman, Hackney, 8 October 1836, 170–71.
35. On a Sunday afternoon in July 2002, I took the tube to one site of pilgrimage, the now-defunct Highbury football stadium in London, and then walked to the location of this church. The building still stands—hence my description—but the church is now Greek Orthodox and was locked for the Sunday. As a result, I can offer no further description of the interior. Zine Magubane notes that Tzatzoe spent "an evening" with the students at Highbury College, a missionary training institution. Magubane quotes a Reverend Thomas Aveling, writing in 1850, to the effect that "vivid recollections" of the visit remained in "many minds": see Magubane, *Bringing the Empire Home*, 44.
36. For "birth," LMS, South Africa, Home Office Papers, Incoming to Committee, Box 6, Folder 11, A, Read Senior to Ellis, Hackney, 21 August 1836. For "not succeed," le Cordeur and Saunders, eds., *Kitchingman Papers*, Read, Senior to Kitchingman, Hackney, 8 October 1836, 170–71. For *Meg Merrilies*, *Missionary Magazine and Chronicle*, December 1836.

GREAT BRITAIN, 1836–1838

1. For Weymouth, TFB, vol. 14, 124, Crump to Buxton, 25 November 1836 and vol. 14, 125, Benson to Buxton, 26 November 1836.
2. Read relates the story of his return to Essex with Tzatzoe for a Missionary Meeting in Cape Town in February 1838; he does not provide a date for the Essex meeting.

Since he writes as Tzatzoe's translator, I am inserting the account into this stretch of meetings, but it might have occurred at any time after Read Junior's departure for the Cape: SACA 21 February 1838.
3. For Oxford, the multiple visits, and James Junior, le Cordeur and Saunders, eds., *Kitchingman Papers*, Read Senior to Kitchingman, Hackney, 8 December 1836, 172–73.
4. For Rotherham, le Cordeur and Saunders, eds., *Kitchingman Papers*, Read Senior to Kitchingman, Hackney, 26 January 1837, 173–76.
5. BL *North Derbyshire Chronicle* and *Chesterfield Advertiser*, 24 December 1836.
6. GTJ, 27 April 1837. Philip and Read had been directly addressing the *Journal's* aspersions on Tzatzoe's character throughout his time in Britain: see, for example, Philip's comments to a missionary meeting in September 1836: "In a paper published at the Cape, in allusion to the chief who had just addressed them, it was said he was a poor weak creature, meaning that he was devoid of intellect; but if the specimen they had seen was weak, what must be the Caffre who was strong? He could positively assert that he had never found a people of finer feelings or possessed of quicker perception, than that race which had been so much calumniated," BL *Bristol Mercury, Monmouthshire, South Wales, and West of England Advertiser*, Saturday 24 September 1836.
7. The information on the Sheffield meeting is drawn from BL *Sheffield Mercury and Hallamshire Advertiser*, 31 December 1836; *Nottingham Review*, 23 December 1836; *Sheffield Independent*, 24 December 1836.
8. For biblical resonance, personal communication with Tina Campomizzi, July 2008.
9. BL *Sheffield Independent*, 31 December 1836. The letter makes for wonderful reading in full. Despite the contemporary ridicule heaped upon (particularly the female) humanitarian public, the letter seems to move beyond the cultural chauvinism usually ascribed to the humanitarians (whereby Africans would be redeemed through British Christian civilization): The "Ladies" blame the "attempt to extend the reign of colonial misrule over the countries" of the Xhosa as the cause of the frontier war of 1834–1835. The issue of naming is particularly interesting given the controversy in post-apartheid South Africa over the renaming of significant locations and geographic features. Marginalized by men in the abolitionist era of the late eighteenth and early nineteenth centuries, women become increasingly active in humanitarian and anti-slavery campaigns in the 1820s and 1830s: see Marika Sherwood, *After Abolition*, 146–48. For the British public, evangelicalism and the missionary movement at home and abroad, see Thorne, "Religion and Empire at Home."
10. BL *Sheffield Independent*, 31 December 1836. See Comaroff and Comaroff, *Of Revelation* 1:49–85, for a discussion of the ideological background from which most humanitarians emerged, including issues of free trade and free labor.
11. For Cutler's Hall, BL *Sheffield Independent*, 7 January 1837.
12. For snow and Bath, le Cordeur and Saunders, eds., *Kitchingman Papers*, Read Senior to Kitchingman, Hackney, 26 January 1837, 173–76.
13. For Meg Merrilies, *Missionary Magazine and Chronicle*, May 1837. For Stoffels, *Missionary Magazine and Chronicle*, April 1838.

14. For new dispensation in the eastern Cape, see Mostert, *Frontiers*, 790–98; Lester, *Imperial Networks*; Keegan, *Colonial South Africa*. Natasha Erlank covers the unsettled decade from 1836 to 1847 in the eastern Cape from a gender perspective, focusing the insecurity and upheaval in Xhosa society as a result of colonial cattle theft across the border: see Natasha Erlank, "Gendered Reactions to Social Dislocation and Missionary Activity in Xhosaland, 1836–1847."
15. Thomas F. Buxton to Gurney, 18 March 1837, in Buxton, *Memoirs*, 3d ed., 1849, 311.
16. GTJ 15 December 1836.
17. For 1836 quote, AB, 1:575. In the transcript Philip is examined and given the chance to prepare a rebuttal. Tzatzoe was present at this rebuttal. Unless otherwise indicated, for the renewed complaints, AB, 2:22–28, 47–48.
18. For "day's rest," le Cordeur and Saunders, eds., *Kitchingman Papers*, Read Senior to Kitchingman, Hackney, 11 April 1837, 176.
19. Equiano and other African or Anglo-African campaigners for abolition had employed similar rhetoric since the 1780s. As with the case of Equiano, Jan Tzatzoe personalized and appropriated the language of the abolitionist movement throughout his many speeches in Great Britain and upon his return to Cape Town. Carretta notes that Equiano "skillfully and creatively fashion[ed]" the story of his "own life," merging it with that of countless others from the Atlantic world, to become "*the* African," so that he could speak to the redeeming power of abolitionism and evangelism. In doing so, Equiano "gave the abolitionist cause the African voice it needed." Tzatzoe's speeches and literary productions must be seen in the same light, that of an individual who created a story of his own life—in his case one that allowed his audience to appreciate the power of evangelical humanitarianism in redeeming the colonial subjects of the emerging British Empire, who were traveling from "darkness into light," and from oppression into a full legal citizenship. Tzatzoe positioned himself as an African voice for African colonial subjects. As I have argued elsewhere in the notes, while Tzatzoe's speeches bear the imprint of the Reads and John Philip, I am convinced that they were largely his own work. See Carretta, *Equiano*, 366–67. The notion of the mark of slavery was often mobilized and was itself informed by biblical verse. Reviewing Equiano's work, Mary Wollstonecraft noted that it was a "favourite philosophic whim to degrade the numerous nations on whom the sun-beams more directly dart, below the common level of humanity, and hastily to conclude that nature, by making them inferior to the rest of the human race, designed to stamp them with a mark of slavery" (Wollstonecraft, quoted in Carretta, *Equiano*, 331). While the mass movements of abolitionism, and later humanitarianism—and in particular their rhetorical flourishes—were repeatedly alluded to in the 1830s, scholars are divided on whether the movements were ultimately effective. Michael Rutz sees in them a reordering of British politics from a "patronage-ridden" system to one that was expected to redress public grievances: see Rutz, "'Meddling with Politics'" and "The Politicizing of Evangelical Dissent, 1811–1813." Sherwood describes the activism, "meaningless Acts," and "almost annual Select Committees" as "just good publicity," or "propaganda," for a colonial and imperial system that continued to greatly enrich the British government and many of its citizens: see Sherwood, *After Abolition*, esp. 175–77.

20. For meeting, *Missionary Magazine and Chronicle*, June 1837, and GTJ 31 August 1837. Tzatzoe's rhetoric anticipates the "particularly utopian moment" of the emancipation of slaves in the British Empire (1 August 1838), in which Catherine Hall suggests the British (especially certain "missionary abolitionists") attempted to incorporate the respectable black elite of Jamaica. A Jamaican Baptist missionary, William Knibb, called for full rights to be granted to freed slaves as "Black Britons"; the Black elite would be the "fathers and patriarchs of the new Jerusalem." Hall argues that the British, committed to the project of empire, wanted to protect British interests while recognizing the brotherhood and sisterhood of black people as part of a reformed and revitalized Britain. Tzatzoe's speech suggests that the utopian moment was more widespread than has been acknowledged and, critically, that the "new Black subjects" of the British colonial world were capable of mobilizing the abolitionist rhetoric to their own ends: see Hall, *Civilizing Subjects*, 84–139, and idem, "William Knibb and the Constitution of the New Black Subject." For "blackness" in England and South Africa, see Zine Magubane, *Bringing the Empire Home*. My thanks to Andrew Bank for suggesting the apparent temporal and geographic breadth of Hall's "utopian moment" revealed in the Tzatzoe material.
21. For "visit from the Africans," le Cordeur and Saunders, eds., *Kitchingman Papers*, Read Senior to Kitchingman, Hackney, 11 April 1837, 176. For "impression" and "prospect," LMS, Box 7, Folder 1, Read to Ellis, 25 July 1837.
22. WITS Philip Papers 1.2 Letters to Miss Wells, Durant Philip to "My very dear Friend," Glasgow, 19 July 1837.
23. For "spoke in English," WITS Philip Papers Cc (3) Durant Philip to Eliza Philip, Glasgow, 28 June 1837. I read Philip's letter the morning after I arrived in Johannesburg in December 2005 on a direct flight from Atlanta. It was an immense relief. I had been deliberating whether the newspaper account could pass muster as a single source on Tzatzoe's successful attempt to learn English while in Britain. The University of Witwatersrand was shutting down the next day for a two-week Christmas holiday break. For Cape Town missionary meeting, SACA 12 February 1838.
24. Information and quotations from the meeting are taken from BL *Kelso Chronicle*, 4 August 1837.
25. Comaroff and Comaroff's two-volume *Of Revelation and Revolution* remains the most comprehensive work on the ideology behind the evangelical and humanitarian move into southern Africa.
26. For the account of the Cape Town Missionary Meeting, SACA, 21 February 1838. The *Graham's Town Journal* did not report on the event.
27. Yale University microfilm collection, the *Sun* (London) 18 May 1838.
28. For "incontrovertible right," AB 2:5; for "remote cause," AB 2:43.
29. Information on gutting of report from Macmillan, *Bantu, Boer*, 188–89, quoting Buxton to Gurney, 17 June 1837 and Priscilla Johnston to Philip, 25 August 1837. See also Laidlaw, "'Aunt Anna's Report.'" The censoring focused on the excision of commentary relating to the Cape Colony in particular: see Laidlaw, "'Aunt Anna's Report,'" 18. Still, the document has retained its status as a high-water mark in the development

of the humanitarian ideology: see Laidlaw, "'Aunt Anna's Report,'" 21, n3 and n4. According to Andrew Bank, the report (as a "passionate defence of the rights of indigenes and a damning critique of colonialism") was interjected into a "racially structured historiography" through which an "ideological debate about race and racial politics" was conducted in South Africa and in the metropole in the 1820s and 1830s: see Bank, "The Great Debate and the Origins of South African Historiography," 261–81, esp. 261 and 275. For the report and the origins of South African historiography in this period, see Robert Ross, "Donald Moodie and the Origins of Historiography."

30. For news of the death of William, SACA, 13 September 1837. For the decline of humanitarian liberalism, see Bank, "Liberals and their Enemies," chap. 8, and idem, "Losing Faith."

31. For the Farewell Meeting, GTJ, 25 January 1838; *Missionary Magazine and Chronicle*, November 1837; *Morning Chronicle*, 18 October 1837; le Cordeur and Saunders, eds., *Kitchingman Papers*, Read to Kitchingman, Hackney, 22 October, 1837, 177.

32. SACA, 6 January 1838.

33. For "poor sister," le Cordeur and Saunders, eds., *Kitchingman Papers*, Read to Kitchingman, Hackney, 22 October 1837, 177. For "resignation," Brent Ms. 183/3 Jane Philip letters, 183/3/12 Jane Philip to Kitchingman, Cape Town, 3 August 1837.

34. For David Scott and "wife for Mr. Blore," *Missionary Magazine and Chronicle*, January 1838, and le Cordeur and Saunders, eds., *Kitchingman Papers*, Read to Kitchingman, Hackney, 22 October 1837, 177. For the sea journey from Britain to Cape Town, LMS, South Africa, Incoming, H-2130, Box 16, Folder 1, A, Read Senior to Ellis, Cape Town, 8 February 1838; and LMS, South Africa, Incoming, Box 16, Folder 1, B, Schreiner to Ellis, *David Scott*, 2 February 1838.

TZATZOE IN KURUMAN

1. This account is a factual rendering of my visit to the Mission, which had experienced a recent turnover in leadership. The gentleman who showed me around did not know where the painting was located.
2. Information on repatriation as documented by the Moffat Mission Trust informational plaque.

KING WILLIAM'S TOWN, 1838–1845

1. For the "present," the *Sun*, 18 May 1838. For the voyage to Port Elizabeth and the journey to the Kat River, LMS, South Africa, Incoming, Box 16, Folder 1, C Read to Ellis, Philipton, 9 June 1838.
2. On Tzatzoe's return to Maqoma, the other Xhosa chiefs, and the amaNtinde, LMS, South Africa, Incoming, Box 16, Folder 2, Tzatzoe to Directors, Philipton, 1 September 1838.
3. James Backhouse, *Narrative of a Visit*, 253.

4. It appears that the most fascinating aspects of his journey across worlds involved familiar objects or rituals transformed, as opposed to discoveries that lie outside the scope of everyday experience. As one example, in a documentary televised on TLC in July 2007, "The Boy with a New Head," a young Ugandan boy, Petero Byakatonda, afflicted with Crouzen's Syndrome and a pariah in his home village, goes to Dallas, Texas, for a complete facial reconstruction. Upon his return, he is no longer shunned for his looks. Instead, at school, he has a rapt audience, and the camera catches him talking about doors that open and close by themselves and buildings that revolve around in circles.
5. For "adverse effect" and Oursen, SOAS, Annual Reports, Forty-Third Report of the Missionary Society, 1837. For "secular duties," SOAS, Annual Reports, Forty-Fifth Report of the Missionary Society, 1839.
6. For the Suthu incident, KAB LG 396 Stretch, case of Tzatzoe, KWT, 20 October 1836, and Stretch to Hudson, KWT, 25 October 1836. In an unrelated but troubling turn of events, several of the amaNtinde turned on Brownlee's mission station, attacking the Mfengu living there, seizing and torturing a boy, killing two cattle, and insulting Brownlee himself. Unfortunately, the only data available on these incidents in 1837 are from the GTJ 28 December 1837. This year-in-review issue may have conflated the incidents of October 1836 with their description of an "eating up" by the "Gaika clans" of Jan Tzatzoe's people. Or, it may have been a separate aggression.
7. The entire Pato/Tzatzoe incident is taken from KAB LG 425, 426, 427, 608. LG 426 includes Bowker to Hudson, Fort Peddie, September and October 1838, 5 October for postscript, Cyrus affidavit, Umbeenba (Tzatzoe's half-brother's actions), affidavit of Umhaa and Nonjola, 23 September Tzatzoe to Stretch, for Tzatzoe letter. LG 427 includes Bowker to Hudson, Peddie, 28 November which has an account of the mediation. LG 608, Stretch, December 1838, for Tyalie's comments on the conflict. In a final postscript to his letter conveying Tzatzoe and Brownlee's letters on the affair, Bowker adds: "It is "Pato's duty to detain cattle passing through his country, [until they can be shown to have been] obtained honestly. I think it is only proper to mention that the cattle have often been detained from persons who had no certificate to shew for them. I have given those persons papers to return to the colony where they have obtained the necessary documents. This Jacob is the first to refuse to return," LG 426 Bowker to Hudson, Fort Peddie, 5 October 1838. Yanna Yannakakis reminds us that violence or the threat of violence is always present when intermediaries, local subjects, and the colonial state are contesting political structures and identities formed during colonialism: Yannakakis, *Art of Being In-between*.
8. Describing the same scene a few years later, a more effusive writer noted: "The scene was certainly very beautiful. Imagine a vast plain of fair green meadow-land, intersected, and in fact divided into parterres, by tall thick bushes, which here and there grew in clumps and copses, giving the ground the appearance of a vast park laid out with a great deal of attention to taste,—an ampitheatre [sic] of hills and mountains rising one behind the another, till the summits in the distance blended with the clouds, gorgeously illuminated by the rays of the declining sun, whose glory was soon succeeded by the milder light of the 'gentle moon.'" (Harriet Ward, *Five Years in Kaffirland*, 68). For anthills, ibid., 77.

9. James Backhouse, *Narrative of a Visit*, 154–251.
10. For the Philipses' visit, LMS, South Africa, Incoming, Box 16, Folder 5, A, account of Jane Philip's travels to mission stations, June 1839.
11. For respectability, see Ross, *Status and Respectability*. For the disillusionment of humanitarians like Philip, see Bank, "Losing Faith in the Civilizing Mission," in Daunton and Halpern, eds., *Empire and Others*.
12. For Brownlee letter and quotes, BRWN Brownlee to Ellis, William's Town, 14 February, (1839).
13. BRWN Brownlee to Ellis, William's Town, 15 October 1838.
14. While Brownlee was withholding the salary due to Tzatzoe for the Buffalo (or King William's Town) Mission, the LMS (likely acting on Brownlee's reports) continued to list him as a "missionary" or "assistant missionary" in its Annual Reports: SOAS, Annual Reports. In the Forty-fifth Report of the Missionary Society for 1839, Tzatzoe is the only African among the Society's Missions who is listed as a "Missionary." In the Annual Report for 1840 he is listed as an assistant missionary, alongside two "native teachers." From 1841 through 1846 he is listed as an assistant missionary.
15. For Napier meeting, KAB OPB 1/11 Correspondence to and from the Frontier for 1836–1845, George Napier to Lord Russell, GT, 11 December 1840; extract from the *Cape Frontier Times*, GT, 9 December 1840.
16. For Stretch's comments on the evening and being in Tzatzoe's company, Rhodes, Bodleian Library, "Memorandum in which Stretch reviews the Treaty System, 1839 to 1846." For the burning in effigy, see Mostert, *Frontiers*, 843. For background to this turbulent period, see Mostert, *Frontiers*, 827–49; Bank, "Losing Faith"; Keegan, *Colonial Order*.
17. The information from Stretch is from Rhodes, Bodleian library, "Memorandum in which Stretch reviews the Treaty System, 1839 to 1846," undated. Another example of Tzatzoe's work as a high-level diplomatic envoy and his presence as part of the highest level of the Xhosa leadership hierarchy is revealed in Colonel Hare's report of a meeting between the Gaika chiefs and himself to mediate a dispute between Eno and Tola. The chiefs wanted Tola to be allowed to retake land in the old Ceded Territory. Hare mentions that Sandile's proposal was seconded by Jan Tzatzoe and Macomo. A final document was signed by all the chiefs who were present, and Tzatzoe alone signed his name. The other leaders make an X, KAB OPB 1/11 Correspondence to and from the Frontier for 1836–1845, Hare to Napier, For Beaufort, 3 October 1843.
18. BRWN Brownlee to Ellis, King William's Town, 27 December 1844. Brownlee wrote during a tense period of the "reformulation of missionary liberalism" amidst the LMS missionaries in South Africa. The LMS missionaries wanted to project themselves into the realm of British respectability and they were coming to resent efforts by their congregations at self-governance, and even small acts of self-assertion. Increasingly, the LMS agents sought full control and authority over ownership of the Gospel: Elbourne, "Whose gospel? Conflict in the LMS in the early 1840s," in de Gruchy, ed., *The LMS in South Africa*, 132–55, and Elbourne, *Blood Ground*, chap. 9.
19. For "savage-born," *Missionary Magazine and Chronicle*, September 1836, 67. The historiographical debate began as a response to Philip's *Researches*, published in 1828, but also featured the refutation of the testimony before the Aborigines Committee,

and the committee's report. In particular Robert Godlonton reprised the editorial bent and content of the GTJ in his *A Narrative of the Irruption of the Kaffir Hordes*. For the historiographical presentations and debate, see Bank, "The Great Debate," and Ross, "Donald Moodie," in *Beyond the Pale*. It is interesting to note that James Read presented the life of Andries Stoffels as a redeemed African (long after the latter's death): *The African Witness: or, a Short Account of the Life of Andries Stoffles*. Tzatzoe and Stoffels were lauded in this fashion by the LMS in their annual volume, *The Christian Keepsake, and Missionary Annual*, 1838, in a lead article, "The African Witnesses": Ellis, ed., *Christian Keepsake*.

20. The re-production of Tzatzoe's life by Brownlee in this period, as with his presentation as a civilized Christian chief in Britain, or the caricature presented by the settler interests, were all examples where Tzatzoe's life was produced to fit a biographical narrative: Rassool, "The Individual, Auto/Biography and History." As his life continued, Tzatzoe had less and less of an ability to affect these presentations, which hardened around the portrayal of Brownlee and the settlers.

21. LMS, South Africa, Incoming, Box 21, Folder 3, B, Tzatzoe, Jan to Arundel, 8 October 1845. Holt mentions in an aside, which he does not cite, that Brownlee, at the end of 1845, speaks of Tzatzoe's continuing itinerating in kraals four or five miles from King William's Town: Holt, *Greatheart*, 115.

BRITISH KAFFRARIA, 1845–1868

1. KAB OPB 1/10 1 Prelude and Conduct of War, 1846, LG Hare to Maitland, GT, 28 March 1846 quoting Stretch on "determination"; Maclean to Maitland, 26 March 1846 quoting Brownlee's request for arms.
2. For Maitland meeting and Sandile and Tzatzoe, below, OPB 1/10 1 Prelude and conduct of war, 1846, Stretch, Diary of Tyumie residency, 3–10 September 1845. Stretch reports the address to the chiefs in his journal for this week.
3. See Levine, "African Ferocity."
4. For "wagons have been burnt," LMS, South Africa, Freeman papers and Philip odds, Box 1, Folder 3, C, copy of a letter from Jan Tzatzoe intended for Dr. Philip but not sent, Spring 1849 (no further explanation provided). Holt, *Greatheart*, 117–20, cites an extensive letter from Brownlee detailing his experiences in Peddie, including how the children in the fort spent the days following the battle, "amusing themselves in showing every mark of indignity to their fallen enemies." Description of Peddie from Cory Library, Cory Collection, MS 104, Oral interview with Mrs. E. E. Gaylard, 14 January 1910.
5. For "beautiful sight," Harriet Ward, *The Cape and the Kaffirs*, 111. For battle itself, Mostert, *Frontiers*, 880–85. Ward describes the "greater part of the cattle" having been driven off: Ward, *Five Years*, 280.
6. For Tzatzoe's safeguarding (and return) of Brownlee's cattle and church services, see "Declaration."
7. For Tzatzoe's visit to Maclean and subsequent mediation, see Frye, ed., *The War of the Axe*, 98, 101. The information is derived from the Reverend J. W. Appleyard, who was

not present at Tzatzoe's meeting with Maclean, but was a confidant and correspondent of the Colonel. Appleyard speaks directly in November 1846 quote.

8. For the Lieutenant-Governor's quote, KAB GH 19/8 LG Berkeley to Pottinger, GT, 25 October 1847. On the surrender, KAB GH 19/8 Minutes of the Communication that took place with Sandilli while "I [Shepstone] acted as Interpreter on Thursday the 21st and Friday the 22nd October 1847." Further evidence is located in GH 19/8, GH 8/45 and GH 8/46. This was William Shepstone, the father of Theophilus Shepstone, who went to Natal in the early 1840s.

9. For the Brownlee quotes on Tzatzoe, BRWN Brownlee to Tidman, Fort Peddie, 28 December 1846. In 1855 Charles Brownlee noted that "in consequence" of his actions in 1846 Tzatzoe was "cut off from direct Church membership by the Rev. Mr. Brownlee," KAB BK 89, Gaika Commissioner's report of the Chief, Jan Tzatzoe, 18 February 1855.

10. For removal, see "Declaration." Writing in 1858 to Fairbairn, editor of the SACA, Tzatzoe recalls, "In 1846 I occupied the house in King William's Town now used as a prison—at the request of the military I left the town and built a new house," Rhodes Bodleian Philip Papers MSS Afr. s. 219 Misc, #75 Jan Tzatzoe to Fairbairn, KWT, 10 May 1858. In 1849 a visitor from the LMS, J. Freeman, described Tzatzoe's location as "four miles distant from the town . . . a fine piece of land, which he is cultivating. He has one or two wagons and spans of oxen. He has also rebuilt a cottage." Perhaps referring to Tzatzoe's "colonial persona," Freeman added: "I fear he still retains much of the 'apathetic' character that belongs to the native,—the want of an internal spring of action, in pursuing what is good and noble," J. J. Freeman, *A Tour*, 103.

11. For list of goods lost, see "Declaration," Spring 1849. Mostert, *Frontiers*, 874, mentions that *The Wrongs of the Caffre Nation* was one of the books, but does not footnote this information, which is located in Rev. J. W. Appleyard's journal of the war. In his entry dated 28 July Appleyard's contempt for the old humanitarian liberalism of Philip and Read, and the possibilities of respectability once held out to Africans, is biting: "It is feared that Jan Tshatshu has given in to the war party. His house was the only one standing when the troops arrived, and they completed the scene of desolation by burning it. He has written to Col. Hare, and at the close of the epistle he adds, this must be put in the paper, the word must be underlined. In his house the 'Wrongs of the Kafirs' [*sic*] was found, inscribed Miss Mary Tshatshu from her sincere friend." The scorn lavished on Tzatzoe for demanding his complaints be heard and on an unnamed benefactor for addressing Mary Tzatzoe as "Miss" is a crystalline example of the emerging racial ideology of the eastern Cape: see Frye, ed., *The War of the Axe*, 87.

12. KAB GH 8/46, Address to Gaika Chiefs, H. Calderwood to R. Woosnam, Sec. to High Commissioner, Fort Hare, 17 March 1846.

13. For an account of Smith's meeting, OPB 1/10 3 Smith to Grey, KWT, 7 January 1848. This meeting was yet another instance of biographical production in Tzatzoe's life.

14. LMS, South Africa, Incoming, Box 23, Folder 5, C, Philip to Tidman, Hankey, 28 March 1848, enclosing Niven to Philip, Bethelsdorp, 6 January 1847.

15. OPB 1/10 4 Smith to Earl Grey, Cape Town, 21 October 1848. This retort to Smith is mentioned in several other secondary texts, including *Frontiers*. It is likely the

best-known episode in Tzatzoe's life. As with almost all of the evidence relating to Tzatzoe, this conversation is only preserved in the archive in English, which likely would have been a translation from the Dutch or isiXhosa being spoken at the meeting. Nevertheless, there is no question of the authenticity or authorship of the remark, and it conforms to the voice that Tzatzoe developed over his life in the public arena.

16. LMS, South Africa, Freeman papers and Philip odds, Box 1, Folder 3, C, copy of a letter from Jan Tzatzoe intended for Dr. Philip but not sent. In his "Declaration" on his conduct in the war, also written in the spring of 1849, Tzatzoe tries to excuse his choice to a greater degree, saying that Sandile was "threatening vengeance on those who would not take to arms": LMS, South Africa, Freeman papers and Philip odds, Box 1, Folder 3, C, Declaration of Jan Tzatzoe (respecting his money concerns and joining in the war), Spring 1849.

17. LMS, South Africa, Freeman papers and Philip odds, Box 1, Folder 3, C, Declaration of Jan Tzatzoe (respecting his money concerns and joining in the war), Spring 1849, and LMS, South Africa, Freeman papers and Philip odds, Box 1, Folder 3, C, copy of a letter from Jan Tzatzoe intended for Dr. Philip but not sent. The copies I consulted were in English, and not of Tzatzoe's hand, with no note of whether the originals were in English, Dutch, or isiXhosa, or who was responsible for translation.

18. LMS, South Africa, Freeman papers and Philip odds, Box 1, Folder 3, C, copy of a letter from Jan Tzatzoe intended for Dr. Philip but not sent.

19. Freeman, *A Tour*, 60–104.

20. KAB BK 436 Maclean to Mackinnon, Fort Murray, October 1850.

21. Appleyard's journal states: "Jan Tshatshu is gone to stay at Ft. Murray. He cannot control his people. Most of them are disaffected": see Frye, ed., *The War of the Axe*, 124–27.

22. For "arise," OPB 1/11 2 Smith with enclosures to Grey, 31 October 1850. KAB A47 Private letters Smith to Godlonton, marked confidential, Smith to G, Fort Cox, 26 December 1850; for "different enemy," ibid., Smith to Godlonton, 7 January 1851.

23. WITS A43 Godlonton collection, (51) Calderwood to Godlonton, Fort Hare, 8 January 1851, (61); Southey to Godlonton, Graaff Reinet, 17 May 1851; KAB A47 Private letters Smith to Godlonton, marked confidential, Smith to G, Fort Cox, 26 December 1850.

24. As in "England," the likely meaning of "extermination" in this context is extrusion, but the banner might reveal a new ambivalence that at least backgrounds a genocidal intent: personal communication, Andrew Bank, March 2008. For date of death, see Mostert, *Frontiers*, 1148. For Read's quote, LMS, South Africa, Incoming H-2130, Box 26, Folder 2, Read Senior to Freeman, Alice, 9 July 1851.

25. On Tzatzoe's defense of the road, BK 74 Maclean to Mackinnon, Fort Murray, 24 March 1851. Maclean accuses Tzatzoe of "altogether disregard[ing] my commands in carrying out measures for the safety of the Queen's Road."

26. For Smith, Smith to Earl Grey, King William's Town, 5 April 1851, in KAB OPB 1/11 4 Smith With Enclosures, First Months of War, 1851.

27. For the indictment of "younger brother of Tzatzoe" and his "councilor," "Statement of Gora of Jan Tzatzoe's tribe," 29 May 1855, which claims that ninety of Tzatzoe's "followers" joined the "Rebellion," while "thirty remained with their chief. . . but these however at different periods joined the war party." "Statement of Mali," 7 March 1855, claims that the "greater part" of the amaNtinde "joined. . . . [T]hose that remained attacked the patrols as they left King William's Town." In Maclean to Liddle, Private Secretary to H. E. the Governor, Fort Murray, 4 November 1855, in KAB GH 8/27 Documents submitted for the consideration of His Excellency the High Commissioner, Fort Murray, 12 November 1855; Various documents relative to the conduct of Jan Tzatoze, and of his tribe, during the late Rebellion. Also, in 1855, Charles Brownlee, adamant in his defense of Tzatzoe, stated that only 48 of Tzatzoe's followers "engaged in war," while 112 remained at King William's Town. KAB BK 89 Charles Brownlee to Maclean, Dohne, 20 February 1855.
28. KAB A47 Private Letters, Sir Harry Smith to Earl Grey, Brownlee to Smith, KWT 19 December 1851. Smith tells Grey that he instructed Brownlee to say "before the Chief Tzatzoe—Who is Sandile? And where is Mlanjeni?," KAB A47 Private Letters, Sir Harry Smith to Earl Grey, Smith to Grey, KWT, 24 December 1851. In June Toise accuses Tzatzoe of spying for Maqoma, BK 74 Maclean to Mackinnon, Fort Murray, 14 June 1851. Again, in mid-January 1852, after a large meeting of the Ngqika chiefs at Wolf River, Tzatzoe brought two key councilors to the Ngqika commissioner, OPB 1/13 2 Smith to Grey, KWT 16 January 1852.
29. For "double part" and Tzatzoe's comment to Pato, KAB BK 74 Maclean to Mackinnon, Fort Murray, 24 March 1851.
30. For "tactical information," KAB BK 437 Maclean to Mackinnon, Fort Murray, 14 June 1851. In June 1852 Maclean draws upon the testimony of "Nyakatya" and "Nonyheke" of Toise's Tribe employed as spies to accuse the "Gaika Chief 'Jan Tzatzoe'" of "furnish[ing] the rebel Chief 'Macomo' with gunpowder within the last week." Maclean asserts the veracity of the information, because "'Jan Tzatzoe's' treacherous conduct is not a new feature in his character." Maclean further asserts that "'Jan Tzatzoe's' Kaffirs" are in "constant communication" with "Uithaalders laager," by which he means the military encampment of leading Khoisan general: KAB BK 89 John Maclean, Hlambi Commissioner to Colonel Mackinnon, Chief Commissioner, Fort Murray, 9 June 1852.
31. On the Cathcart order, KAB BK 1, Cathcart to Mackinnon, Fort Beaufort, 15 June 1852. Sir Harry Smith had been dismissed by the British colonial office for failing to bring the war to a speedy conclusion: see Mostert, *Frontiers*, 1136–37.
32. The chiefs were Siwani and Toise; for the confiscation, Charles Brownlee to Maclean, Gaika Commissioners report of the Chief Jan Tzatzoe, 18 February 1855, in KAB GH 8/27.
33. For "speaking in Exeter Hall," GTJ 3 September 1853.
34. For "most barren," Bodleian Library, Philip Papers, MSS Afr. s. 219 Misc, (75) Jan Tzatzoe to Fairbairn, KWT, 10 May 1858. Information on the sale of land and the reduction in size of the amaNtinde allotment is from KAB CCP 1/2/2/1/31, Report of the Select Committee on the Petition of Jan Tshatshu, 1883.

35. The letter is in two versions. There is an English transcription, and there is an original in isiXhosa that appears to be in the same script as Tzatzoe's signature, as it appears in this letter and in other instances (for example, below the engraving made of his portrait in 1836.) This is a rare archival record of Tzatzoe's ability to write script, but it does not prove or disprove his literacy: Tzatzoe to Grey, Encmeza, 15 September 1855, and the other documents in KAB GH 8/27 Documents submitted for the consideration of His Excellency the High Commissioner, Fort Murray, 12 November 1855; Various documents relative to the conduct of Jan Tzatoze, and of his tribe, during the late Rebellion. For Grey, see Mostert, *Frontiers*, 1165–77, and for Grey's involvement in the Cattle Killing, see Peires, *Dead Will Arise*.
36. Maclean to Liddle, Private Secretary to H. E. the Governor, Fort Murray 4 November 1855, in KAB GH 8/27 Documents submitted for the consideration of His Excellency the High Commissioner, Fort Murray, 12 November 1855; Various documents relative to the conduct of Jan Tzatzoe, and of his tribe, during the late Rebellion.
37. The letter is in two versions. There is an English transcription, and there is an original in isiXhosa that appears to be in the same script as Tzatzoe's signature, as it appears in this letter and in other instances (for example, below the engraving made of his portrait in 1836.) This is a rare archival record of Tzatzoe's apparent literacy, Tzatzoe to Grey, Encmeza, 15 September 1855 and the other documents in KAB GH 8/27 Documents submitted for the consideration of His Excellency the High Commissioner, Fort Murray, 12 November 1855; Various documents relative to the conduct of Jan Tzatzoe, and of his tribe, during the late Rebellion.
38. For "remained at peace" and orchards, Charles Brownlee (Gaika Commissioner) to Cathcart, 18 February 1855. For wagons, cattle, and "messengers," Brownlee to Maclean, 20 February 1855, both in KAB GH 8/27. In his letter of 18 February Brownlee is by no means complimentary of Tzatzoe's past—he describes Tzatzoe's trip to England "when he was passed off as an important Chief, and encouraged to make statements regarding grievances and oppressions toward his Tribe and Nation, which grievances did not exist"—but he does appear to believe in his loyalty during the war itself. Brownlee adds: "Jan returned to Kaffraria a changed man, he had learnt to love wine, and to this visit is his ruin to be attributed."
39. Tzatzoe reported to his local colonial administrator on 1 July 1856 that a messenger from Sarhili had brought the following message: "That one of Kreli's [Sarhili's] people named Umhlakaza had frequent communication with a strong people who had lately made their appearance near the sea in Kreli's Country, that these people are the forefathers of the Kaffir chiefs and also the forefathers of many of the common Kaffirs who died in former times, and that these people will assist the Kaffirs in driving all the white faces out of the land—That the Cattle at present possessed by the Kaffirs are bewitched and that they must sacrifice them, for others which will be obtained from this new people." Information communicated to the Chief Commissioner, Fort Murray, 1 July 1856, KAB GH 8/29.
40. Elbourne adds that Tzatzoe rode "with missionary envoys around Xhosaland, attempting in vain to persuade the desperate chiefs that God spoke through missionaries,

and not through the mouth of a nine-year-old prophetess," Elbourne, *Blood Ground*, 292.
41. For "collect together," Fielding to Maclean, 11 January 1857 in KAB BK 89, also Information from Jan Tzatzoe, 13 October 1856; KAB GH 8/29 Fielding to Maclean, Fort Murray, 14 October 1856; KAB GH 8/31 Fielding to Maclean, Fort Murray 7 January 1857, all in KAB BK 89, which contains an extensive set of correspondence involving Tzatzoe and reports on the disturbances. The historiography of the Cattle Killing is growing rapidly. Peires, *The Dead Will Arise*, remains the standard, although recent scholarship is beginning to question its central argument that the movement was a "logical and rational response" to a set of dire circumstances, most prominently instances of lungsickness. For additional critiques, see Helen Bradford, "Women, Gender and Colonialism," and special issues of *African Studies* (2008) and *South African Historical Journal* (1991). My reading of the sources suggests that events were driven by multiple prophets, without the centrality of Mhlakaza and Nongqawuse. I also think the events are better described as a millenarian movement steeped in evangelical Christianity. See also Crais, *White Supremacy and Black Resistance*, and Mostert, *Frontiers*.
42. KAB BK 44, Memorial of Jan Tzatzoe to Sir George Grey, KWT, 7 June 1857. Tzatzoe's signature appears on the archival copy, which is in English, so it was likely transcribed by a colonial official or missionary. As with the letters of 1833 I would argue the Memorial reflects Tzatzoe's understandings; it may even be a production of his dictation. The amaNtinde's situation grew more dire in the coming year, and in May 1858 Tzatzoe wrote a petition to Fairbairn pleading for help in gaining restitution of the land. The following extract is from Mears's notes on the letter from Tzatzoe to Fairbairn in 1858. "In 1846 I occupied the house in King Williams Town now used as a prison—at request of military left the town and built a new house in the lands—in war of 1850 moved to a spot 3 miles from King on Fort Murray side on instructions of Colonel Maclean—this most barren. At end of war I was not able to return as the land was given to Col. Bisset and Fingos, although Col. Bisset neither occupies nor ploughs the land. Tzatzoe and his people starving. Made a petition to Grey in presence of Maclean—Grey promised the restoration of land—hitherto petitions have failed to obtain land, tho' Mr Chas. Brownlee had even read in a paper that the governor had given back the land. Fairbairn's help asked." UCT BC 312 (75) Mears's notes on Philip Papers, Jan Tzatzoe to Fairbairn, Kingwilliamstown, 10 May 1858. In 1883, the House of Assembly of the Cape Colony inquired into the "Petition of the Amatinde tribe of Kafirs, under the Chief Tshatshu," which alleged that the amaNtinde faced continued alienation of the land to which Jan Tzatzoe had relocated himself during the war of 1850–1853, without consultation or due compensation, and in the "face of a formal protest against such alienation." As a result the amaNtinde were "greatly impoverished," occupying a "strip of poor ground, very little being capable of cultivation." The petition asked for *reasonable compensation for the great loss they have sustained*, preferably in the form of a location near East London with individual "garden lots of ten acres" for each adult male, in addition to a "commonage." A Johannes Tshatshu

signed the petition on behalf of his people. He could only do so by marking his X. I have been unable to establish how Johannes became the amaNtinde leader, or his relationship to Jan Tzatzoe. The committee heard from John Harper, "Missionary to Tshatshu's People," who asked the Secretary for Native Affairs to "do these poor ignorant Kafirs justice in the matter." In an 1879 letter Jan Tzatzoe's old supporter Charles Brownlee supported the amaNtinde land claims. J. Rose Innes, Under Secretary for Native Affairs and former Civil Commissioner of King William's Town testified: "Would they have an equitable claim to consideration? Clearly." After all of Jan Tzatzoe's failed Memorials, his descendants succeed; the committee was "of opinion that the allegations set forth in the Petition are correct." Yet the amaNtinde were never granted new lands near East London (Tshatshu township or location is about ten kilometers from King William's Town), and likely, were not compensated for their ongoing losses. KAB CCP 1/2/2/1/31, Report of the Select Committee on the Petition of Jan Tshatshu, 1883.

43. For an experimental history of the Royal Visit and the colonial world of South Africa at the time, see my "Prince William in King William's Town." The Prince spent most of his time hunting. He had one close scrape with an enraged bull elephant near Knysna: see Roger Levine, "Changes and Markets in the Knysna and Witwatersrand Landscapes to 1899," Unpublished B.A. thesis, Yale University, May 1995. For Alfred's visit, and the British Royal Tour, see Price, *Making Empire*, 345–51. A visitor in 1864 did not offer as optimistic an assessment of King William's Town or the security of its surrounding frontier. The "whole of the houses in the town are of the most squat and temporary appearance, being generally built of inferior brick or wattle-and-daub, a wickerwork sort of erection plastered over with mud . . . [the] poor appearance of town . . . [reflects the] scarcity of money throughout the whole of British Kaffraria . . . mostly because of Kreli [Sarhili] and his marauding Kaffirs. . . . [The] whole country once belonged to him. . . . [The next war will be one] of "extermination.". . . [T]he colonists are so exasperated at the continual panics and rumours of war . . . [they have been] left beggars. . . . [I]s it to be wondered . . . that they should damn the policy that gives the Native so much latitude and consequently brings on such an unsettled state of things?" See *Captain James Briggs, Hunting and Sotho War Diaries, 1864–1865*, edited by Karel Schoeman, Cape Town, Human & Rousseau, 1985.

44. As the introduction to *The Progress of Prince Alfred* notes in a celebratory manner. "And most auspicious of all, and most gratifying to our countrymen at home, the long series of our miserable Kafir wars have to all human appearance come to a final termination. The Kafir tribes that for half a century had molested our frontiers, and involved us in bloody and prolonged and costly struggles are now, partly . . . by national suicide . . . by Sir George Grey's native policy, become dispersed throughout the country, and are occupying the position of labourers and herdsmen over the whole land from Kaffraria to Cape Town. . . . Those of them who still remain on their ancestral homes are subjected to the restraints and accustomed to the improvements of civilized life. The political power of the Kafirs is hopelessly broken. . . . [The chiefs are imprisoned on Robben Island]. . . . British law has superseded the crude though not uninteresting laws and usages of the self-outwitted and defeated savage," *The Progress of His Royal*

Highness Prince Alfred Ernest Albert through the Cape Colony, British Kaffraria, the Orange free state, and Port Natal in the year 1860, Cape Town: Saul Solomon, 1861.
45. Ibid., 50.
46. I have been unable to resolve satisfactorily the question of whether Boy Henry Duke of Wellington is Sanna Oursen's son. I do not have a date of death for Oursen (who might have outlived her husband). If Oursen continued to have children into her forties, and Henry Duke is in his twenties, the ages do not necessarily conflict.
47. SAL MSB 223, 5 (6) and (7), George Mandydi Macomo to Sir George Grey, Nuneaton, 1 October 1860, and Boy Henry Duke Tshatshu to Sir George Grey, Nuneaton, 4 January 1861. André Odendaal suggests that Tzatzoe's son was named Boy Henry Duke of Wellington Tshatshu, and that he, along with the sons of other Xhosa chiefs, gave themselves heroic names while in school at Cape Town's Zonnebloem College. Central to their new identity was participation in cricket. Indeed, African interest in, and success at, cricket is concentrated in the eastern Cape to this day: André Odendaal, *The Story of an African Game* (for Henry Duke, specifically, 26). Cricket had been seeping into African and European frontier consciousness since at least the 1830s. Barker, writing to Philip in 1831, mentions that "young men played cricket on Sunday next to the Hottentot church": see UCT BC 312 8 Barker, Theophilus to Philip, 7 April 1831, WGA Mears summaries of letters in Gubbins collection of Philip's Papers at Wits, copied by Mears in 1927, burnt in 1931. The *Graham's Town Journal*, in 1853, had predicated this development in its own way. Commenting on a match in King William's Town between the 43rd Regiment and the local garrison (won by 21 runs by the 43rd), the paper editorialized: "The few spectators were chiefly Kaffirs, who appeared to take such a lively interest in the game, that a philanthropist would have wept for joy at the probability of taming these savages by the aid of cricket. A few contumacious steady underhand bowlers to begin with might be sent out at a small expense by the supporters of Exeter Hall, and there is no doubt that ere long each Tribe would have its eleven" (GTJ 11 June 1853). A fourth C to add to the infamous missionary's famous phrase: Christianity, Commerce, and Civilization!

I could only find two more archival references to possible direct descendants of Jan Tzatzoe, although the Tshatshu's of King William's Town have a fascinating story of their own to tell about the segregation and apartheid eras. A Herman Tshatshu, writing from Trinity Mission, Fort Beaufort, on February 13 1872, asks to be admitted to Government Service as a "clerk and interpreter. I have been bred and brought up in the Kaffir College School Cape Town and for these last two years being the date I left school, am labouring in the missionary [sic] as government schoolmaster. . . . [I have expressed a] constant desire [for] civil service. . . . [I can provide a] reference from Reverend Pastor Thom Henchman" (KAB CO 4176). Even more tangentially, an Eliza Jane Tshatshu died at Rocklands, Askeaton, on 27 August 1952, aged 65; she had married a Charles Tshatshu, and the fact that her given names are that of John Philip's daughter and wife is, perhaps, entirely coincidental. KAB MOOC 6/9/20379 6499/52. There are numerous amaNtinde or Tshatshu genealogies available online, but none that are sourced. For example, the following taken from http://rulers.org/safrtrad.html, accessed on 5 September 2009: (11) amaNtinde . . . Ntinde a Togu;

Ngethani a Ntinde; *1779* Bange a Ngethani; Cika a Bange; 1825 Tshatshu a Cika; 1825–28 Feb 1868 Dyani a Tshatshu; 1868–1885 Mthikrakra a Dyani; 1885—Duku a Mthikrakra;—1906 Ziwengu a Duku; 1906–1915 rulership suspended; 1915–11 Jun 1941 Mgcawezulu a Nonqane (acting to 1 Jul 1919); 1941–16 Sep 1946 Elizabeth Tshatshu (f) (acting); 16 Sep 1946—Zwelitsha a Mgcawezulu. Nancy Jacobs notes that many such genealogies were produced during the early apartheid period: personal communication, March 2009.

48. SACA, 7 November 1832.
49. *King William's Town Gazette*, 14 November 1857. Soga represents the second generation that followed Tzatzoe, who came of age after the establishment of the colonial order with a greatly heightened European presence. He was educated in mission schools, studied in England, and wrote and spoke in English. None of the studies on Soga (or Soga himself) mention Jan Tzatzoe as a man who prepared the ground for men like Soga. The first such study was Henry Cousins, *From Kafir Kraal*. See also Donovan Williams, ed., *The journal and selected writings of the Reverend Tiyo Soga*, and idem, *Umfundisi*.
50. Date of death from George S. Hofmeyr, "King William's Town and the Xhosa, 1854–1861: The Role of a Frontier Capital During the High Commissionership of Sir George Grey," Unpublished M.A. thesis, University of Cape Town, 1981, 76. Hofmeyr cites the *Dictionary of South African Biography* as his source, and the DSAB does not cite its source. Thanks to Gregory M. Blanton for tracking down this source at the last minute.

EPILOGUE

1. For an evocative biographical approach to the historical legacy of a South African figure, see "Ghosts of Sara Baartman," in Crais and Scully, *Sara Baartman and the Hottentot Venus*.
2. Wilson Armistead, *A Tribute for the Negro*. See also, Henry Gardiner Adams, ed., *God's Image in Ebony*.
3. Armistead, *Tribute*, xi, on Tzatzoe, 359–73. I have also located a trace of Tzatzoe's life in an 1867 volume, *Anecdotes of Aborigines, or, Illustrations of the coloured races being "men"* but have been unable to access the volume. It contains the intriguing chapter heading: "The Judgment of Tzatzoe."
4. James Cowles Prichard, *The Natural History of Man*, 2, 375. I was unable to locate Prichard's diaries to confirm that he, in fact, saw Tzatzoe speak in Bristol.
5. The best introduction to Prichard is found in George W. Stocking, Jr., "From Chronology to Ethnology." Stocking has a seminal discussion of the rise of social Darwinism and scientific racism in nineteenth-century English thought: Stocking, *Victorian Anthropology*.
6. The letter is in SAL MSB 858 WP Schreiner Collection 2 (B) LMS (Misc). I could not locate a reply to Jones from either Schreiner brother in their archival holdings. In a fascinating twist, Anna Jones and her children are living as "European" citizens of the Union. Anna writes of the "prejudice" and "racial feeling" they face, in particular

from W. C. Scully (I could find no record of this contumely in Scully's published and unpublished writings). Anna defends the "deeds" of her grandfather and father "for the Christian cause & the Empire" as "irreproachable." "No one is more against inter marriage than I am," Jones concludes, "but what is done can't be undone." Elizabeth Elbourne uses the letter in *Blood Ground* with no discussion of any further history of the boxes. She contends that Jones was writing directly to the archivist of the South African Library who rejected the request. I think the letter was more speculative and intended for Will Schreiner as per his note to Theo Schreiner, but perhaps the archivist sent the letter to Schreiner. See Elbourne, *Blood Ground*, 375–76. The meaning and import of the letter does not change materially whether it was written for the archivist, or for Will Schreiner: personal communication, Elizabeth Elbourne, April 2010. As noted, I was unable to trace the Read descendants past the 1960s, but if any are still reading this note who know of a box of old papers, please send word. Many books would need to be written and re-written in this new light!

7. I wish to thank Elvis Ntozini Tshatshu, who worked at King Williams's Town's Amathole Musuem in 2003, for facilitating the visit to Maritz Ngobe. Tshatshu also took me to see the chief of the amaNtinde, Lindele Tshatshu, in Tshatshu location. Chief Tshatshu spoke no English. Elvis Tshatshu told him I was there to find out about the old chief. We were ushered inside a well-appointed living room of a two-room township house. The chief pointed to the wall and there they were—the old Tshatshu chiefs, housed in oval frames, regal in bearing and unmistakably dressed in the uniforms of soldiers of the Great or First World War. The anthropologists and historians of the Amathole Museum were not aware of an oral tradition among the amaNtinde reaching back to Jan Tzatzoe. The particular difficulties of reconstructing the past through Xhosa oral tradition are discussed in the work of Jeffrey Peires and Timothy Stapleton. See, in particular, Peires, *House of Phalo*, 170–91. I returned to the mission house in December 2005. It was a Sunday and neither it nor the Amathole museum were open. The mission house was surrounded by a locked fence and its grounds had been cleaned: there was no more long grass, no hand-painted scriptural signs, and no indication that Maritz Ngobe had remained. The tidy and sanitized garden did reveal stunning examples of local vegetation.

8. For Biko and Christianity, see Steve Biko, "The Church as seen by a young layman." See also Bishop Desmond Tutu in *I write what I like*. Mostert ends his epic *Frontiers* with a personal account of the funeral: see Mostert, *Frontiers*, 1277–80. For Biko's life and ideology, see Gail Gerhart, *Black Power in South Africa*. Pallo Jordan, who inherited the heritage of Eastern Cape literacy and cultural interaction and who was a contemporary of Biko, links Tzatzoe's legacy directly to that of Mandela: "In a sense Mandela is part of a continuum of Xhosa history. . . . The earliest modern political leaders came from the Eastern Cape. . . Dyani Tshatshu [Jan Tzatzoe] could be called the first modern African political leader in that he was trying to act within the colonial framework, rather than outside it. So I think Mandela is part of that continuum." See also Maharaj and Kathrada, eds., *Mandela: The Authorized Portrait*, 16.

BIBLIOGRAPHY

ARCHIVAL PRIMARY SOURCES

Amathole Museum, King Williams Town, South Africa
(BRWN) Collection of correspondence between John Brownlee and the London Missionary Society collected and typed. Courtesy of Killie Campbell Africana Library.

Brenthurst Library, Johannesburg, South Africa
(BRENT) Kitchingman Papers, Philip letters MS 183/4, 1–108; Jane Philip Letters, MS 183/3/1–12.

(KAB) Cape Archives, Cape Town, South Africa
A519: Papers of Sir Benjamin D'Urban
A559: Records of Bethelsdorp
A1415: Diverse collection
(BK) British Kaffraria: Multiple Files
CCP 1/2/2/1/31 Report of the Select Committee on the Petition of Jan Tshatshu, 1883.
(CO) Colonial Office: Multiple Files
(GH) Government House: Multiple Files
MOOC 6/9/20379 6499/52
(OPB) Imperial Blue Books of South Africa: Multiple volumes

Cory Library, Rhodes University, Grahamstown, South Africa
Pamphlet Box 70, Bokwe, *Ntsikana: The Story of an African Hymn*
MS 9063, N. Falati, "The Story of Ntsikana: A Gaika Xhosa," 1895.
MS 109 conversation with Somana and Tanco, Jan 22 1910.
MS 104
Cory Burton papers 14,610 (2), (18)
Cory Burton papers 14, 619 F
South African Library, Cape Town, South Africa

Sir George Grey Collection: Multiple Files
(QAP) Records of the Province of Queen Adelaide, consisting chiefly of the private and confidential correspondence between Governor Sir Benjamin D'Urban, Colonel H. G. Smith, Lieutenant-Colonel H. Somerset and other high officials; copied and arranged by George McCall Theal, 1913.
Graham's Town Journal (1850s)

(UCT) Manuscripts and Archives, University of Cape Town, South Africa
BC 312 WGA Mears summaries of letters in Gubbins collection of Philip's Papers, copied by Mears in 1927, burnt in 1931

(WITS) Historical Papers, University of Witwatersrand, Johannesburg, South Africa
Philip Papers
Guide to the Archives Housed at Historical Papers, Wits
A43 Godlonton collection (51)

Bodleian Library, Rhodes House, Oxford University, England
Philip Papers; MSS Afr. s. 217, 1834–1842
MSS Afr. s. 219 Misc, #75
Philip papers V, 1836–1838
Patriot, Mss. British Empire S.44, Volume 41
"Memorandum in which Stretch reviews the Treaty System, 1839 to 1846."

School of Oriental and African Studies, London, England
(SOAS) Annual Reports
(LMS) Council for World Missions Archives, London Missionary Society Series:
South Africa Incoming (Microform)
South Africa Journals (Microform)
Home, Personal
South Africa, Freeman papers and Philip odds

Sterling Memorial Library Microform Collection, New Haven, Connecticut
(TFB) Thomas Fowell Buxton Collection.
Houghton Library, Cambridge, Massachusetts
American Board Mission records: Miscellaneous Foreign Letters

PRINTED PRIMARY SOURCES

(AB) Reports of the House of Commons Select Committee on Aborigines (British Settlements), two volumes. British and Cape of Good Hope Parliamentary Papers.
Henry Gardiner Adams, ed. *God's Image in Ebony: Being a Series of Biographical Sketches, Facts, Anecdotes, Etc., Demonstrative of the Mental Powers and Intellectual Capacities of the Negro Race.* London: Partridge and Oakey, 1854.
Alexander, Captain James. *Narrative of a Voyage and a Campaign in Kaffirland.* London: Henry Colburn, 1837

Appleyard, John W. *An Apology for the Kafir Bible: Being a Reply to the Pamphlet Entitled, "Rev. J. W. Appleyard's Version Judged by Missionaries of Various Denominations and Others."* Mount Coke, South Africa: Wesleyan Mission Press, 1867.

Appleyard, J. W., with John Frye, ed. *The War of the Axe and the Xhosa Bible: The Journal of the Rev. J. W. Appleyard.* Cape Town: C. Struik, 1971.

Armistead, Wilson. *A Tribute for the Negro: Being a Vindication of the Moral, Intellectual, and Religious Capabilities of the Coloured Portion of Mankind; with Particular Reference to the African Race.* Manchester: William Irwin, 1848.

Alberti, Ludwig. *Account of the Tribal Life and Customs of the Xhosa in 1807.* Cape Town: Balkema, 1968.

Backhouse, James. *A Narrative of a Visit to the Mauritius and South Africa.* London: Hamilton, Adams, and Co., 1844.

Brownlee, Charles. "The Old Peach Tree Stump: A Reminiscence of the war of 1835." In *Cape Monthly Magazine* 7 (September 1873): 129–43, as reprinted in A. M. Lewin Robinson, ed., *Selected Articles from the Cape Monthly Magazine* (New Series 1870–76). Cape Town: Van Riebeeck Society, 1978.

Bokwe, John Knox. *Ntsikana: The Story of an African Convert.* Lovedale: Lovedale Mission Press, 1914.

Boyce, W. B. *Notes on South African Affairs, from 1834 to 1838; with reference to the civil, political, and religious condition, of the Colonists and Aborigines.* Graham's Town: Aldum and Harvey, 1838. Reprint, Cape Town: C. Struik, 1971.

Buxton, Charles. *Memoirs of Sir Thomas Fowell Buxton, baronet. With selections from his correspondence. Edited by His son, Charles Buxton.* Third Edition. Philadelphia: H. Longstreth, 1849).

Casalis, Eugene. *My Life in Basutoland.* Cape Town: C. Struik, 1971.

Cousins, Henry. *From Kafir Kraal to Pulpit: The Story of Tiyo Soga, first ordained preacher of the Kafir Race.* London: S. W. Partridge and Co., 1899.

Darwin, Charles. *Charles Darwin's Diary of the Voyage of H.M.S. "Beagle," Edited from the Manuscript by Nora Barlow.* New York: Macmillan, 1933.

Davis, Rev. W. J., revised by Rev. William Hunter. *An English-Kaffir Dictionary Principally of the Xosa-Kaffir but including also many words of the Zulu-Kaffir Dialect.* Cape Town: Methodist Publishing Office, 1903.

"The African Witnesses," in Ellis, Reverend William, ed. *The Christian Keepsake and Missionary Annual for 1838.* London: Fisher, Son, and Co., 1838.

Freeman, J. J. *A Tour in South Africa.* London: John Snow, 1851.

Godlonton, Robert. *A Narrative of the Irruption of the Kaffir Hordes into the Eastern Province of the Cape of Good Hope, 1834–1835.* Cape Town: C. Struik, 1965.

Holy Bible. Oxford, U.K.: Samuel Collingwood and Co., 1823.

Johnston, Priscilla. *Extracts from Priscilla Johnston's Journal and Letters, edited by E. Macinnes.* Carlisle: Charles Thurnam and Sons, 1862.

Kay, Stephen. *Travels and researches in Caffraria: describing the character, customs, and moral condition of the tribes inhabiting that portion of southern Africa: with historical and topographical remarks illustrative of the state and prospects of the British settlement in its borders, the introduction of Christianity, and the progress of civilization.* London: John Mason, 1833.

Kayser, F. G., in Chris Hummel, ed. *Rev. F. G. Kayser: Journal and Letters*. Grahamstown: Maskew Miller Longman, 1990.

(KITCH) le Cordeur, Basil, and Christopher Saunders, eds. *The Kitchingman Papers: Missionary Letters and Journals, 1817–1848 from the Brenthurst Collection, Johannesburg*. Johannesburg: Brenthurst, 1976.

Kropf, Rev. Albert. *A Kaffir-English Dictionary*. Lovedale, South Africa: Lovedale Mission, 1899.

Noyi, Robert Balfour. "The Kafirs and their Country." In Bokwe, *Ntsikana: The Story of an African Convert*. Lovedale: Lovedale Mission Press, 1914.

Philip, John. *Researches in South Africa: Illustrating the Civil, Moral, and Religious Condition of Native Tribes*. Two volumes. London: James Duncan, 1828.

Prichard, James Cowles, and George W. Stocking, Jr., eds. *Researches into the Physical History of Man*. Chicago: Chicago University Press, 1973.

———. *The Natural History of Man; Comprising Inquiries into the modifying influence of Physical and Moral Agencies on the Different Tribes of the Human Family*. Two volumes. London: H. Bailliere, 1855.

Pringle, Thomas. *African Sketches*. London: Edward Moxon, 1834.

Read, James Senior. *The African Witness: or, a Short Account of the Life of Andries Stoffles; Published with Josiah Basset, The Life of a Vagrant, or the Testimony of an Outcast*. London: 1850.

Rose, Cowper. *Four Years in Southern Africa*. London: Henry Colburn and Richard Bentley, 1829.

Saul Solomon and Co. *The Progress of His Royal Highness Prince Alfred Ernest Albert through the Cape Colony, British Kaffraria, the Orange free state, and Port Natal in the year 1860*. Cape Town: Saul Solomon and Co., 1861.

Shaw, William. *The Story of My Mission in South-Eastern Africa: comprising some account of the European colonist; with extended notices of the Kaffir and other native tribes*. London, Hamilton, 1860.

Soga, John Henderson. *The Ama-Xosa: Life and Customs*. Lovedale: LovedalePress, 1931.

Theal, George McCall. *Records of the Cape Colony: from February 1793 to April 1831*. Cape Town: Government of the Cape Colony, 1897–1905.

———. *History of South Africa, 1795–1834*. London: Swan Sonnenschein and Co., 1891.

Ward, Harriet. *The Cape and the Kaffirs*. London: Henry G. Bohn, 1851.

———. *Five Years in Kaffirland*. Volume 1. London: Henry Colburn, 1848.

Williams, Donovan, ed. *The Journal and Selected Writings of the Reverend Tiyo Soga*. Cape Town: A. A. Balkema, 1983.

Willoughby, W.C. *Nature-worship and Taboo: Further Studies in "The Soul of the Bantu."* Hartford: Hartford Seminary Press, 1932.

———. *The Soul of the Bantu: A Sympathetic Study of the Magico-Religious Practices and Beliefs of the Bantu Tribes of Africa*. Garden City, N.Y.: Doubleday, Doran and Co., 1928.

Young, Robert. *African Wastes Reclaimed, Illustrated in the Story of the Lovedale Mission*. London: J. M. Dent, 1902.

NEWSPAPERS AND PERIODICALS

(BL) British Library Newspapers Collection, Colindale, England
Bristol Advocate
Bristol Mercury, Monmouthshire, South Wales, and West of England Advertiser
Morning Chronicle
North Derbyshire Chronicle and Chesterfield Advertiser
Nottingham Review
Sheffield Independent
Sheffield Mercury and Hallamshire Advertiser
Patriot
Yorkshire Gazette
Yorkshireman

Sterling Library Microform Collection, CRL, New Haven, Connecticut

(GTJ) *Graham's Town Journal*
(SACA) *South African Commercial Advertiser*
Missionary Magazine and Chronicle
Sun (London)

South African Library, Cape Town, South Africa

Graham's Town Journal
King William's Town Gazette
Evangelical Magazine and Missionary Chronicle

PUBLISHED SECONDARY SOURCES

Anderson, Allan A., and Gerald J. Pillay. "The Segregated Spirit: The Pentecostals," in Elphick and Davenport, *Christianity in South Africa*.

Ashforth, Adam. *Witchcraft, Violence, and Democracy in South Africa*. Chicago: University of Chicago Press, 2005.

———. *Madumo: A Man Bewitched*. Cape Town: David Philip, 2000.

Axtell, James. *The Invasion Within: The Contest of Cultures in Colonial North America*. New York: Oxford University Press, 1985.

Bank, Andrew. *Bushmen in a Victorian World: The remarkable story of the Bleek-Lloyd Collection of Bushman folklore*. Cape Town: Double Storey, 2006.

———. "Losing faith in the civilizing mission: the premature decline of humanitarian liberalism at the Cape, 1840–1860,"in Martin Daunton and Rick Halpern, eds. *Empire and Others: British Encounters with Indigenous Peoples, 1600–1850*. London: UCL Press, 1999.

———. "The Great Debate and the Origins of South African Historiography," *Journal of African History* 38 (1997).

Bayly, C. A. "The British and Indigenous Peoples, 1760–1860: Power, Perception, and Identity." In Daunton and Halpern, eds. *Empire and Others: British Encounters with Indigenous Peoples, 1600–1850.*

Bederman, Gail. *Manliness and Civilization: A cultural history of gender and race in the United States, 1880–1917.* Chicago: University of Chicago Press, 1995.

Benjamin, Walter. "The Task of the Translator," in *Illuminations*, ed. Hannah Arendt. New York: Schocken, 1969.

Biko, Steve. "The Church as seen by a young layman." In *I Write What I Like: A Selection of His Writings.* Johannesburg: Ravan Press, 1978.

Blackburn, Julia. *Daisy Bates in the Desert.* London: Secker and Warburg, 1994.

Blakely, Thomas D., Walter E. A. van Beek, and Dennis Thomson, eds. *Religion in Africa: Experience and Expression.* Portsmouth, N.H.: Heinemann, 1994.

Bradford, Helen. "Women, Gender and Colonialism: Rethinking the History of the British Cape Colony and Its Frontier Zones, C. 1806–70." *Journal of African History* 37, no. 3 (1996).

Bredekamp, Henry, and Robert Ross, eds. *Missions and Christianity in South African History.* Johannesburg, Witwatersrand University Press, 1995.

Breen, Louise A. "Praying with the enemy: Daniel Gookin, King Philip's War and the dangers of intercultural mediatorship," in Daunton and Halpern, eds, *Empire and Others.*

Calloway, Colin G. *New Worlds For All: Indians, Europeans, and the Remaking of Early America.* Baltimore: The Johns Hopkins University Press, 1987.

Cannadine, David. *Ornamentalism: How the British Saw Their Empire.* New York: Oxford University Press, 2001.

Carretta, Vincent. *Equiano, the African: Biography of a Self-made Man.* Athens: University of Georgia Press, 2005.

Cayton, Andrew R. L. *Frontier Indiana.* Bloomington: Indiana University Press, 1996.

Cell, John Winston. *British Colonial Administration in the Mid-nineteenth Century: The Policy-Making Process.* New Haven: Yale University Press, 1970.

Chidester, David. *Savage Systems: Colonialism and Comparative Religion in Southern Africa.* Charlottesville: University of Virginia Press, 1996.

Christiansen, Rupert. *The Visitors: Culture Shock in Nineteenth-Century Britain.* London: Chatto and Windus, 2000.

Clive, John. *Not By Fact Alone: Essays on the Writing and Reading of History.* New York: Alfred A. Knopf, 1989.

Coleman, Jon T. *Vicious: Wolves and Men in America.* New Haven: Yale University Press, 2004.

Colley, Linda. *Britons: Forging the Nation 1707–1837.* New Haven: Yale University Press, 1992.

Comaroff, Jean, and John L. Comaroff. *Of Revelation and Revolution: The Dialectics of Modernity on a South African Frontier.* Chicago: Chicago University Press, 1997.

——— . *Of Revelation and Revolution: Christianity, Colonialism, and Consciousness in South Africa.* Chicago: University of Chicago Press, 1991.

Cooper, Frederick, and Ann Laura Stoler. "Between Metropole and Colony: Rethinking a Research Agenda," in Cooper and Stoler, eds. *Tensions of Empire*.
Cooper, Frederick, and Ann Laura Stoler, eds. *Tensions of Empire: Colonial Cultures in a Bourgeois World*. Berkeley: University of California Press, 1997.
Couzens, Tim. *Murder at Morija: faith, mystery, and tragedy on an African mission*. Charlottesville: University of Virginia Press, 2005.
———. *Tramp Royal: The True Story of Trader Horn*. Johannesburg: University of Witwatersrand Press, 1992.
Crafford, D. "Jan Tshatshu," in *Trail-Blazers of the Gospel: Black Pioneers in the Missionary History of Southern Africa*. Pretoria: Institute for Missiological Research, 1991.
Crais, Clifton. *The Poetics of Evil: Magic, State Power, and the Political Imagination in South Africa*. New York: Cambridge University Press, 2002.
———. *White Supremacy and Black Resistance in Pre-Industrial South Africa: The Making of the Colonial Order in the Eastern Cape, 1770–1865*. Cambridge: Cambridge University Press, 1992.
Crais, Clifton, and Pamela Scully. *Sara Baartman and the Hottentot Venus: A Ghost Story and a Biography*. Princeton: Princeton University Press, 2008.
Crampton, Hazel. *The Sunburnt Queen: A True Story*. Johannesburg: Saqi, 2006.
da Costa, Emilia Viotti. *Crowns of Glory, Tears of Blood: The Demerara Slave Rebellion of 1823*. New York: Oxford University Press, 1994.
Daunton, Martin, and Rick Halpern, eds. *Empire and Others: British Encounters with indigenous peoples, 1600–1850*. London: UCL Press, 1999.
———. "Introduction: British identities, indigenous peoples, and the empire," in *Empire and Others: British Encounters with indigenous peoples, 1600–1850*. London: UCL Press, 1999.
Davis, Natalie Zemon. *Women on the Margins: Three Seventeenth-Century Lives*. Cambridge: Harvard University Press, 1997.
de Gruchy, John, Ed. *The London Missionary Society in Southern Africa: Historical Essays in celebration of the LMS in Southern Africa, 1799–1999*. Cape Town: David Philip, 1999.
Demos, John. *The Unredeemed Captive: A Family Story from Early America*. New York: Knopf, 1994.
Denning, Greg. "Texts of Self," in Hoffman et al., *Through a Glass Darkly*.
Doke, Clement. "Scripture Translation into Bantu Languages." *African Studies* 17, no. 2 (1958).
Duffield, Ian. "Skilled Workers or Marginalized Poor?: The African Population of the United Kingdom, 1812–52," in *Africans in Britain*.
Edwards, Paul, ed. *Equiano's Travels: The Interesting Narrative of the Life of Olaudah Equiano or Gustavus Vassa the African*. Long Grove, Illinois: Waveland Press, 1996.
———. "Unreconciled Strivings and Ironic Strategies: Three Afro-British Authors of the late Georgian Period (Sancho, Equiano, Wedderburn)," in David Killingray, ed., *Africans in Britain*.
Elbourne, Elizabeth. *Blood Ground: Colonialism, Missions, and the contest for Christianity in the Cape Colony and Britain, 1799–1853*. Montreal: McGill-Queen's University Press, 2002.

———. "Word made flesh: Christianity, Modernity, and Cultural Colonialism in the Work of Jean and John Comaroff." *American Historical Review.* 108, no. 2 (June 2003).

———. "The Sin of the Settler: The 1835–36 Select Committee on Aborigines and Debates over Virtue and Conquest in the Early Nineteenth-Century British White Settler Empire." *Journal of Colonialism and Colonial History* 4, no. 3 (2003).

———. "Whose gospel? Conflict in the LMS in the early 1840s," in de Gruchy, ed., *The LMS in South Africa.*

Elphick, Richard. *Kraal and Castle: Khoekhoe and the Founding of White South Africa.* New Haven: Yale University Press, 1977.

———. "Writing Religion into History: The Case of South African Christianity," in Bredekamp and Ross, eds. *Missions and Christianity in South African History.*

Elphick, Richard, and Rodney Davenport, eds. *Christianity in South Africa: A Political, Social and Cultural History.* Berkeley: University of California Press, 1997.

Elphick, Richard, and Hermann Giliomee, eds. *The Shaping of South African Society, 1652–1840.* Middletown, CT: Wesleyan University Press, 1988.

Enklaar, Ido H. *Life and Work of Dr. J. Th. van der Kemp, 1747–1811: Missionary, Pioneer and Protagonist of Racial Equality in South Africa.* Cape Town and Rotterdam: A. A. Balkema, 1998.

Erlank, Natasha. "Jane and John Philip: Partnership, Usefulness and Sexuality in the Service of God," in de Gruchy, ed., *The London Missionary Society in South Africa.*

———. "Gendered Reactions to Social Dislocation and Missionary Activity in Xhosaland, 1836–1847," *African Studies* 59, no. 2 (2000).

———. "Re-examining initial encounters between Christian missionaries and the Xhosa, 1820–1850: the Scottish case," *Kleio* 31 (1999).

Etherington, Norman. *The Great Treks: the transformation of Southern Africa, 1815–1854.* Harlow, England: Longman, 2001.

Etherington, Norman, ed. *Missions and Empire.* New York: Oxford University, 2005.

Feierman, Steven. *Peasant Intellectuals: Anthropology and History in Tanzania,* Madison: University of Wisconsin Press, 1990.

Gerard, Albert S. *Four African Literatures: Xhosa, Sotho, Zulu, Amharic.* Berkeley: University of California Press, 1971.

Gerhart, Gail. *Black Power in South Africa: The Evolution of an Ideology.* Berkeley: University of California Press, 1978.

Geschiere, Peter. *The Modernity of Witchcraft: Politics and the Occult in Postcolonial Africa.* Charlottesville: University of Virginia Press, 1997.

Gevisser, Mark. *Thabo Mbeki: The Dream Deferred.* Johannesburg: Jonathan Ball, 2007.

Gilmour, Rachael. "Missionaries, Colonialism and Language in Nineteenth-Century South Africa." *History Compass* 5/6 (2007).

———. *Grammars of Colonialism: Representing Languages in Colonial South Africa.* New York: Palgrave Macmillan, 2006.

Glaser, Clive. *Bo-Tsotsi: The Youth Gangs of Soweto, 1935–1976.* Portsmouth: Heinemann, 2000.

Goodman, James. *Stories of Scottsboro.* New York: Vintage, 1994.

Gould, Stephen Jay. *Wonderful Life: The Burgess Shale and the Nature of History*. New York: W. W. Norton, 1989.
Gray, Richard. *Black Christians and White Missionaries*. New Haven: Yale University Press, 1990.
Guy, Jeff. *The View Across the River: Harriette Colenso and the Zulu Struggle against Imperialism*. Charlottesville: University Press of Virginia, 2001.
Hall, Catherine. *Civilizing Subjects: Metropole and Colony in the English Imagination 1830–1867*. Chicago: University of Chicago Press, 2002.
———. "William Knibb and the Constitution of the New Black Subject." In Martin Daunton and Rick Halpern, eds. *Empire and Others: British Encounters with Indigenous Peoples, 1600–1850*. London: UCL, 1999.
Hall, Catherine, and Sonya O. Rose, Eds. *At Home with Empire: Metropolitan Culture and the Imperial World*. New York: Cambridge University Press, 2006.
Harms, Robert W. *The Diligent: A Voyage through the Worlds of the Slave Trade*. New York: Basic, 2002.
Hilton, Boyd. *A Mad, Bad, and Dangerous People? England, 1783–1846*. Oxford: Oxford University, 2006.
———. *The Age of Atonement: The Influence of Evangelicalism on Social and Economic Thought, 1795–1865*. New York: Oxford University Press, 1988.
Hiney, Tom. *On the Missionary Trail: A Journey Through Polynesia, Asia, and Africa with the London Missionary Society*. New York: Atlantic Monthly, 2000.
Hochschild, Adam. *Bury the Chains: Prophets and Rebels in the Fight to Free an Empire's Slaves*. Boston: Houghton Mifflin, 2005.
Hodes, Martha. *The Sea Captain's Wife: A True Story of Love, Race, and War in the Nineteenth Century*. New York: W. W. Norton, 2006.
Hodgson, Janet. "A Battle for Sacred Power: Christian Beginnings among the Xhosa," in Richard Elphick and Rodney Davenport, eds. *Christianity in South Africa: A Political, Social and Cultural History*. Berkeley: University of California Press, 1997.
———. "A Study of the Xhosa Prophet, Nxele." *Religion in Southern Africa* 6, no. 2 (July 1985) and 7, no. 1 (January 1986).
———. *The God of the Xhosa: A Study of the Origins and Developments of the Traditional Concepts of the Supreme Being*. Cape Town: Oxford University Press, 1982.
———. *Ntsikana's Great Hymn: A Xhosa Expression of Christianity in the Early Nineteenth-Century Eastern Cape*. Cape Town: Centre for African Studies, 1980.
Hoffman, Ronald, Mechal Sobel, and Fredrika Teute, eds. *Through a Glass Darkly: Reflections on Personal Identity in Early America*. Chapel Hill: University of North Carolina Press, 1997.
Hofmeyr, Isabel. *The Portable Bunyan: A Transnational History of the The Pilgrim's Progress*. Princeton: Princeton University Press, 2004.
Holt, Basil. *Greatheart of the Border: A Life of John Brownlee, Pioneer Missionary in South Africa*. King William's Town: The South African Missionary Museum, 1976.
———. *Joseph Williams and the Pioneer Mission to the Southeastern Bantu*. Lovedale: Lovedale University Press, 1954.

Hunt, Nancy Rose. *A Colonial Lexicon of Birth Ritual, Medicalization, and Mobility in the Congo.* Durham: Duke University Press, 1999.
Hunt, Tristam. *Building Jerusalem: The Rise and Fall of the Victorian City.* New York: Henry Holt, 2005.
Jasanoff, Maya. *Edge of Empires: Lives, Culture, and Conquest in the East, 1750–1850.* New York: Alfred A. Knopf, 2005.
Johnson, Walter. "On Agency," *Journal of Social History* 37, no. 1 (2003).
Jonas, P. J. "Jan Tshatshu and the Eastern Cape Mission—A Contextual Analysis." *Missionalia* 18 (1990).
Joubert, Elsa. *Poppie Nongena: One Woman's Struggle against Apartheid.* New York: Henry Holt, 1980.
Kaplan, Steven, Ed. *Indigenous Responses to Western Christianity.* New York: New York University Press, 1995.
Karttunen, Frances. *Between Worlds: Interpreters, Guides, and Survivors.* New Brunswick: Rutgers University Press, 1994.
Keegan, Timothy. *Colonial South Africa and the Origins of the Racial Order.* Charlottesville: University of Virginia Press, 1996.
Killingray, David, ed., *Africans in Britain.* Portland: Frank Cass, 1994.
———. "Africans in the United Kingdom: An Introduction," in *Africans in Britain.*
Kopytoff, Igor. *The African Frontier: The Reproduction of Traditional African Societies.* Bloomington: Indiana University Press, 1987.
Kreike, Emmanuel. *Re-Creating Eden: Land Use, Environment, and Society in Southern Angola and Northern Namibia.* Portsmouth: Heinemann, 2004.
Kynoch, Gary. *We are Fighting the World: A History of the Marashea Gangs in South Africa, 1947–1999.* Athens: Ohio University Press, 2005.
La Hausse, Paul. *Restless Identities: Signatures of Nationalism, Zulu Ethnicity, and history in the lives of Petros Lamula (c. 1881–1948) and Lymon Maling (1889–c.1936).* Pietermaritzburg: University of Natal Press, 2000.
LaDow, Beth. *The Medicine Line: Life and Death on a North American Borderland.* New York: Routledge, 2001.
Laidlaw, Zoë. *Colonial Connections, 1815–45: Patronage, the Information Revolution and Colonial Government.* New York and Manchester: Manchester University Press, 2005.
———. "'Aunt Anna's Report': The Buxton Women and the Aborigines Select Committee, 1835–1837," *Journal of Imperial and Commonwealth History* 32, no. 2 (May 2004).
Lalu, Premesh. *The Deaths of Hintsa: Postapartheid South Africa and the Shape of Recurring Pasts.* Cape Town: HSRC Press, 2009
———. "The Grammar of Domination and the Subjection of Agency: Colonial Texts and Modes of Evidence." *History and Theory* 39 (December 2000).
Lamar, Howard and Leonard Thompson, eds. *The Frontier in History: North America and Southern Africa Compared.* New Haven: Yale University Press, 1981.
Lambert, David, and Alan Lester, Eds. *Colonial Lives Across the British Empire: Imperial Careering in the Long Nineteenth Century.* New York: Cambridge University Press, 2006.
Lan, David. *Guns and Rain: Guerrillas and Spirit Mediums in Zimbabwe.* Berkeley: University of California, 1995.

Landau, Paul S. *The Realm of the Word: Language, Gender, and Chrisianity in a Southern African Kingdom.* Portsmouth: Heinemann, 1995.

———. "'Religion' and Christian Conversion in African History: A New Model." *Journal of Religious History* 23, no. 1 (February 1999).

———. "Explaining Surgical Evangelism in Colonial Southern Africa: Teeth, Pain and Faith." *Journal of African History* 37, no. 2 (1996).

Lawrance, Benjamin N., Emily Lynn Osborn, and Richard L. Roberts, eds. *Intermediaries, Interpreters and Clerks: African Employees in the Making of Colonial Africa.* Madison: University of Wisconsin Press, 2006.

Lehmann, Joseph H. *Remember You Are an Englishman: A Biography of Sir Harry Smith, 1787–1860.* London: Jonathan Cape, 1977.

Lepore, Jill. *The Name of War: King Philip's War and the Origins of American Identity.* New York: Vintage, 1999.

———. "Historians Who Love Too Much: Reflections on Microhistory and Biography." *Journal of American History* 88 (2001).

Lester, Alan. *Imperial Networks: Creating Identities in Nineteenth-Century South Africa and Britain.* New York: Routledge, 2001.

Levine, Roger S. "Prince Alfred in King William's Town, South Africa: 13 August 1860." *Rethinking History: Journal of Theory and Practice* 14, no. 1 (2010).

———. "An Interpreter Will Arise: Resurrecting Jan Tzatzoe's Diplomatic and Evangelical Contributions as a Cultural Intermediary on South Africa's Eastern Cape Frontier, 1816–1818." In Lawrance, Osborn, Roberts, eds., *Intermediaries, Interpreters and Clerks.*

———. "'African Warfare in All Its Ferocity': Changing Military Landscapes and the Study of Precolonial and Colonial Conflict in Southern Africa," in Richard Tucker and Ed Russell, eds. *Natural Ally, Natural Enemy: Toward an Environmental History of Warfare,* Eugene: University of Oregon, 2004.

Lindfors, Bernth, Ed. *Africans on Stage: Studies in Ethnological Show Business.* Bloomington: Indiana University Press, 1999.

———. "Charles Dickens and the Zulus," in *Africans on Stage.*

Lovett, Richard. *The History of the London Missionary Society, 1795–1895.* Two Volumes. London: H. Frowde, 1899.

Mabona, Mongameli. *Diviners and Prophets among the Xhosa, 1593–1856: A Study in Xhosa Cultural History.* Piscataway: Transaction, 2004.

Maclennan, Ben. *A Proper Degree of Terror: John Graham and the Cape's Eastern Frontier.* Johannesburg: Ravan, 1986.

Macmillan, W. W. *Bantu, Boer, and Briton: The Making of the South African Native Problem.* Oxford: Clarendon, 1963

Magubane, Zine. *Bringing the Empire Home: Race, Class, and Gender in Britain and Colonial South Africa.* Chicago: University of Chicago Press, 2004.

Maharaj, Mac, and Ahmed Kathrada, eds. *Mandela: The Authorized Portrait.* Kansas City: Andrews McMeel, 2006.

Malherbe, V. C. *Krotoa, called "Eva": A Woman Between.* Rondebosch, South Africa: Centre for African Studies, University of Cape Town, 1990.

Mamdani, Mahmood. *Citizen and Subject: Contemporary Africa and the Legacy of Late Colonialism*. Princeton: Princeton University Press, 1996.

Mandela, Nelson. *Long Walk To Freedom: The Autobiography of Nelson Mandela*. Boston: Little Brown, 1994.

Margadant, Jo Burr. "Introduction: Constructing Selves in Historical Perspective," in Margadant, ed., *The New Biography*.

Margadant, Jo Burr, ed. *The New Biography: Performing Femininity in Nineteenth-Century France*. Berkeley: University of California Press, 2000.

Marks, Shula. *Not Either an Experimental Doll: The Separate Worlds of Three South African Women*. Bloomington: Indiana University Press, 1987.

———. *The Ambiguities of Dependence in South Africa: Class, Nationalism, and the State in Twentieth-Century Natal*. Baltimore: The Johns Hopkins University Press, 1986.

Martin, Joel W. *Sacred Revolt: The Muskogees' Struggle for a New World*. Boston: Beacon, 1991.

Mbiti, John S. *African Religions and Philosophy*. New York: Frederick A. Praeger, 1969.

McAllister, Patrick A. *Xhosa Beer Drinking Rituals: Power, Practice and Performance in the South African Rural Periphery*. Durham: Carolina Academic, 2006.

McClendon, Thomas. "The Man Who Would Be Inkosi: Civilising Missions in Shepstone's Early Career." *Journal of Southern African Studies* 30, no. 2 (June 2004).

McClintock, Anne. *Imperial Leather: Race, Gender and Sexuality in the Colonial Contest*. New York: Routledge, 1995.

———. "The Scandal of Hybridity: Black Women's Resistance and Narrative Ambiguity," in *Imperial Leather: Race, Gender and Sexuality in the Colonial Contest*.

McKenzie, Kirsten. *Scandal in the Colonies: Sydney and Cape Town, 1800–1850*. Melbourne: University of Melbourne Press, 2004.

Merrell, James H. *Into the American Woods: Negotiators on the Pennsylvania Frontier*. New York: W. W. Norton, 1999.

———. *The Indians' New World: Catawbas and Their Neighbors from European Contact through the Era of Removal*. Chapel Hill: University of North Carolina Press, 1989.

Merwick, Donna. *Death of a Notary: Conquest and Change in Colonial New York*. Ithaca: Cornell University Press, 1999.

Merry, Sally Engle. "Hegemony and Culture in Historical Anthropology: A Review Essay on Jean and John L. Comaroff's *Of Revelation and Revolution*." *American Historical Review*, 108, no. 2 (June 2003).

Milton, John. *The Edges of War: A History of Frontier Wars (1702–1878)*. Cape Town: Juta and Co., 1983.

Mngxitama, Andile, Amanda Alexander, and Nigel C. Gibson, eds. *Biko Lives!: Contesting the Legacies of Steve Biko*. New York: Palgrave Macmillan, 2008.

Moore, Henrietta L., and Todd Sanders, eds. *Magical Interpretations, Material Realities: Modernity, Witchcraft and the Occult in Postcolonial Africa*. London: Routledge, 2001.

Mostert, Nöel. *Frontiers: The Epic of South Africa's Creation and the Tragedy of the Xhosa People*. London, Pimlico, 1993.

Mottram, R. H. *Buxton the Liberator*. London: Hutchinson and Co., 1946

Muir, Edward, and Guido Ruggiero, eds. *Microhistory and the Lost Peoples of Europe*. Baltimore: The Johns Hopkins University Press, 1991.
Musopole, A. C. "Witchcraft Terminology, the Bible, and African Christian Theology: An Exercise in Hermeneutics" *Journal of Religion in Africa* 23, no. 4 (1993).
Myers, Norma. *Reconstructing the Black Past: Blacks in Britain, 1780–1830*. Portland: Frank Cass, 1996.
Nandy, Ashis. *The Intimate Enemy: Loss and Recovery of Self under Colonialism*. New York: Oxford University Press, 1983.
Ndletyana, Mcebisi, ed., *African Intellectuals in 19th- and early 20th-Century South Africa*. Cape Town: HSRC, 2008.
Newton-King, Susan. *Masters and Servants on the Cape Eastern Frontier, 1760–1803*. Cambridge, U.K.: Cambridge University Press, 1999.
Niehaus, Isak, with Eliazaar Mohlala and Kally Shokane. *Witchcraft, Power and Politics: Exploring the Occult in the South African Lowveld*. London: Pluto, 2001.
Nobles, Gregory. *American Frontiers: Cultural Encounters and Colonial Conquest*. New York: Hill and Wang, 1997.
Odendaal, André. *The Story of an African Game*. Cape Town: David Philip, 2003.
Osborn, Emily Lynn. "'Circle of Iron': African Colonial Employees and the Interpretation of Colonial Rule in French West Africa." *Journal of African History* 44 (2003).
Parrinder, Geoffrey. *African Traditional Religion*. London: Sheldon, 1962.
Parsons, Neil. *King Khama, Emperor Joe, and the Great White Queen: Victorian Britain through African Eyes*. Chicago: The University of Chicago Press, 1998.
Peel, J.D.Y. "For Who Hath Despised the Day of Small Things? Missionary Narrratives and Historical Anthropology." *Comparative Studies in Society and History* 37, no. 3 (1995).
Peires, J. B. *The Dead Will Arise: Nongqawuse and the Great Xhosa Cattle-Killing Movement of 1856–57*. Bloomington: Indiana University Press, 1989.
———. *The House of Phalo: A History of the Xhosa People in the Days of their Independence*. Johannesburg: Ravan, 1981.
Penn, Nigel. *The Forgotten Frontier: Colonist and Khoisan on the Cape's Northern Frontier in the 18th Century*. Cape Town: Double Storey, 2005.
Peterson, Derek. "Translating the Word: Dialogism and Debate in Two Gikuyu Dictionaries." *Journal of Religious History* 23 (1999).
Picard, Liza. *Victorian London: The Life of a City, 1840–1870*. New York: St. Martin's, 2005.
Pirouet, M. Louise. *Black Evangelists: The Spread of Christianity in Uganda 1891–1914*. London: Rex Collings, 1978.
Poignant, Roslyn. *Professional Savages: Captive Lives and Western Spectacle*. New Haven: Yale University Press, 2004.
Porter, Roy. *London: A Social History*. Cambridge, MA: Harvard University Press, 2001.
Pratt, Mary Louise. *Imperial Eyes: Travel Writing and Transculturation*. New York: Routledge, 1992.
Price, Richard. *Making Empire: Colonial Encounters and the Creation of Imperial Rule in Nineteenth-Century South Africa*. New York: Cambridge University Press, 2008.

Pyne, Stephen J. *Fire: A Brief History*. Seattle: University of Washington Press, 2001.
Ranger, T. O. and I. N. Kimambo, eds. *The Historical Study of African Religion*. Berkeley: University of California Press, 1972.
Richter, Daniel K. *Facing East from Indian Country: A Native History of Early America*. Cambridge: Harvard University Press, 2001.
Rosenstone, Richard A. *Mirror in the Shrine: American Encounters with Meiji Japan*. Cambridge, MA: Harvard University Press, 1988.
Ross, Andrew. *John Philip (1775–1851): Missions, Race and Politics in South Africa*. Aberdeen: Aberdeen University Press, 1985.
Ross, Robert. *Status and Respectability in the Cape Colony, 1750–1870: A Tragedy of Manners*. New York: Cambridge University Press, 1999.
———. *Beyond the Pale: Essays on the History of Colonial South Africa*. Hanover: University Press of New England, 1993.
———. *A Concise History of South Africa*. Cambridge: Cambridge University Press, 1999.
———. "Hermans Matroos aka Ngxukumeshe: A Life on the Border." *Kronos: Journal of Cape History/Tydskrif vir Kaaplandse Geskiedenis*, 30 (November 2004).
———. "Donald Moodie and the Origins of Historiography." In *Beyond the Pale*.
Rutz, Michael. "'Meddling with Politics': The Political Role of Foreign Missions in the Early Nineteenth Century." *Parliamentary History* 27, no. 1 (2008).
———. "The Politicizing of Evangelical Dissent, 1811–1813." *Parliamentary History* 20, no. 2 (2001).
Sachs, Aaron. *The Humboldt Current: Nineteenth-Century Exploration and the Roots of American Environmentalism*. New York: Viking, 2006.
Sagner, Andreas. "The Abandoned Mother: Ageing, Old Age and Missionaries in Early and Mid- Nineteenth-Century South-East Africa." *Journal of African History* 42, no. 2 (July 2001).
Sales, Jane. *Mission Stations and the Coloured Communities of the Eastern Cape, 1800–1852*. Cape Town: Balkema, 1974.
Sampson, Anthony. *Mandela: The Authorized Biography*. New York: Knopf, 1999.
Sanneh, Lamin. *Translating the Message: The Missionary Impact on Culture*. Maryknoll: Orbis, 1989.
Schoffeleers, J. Matthew. *River of Blood: The Genesis of a Martyr Cult in Southern Malawi, c. A.D. 1600*. Madison: University of Wisconsin Press, 1992.
Scully, Pamela, and Clifton Crais. "Race and Erasure: Sara Baartman and Hendrik Cesars in Cape Town and London." *Journal of British Studies* 47 (April 2008).
Scott, James C. *Seeing Like a State: How Certain Schemes to Improve the Human Condition Have Failed*. New Haven: Yale University Press, 1998.
Shanafelt, Robert. "How Charles Darwin Got Emotional Expression out of South Africa (and the People Who Helped Him)." *Comparative Studies in Society and History* 45 (2003).
Shepherd, R.H.W. *Bantu Life and Literature*. Lovedale: Lovedale, 1955.
Sherwood, Marika. *After Abolition: Britain and the Slave Trade Since 1807*. New York: I. B. Tauris, 2007.

Snell-Hornby, Mary. *Translation Studies: An Integrated Approach.* Amsterdam and Philadelphia: John Benjamins, 1988/1995.
Spear, Thomas, and Isaria N. Kimambo, Eds. *East African Expressions of Christianity.* Athens: Ohio University Press, 1999.
Spitzer, Leo. *Lives in Between: Assimilation and Marginality in Austria, Brazil, and West Africa, 1780–1945.* New York: Cambridge University Press, 1989.
Stapleton, Timothy. *Faku: Rulership and Colonialism in the Mpondo Kingdom (c. 1780–1867).* Waterloo, Canada: Wilfrid Laurier University Press, 2001.
———. *Maqoma: Xhosa Resistance to Colonial Advance, 1798–1873.* Johannesburg: Jonathan Ball, 1994.
Stocking, George W. *Victorian Anthropology.* New York: Free Press, 1987.
Stocking, George W. Jr. "From Chronology to Ethnology: James Cowles Prichard and British Anthropology, 1800–1850." In James Crowles Prichard, *Researches into the Physical History of Man.*
Spence, Jonathan D. *The Question of Hu.* New York: Knopf, 1988.
Switzer, Les. *Power and Resistance in an African Society: The Ciskei Xhosa and the Making of South Africa.* Madison: University of Wisconsin Press, 1993.
Szasz, Margaret Connell, ed. *Between Indian and White Worlds: The Cultural Broker.* Norman: University of Oklahoma Press, 1994.
Taylor, Alan. *The Divided Ground: Indians, Settlers, and the Northern Borderland of the American Revolution.* New York: Knopf, 2006.
Thompson, Leonard Monteath. *A History of South Africa,* rev. ed. New Haven: Yale University Press, 1995.
———. *Survival in Two Worlds : Moshoeshoe of Lesotho, 1786–1870.* Oxford: Clarendon, 1975.
Thorne, Susan. *Congregational Missions and the Making of an Imperial Culture in Nineteenth-Century England.* Stanford: Stanford University Press, 1999.
———. "Religion and Empire at Home." In Catherine Hall and Sonya O. Rose, eds. *At Home with Empire.*
———. "'The Conversion of Englishmen and the Conversion of the World Inseparable': Missionary Imperialism and the Language of Class in Early Industrial Britain." In Cooper and Stoler, eds. *Tensions of Empire*
Thornton, John K. *Kongolese Saint Anthony: Dona Beatriz Kimpa Vita and the Antonian Movement, 1684–1706.* Cambridge: Cambridge University Press, 1998.
Trüper, Ursala. *The Invisible Woman: Zara Schmelen African Mission Assistant at the Cape and in Namaland.* Basel: Basel Afrika Bibliographien, 2006.
Tutu, Desmond. Preface, in *I Write What I Like.*
van Onselen, Charles. *The Seed is Mine: the Life of Kas Maine, a South African Sharecropper, 1894–1985.* New York: Hill and Wang, 1996.
Vaughan, Meghan. *Curing Their Ills: Colonial Power and African Illness.* Cambridge: Polity, 1991.
Vera, Yvonne. *The Stone Virgins.* New York: Farrar, Straus and Giroux, 2003.
West, Harry G. *Kupilikula: Governance and the Invisible Realm in Mozambique.* Chicago: University of Chicago Press, 2005.

Wood, James. *How Fiction Works*. New York: Farrar, Straus and Giroux, 2008.
Worden, Nigel, ed. *Contingent Lives: Social Identity and Material Culture in the VOC World*. Rondebosch: Historical Studies Department, University of Cape Town, 2007.
White, Landeg. *Magomero: Portrait of an African Village*. New York: Cambridge University Press, 1987.
White, Luise. *Speaking with Vampires: Rumor and History in Colonial Africa*. Berkeley: University of California Press, 2000.
White, Richard. *The Middle Ground: Indians, Empires, and the Republics in the Great Lakes Region, 1650–1815*. New York: Cambridge University Press, 1991.
Willan, Brian, ed. *Sol Plaatje: Selected Writings*. Athens: Ohio University Press, 1997.
———. *Sol Plaatje: South African Nationalist, 1876–1932*. Johannesburg: Ravan, 1984.
Williams, Donovan. *Umfundisi: a biography of Tiyo Soga, 1829–1871*. Lovedale: Lovedale, 1978.
Wilson, Monica Hunter. "The Interpreters." Grahamstown: 1820 Settlers' National Monument Foundation, 1972.
———. *Reaction to Conquest: Effects of Contact with Europeans on the Pondo of South Africa*. London: H. Milford, 1936.
Wilson, Monica Hunter, and Leonard Thompson, eds. *The Oxford History of South Africa, Vol. 1: South Africa to 1870*. New York: Oxford University Press, 1969.
Worger, William. "Parsing God: Conversations about the Meaning of Words and Metaphors in Nineteenth-Century South Africa." *Journal of African History* 42 (2001).
Wylie, Diana. *Art + Revolution: The Life and Death of Thami Mnyele*. Charlottesville: University of Virginia Press, 2008.
Yannakakis, Yanna. *The Art of Being In-between: Native Intermediaries, Indian Identity, and Local Rule in Colonial Oaxaca*. Durham: Duke University Press, 2008.

UNPUBLISHED SECONDARY SOURCES

Bank, Andrew. "Liberals and Their Enemies: Racial Ideology at the Cape of Good Hope, 1820–1850." Ph.D. dissertation, Cambridge University, 1995.
Beck, Roger. "The Legalization and Development of Trade on the Cape Frontier, 1817–1830." Ph.D. dissertation, Indiana University, 1987.
Hofmeyr, George S. "King William's Town and the Xhosa, 1854–1861: The Role of a Frontier Capital During the High Commissionership of Sir George Grey." M.A. thesis, University of Cape Town, 1981.
Lalu, Premesh. "In the Event of History." Ph.D. dissertation, University of Minnesota, 2003.
Levine, Roger S. "Sable Son of Africa: The Many Worlds of an African Cultural Intermediary on the Eastern Cape Frontier of South Africa, 1800–1848." Ph.D. dissertation, Yale University, 2004.
———. "Changes and Markets in the Knysna and Witwatersrand Landscapes to 1899." B.A. thesis, Yale University, May 1995

Rassool, Ciraj. "The Individual, Auto/Biography and History in South Africa." Ph.D. dissertation, University of the Western Cape, 2004.

Volz, Stephen C. "From the Mouths of Our Countrymen: The Careers and Communities of Tswana Evangelists in the Nineteenth Century, Ph.D. dissertation, University of Wisconsin, Madison, 2006.

INTERVIEWS

Maritz Ngobe, King William's Town, 18 July 2003
Elvis Tshatshu, Tshatshu Township, 18 July 2003

INDEX

abolitionism, 2, 107–8, 169, 203n21, 249n19. *See also* humanitarianism; slavery
Aborigines Committee (British Parliamentary group), 128, 137–38, 149, 154–55
Aborigines (of Australia), 1
Africans: as authors, 4, 96–97, 139, 216n4, 233n6, 255n15; displayed or exhibited by Europeans, 4, 112, 203n21, 240n25, 244n15; in Britain, 125–57; intellectual tradition of, 5, 199n8. *See also* colonial encounter; colonialism; Great Britain; Khoisan; missionaries; Xhosa; *specific leaders, groups, missions, rivers, mountains*
Afrikaners. *See* Boers
agency (in history), 3, 201n14
Albany province, 66–68
Prince Alfred, 190
Algoa Bay, 11–12, 14, 66, 148, 163–64, 206n1
amaGqunukhwebe (group), 165
Amakholwa, 202n17
amaNtinde (group): affiliations of, 13, 116–17, 165, 167–70, 207n14; evangelism among, 26, 56, 71, 77–78, 86; leadership of, 1, 11, 41, 119, 127, 174, 180; in wars, 101, 111–12, 175–77, 185–87
amaTembu (people), 19
Amathole mountains, 67, 74, 79, 162, 175, 190, 221n1

amaXhosa. *See* Xhosa
Armistead, William, 193
authorship (authenticity of in colonial encounter), 4, 96–97, 139, 216n4, 233n6, 255n15
Auxiliary Mission Society, 79
Ayliff, John, 115

Backhouse, James, 167–68
Baines, Edward, 137–38
Barker, George, 50, 65, 79–80
Baushe, Jacob, 165–67
Beagle, 124
Bethelsdorp (mission): as LMS missionary institution in South Africa, 47–51, 66, 79, 167; revival in, 23–25, 48, 94; role of, in Jan Tzatzoe's education, 11–13, 21–33, 36, 43, 116
Biko, Steve Bantu, 196
biography (genre), 3
Bird, Christopher, 34, 53–54, 74, 218n27
Black Consciousness movement, 196
Boers (Dutch colonists), 13, 34, 52–53, 59–62, 104, 119
Boklo (Xhosa leader), 42
Bolivar, Simon, 2
border regions: cultural exchange in, 12, 77; denizens of and trades in, 49; lingua franca of, 55; relative freedom

283

border regions (*continued*)
of movement in, 56; religion in, 54; as requiring intermediaries, 4–5; rumor in, 217n24; terminological difference of, from "frontier," 203n22; uncertainty as characteristic of, 4, 28, 59, 180; violence in, 13 *See also* Boers; wars; Xhosaland; *specific religious and political figures*
Botman. (Xhosa chief). *See* Botomane
Botomane (Xhosa leader), 60, 62, 88, 113, 117
Bowker, John, 166–67, 252n7
Brereton, Thomas, 67
British Empire. *See* Great Britain
British Kaffraria, 179, 184
Brownlee, Charles, 186, 188, 257n27
Brownlee, John: changing relationship with Tzatzoe, 111, 156, 169–70, 173, 175–76, 178–80; Chumie mission and, 78–79; evangelism of, 76, 87, 93, 100; on illnesses and disease, 84; instructional materials of, 83; as James Read's replacement, 74; missionary life of, 168; preaching of, 82; pressure on, by LMS, 98; testimonials of, 76; as town founder, 193; veiled racism of, 83–84
Buffalo River, 43, 78, 112
Bushman's River, 66
Bushmen. *See* Khoisan
Buttanje (translator), 60
Buxton, Thomas Fowell: as host and sponsor of Tzatzoe, 125–26, 129–31, 142, 145, 148–49, 164, 179; humanitarianism of, 107–11, 119; role of, on Aborigines Committee, 155

Caffres. *See* Xhosa
Calderwood, Reverend, 183, 185
Campbell, John, 75–76
Cape Colony. *See specific governors, languages, policies, and peoples*
Cape Dutch (language), 5

Cape State Archives, 194
Cape Town: as LMS and colonial headquarters, 21–23, 31–35, 46, 72, 76–77, 80, 94, 100–101, 109, 112, 136, 153–54, 164, 171, 179, 181, 194, 197n2, 261n46; as port, 12, 108, 117–19, 123–24, 148, 151, 157, 163
Cape Town Missionary Meeting, 153
Casalis, Eugene, 118
Cathcart, George, 186–88
cattle: importance of, to Xhosa, 14–18, 51, 177, 188–89; theft of, as major problem, 45, 52–54, 56, 59, 61–62, 101, 165–66, 171, 178, 215n21
the Cattle Killing, 188–89, 230n39
Chesterfield Advertiser (newspaper), 143
Christianity: as civilizing force, 4; in comparison with other religions, 134; missions and missionaries of, 3–4, 30, 34–48; role of, in colonialism, 5, 49, 53–56, 108; services of, 17; spread of, in Xhosaland, 28–30. *See also* Jesus Christ
Chumie River, 71, 74, 79, 175
colonial encounter, 2–5, 153, 204n26, 228n33, 230n39. *See also* border regions; intermediaries; translation; *and specific people, places, agencies, and incidents*
colonialism: brutality of, 1, 22, 102, 107–10, 112–13, 170; civilizing mission of, 3–4, 31–36, 49, 77–80, 91, 94, 100, 107, 128, 130; Dutch, 4, 150; misrule in, 142–47, 154–55; rebellions against, 2, 5, 144, 171–79; religion's role in, 5. *See also* Boers; Christianity; Great Britain; wars
Commandos (and commando system): moral ambivalence of, 56, 140, 171; resentment of, 101, 109, 126; specific incidents, 61–63, 67, 95–96, 185, 220n5
contingency (in history), 203n23, 205n31
Cree Indians, 1
Creek Indians, 1

cultural chauvinism, 91, 169–70, 173, 176, 199n8
Cuyler, Jacob, 11, 19–20, 31–32, 34–35, 42, 45, 47, 60, 207n6
Cyrus, George, 166

Darwin, Charles, 123–24
David Scott (ship), 156
diplomacy, 1, 18, 42–77, 97, 135–48, 168–78, 186, 219n32, 253n17
disease and illness, 84–90
diviners, 41, 55–58, 82–93, 114–15, 179, 188–89, 226nn29–31, 229n38
Donkin, Rufane, 126–27
Duff (ship), 14, 128
Dundas, William, 80
D'Urban, Benjamin, 101–18, 127, 130, 144–48, 165, 179
Dutch East India Company, 12
Dutch settlers. *See* Boers

Eksteen, Windvogel, 51
Ellis, William, 110–12, 132, 150
Ely (reverend), 139
emancipation (of slaves), 103–4, 238n8
empire. *See* Great Britain
England, Richard, 102
Enno (Xhosa leader), 60
Equiano, Olaudah, 193, 234n6, 249n19
Evans, John, 25, 48
evolution, theory of, 124
Exeter Hall, 132–33, 139, 146, 149–55, 164, 187, 196
exhibition (or display of Africans). *See* Africans
experimental history, 199n7
extermination (term), 130, 185, 246n24, 260n43

Fairbairn, John, 94
Fawcett, John, 115
Fielding, R. (colonel), 188

Fish River (as boundary), 12, 28–29, 37, 47, 51, 66, 73, 104, 106, 113, 148
forced removal (of indigenous people), 110–11, 178–82, 190–91
Fort Peddie, 165–66, 172, 176–81
Fort Willshire, 68
Fraser, George, 53–54, 62–63, 95–96, 126, 196, 220n15
Frontiers (Mostert), ix, x, 263n8
Frontier War of 1811. *See* Graham's War
Frontier War of 1818. *See* Makana's War
Frontier War of 1835, 13, 103–6, 109, 126–27, 144, 146
Frontier War of 1845, 175–77
Frontier War of 1850. *See* Umlanjeni

Geertz, Clifford, 200n9
German Legion, 189
gift-giving ceremonies, 72
Gilfillan, William, 95, 97
Glasgow (city), 125, 151
Glasgow society, 76
Glenelg, Charles Grant (Lord), 109–10, 148, 164
Glenelg dispatch, 148
Godlonton, Robert, 94, 138, 184–85
Graaff-Reinet (town), 23
Graham, John, 22, 66
Graham's Town, 22, 28, 37, 39, 61–68, 80, 100–103, 167, 177, 184, 210n4
Graham's Town Journal (newspaper), 94–97, 103, 111, 138–39, 143–44, 148–50, 187, 233n6, 248n6, 261n47
Graham's War, 28–29
Great Britain: antislavery movements in, 2, 107–8, 169, 203n21, 249n19; attitudes of, toward colonized people, 94; chauvinism of, 91, 98–100, 169–73, 176, 178–83, 199n8; as colonial center of Christianity, 46; colonial government of, 22–23, 29, 32, 34, 45, 47, 74, 103, 106–7, 113–14, 145, 166, 172–73, 179, 181–83; colonization

Great Britain (*continued*)
practices of, 12, 49, 53–55, 59, 61, 67–68, 76, 91, 102, 106–10, 113–14, 127, 154, 176, 178–79, 198nn3–4; empire and imperialism of, 4, 145, 149–50, 152, 176, 198n3, 243n9, 249n19, 250n20; hypocrisies of, 140, 145–47, 154–55, 166, 171–72, 178–79, 182–83; parliament of, 108, 126; political campaigns, 4, 110–12, 245n16; role of, in intratribal disputes, 42; 1820 settlers from, 66–67, 74–75, 220n2, 222n2, 233n52; Tzatzoe's sojourn in, 119–57; use of Jan Tzatzoe as symbol, 4, 115–17, 138, 180. *See also* colonialism; *specific colonies*
Great Fish River. *See* Fish River
Great Kei River. *See* Kei River
Great Trek, 110
Grey, George, 108–9, 155, 187–89, 191, 260n44
Gurney, Anna, 109–10, 148, 155, 239n14

Hackney, 125, 141
Hans, William, 51
Hare, John, 176
Hart, Robert, 65
Hay, John, 131
healers (traditional), 41, 55–58, 82–93, 114–15, 179, 188–89, 226nn29–31, 229n38
Hintza (aka Hintsa), 67, 104, 109, 155, 181, 236n33
history (academic discipline and method). *See* experimental history; microhistory; narrative history
Hottentots. *See* Khoisan
House of Commons Select Committee, 126–27, 238n8
humanitarianism (in British politics): arrogance and paternalism of, 169–70, 173–74, 179, 238n12; decline of, 169–82; effect of, in the colonies, 166, 194, 255n11; tenets of, 94, 97–99, 102; uses of native peoples, 2, 101–2, 107–11, 130–32, 145, 149–50, 154–55, 245n15. *See also* abolitionism; colonialism; paternalism
hunting, 12–18, 44, 59, 73, 210n25

illness and disease, 84–90
imperialism. *See* Great Britain
India, 108
indirect rule, 61, 106–7, 199n6, 218n26, 237n3. *See also* colonialism; Great Britain; missionaries
Industrial Revolution, 1, 125
infant schools, 136, 140, 168
interaction (term), 2, 199n8
intermediaries, 1–5, 199n9, 200nn10–11, 202n20, 230n39, 252n7. *See also* Tzatzoe, Jan
intimacy and intimate relationships, 21, 48, 64, 71, 116, 210n2, 216n3
isiXhosa (language). *See* Xhosa

Jager, Catherine de, 74
Jalousa (Xhosa leader), 60
Jesus Christ (as Great Physician), 90, 196, 227n32, 231n46
Joris, Mattroos, 51

Kaarlus, William, 51
Kafirs. *See* Xhosa
Kama (Xhosa leader), 113, 181
Kat River, 45–46, 48, 83, 115, 136, 163
Kat River mission, 49–65, 71, 76–77, 81–85, 88, 91–94, 163
Kay, Stephen, 67, 70–73, 75
Kayser, Friedrich Gottlob, 84, 86–90, 94, 100–101, 111, 169, 230n39
Kei River, 12, 61, 106, 113, 148, 164
Keiskamma River, 43, 106, 114
Kelso, 7, 151–53
Kelso Chronicle (newspaper), 7, 152
Khoisan (language), 41, 119, 130
Khoisan (people): clothing of, 23; definition of, 208n12; mistrust of missionaries, 63, 65; as oppressed people, 76, 103;

Index

relationships of, to Xhosa, 13, 22, 25, 28, 68; religiosity of, 24–28, 32, 34, 46, 117, 135–36, 146; in wars, 91, 100, 112, 184
King William's Town, 112–13, 116, 127, 148
Kitchingman, James, 143
Kobus Congo (Xhosa chief), 39, 42
Kuruman (place and mission), 161–62, 193

Landau, Paul, 225n27
languages. *See specific languages*
Lattakoo (station location), 48, 74
Leeds, 125
Lepore, Jill, 2
Links, Jan, 51
Liverpool, 125
Livingstone, David, 161–62
LMS (London Missionary Society). *See* London Missionary Society
London (city), 125
London Missionary Society (LMS): auxiliary meetings of, 80; humanitarianism of, 94, 96, 107, 206n2; James Read as missionary for, 11–20, 29, 34, 45, 47–48; Jan Tzatzoe's relationship with, 112, 126–39, 149, 155, 163, 169, 178, 180, 183, 190; John Brownlee as missionary for, 74, 83, 169, 178; John Philip as missionary for, 75–77; Joseph Williams as missionary for, 55, 58; publications of, 50
A Long Walk to Freedom (Mandela), 3
L'Ouverture, Toussaint, 193
Luza, Jan, 53

Mackinnon, George Henry, 186
Maclean, John, 175, 178, 184, 186–87
Maitland, Peregrine, 172, 175–76
Makana (leader): resistance of, to colonial rule, 2; secular power of, 45, 51; spirituality of, 29–30, 38–44, 47, 54, 57, 184, 217n12, 220n5, 229n34; war and, 67–68, 71–72, 83

Makana's War, 67–68, 83
Mandela, Nelson, 3, 196
Maqoma (Xhosa leader): ascent of, 57, 60; as chief, 91, 94, 101, 110, 165, 186, 191; reception of Tzatzoe, 163; as warrior, 67, 112–13, 176
Margadant, Jo Burr, 3
mark of slavery (trope), 249n19. *See also* racism; slavery
Matroos (preacher), 25
Meg Merrilies (ship), 141, 148
Messer, John George, 27
microhistory, 2, 199n7
millenarian movements, 188–89, 230n39
missionaries: efficacy of, in evangelical terms, 110–11; ideological shifts of, 76; place of, in South African life, 1–2; political impotence of, 52–53; role of, in colonization, 76. *See also* London Missionary Society; *specific missions and missionaries*
missionary meetings (in England), 128–56
missions. *See* Bethelsdorp; Kat River mission; *specific missionaries and other specific missions*
Mlanjeni. *See* Umlanjeni
Mlanjeni's War, 184, 200n12
Moffat, Robert, 74, 161, 183
Mostert, Noel, ix, x, 219n33, 238n8, 263n8
Mzilikazi, 161

Napier, George, 163, 171
narrative history, 2, 199n7
"Native agency" (colonial-evangelical institution), 98
Natural History of Man (Prichard), 193–94
Ndlambe (Xhosa leader), 42–43, 59–60, 62, 67, 74, 76, 98–100
The New Biography (Margadant), 3
newspapers, 94–97. *See also specific publications*
Newton, Isaac, 131
Ngobe, Maritz, 195–96

Ngqika (Xhosa leader): as chief, 42, 44–46, 52–75, 217n21, 219n33; as Christian convert, 83, 87, 150; death of, 165; lineage of, 167, 175, 181
Niven, Robert, 178
Noeka, Hendrik, 44, 54, 61
Nolo, 165
North Derbyshire Chronicle (newspaper), 143
Ntsikana (religious leader), 40, 66, 191, 228–29nn33–34

Opperman, Philip, 53
Oursen, Sanna, 25, 48, 51, 64, 77, 116, 168
Oxford, x, 142, 148

Paris Evangelical Mission Society, 118
Parliament (British), 108, 126. *See also* Africans; Buxton, Thomas Fowell; Tzatzoe, Jan
paternalism, 98–102, 108–14, 130–32, 145, 149–50, 169–73. *See also* humanitarianism; racism
Pato (Xhosa leader): as chief, 42, 67, 72, 103, 113, 181, 185–86; relationship of, to colonists, 165–66, 172, 252n7
patrol system. *See* commandos
petitions (to the colonial government), 110, 131, 140, 187, 259n42
Philip, Durant, 151
Philip, John: colonists' resentment of, 171; as defender of the Xhosa, 102–3, 107–9, 126, 180–81, 183; disappointment of, in Tzatzoe, 168–70, 178; Tzatzoe's importance to, 77–78, 94, 98, 111–17, 128, 131–42, 149, 151, 155
Philipton, 167–68
Plaatje, Windshut, 51
Port Elizabeth, 163, 167, 184, 206n4
Portland Place, 125, 129
present tense (in historical writing), 5, 205n33
Prichard, J. C., 193–94

printing technology, 94
prophets, 41, 55–58, 82–93, 114–15, 179, 188–89, 226nn29–31, 229n38. *See also* specific prophets

Quakers, 167
Queen Adelaide province, 105, 107, 109–10, 130, 147–48, 165, 179–80

racism: Christianity and, 26, 83–84, 98, 138–39, 170, 175, 183, 185; colonial policy and, 111–12, 115; Darwin and, 124
rainmakers, 82, 114–15
Read, Elizabeth, 21
Read, James: as diplomat, 44–45, 58, 76, 100, 103, 111; evangelism of, 28–30, 34–48; homecoming of, 128–29; as humanitarian, 76; infidelity of, 47, 74–75; journey of, to take in Tzatzoe, 11–20; popularity of, among the Xhosa, 91; representations of Tzatzoe, 47; in role as Tzatzoe's spiritual parent, 44, 112; as suspected spy, 42, 126; testimonies of, 21–22, 127; as translator, 142; upbringing of, 14; use of Tzatzoe's intermediary status, 31
Read Junior, James: birth of, 21; descriptions of, 118; humanitarianism of, 140–41; role of, in transcribing and translating Tzatzoe, 97–98, 133; Tzatzoe's traveling companion, 112, 127–29, 148
religions. *See* Christianity; witches and witchcraft; Xhosa
Resident agents. *See* Fielding, R.; *other specific agents*; Stretch, Charles
respectability, 77, 95, 150, 178, 241n1, 250n20
ritual specialists, 41, 55–58, 82–93, 114–15, 179, 188–89, 226nn29–31, 229n38. *See also* diviners; prophets; *specific rituals and ceremonies*
Robben Island, 68, 124
Room (painter), 128, 161–62

Royal African Corps, 67
Russell, John (Lord), 171

Sandile (Xhosa leader), 167, 176–78, 182, 185–86, 189
Sarhili (Xhosa leader), 189, 258n39
Schoeman, Coenraad, 104
Schreiner, Gottlieb, 156, 194
Scotland, 7, 150–51
Secession Church, 7, 151, 153
Select Committee on Aborigines, 128, 137–38, 149, 154–55
Sermon on the Mount, 26, 36
settler lobby, 101, 174
settlers. *See* Boers; Great Britain
Shaw, William, 66, 70–71, 75
Sheffield Independent (newspaper), 145–46
Shepstone, William, 75
Sibi (Xhosa chief), 14–15
Sikhs (group), 1
slavery, 2, 101, 107–8, 118, 169, 174, 249n19. *See also* abolitionism; Equiano, Olaudah
Slavery Abolition Act, 107–8
Smith, Harry, 101–18, 147, 165, 179–80, 184
Smith, Joseph, 40
Soga, Tiyo, 191
Soko (Tzatzoe's half brother), 84–87, 93–94
Somerset, Henry, 60–62, 65, 67, 96, 102
Somerset River. *See* Buffalo River
sorcery and counter-sorcery, 41, 55–58, 82–93, 114–15, 179, 188–89, 226nn29–31, 229n38
South Africa. *See* Boers; colonialism; Great Britain; Xhosaland; *specific peoples, politicians, and missionaries*
South African Commercial Advertiser (newspaper), 94–97, 113, 119, 138, 156, 164
South African Library, 194
Southey, William, 95, 97, 185
spoor law, 61, 96

Stephen, James, 109
Stockenstrom, Andries, 60, 148, 171, 175, 185
Stoffels, Andries, 118–19, 127–28, 138, 141, 148, 246n26
A Story of an African Farm (Schreiner), 156
Stretch, Charles, 165, 171–72, 175–76, 182, 253n17
Sundays River, 37
Sun (newspaper), 154
Suthu (Xhosa leader), 165, 167, 189

Table Bay, 68, 123–24, 148, 157
Tecumseh (leader), 2
Theopolis, 37, 65–66, 78–79
Threlfall, William, 67
Thyumie river. *See* Chumie River
Transactions (LMS publication), 50
translation, 52, 56–75, 83, 87, 90–99, 133, 142, 168, 230n39, 231n46
Treaty system, 171–72, 175
A Tribute for the Negro (Armistad), 193
Tshatshu, Dyani, 206n3. *See also* Tzatzoe, Jan
Tshawe (Xhosa ancestor), 12, 41, 206n4
Tyalie (Xhosa leader), 113
Tzatzoe, Jan: acculturation of, to European lifeways, 19–20, 23; as ambassador of Christianity, 1, 54, 66, 77; ambivalent position of, 63, 83–84, 95, 101–5, 111, 127, 164–66, 184–86, 249n19; at-homeness of, 79; authenticity as author, 4, 96–97, 139, 216n4, 233n6, 255n15; as chief of amaNtinde, 1, 54–56, 60, 62, 64, 81, 92, 113, 144, 164–66, 169–78, 183, 186, 189; Christianity of, 2, 23–24, 70, 86, 91, 133, 166, 173, 178–81; as colonial exemplar in London, 112–13, 115, 125–62; colonial persona of, 95–97, 119, 126–27, 181–89; coming of age of, 18, 116; as diplomat, 1, 42, 54, 59–77, 97, 125–57, 167, 171–78, 186, 253n17; disagreements of, with

Tzatzoe, Jan (*continued*)
Kote, 81, 85; disappearance of, from history, 193–96, 197n2, 223n11; evangelism of, 5, 25–28, 44, 70, 78–81, 88–89, 127–29, 145, 150–52, 164–65; expulsion of, from his own land, 179; hybridity of, 3, 5, 60–63, 65, 83–84, 145; impressions of England, 129–32, 153–54; initial meeting of, with Read, 11–20, 164; as intermediary, 25, 30, 32, 45, 47, 51, 63, 72, 84, 90, 119, 172, 176–78, 180–83, 186, 190, 253n17; journeys of, 2, 4, 19, 66–67, 77, 115–18, 150, 163; languages of, 19, 23, 136, 142; letters and articles of, 32, 34, 61, 94–99, 183, 189–90, 234n6; lifespan of, 1; marriage of, 48, 116, 168–69; oratory of, 7, 36–39, 43, 46, 115–16, 126–27, 133–35, 138–40, 142–44, 147, 149–54, 156; others' opinions of, 76, 80, 83, 96, 98–100, 111, 114–18, 138–39, 142–46, 148–50, 152; presentation of, to various groups, 35, 127–28, 130; reception of, by Xhosa, 163–64; royal derivation of, 7, 13, 153; self-representations of, 36, 154; suspected espionage and, 42, 186–88; suspected polygamy and, 64; testimonies of, 132, 149, 218n29, 240n34, 242n3; time with the Reads, 21; traditional religions and, 55–56; as translator and interpreter, 52, 56, 58–59, 64, 69–70, 75, 83, 87, 90–92, 94, 99, 168, 230n39, 231n46; use of English in speeches, 151–153

Tzatzoe, Kote: decision to send Jan to Bethelsdorp, 11; disagreements of, with Jan, 81, 85, 116–17; as Jan's father, 7, 70, 78; kraal of, 16; openness of, to Christianity, 43–44, 55; traditional healing and, 84–91, 93–94; view of Jan Tzatzoe, 37; as Xhosa chief, 1, 7, 11, 42–43

Uitenhage (town), 11, 25, 28, 32, 35
Umhala (Xhosa leader), 189

Umhlakaza (Xhosa prophet), 188–89, 258n39
Umlanjeni (prophet), 184, 200n12
United States, 1–2, 94

Van der Kemp, Johannes: care of, for Tzatzoe, 11–12, 19, 39, 126; criticisms of, 75–76; evangelism of, 29, 36, 40–41, 47, 74, 89, 136, 169, 172–73; testimonies of, 21–22
Van der Lingen (religious figure), 39
Van Diemen's Land, 108
Queen Victoria, 155, 190–91

Walker, George, 167
war doctors, 41, 55–58, 82–93, 114–15, 179, 188–89, 226nn29–31, 229n38
War of Hintza. *See* Frontier War of 1835
War of the Axe, 175–77
wars: Frontier War of 1835, 100, 103–6, 109–10, 113, 126–27, 144, 155, 236n33; Frontier War of 1846, 176–87, 255n11; Graham's War, 28–29; Makana's War, 67–68, 83
Watt's Catechism, 83
Wesleyan Methodist Society, 131, 141
Wesleyans (sect), 66, 76, 139, 172
Wesleyville, 75, 103
Wheatley, Phillis, 193
Wilberforce, William, 22, 107
King William IV, 113, 155
Williams, Elizabeth, 50–51, 59, 64, 76, 216n4
Williams, Joseph: as assisted by Tzatzoe, 98; death of, 76–77; evangelism of, 34–35, 41–56, 81, 85
Wilson, Monica, 200n9
Windsor Castle, 150
Winterberg, 37
witches and witchcraft, 41, 55–57, 82, 84–90, 92–93, 114–15, 179, 188–89, 226nn29–31, 229n38. *See also* sorcery and counter-sorcery

Wollstonecraft, Mary, 249n19
Worger, William, 5
The Wrongs of the Caffre Nation (humanitarian tract), 179

Xhosaland: colonization of, by Europeans, 12; encroachment upon, by colonial powers, 62–63, 67, 106–10, 117, 127, 147, 171, 175–76, 178–79, 189; missions and missionaries in, 51–53, 66–67, 73–75; as state, 1, 12, 42, 54–61, 140, 165, 167, 182. *See also* Commandos (and commando system); Great Britain; *and specific languages, peoples, chiefs, and missions*
Xhosa (language), 12–13, 18, 41, 46, 82–83, 87–89, 98–99, 130, 187, 224n25
Xhosa (people): attacks upon colonists, 100–104; Britons' opinions of, 107–10; campaigns against, by colonial government, 22–23, 62–63, 67; Christianity and, 28–29, 40–48; clothing of, 19; diplomatic etiquette of, 52, 57, 71–72; Europeanization of, 49; exploitation of, by settlers, 53–54; forced relocations of, 110–11, 178–82, 190–91; histories and clans of, 12; housing of, 15–16; hunting and, 12–18; initiation rituals of, 18–19, 24, 168; insurrections of, against colonial rule, 28, 31, 34, 126, 144; leadership responsibilities of, 81; lineages of, 1, 7, 11, 41–43, 52–76, 78, 98–100, 167, 175, 181; livestock's importance to, 12–13; marriage norms of, 42; military training of, 12–18, 100–102; oratorical idioms of, 135, 139, 246n20; political structure of, 1, 39, 42, 54, 56–57, 59–61, 140, 165, 167, 182; relations of, with other African groups, 13; religions of, 40, 55–57, 82–88, 90, 134–35, 188–89, 224n20, 225nn27–28, 226n31, 232n49; skepticism of, toward Christianity, 70, 93; trade of, with colonizers, 68, 146. *See also specific chiefs and prophets; specific families, couples, filial relationships*
Xoxo (Xhosa leader), 101, 126

Young, John, 136–37

Die Zuid-Afrikaan (Newspaper), 138